D1171523

Legacies of Childhood

HARVARD EAST ASIAN MONOGRAPHS
136

Toddler in North China, 1908. Courtesy, Essex Institute, Salem, Mass.

LEGACIES OF CHILDHOOD

Growing up Chinese in a Time of Crisis
1890–1920

JON L. SAARI

Published by COUNCIL ON EAST ASIAN STUDIES, HARVARD
UNIVERSITY, and distributed by HARVARD UNIVERSITY PRESS,
Cambridge (Massachusetts) and London   1990

Copyright 1990 by the President and Fellows of Harvard College

Printed in the United States of America

The Council on East Asian Studies at Harvard University publishes a mono-graph series and, through the John King Fairbank Center for East Asian Re-search and the Edwin O. Reischauer Institute of Japanese Studies, administers research projects designed to further scholarly understanding of China, Japan, Korea, Vietnam, Inner Asia, and adjacent areas.

Some of the material in Chapter Eight was originally published in *Social Inter-action in Chinese Society,* edited by Sidney L. Greenblatt, Richard W. Wilson, and Amy Auerbacher Wilson, and is reprinted with the permission of Praeger Publishers/Greenwood Press of Westport, Connecticut, 06881.

Library of Congress Cataloging-in-Publication Data

Saari, Jon L.
  Legacies of childhood.

  (Harvard East Asian monographs ; 136)
  Includes bibliographical references.
  1. Children—China—Social conditions.   2. Child
rearing—China—History—19th century.   3. Child rearing—
China—History—20th century.   I. Title.   II. Series.
HQ792.C5S22   1989   305.23'0951'09041   89-24005
ISBN 0-674-52160-9

To my mother,
Helen Ann Luebchow Saari,
and to the memory of my father,
Leonard Victor Saari
(1906–1987)

Preface

A very ancient Chinese expression, *tso jen,* defined the landscape of ideal Chinese behavior. I would translate it into English as "the struggle to be fully human." It mapped the valleys of shame, the plains of decency, and the slopes of virtuous achievement. It pointed to a pathway trod by millions of Chinese youngsters who upon reaching the age of six or seven years were exhorted by nurses, parents, and elders to *ch'eng jen,* to become human, to realize their nature, to bring their innate humanity to expression and completion.[1] Becoming human implied certain behaviors that were known, valued, and stressed by parents and educators. The scholar Chang Po-hsing (1652–1725), in a 1713 preface to a commentary on the Neo-Confucian philosopher Chu Hsi's *Hsiao hsueh* (Learning for the young), wrote of this influential childhood primer as "establishing the model for becoming human" *(tso jen yang-tzu).*

> Before Confucius there was no book for adult learning [*ta hsueh*]; after Confucius created one, the gateway to virtue existed. Before Chu Hsi there was no book for elementary learning [*hsiao hsueh*]; after Chu Hsi wrote one, the way to become fully human existed.[2]

This pathway, defined via the concept of Confucian self-fulfillment, was surveyed by Thomas A. Metzger in *Escape from Predicament* (1977), following the works of T'ang Chün-i and other neo-traditionalists. Individual moral goals and striving are framed against a recalcitrant world, a perspective which produced in China after the twelfth century a world

view with a profound sense of predicament. But growing children themselves are almost invisible in Metzger's study; the concepts seem always
to describe mature or maturing adults. The exception is a short discussion on intangible moral gratifications in Chapter One of Metzger's book.
This discussion is intended to provide an alternative viewpoint to a widely
held assumption that traditional Chinese socialization instilled pervasive
dependency anxieties in children and created many deep-seated problems
in dealing with authority figures, whether in the family or the polity.
Metzger argues that for children, acting morally had its own gratifications that partially compensated for dependency anxieties.[3]

These dependency anxieties were the focus of part of an earlier book
by Richard H. Solomon, *Mao's Revolution and the Chinese Political Culture*,
which Metzger acknowledges as a major catalyst for his own study.[4]
Indeed, Solomon's essay on "The Traditional Chinese Socialization Process" still has to be viewed as a substantial achievement in an underdeveloped field of understanding how Chinese children actually grew up
within late imperial China. Solomon's critics have faulted him for an
inadequate grasp of traditional society, for decorative Sinology, for cul-
ture-bound assumptions, for ideological bias, and for outright arrogance
in assuming that he had uncovered psychocultural phenomena that could
explain Mao's revolution.[5] The critics, however, do not seem to have
contested the centrality of the issue of authority in Chinese socialization
that Solomon raised nor the validity of a psychocultural approach if properly
and sensitively executed.

The present book has been written under the shadow of the criticism
meted out to Solomon's book, and in foreknowledge of the resistance
that such terms as "political culture" and "psychohistory" arouse in some
readers. I have no special allegiance to either group of specialists in these
subfields, but I have attempted to build on criticisms of their work in a
constructive way. The authority-related issues of dependency and autonomy, for example, have dominated the political culture perspective. While
not denying their importance, I have sought a better balance by emphasizing the minority phenomenon of mischievous children, by questioning what autonomy and independence meant in a Chinese context, and
by exploring the limits of conformist behavior in various Chinese settings. I have also sought to broaden the agenda of scholarly concerns in

this field of traditional Chinese socialization by including such issues as the emergence of a sense of hope and trust in infants and a sense of efficacy and competence in older children. Above all, I have tried to keep aware that the nature and significance of childhood can only be found within particular Chinese historical and cultural contexts and within actual documented lives. There is no Childhood Abstracted, only children of different classes, genders, ethnic groups, and regions experiencing the world and trying to make sense of it. The children whose lives I have chosen to focus upon were those who became part of the generation of educated youth in the early twentieth century. Because of access to education, they were mostly boys from rich peasant, merchant, or upper-class families. They were a special generation, the last to have the world of Confucian learning etched into their memories as schoolboys, yet the first as a group to confront the intrusive Western world forcing itself into Chinese territory and Chinese minds. This was the generation of Mao Tse-tung (b. 1893), when many, like the young Mao, sought a Way Out of an unprecedented historical crisis for their ancient land.

We cannot free our retrospective search for the children of the past entirely from present-day ideological and theoretical preferences, but we can adopt the defensive strategy of directing as much scrutiny towards our own minds as historians have traditionally directed towards their sources. For it is in the interplay of minds and sources that facts are discerned and generalizations discovered. With what set of attitudes and techniques shall we approach the sources? Solomon expressed the hope that "through the techniques of social science analysis—interviews using controlled sampling procedures and structured questioning, psychological projective tests, content analysis of published documents, and interpretation of data on the basis of social theory—it would be possible to come to some understanding of the Chinese revolution on Chinese terms."[6] But Solomon, like most enterprising analysts, was held in a harness of theories not necessarily shared by his Chinese subjects. Some of these theories come out of the Freudian psychoanalytic tradition, like the concepts of orality and anality; others reflect diverse traditions of social theory, from Max Weber on shared cultural orientations to more recent political cultural theorists. It is no easy task to reconcile Western-derived theories with an understanding based "on Chinese terms." The chosen theories must be applicable to the problems at hand without being parochially grounded in Western normative frameworks.[7] The further we move beyond Chinese-defined meanings and interpretations, the more tenuous and hazardous our scholarly undertakings become. A corollary of the defensive strategy, therefore, is to try to determine what different experiences seemed to mean to the actors themselves, that is, to decipher the texts they used to understand the world, whether these were a belief in spirit sadism, a proverb, a philosophical essay, an autobiography, a short story, the rules of an academy *(shu-yuan)*, the concept of face *(lien)*, or a model of becoming human *(tso jen)*. We must also acknowledge that such meanings range from conscious understandings to a seldom articulated shared grammar of beliefs to unconscious assumptions.

Conscious reliance upon some theoretical perspective is unavoidable when the past actors are children. Adult memory seldom reaches back before age five and the significance of what is happening in those early years is not apparent in the outer, visible behavior of children. For this reason, anthropologists, sociologists, social psychologists, psychologists—those who can observe living behavior in its fullness and complexity—must be consulted and their theoretical insights used to help historians connect the surviving fragments from the past. I have used the perspectives of various theorists, ranging from sociologists Peter Berger, Helen Lynd, Robert LeVine, and Talcott Parsons to psychologist Erik Erikson and anthropologist Francis L. K. Hsu, as they have seemed appropriate and useful in illuminating the sources. It is by default that the theories of outside observers, whose studies of humanization derive mostly from Western cultures in contemporary settings, must still be used; for no modern theory of human development or of the self in culture has appeared based primarily upon the Chinese variety of the human experience. At most, a critique is emerging that views individualism as a Western cultural and ideological phenomenon of limited usefulness in understanding human behavior and of mixed value as a social virtue.[8]

Chinese understandings do provide the framework for Metzger's analysis, but we as readers are still left wondering just how the abstract formulations of Confucian self-fulfillment connect with the actual feelings, needs, and ideas of growing children. The connection I have come to see, explored in Chapter One, was the widespread parental and philosophical perception of childhood as a time of crisis, when vulnerable and even defenseless children struggled against ever-recurring threats, both in the outside world and within themselves. This crisis was understood in terms of a physical and moral endowment that influenced the child's development, and in some cases determined that development. A Western-based theoretical framework that has some resonance with this Neo-Confucian view is the life cycle or epigenetic theory of Erik Erikson. Erikson's concept portrays self-identity as accruing over time through a succession of developmental crises, no one of which is decisive for adult life, but each of which can promote or undermine the evolution towards a healthy and mature adulthood. Individual development is also strongly linked to the emergence of certain social virtues important to the human community as a whole, such as faith, hope, purposefulness, competence, and a sense of responsibility and caring. In both the Chinese Neo-Confucian view and Eriksonian epigenesis, human development is not easy, natural, and inevitable but a contingent achievement in which the human mind and will face numerous hazards. The traditional Chinese insights into this uncertain and conditional outcome, phrased in the lexicon of physical endowment and moral struggle, is not worlds apart from some contemporary Western claims that the full development of human potential depends upon a complex biological-historical-sociocultural matrix.[9]

The sources that permit us to piece together the actual lives of children growing up in the period from 1890 to 1920 are the traditional types of personal documents: memoirs, written autobiographies, oral life stories. My reconstruction draws upon numerous life histories, some in the form of written autobiographies and others collected orally in Taiwan and Hong Kong in 1969. These personal documents afford us the chance to see and feel the years of growing up as they are caught in memory. Frozen scenes remain from the earliest years; a recollected flow of encounters and events emerges in later childhood. In *A China Childhood* Ida Pruitt objectifies herself as "the little girl," perhaps a year-and-a-half old in 1889 leaning against the pole of a mule litter in a Chinese courtyard, her fingers pricked by the roughness of the wood grain.

> "This is not me," she thought with surprise. She lifted her head and looked out into the courtyard. Huge blue figures loomed and moved and were unfocused shapes in the distance that meant nothing. More "not me." How much "not me" there was. The rest of her life was to be spent in learning about "me" and "not me," in trying to understand them both in ever widening circles—of experience, of thought, and of understanding, widening ever outward like the circles curving away from a stone dropped into a pond.

The next event she could remember occurred four and a half years later when she was six years old. Ida Pruitt, as narrator, now switches to the first person, as a girl growing up within the "outer shell" of a Chinese family courtyard home in a Shantung village. Progressively she moved out beyond the family courtyard into the village streets, learning to define the "me" and "not me" dialectically in ever more precise and comprehensive ways. [10]

The paradigm of the objectified child, the adult who remembers and narrates, and the researcher who interviews, listens, and interprets is inherent in the life history approach, and forces us to address certain methodological concerns. The child, being accessible only indirectly through memory, is a creation of the two adults who aspire to bring the child back to life. The narrator will recover the child within the boundaries of his or her memory, and should be aware, or made aware, of how selective and mythmaking the remembering ego can be; sore points may be skirted and later adult identities may distort—negatively or positively—the characterization of childhood. [11] The researcher should be aware of this interaction between the narrating adult and the remembered child, between present and past, and the impossibility of fully recovering that child's world as it actually emerged. The researcher must also be aware of the forces of attraction and repulsion occurring between himself or herself and the narrating subject, and the degree to which trust, respect, and intimacy have developed in the relationship. [12] Given these constraints in the life history approach, it is necessary, or at least methodologically wise, to supplement life histories with the observations of actual children in Chinese settings by more or less trained observers in the past, from missionaries to anthropologists.

It is finally our own questions and chosen themes—not the techniques and the sources—that organize our presentation of history. What was the significance of childhood for this transitional generation of educated young Chinese? Their life records frame the question of the significance of childhood in an illuminating, possibly novel way: did early experiences help the growing child to see and grasp change as an opportunity, or did they bias the child to look for security and order within conventional patterns, only to be bewildered and paralyzed by the mounting disharmony within society? For this was a world breaking up, a disjointed world of ideas and experience, where traditional wisdom was less and less reliable as a compass. Late Ch'ing China, dislodged from its ancient moorings, had been pushed out into the turbulent stream of worldwide change. What was needed was the ability to keep a footing in the turbulence, to discern the shallows and the depths, the twists and turns of the current, and to find the faith and courage to act and to create in this era of great uncertainty. This framework of dislocation led me to focus on two persistent childhood legacies: the strengths and weaknesses the young children had as actors amidst the brokenness and opportunities, and the diffuse symbolic meanings through which they came to understand this chaotic world. Part One looks at the children of the late Ch'ing as heirs, born into a specific cultural and historical situation; Parts Two, Three, and Four see them growing up as actors, struggling to establish their individual character and direction amidst the claims of the filial system and the pressures and contradictions of the era. Some of these young people—only a few as I will argue—were able to see, grasp, and make creative reconnections among the fragmented traditions of the past and their hopes and visions for the future. But through them the ancient life-goal of *tso jen* was given twentieth-century meaning.

Living means forever trying to comprehend an often incomprehensible world, to make a home in an often hostile environment. In these struggles the gains and losses to the bitch-goddesses of Change and Progress are not easily weighed and sometimes surprising. There is no mythic highway from Tradition to Modernity; there are only thousands of footpaths in the underbrush, some of them becoming roads, as the writer Lu Hsun noted, because many people went that way.[13] And there was no one-way transmission from a dynamic West to a static, unchanging China. "It's all transient, these changes in nations, the giving and taking in history," I was told by an older man in Taiwan in 1969, who must have been bemused that the young American could not free himself from recounting the perennial Western challenge and the perpetual Chinese response. "Do not think of this modern history of China as the experience of an 'underdeveloped' or 'Oriental' society," he warned. "Social disintegration is a worldwide crisis, and so are the powerful passions and ideas of youth. Historians have been too parochial, and have made the world ignorant that the pains and pleasures of all are similar and inseparable." [14] Fifteen years of aging have made a difference in the writing of this book, and the difference lies mainly in the perspective of the observer and the teller.

Acknowledgments

What seemed like a lonely, private undertaking appears in retrospect, as usual, as a collective achievement. I thank my graduate advisors at Harvard, Benjamin I. Schwartz, John King Fairbank, and Ernest R. May, for the expectation that graduate students do something unusual, and for the time and intellectual space within which to do it. Certain colleagues have critiqued parts of the many revisions as the manuscript progressed from dissertation to book: Paul Cohen, Leo Ou-fan Lee, Parker Po-fei Huang, Sherman Cochran, and Ken Waltzer. For assistance with Chinese translations, I thank Paul Heng-chao Ch'en from my graduate student days, and more recently, Zhuang Zhong and Jian Yili. External support for the research came initially from the Social Science Research Council and the Ford Foundation; they funded a semester of specialized coursework at Harvard and MIT, followed by a year abroad in Taiwan and Hong Kong in 1968–1969. The John King Fairbank Center for East Asian Research at Harvard assisted through two stints at the center as a Research Associate in 1973 and 1977.

Within Northern Michigan University, institutional support for sabbatical leaves in 1977–1978 and 1985–1986 as well as for several periods of released time for writing has come from a succession of administrators, in particular Academic Vice-Presidents Robert Glenn and Alan Donovan, Dean of Arts and Science Donald H. Heikkinen, and Heads of the Department of History Steven Barnwell, Barry Knight, and Ruth Roebke-Berens. Members of their secretarial staffs were particularly essential in typing the manuscript, especially Linda Cleary, Kim Ericson, and Alice McKinney. Six months of the first sabbatical leave were spent at my wife's mountain farm in Upper Austria, where Andrei Fuchs-Robetin graciously provided for me a daytime study in his villa in the valley.

Emotional support has come above all from my wife Christine, as companion on the research treks, gadfly during the long dormant periods when little was happening, and anchor during the periods of intense writing and revision. Our two sons, Alexander and Matias, grew up alongside this book; their lives provided an unusual parallel with my reconstruction of Chinese childhoods in the past, a parallel that helped my awareness both as a parent and as an interpreter of other childhoods.

Katherine Keenum, my editor at the Council on East Asian Publications, Harvard University, has made the most direct contribution to this book through her relentless questioning and attention to detail. She was my harshest critic. At one time, because of her, the revision stretched before me like an endless range of mountains, of problems within problems; but she also helped bring the task towards closure, towards a place of relative clarity, focus, and stillness. I do not hope, at least for now, for any more.

Jon L. Saari
Marquette, Michigan
April 1989

Contents

Prologue

There is perhaps no end to the surprise of finding ourselves when trying to tell the tales of others. The legacies of childhood are not obvious. The very emphasis upon the centrality of childhood as a basis for adult life may in fact be a Western bias. As Arthur Kleinman has argued, the dominant theories of the self derived from the Western cultural tradition's models (psychoanalytic, behaviorist, cognitive, and so forth) tend to see the self as "unchanging, emerging progressively from childhood experience and strongly anchored in it . . . and consisting of a deeply private, authentic, stable interiority at odds with changing surface impressions."[1] An alternative theoretical conception, which he among others envisions, is derived from anthropology and posits a much more fluid sense of self as a locus of relations with the rest of the world, from people to nature. This is a self that is created in social interaction, whose habits and choices are negotiated in local webs of relationships and informed by cultural orientations. As local settings and orientations may change, so may this integrating self, caught up in resistance to the lived world, in a continual process of trying to make sense of events and experience.[2] Gone is the deep, private interior, gone is the hard core of a personality with certain enduring traits and characteristics, gone is the anchoring of the adult in childhood.

Or are they? They are "gone" or "present' only if we accept the theories in our minds, the theories existing in either case in a complex relationship to the specific people, places, and events that fill the records of the past. Alas, these actual subjects fill the records incompletely, remaining suggestive, tantalizing. Yet theory, as the fine threads of assumption that make connections in our understanding of ourselves and the world, inheres in every word we write. Years of reflection upon a generation of educated Chinese youth caught in history have led me to envision the self as both embedded in the world and as embodying the world within itself, a self growing by stages of awareness from the former state towards the latter over the course of a lifetime.

The self as embedded in the world. From the outside in: the things that frame lives. You are an infant born into time and history, vulnerable to the happenstance of accident, illness, pain, and distress, choosing neither the moment nor the place of your birth. You did not determine the health and love of your caretakers, the vigor or decay of your family, the stability of your country's traditional culture, the confrontations with foreigners, the pace and depth of change. You live on the vast Chinese subcontinent, with its mountains and crowded river valleys, its myriad peasant villages, its market towns and cities. You inherit a massive cultural tradition passed down for centuries, awaiting children in the lockets attached around necks to ward off troublesome devils, in the philosophical primers placed in the hands of schoolboys, in the deference accorded to the Young Masters of the scholar-official class, in the derisive looks cast toward the disobedient, the shameless, the poor, the ignorant. You come to discern that people live different lives at different levels within society: upper-class lives of relative material ease, with strong encouragement for learning and an assumed role as social and political leaders; and peasant lives of manual toil, narrow horizons, and third-best choices. Rich or poor, you are made to feel indebted to your family: did family members not feed you, care for you in your long immaturity, teach you language and skills, and instruct you in how to be a worthy human being? They gave you that first world of childhood, whose smells, sounds, feelings and understandings will be a lifelong memory. They gave you themselves, so that you may be like them.

The self as embodying the world within itself. From the inside out: things chosen, or half-chosen, that express the sense of self. As an infant, I gained my sense of self through others: I am me, reflected in my mother's smile, smiling back to her. As a toddler, I am what I can assert and get away with, exploring the family courtyard with uncertain steps, pulling my wet nurse this way and that. For several years I knew myself through my body and its needs, but then I began to be schooled in ideas and my body slowed and shrank. I am what I am told by others I should be and do: a filial son, a diligent student, a quiet presence, a credit to my ancestors. I am many selves: a private, inner self that talks only to itself; a social self that does what others require; perhaps another self that lives in the past or an ideal self that dreams about possible futures. As a schoolboy, I am what I can do well: a reciter of whole passages in old classics by heart, an inventor of ways to be a truant, a commander of an army of children in the streets of the city. I am what I can assume responsibility for: a caretaker for my pet pigeons, a companion to my fellow cow herders, a contributor to the family's welfare by hard work and personal diplomacy, a success in pursuing my own education, a helper to my younger brothers and sisters. As a young adult, I am the principles I have chosen to stand for: a follower of Confucius, remedying hidden faults through introspection and self-cultivation of my moral character; a revolutionary activist, sacrificing my own individual self for the perceived interests of China, the masses, or historical progress; an independent thinker, maintaining my personal integrity by refusing to bend to the power of the group and shame; a restless explorer of boundaries, of my self in society, of my country within the world, of the past as part of the future, of the human order within the cosmos.

PART ONE
Children as Heirs

Shansi landscape with temple, ca. 1900. Courtesy, Essex Institute, Salem, Mass.

ONE

Childhood as Crisis: A Cultural Perspective

The persons in a past society most difficult to characterize are the illiterate, the dissident, the powerless; for the surviving historical records present them as they were seen by others, not necessarily as they saw themselves. The approach to young children is particularly hard, for they are one of the most powerless and dependent parts of a society. How can we know their inner worlds, what was shared and not shared among them in the process of growing up? How can we know that what we describe as the child's reality is anything more than the projections of outsiders, whether foreign scholar or Chinese adult, or the hazy and perhaps inaccurate remembrance of an adult who had once been a child? We can turn this apparent difficulty to partial advantage, however, by acknowledging that parental perceptions, distorted or not, are an integral part of the structure of childhood. Children are imperfect mirrors held up to the adult world; and by looking at that world, we can catch revealing glimpses of how children were treated and understood.

In late Imperial China, parental views of the child and childhood were anchored in an overall adult world view. Two assumptions, one about the outer environment and one about human development, were particularly relevant to children and seem to have been widely shared among Chinese adults within both folk culture and elite culture during the late Ch'ing period. The first was that the world was a threatening place to be born into because human understanding and control were too often incomplete, if not impotent, in the face of the environment.

The second assumption, muted among peasants and revealed most systematically in the Neo-Confucian philosophical understanding of human
development, was that childhood was the setting for an either/or struggle to become a moral being, in which the odds were on the side of
losing. Any such underlying assumptions, whether systematized as universal philosophy or simply expressed in folk religion and in common-
sense notions, are rooted in our existence as cultural and historical beings.
We see mostly what our own cultural fragment and era have prepared
us to see; we seek answers to those questions that we as finite men and
women enmeshed in our own confining present can imagine and find
worth asking. The convincingness of these answers depends not only
upon their demonstrable reasonableness but also upon the resonance that
the underlying assumptions evoke in us as living, thinking, feeling persons.[1]

Throughout the years of childhood, the basic pattern of Chinese child-
rearing was governed by the image of children as weak, vulnerable, and
dependent beings that had to be closely protected and strictly instructed
if they were to survive and become worthy adults. A period of early
indulgence and protective restraint, from conception to age six, when
various taboos were observed and children kept close, satisfied, and out
of any conceivable danger, was followed by a period of strict instruction
in the ways of life that ended around age fourteen. During this entire
period, adults attempted to control the milieu of children, to shield
them from dangers and temptations in the outer world that could destroy and corrupt their emerging lives. What thoughts and emotions
encouraged so many Chinese adults to see children as weak, vulnerable,
and dependent beings? Did this image fit because of their own self-
image as weak and vulnerable in the face of an indifferent, even hostile
environment? Could parents give their children more scope than they
had learned it was wise to give themselves?

VULNERABILITY AND STRUGGLE IN THE FACE OF THE ENVIRONMENT

The world view of the peasant villager, including the governing image
of the child as weak and vulnerable, was continually reborn and confirmed in the existential struggle waged with the land, with disease and

death, and with recurrent social disorder. The implicit message of hundreds of events that occurred and reoccurred in daily life was the need for cautious watchfulness, restraint, and perseverance. Peasant parents had ambivalent feelings about having children in the first place. The longing for a rest from labor in old age, and the hopes and fears connected with continuity of ancestor worship, made having children, especially sons, an important personal and family act. Yet high infant mortality pointed to the frequency of defeat and loss. The parents' desire to limit the family to the size of their piece of land was also strong, for those tiny plots needed only so much labor and could support only so many mouths. To exceed this limit would only mean destitution and crime; and to forestall this prospect, individual families practiced abortion and infanticide. The children that were born and survived were highly valued for ritual and security purposes, but felt by peasant parents to have been born into an external environment that valued children hardly at all and that constantly threatened their lives. And the parents were partially correct.

THE LIMITATIONS OF GEOGRAPHY AND TECHNOLOGY. The adult Chinese peasant as cultivator in the late Ch'ing period faced certain natural conditions that severely limited what R. H. Tawney has called "the possibilities of scientific knowledge and the social art." Among these were exhaustion of the soil (especially in the south), irregular rainfall (especially in the north), deforested hills, great rivers prone to periodic flooding, mountains and deserts encroaching on the cultivable land area, and an immense number of human beings to support. These last two conditions set up the dynamic that operated throughout rural China, despite great diversity of crops and regions, namely the necessity of extracting every bit of nutriment from such land as there was. A gardening style of agricultural production on small, dispersed plots of land absorbed the available labor supply; but it hampered the development of an agricultural technology superior to the technology of the hoe, the rake, the simple plow, and the sickle. It even precluded the extensive use of animal power and the use of land for breeding livestock, while seldom providing any margin of security for the individual cultivator, who was driven by ruthless demands for greater economy and reduced consumption. Economy, as Tawny stressed, was the keynote of the system: "economy of space, economy of materials, economy of implements, economy of fuel, economy of waste products, economy of everything except the forest, which had been plundered . . . and of the labor of human beings, whom social habits have made abundant and abundance cheap."[2]

What material security there was for the well-to-do contrasted with the desperate equilibrium of the peasant family. For this peasant family, the margin between life and death was so slight that "scarcity," a relative condition, threatened to slip into starvation whenever the normal balance between humans and land was disturbed. Population, estimated at 150 million in 1600, 313 million in 1794, and 430 million by 1850, increased dramatically during the Ch'ing period. Despite the concurrent expansion of arable land and the introduction of foreign food crops, the balance of humans and resources became strained. The fragmented nature of peasant holdings along with the lack of primogeniture helped make downward mobility common and movement outward from the village increasingly necessary. Internal migration away from the densely settled countryside of Central and North China and emigration abroad from South China were not sufficient to moderate the development of a rural subproletariat in the wake of the great mid nineteenth-century rebellions. This group of migrant paupers was completely destitute, with no fixed livelihood or regular residence, ever vulnerable to famines, epidemics, natural disasters, and to the slightest change in taxes, rents, harvests, or health.[3] By the first decades of the twentieth century, the situation had become desperate indeed. Two and a quarter acres of land were required to supply the basic food needs of a family of five, irrespective of housing, farm equipment, clothing, and fuel; by this standard, between 40 and 50 percent of peasant families in 1917 had land insufficient to provide then with food alone.[4] Food expenditures absorbed a large part of peasant budgets, an average of about 50 percent, but often going much higher among tenant and landless families. Destitution was held at bay by accepting low standards in housing and clothing; by eating no meat; by limiting the size of the family through infanticide, abortion, and the sale of women and children; by laboring continuously and unrelentingly in the fields and elsewhere during the slack periods of the rural cycle; and by using up limited physical capital.[5]

This basic rural situation made certain conclusions about "the facts of life" seem logical, even compelling. Inside the village, according to Fei Hsiao-t'ung's observations for rural communities in Yunnan in the 1940s, peasants thought in terms of limited and unexpanding resources, in terms of the distribution of wealth, not the multiplication of wealth. Stability was the elusive goal that men sought, a goal which found a psychological counterpart in the idea of "contentment." Contentment defined a minimum but acceptable state of well-being that ensured a certain level of material consumption as well as a certain freedom from the "sweat and blood" work in the fields. Being doomed to suffer continuous toil in the fields just to subsist was not achieving contentment; but once the state of contentment was reached, many did not work any more than was necessary to maintain it. Leisure time was spent in teahouses in the market towns, or sleeping, loitering, or smoking opium. A villager with an acceptable ratio of work and leisure was held in this pattern by mutual suspicion and envy among families, for striving to increase one's material wealth within the relatively closed economy of the village was viewed as an unsocial exploitation. Although the village community was not homogeneous and contained visible differences of wealth, prestige, power, housing, and land, public opinion worked both to confirm and mitigate such differences by requiring a social display of conspicuous consumption in the proper ceremonials (marriages, funerals, burials, births, general food fortune, and long life).[6]

The traditional paths to wealth all lay outside the village. They ranged from the highly sanctioned and prestigious to the illegal and unapproved, from joining the bureaucracy as an official (military more often than civilian) to engaging in commerce, smuggling, or banditry. Resources and status acquired outside the village could, of course, be used to expand a family's holdings within the village; but such social mobility usually occurred dramatically and without incremental increases over time. For those less desperate or less ambitious who did not leave the village, wealth was often a fantasy object, something that happened to people by luck, such as discovering buried treasure or being befriended by a wealthy patron. Wealth did not appear to be a function of hard work and thrift, although these qualities over generations could and did gradually place some families on a sounder material footing.[7]

THE PROTECTIVE SCREEN OF POPULAR RELIGION. In normal times, owing to the uncertain behavior of markets, weather, local bullies, landlords, and magistrates, only a fine line separated the "contented" life on the soil from a life of actual destitution; in times of calamity the rural population was almost helpless. Calamity could come in three basic forms: 1) natural disasters, such as flood, drought, locusts, and earthquakes; 2) disease in general and epidemics in particular; and 3) civil disorder, as represented by bandits, plundering soldiers, and organized rebels. Over the centuries human ingenuity and diligence had made some progress in controlling these calamities, or at least their effects. Kinship organizations had been elaborated into multi-purpose bulwarks against insecurities posed by the general environment. The pooling of resources in the basic kinship unit was not only an obvious way to avoid or at least equalize destitution, but also a way in which offensive gains by a single member or two of a clan who "made it" outside the village could be consolidated and the life of many put on a more secure economic basis. Yet such solidarity was often not enough to stave off destitution, and could not protect against the larger disasters. Enormous dikes were constructed to hold in the great rivers, and were maintained by state and local cooperation; but such efforts proved only temporarily effective.[8] The niggardly rainfall in North China was impervious to human will; the populace could only try to save water and to cushion the effects of drought by a system of public granaries. But problems of transportation made this effort effective only locally or regionally at best, and a prolonged drought would wipe out limited savings. An indigenous system of medicine and pharmacology had been developed; and though weak in its methods of diagnosis, it sometimes proved effective in its prescriptions. Yet it made no inroads against the infant mortality rate, let alone epidemics. In all these areas human diligence and ingenuity met final defeat. The knowledge and remedies that could be marshaled were insufficient to the task, and it was necessary for human effort to be supplemented by supernatural help if the pain and anxiety of impotence were to be mitigated and the hope of control kept alive. In the face of these ultimate disasters, a protective screen had been created, one in which factual knowledge was thoroughly interwoven with magical-supernatural elements, making it virtually impossible for the populace to separate the two or say which one was more essential or protective or controlling.[9]

Adult perceptions of children were also caught in this protective screen. To improve chances of survival for the foetus and infant, a whole series of precautions had to be observed to maintain grace and favor with invisible powers. One such step—a reaction to "spirit sadism"—clearly reveals the logic that moved parents to action. Spirit sadism was the belief that the lives of children, especially those sons most highly regarded by their parents, were sought out by devil spirits. The way to protect a boy was to show a lack of interest in him. At the ceremony that celebrated his reaching his first month, for instance, he might be given a name of abuse, like Dog or Pig or Flea or Slave Girl or Buddhist Monk. Or in a pseudo-adoption, he might nominally be given away to someone with greater protective power or influence than the parents, such as a monastery or a family with many surviving children. These widespread practices rested on the belief that the spirits would leave children alone if the parents did not seem to value them too highly.[10] One behavioral consequence of these beliefs was that affection for sons was often carefully concealed behind a mask of indifference.

The French Jesuit Henry Doré observed in 1914 that the naming phenomenon and pseudo-adoption, as well as other customs such as putting an earring on a boy to deceive spirits about his sex, were practiced in special circumstances, such as for an only son of elderly parents or after older children in a family had died. The specialness of such cases, however, does not diminish the general fear and respect which commoner parents bestowed on meddlesome spirits. The soul-stealing devils (*t'ou-sheng kuei*), for example, were believed to be the hungry souls of young girls who had died unmarried and who needed the soul of a male child in order to be reborn male. They were very dangerous but could be tricked or scared off by such devices as burning foul-smelling old shoes or draping a fish net smeared with hog's blood around the child's bed. The *t'ou-sheng kuei* were believed to lose power over children who had passed through "the barrier of the hundred days" (*pai-erh kuan*), which was the ninth of thirty barriers that Taoist priests claimed all children were destined to pass through during the sixteen years of childhood. Parents had to take precautions that each of these difficult barriers, marked by a precise day, month, or year, would be traversed without harm. Protective means were available, but the danger was not over until all thirty barriers had been passed. The greatest danger was in the earliest years, as there were nine barriers in the first hundred days and twenty-three within the first thousand days. The major concern in the early years appears to have been to link the child's soul securely to this visible earthly existence; and symbolic charms to this end included padlocks attached to the neck with a silver chain, copper-cash hung on a red string, and silver dollars worn around the neck.[11]

Resources, both material and psychological, were clearly expended throughout childhood in a continual contest between the child's soul and harmful spirits. These spirit beliefs were projections of the parent's sense of living in an unpredictable if not sadistic environment, where invisible beings and forces had to be propitiated or neutralized by trickery, deception, and counterforce, often with the help of charismatic Buddhist and Taoist priests who understood the workings of the unseen realm. The hold of these beliefs originated less in the inertia of tradition or in the securing of practical benefits for believers than in the recurring experience of the dangers of life in a preindustrial society.[12] The beliefs thrived on the interplay between the possible and the impossible, between the intense human struggles for life and livelihood and human powerlessness before disaster. The western Hunan writer Shen Ts'ungwen (b. 1902) knew well the origin and complexity of this orientation, particularly the place of "fate" as a final comfort and explanation. "As a rule, whenever country people are in a position where there isn't any way out, they almost all use 'fate' to stand up against it, to increase a bit their endurance as well as their adaptability to unfair treatment and the arrival of tragedy, and even to maintain a bit of hope, in case of a miracle." Shen approved of popular superstition as helping support the initiative and confidence of country people, as an "amulet" in the struggle for survival. He deplored the breakdown of this faith, particularly if replaced only by "modern" cynicism.[13]

Villagers in late Ch'ing rural China, like Michelangelo's sculptured slaves, seem embedded in a background that refuses to release them.

There is motion and struggle, but it is struggle against the ever-recurring threats of starvation, natural disasters, disease, and disorder. By exposing the villagers' greatest vulnerabilities, such calamities concentrated their attention and ingenuity, their helplessness and resignation; and out of these responses was created the protective screen of images, beliefs, and techniques. This screen has continued to resist reordering in China, even after the Revolution of 1949 profoundly altered social relationships. The remaking of culture—the transmitted consciousness of the nature of reality—is a more difficult and long-range task than a ten year Cultural Revolution. Not only must the age-old scourges themselves be made more amenable to human control and comprehension, but children must grow up with a sense that environmental mastery is more in their own hands.

The response of the masses in the People's Republic to three years of great disaster, 1959–1962, documents the persistence of the protective screen in the first decades after the Revolution. According to the testimony of hundreds of Cantonese refugees interviewed in Hong Kong during this period, Mao Tse-tung lost the credibility as a new living god which he had gained with many peasants during 1950–1952, the early period of land reform in Kwangtung. Whereas earlier they had thrown out ancestor tablets and kitchen gods and hung up Mao's portrait, now they turned against Mao for failing to provide material benefits and protection against misfortunes and evil spirits. A great revival of ancestor worship, religious rituals, and superstitious practices resulted. The interviewer concluded that "while gods are expendable, the masses would always worship the god or gods who are their material benefactor or protectors . . . and that while old forms of superstitions may be suspended, new patterns of superstition will soon be devised to take their place. This pattern of religious behavior will continue to survive for many decades until China has been fully industrialized and the educational process of the future has succeeded in remolding the personality makeup of the masses."[14] Mao and the Chinese Communist Party certainly weakened the authority of ghosts and gods, but the god-requiring consciousness has not been easily eliminated.

THE PRECARIOUS HOLD OF CIVILIZATION. Against the background of these struggles in the villages and fields and mines and workshops—so repetitive and apparently unchanging, so visible still in the images of *China at Work* recorded by Rudolf Hommel in the 1920s[15]—is the great theme of Chinese history: the slow, cumulative building of a rich and diversified civilization through human efforts and insights. Through the work of millennia, men and women in East Asia were transformed from the beastlike beings reflected in mythology into members of a wealthy imperial state resting upon a base of intensive grain agriculture and a corpus of classical knowledge. To the defenders of this state, the most precious inheritance was the accumulated wisdom of the sages of antiquity; for immersion in their insights was believed to have the power to transform human beings into higher levels of moral and rational being. "Civilization" *(wen-hua)* meant literally "a transformation through literature." Yet this precious accumulation of skills and wisdom, passed on for millennia from adults to children, was ever vulnerable to periodic loss and decay. Looking back into the panorama of the past, the educated late-Ch'ing Chinese adult was reminded of this fact. The cyclical appearance of *luan* or "chaos" and the rise of the devouring tiger of politics bore witness to the precarious hold that civilization held in the world. The arc of the dynastic cycle seemed to turn inevitably downward; awareness of the stereotyped ills behind it had not enabled rulers or officials to reverse the pattern of administrative decay. At least social customs or the *li*—what philosophers honored as natural ethical law—persisted at the local level among conscientious men and women and became a source of continuity within the cycle of dynastic flourishing and waning.[16]

Looking at late-Ch'ing society within and beyond the Great Wall also reminded thoughtful adults of the vulnerability of civilization. Widespread illiteracy among women and the poor, the ineradicable presence of unruly inferior men *(hsiao jen),* and the barbarians outside the pass, all were seemingly immutable features of the scene. These underscored the limitations in the spread of civilization, which had not yet reached all humans inside the Central Kingdom, let alone within the Four Seas. The illiteracy meant that vast numbers had only an indirect encounter with the transforming power of civilization; they learned correct behavior through oral teaching and model emulation, but not through the personal discipline of classical studies. The Legalist-inspired assumption that in practice punitive law was necessary to ensure control and order was a continuing concession to the fractious, ethically obtuse members of society who were not made peaceful by internalizing the *li*. Mencius had taught that a secure material life was a necessary foundation for human receptivity to ethical teaching, yet scarcity and starvation had always haunted the scene. Strong outlying barbarians on horseback and in gunboats, who resisted settled agricultural ways and did not practice the "relations of humanity" *(jen-lun)*, were a recurrent threat to civilization; they kept alive the spectre of a "barbarianized" China.

And among their own kind, the educated elite, moral backsliding was all too common. As Confucius knew so well in his own age over two thousand years before, the man superior in status did not always conduct himself as the ethically "superior man" *(chün-tzu)*. Had it ever been otherwise? Perhaps in the remote past under the legendary Sage Emperors Yao, Shun, and Yü. History seemed at times a weary story of declension, of cycles of order and chaos, prosperity and decay, times when right principles expanded and held sway and times when they contracted and were almost lost to sight. Yet the sense of the absolute rightness of these principles was uncontestable, grounded, as the educated Confucians believed, in the very structure of the cosmos.

THE NATURE OF THE NEO-CONFUCIAN AFFIRMATION

The Great Tradition of the Chinese literati continually affirmed human potential in the face of life conditions that kept so many in China riveted to the basic tasks of survival and that made civilization seem so precarious. Like the peasants' knowledge of the interpenetrating visible and invisible worlds, the wisdom of the high tradition helped to take some terror out of the natural environment and to mitigate human dread and fear and the sense of impotence before death and insecurity. Differentiating, classifying, and naming things was, and is, a powerful tool to increase human strength and self-confidence; and humans have ceaselessly used this ability to frame hypotheses about themselves in relation to the world and the cosmos. Yet these hypotheses differ greatly in their liberating or constricting impact upon the thoughts and actions of individual persons. Within just the Confucian tradition, possible impacts ranged from an encounter with the ever-enlivening vision of the sage Confucius in the *Analects* to a deadening encasement within the institutions of late Ch'ing imperial Confucianism. The most important part of this tradition for us to understand, however, is Neo-Confucianism, a seven-hundred-year-old philosophy that combined a rich metaphysics with a sharp awareness of experiential realities. Neo-Confucian thought informed the assumptions and lives of educated Chinese in the late nineteenth century. It provided an image of the process of becoming human *(tso jen)* in childhood and early adulthood. It dominated education, from the primers read in the tutorial schools of gentry families to the answers favored in the imperial civil service examinations. It governed the sense of orthodoxy in a soon-to-be beleaguered system of thought and institutions. Neo-Confucian thought thus had a wide-ranging impact on the educated young men who grew up and matured in the period from 1890 to 1920; it affected them as children, as students, and as would-be reformers and critics of Chinese society.

The Neo-Confucian version of the Great Tradition was a striking hypothesis about heaven, earth, and humankind, an hypothesis marked by strong tensions if not outright contradictions. It affirmed the cosmos as real with certain regularities in its movement that were accessible to human insight, while it also expressed a deep need for fixed and absolute principles that were said to govern all human life and history. It was a world view in which human beings ranked high enough in the cosmic order to have a sense of self-importance and even moral perfectibility; yet its ablest thinkers and exponents were wracked with anxieties and fears of being unworthy, or perhaps incapable of, this heavenly gift.

This cosmological view reached its most systematic expression in the writings of Sung dynasty philosophers, especially Chu Hsi (1130–1200), who reformulated the indigenous Confucian and Taoist schools of thought in response to the challenge posed by "foreign" Buddhist metaphysics. Reality was perceived in biological metaphors, so much so that Joseph Needham (among others) has characterized the Chinese world view as a "philosophy of organism." In Chu Hsi's thought *ch'i* ("energy-matter") and *li** ("order, pattern, principle of organization") represented the ma-

---

*The Chinese word *li* meaning "order, pattern, principle of organization," is given in this book with an asterisk to distinguish it from the *li* or "social customs."

terial and non-material elements in a basically natural universe.[17] Not translatable into Western dualities of body and soul or matter and form, they were held to be equally important in the universe.[18] They were understood to be in perpetual motion and mutual dependence, never separated; all things, from the inorganic to man, participated in the integrative patterns inherent in natural phenomena, according to their different capacities and levels of organization. All were seen as spontaneously combining into a whole that was constantly forming and reforming, but a whole that had no personalized Creator or Lawgiver and was simply a harmonious interaction of all things, each according to the internal necessities of its own nature. At the level of human nature, this meant the natural emergence of moral values whose full reality was "obstructed" at lower levels of existence. This philosophical system established human ethics within a naturalistic universe, and avoided the dualism of Western thought between mechanical matter and spiritual values.

Yet within this organic whole Thomas A. Metzger has detected an acute sense of predicament suffusing Neo-Confucian thought. The philosophers' goals indeed bespoke an image of human potentiality that made men godlike: total moral purification, total cognitive clarity, social and cosmic wholeness by the perfection of the *wu-lun* (human relationships) and by the achievement of *ta-t'ung* (the great oneness of all people), goals which depended upon the successful linkage of the metaphysical realm and the experiential realm. Humans were theoretically able to achieve this coherence and control in their lives not by unaided individual effort, but by tapping the positive cosmic force that existed in the universe and that was imprinted in their moral nature from birth. But the Neo-Confucian understanding of the given world, including the cosmos and human minds, so militated against the achievement of these goals that Metzger has described the overall effort to achieve them as exquisitely self-defeating, as Sisyphean in quality. The given "outer" world of other men and institutions was a "moral wilderness" that had led Neo-Confucians to despair of its radical transformation; good men, let alone sages, were rare. Evil had an ontological dimension beyond bad individual choices; there were inherently degenerative forces immanent in the very flow of existence, forces that made the good cosmic force elusive and mercurial. Moral principles were only incipient in the mind and selfish feelings all too pervasive; the evaluting mind had to be ever fearful and cautious, never dropping its guard. Certain areas of life, even the moral life, seemed determined by "what heaven had decreed": economic position, social status, longevity, and even the internal capacity to respond to external events. This great gap between goals and the given world, however, did not lead to a passive fatalism in post-Sung elite thought. It did discourage anything more than a "moderate realism" about reforming the governmental order; and under the stimulus of the Ming philosopher Wang Yang-ming (1472–1529), Confucian thought did turn progressively inward in attempting to understand more completely the nature of mind as the given locus for the linkage of metaphysical principle and experience. By the eighteenth century, the moral zeal inherent in the Neo-Confucian quest had declined; and Neo-Confucianism itself had become the high orthodoxy of the imperial system, thoroughly intertwined with the official Ch'ing examination system. [19]

The pervasive fears and anxieties expressed by Neo-Confucian thinkers point not only to a profound awareness of the subtle forms of corruptibility in the experiential world of the mind; they also show how high ideals, projected out into actual environments that were often their obverse, can undermine the self-confidence of the mind and create special needs for self-control. Like the peasantry, Neo-Confucians felt themselves to be subject to hostile environmental forces that often threatened to overwhelm the self; as with the peasantry, the explanation for this feeling can be found partly in projections of inherited beliefs which prejudged the meaning of what they saw and felt. Chu Hsi perceived a widespread turmoil in contemporary affairs and things when he held them up to the ideal models of Yao, Shun, and Yü and the Three Dynasties. The resultant tension, in practical terms, could only be resolved in the mind. The mind had to become the inner ruler exerting control in the face of threatening forces; yet the mind was inherently fragile, vulnerable to "any and all troubling outer stimuli, a thing perfectly designed to be victimized by [affairs and things] and their unremitting onslaught." Unable to sustain such control alone, the mind needed support from fixed principles and cosmic force. Metzger has expertly formulated the felt need for these "external" supports. Fixed principles, he argues, were for Chu Hsi a counterweight to avoid being like "a boat without a rudder" or someone "riding a horse, drifting about without a place to return to." Individuals furthermore "needed to feel supported by immense [cosmic] power transcending the immediate ego" in order to act morally.[20]

Deeply held values are other words for needs; a world view, through all its abstractness, speaks to us because it addresses our feelings, perhaps most particularly our anxieties. It is, or course, impossible to know how acute and widespread this Neo-Confucian moral anguish was among the millions of young men who aspired to or who qualified for literati rank via the examination route during the Ming-Ch'ing period. Obviously not all Neo-Confucians felt and thought alike; Wang Yang-ming did not even share Chu Hsi's contention that the human mind could hold onto the *tao* ("the Way") as a fixed thing, or that moral standards, righteousness, or principle had fixed locations.[21] But many did; and it was easy enough for the personally grasped, living truths of Chu Hsi or Wang Yang-ming to become dead formalistic principles in the hands of followers and students. The ascent to universal principles, cosmic force, and sagehood was understandably aborted for many in favor of reliance upon more proximate authorities, such as parents, teachers, friends, patrons, officials, and emperors, and even their own "selfish" notions and goals. Moral backsliding was the topic in China of countless learned exhortations.[22]

Such moral backsliding was undoubtedly furthered by the elite's embeddedness in the surrounding countryside of peasant villages, a closeness that guaranteed continuing challenges to Confucian rationalism and naturalism, not to mention to its moral zeal about transforming an obdurate environment. The living Neo-Confucian synthesis had to be rediscovered and affirmed by each generation out of its own experience, for this world view was an island existing in the sea of peasant fears and magical-supernatural beliefs. A strong skeptical tradition countered popular supernaturalism as well as such cultivated beliefs as divination and phenomenalism, but how difficult it was to be freed from belief in the spirit world![23] Technically, the spirits *(kuei-shen)* could be considered natural phenomena; but their occasionally capricious actions tended to break up the regularities in the world of humans and nature and introduce an unsettling dependence upon unpredictable forces, as Taoist thinkers had long recognized.[24] The Sung philosopher Chu Hsi personally admitted the existence of "dishonest and depraved *kuei-shen*," which whistled on rooftops and hit people in the dark, or to whom it was customary to offer exorcistic sacrifices. He rationalized the meaning of the old terms from the folk religion for souls and spirits, *hun-po* and *kuei-shen*, but still kept using them. This admission, and the inability to break away from old terms, gives us a glimpse of the effort it required for Confucian thinkers to maintain their naturalism and rationalism amid what Needham has called, in a footnote, "the encircling gloom."[25]

The ability to free oneself from the "encircling gloom," to believe with the Taoists and the Chinese skeptic Wang Ch'ung that "man has his happiness in his own hands, and the spirits have nothing to do with it" was largely a class ability.[26] The sense of control over one's life increased as wealth and education narrowed the areas of necessity and ignorance. Yet there were clear limits to this area of comprehension and control. The anxieties that the common people knew so well also pressed in on gentry families, despite their stronger kinship groups and greater wealth and influence. In times of exceptional stress—flood, drought, rebellion, war—even their hoarded resources could run out or their high-walled courtyards could become targets for plundering mobs. Before disease they were quite powerless. The expensive, exotic drugs that fourteen-year-old Lu Hsun (b. 1881) fetched for his dying father in late 1894 or early 1895 were not effective, and his father's slow death was as mysterious to him as it might have been to the son of a peasant. Unable to help or understand, he was at least able in a few years to get outside the event, to see the hypocrisy of the herbalists who had treated and cheated his father and himself, and eventually to secure training as a Western doctor in Japan.[27] This kind of resolution was, of course, seldom available to the son of a peasant, who was cut off from serious education and had fewer chances to come to understand disturbing experiences.

The sons of the educated were also in continuous contact with the Little Tradition in the village. As youngsters they avidly read the vernacular novels and heard the common folktales from traveling entertainers and servants. The women in the family were often firm believers in the system of popular religion. Great effort was sometimes necessary to free oneself from supernatural beliefs learned during childhood from mothers and nurses. The adolescent experience of Hu Shih (b. 1891) during the late Ch'ing illustrates this pain of extrication. Hu Shih's family split along philosophical and religious lines. His father and fourth uncle were followers of the Neo-Confucian school of *li-hsueh* (the study of principle), while his mother and other women relatives believed in Buddhism and supernatural spirits. From age three on, after his father died, the influence of the women was dominant, and the young Hu Shih came to live with the imagery of hell, rebirth, and the soul. At age ten, he was "enlightened" by reading several passages from the anti-Buddhist scholar Fan Chen (fifth century A.D.) and the historian Ssu-ma Kuang (1019–1086). They argued that the spirit rotted with the body and was simply not around for any hellish tortures. Young Hu began to doubt the very idea of a separate soul; and reincarnation ceased to explain why some were kings and others paupers. For him, this was a liberation from fear, not a simple question of intellectual growth. As he himself retold the experience,

> The cruel shapes of hell portrayed in *Mu-lien chiu-mu* [Mu-lien's descent into purgatory to save his mother], *Yu-li chao-chuan* [The chronicle of Yu-li] and other books appeared before my eyes, but I felt no fear. The pictures of Yin Wang of the Ten Palaces . . . and the 18 levels of hell with every sort of cow-headed and horse-faced devil using steel pitchforks to push the criminals up to Knife Mountain or down to the boiling cauldron of oil, and throw them under the Bridge of Hopelessness to feed hungry dogs and poisonous snakes—every kind of horrible appearance came before my eyes; but I felt no fear. I read the words repeatedly: 'Once the form perishes, the spirit disperses; so although there are tools to saw and beat and punish [spirits], there is no way to do it.' My heart was glad, as though the Buddha of Ti Tsang Wang had pointed the way with his scepter and the door of hell opened . . . In my childhood I had become used to the Buddhist teaching of karma and greatly feared becoming a pig or dog in my next existence. Then suddenly after reading Fan Chen's comparison, my heart was gladdened and took great courage from it. His and Ssu-ma Kuang's essay on the perishing of spirits taught me not to fear hell. His discourse on non-causality taught me not to fear. I was convinced by their words because they taught me not to fear.[28]

After this liberation, Hu Shih gradually became a non-believer, or literally "a person without demons or gods" *(wu-kuei wu-shen ti jen)*. Subsequently, however, he retained a strong interest in religious and philo-

sophical questions, and wrote much in a very negative vein on Buddhism
in China. It is hard to see how elite Chinese could completely free themselves from spirit belief, considering their exposure and participation in
the whole of society. A residue remained as part of their inner imagery,
a residue that required continuous mental work to keep confined and
unthreatening, especially when they were in the Chinese social setting.
As one popular skeptical slogan put it: *"Mi-hsin, mi-hsin, pu te pu hsin,"*
or "Yes, superstitions are superstitions, but one cannot help believing
in them." [29]

The sharing of the world with spirits and unpredictable supernatural
forms—assumed among the peasant masses, combatted with skepticism
among the educated—introduces a discordant element into the philosophical affirmation of reality as a natural whole accessible to human
understanding. The philosophical affirmation of human moral capacity
also becomes more problematic as the emphasis shifts away from human
beings as the measure towards human beings as the ones measured by
fixed ideals, principles, and norms. Starting with assumed principles
could cripple open-ended encounters with people and things by boxing
minds in and confining behavior to traditional categories, definitions,
and styles; proper behavior became conformity or squaring oneself within
the requisite categories. It was common, for example, during the Ch'ing
period to follow the orthodox Ch'eng-Chu school of Neo-Confucianism
in interpreting virtue as the suppression of evil desires in order to manifest the moral nature implanted in all men as principle or *li**. Only a
few innovative Ch'ing thinkers, such as Yen Yuan (1635–1704), Wang
Fu-chih (1619–1692), and Tai Chen (1724–1777) were willing to redefine virtue as the orderly expression and fulfillment of human desires
rather than their absence or suppression. [30] In making *li** secondary to
ch'i in emphasis, they became inclined to reevaluate the assumed antag-
onism between the moral nature implanted in humans and the reality of
human desires, without denying that selfish desires were a moral problem. Wang Fu-chih, in discussing the human fondness for wealth and
sex, best expresses the quality of openness to experience and surprise
that sets his mentality off from one that starts with principles and de-
duces truths.

Let us be broad and greatly impartial, respond to things as they come, look at them, and listen to them, and follow this way [of seeing the open desires of all creatures] in words and actions without seeking anything outside.[31]

Wang also refused to accept ancient institutions and practices as models for posterity, arguing that only the most general principles applied over long periods of time. He criticized the book memorizers for trying to "determine the fundamental standards for ten thousand generations."[32] In these differing areas of life and thought, Wang Fu-chih was expressing a consistent distaste for the closed argument, for the world of a priori assumptions that takes spontaneity out of experience, and for fixed traditions that hobble posterity in its fresh encounters with time and history. He did not reject generalizations and formulated standards but argued "let us investigate principle [*li**] as we come into contact with things, but never set up principle [*li**] to restrict things."[33]

That Wang Fu-chih, one of the most courageous and innovative thinkers in the early Ch'ing period, went unpublished for two hundred years testifies to the high price exacted within the system for nonconformist thought. Indeed, thinkers were not only enmeshed within the rural countryside of peasant villages, but also within an imperial state structure that jealously guarded its ideological perimeter. An illuminating example of the role of the state as guardian of orthodoxy is the sixteenth-century Ming experience with private academies *(shu-yuan)* whose revival was inspired in part by Wang Yang-ming's life and thought. These academies became, in the words of John Meskill, "cells of reform" within Chinese society, not unlike the institutions of the New Learning that became cells for social reform in late nineteenth-century China. The followers of Wang Yang-ming, although not questioning the ideal of sagehood taught by the Ch'eng-Chu school of Sung learning, urged the exploration of new means towards sagehood; in particular, they urged, on the one hand, less book learning and less concern for self-advancement via the examination system and, on the other hand, more experiential understanding of the classics and more introspective examination of the mind and the will. They encouraged freewheeling philosophical discussions within the academies, created a network of local education associations (with some commoners as members) outside the bureaucracy, and were very critical of corruption within official ruling circles. Political vulnerability finally ended the reform movement as the chilling winds of official proscription blew from the capital out into the provinces. But as Meskill argues, it was a general cultural autocracy and suspicion of intellectual independence and innovation that set the boundaries for this experiment. The new regulations within surviving academies restricted debate and instituted tighter and more book-oriented study schedules; they also sought to control student contact with "unedifying types," such as townspeople and other commoners. The thought of Wang Yang-ming was criticized by its detractors for irreverence towards tradition, for fallacious and heterodox reasoning, and for unleashing licentious behavior among many students that lured them away from their proper role and pursuits. This concern with the contamination of young minds as well as with the dangers of reform-minded and nonbureaucratic political associations combined to end at least the institutional side of the reform movement, if not to contain the influence of Wang Yang-ming's thought.[34]

From a late twentieth-century viewpoint, we can see that the orthodox Neo-Confucian tradition constricted life and thought within categories that were as much social and economic as universal, as much political and psychological as philosophical. Even its staunch contemporary defenders concede that Confucianism in its inherited form was an "impure" system, and that distinctions must be made between its essence and accidental and transient aspects, such as the institutions of feudalism, monarchy, and patriarchy.[35] This philosophical tradition, so dynamically formulated by Chu Hsi and Wang Yang-ming, consistently imparted to some of its adherents a sense of creative purpose within the natural cosmic order. Nevertheless, the recurrent ambivalence within that tradition about disruptive spiritual beings, the preference for reasoning from fixed and assumed norms, the measuring of the historical present by ancient ideal types, and the view of human desires as evil were signs of a faltering courage to sustain the dynamism of older discoveries and to prevent living truths from becoming lifeless principles. High moral idealism probably cannot be sustained indefinitely throughout a whole society, nor can corruptibility and vulgarity in human endeavors be eliminated. Over many long centuries, human initiative had pressed forward but remained thwarted in many ways; and this fact encouraged most human beings to live by the values of contentment, stability, moderate realism, and adjustment within the "immutable" natural, social, and political order. The distinctive Neo-Confucian image of the individual moral hero against the backdrop of an often corrupted society and polity was perhaps emblematic of the cultural pattern: neverending, persistent human action in the face of ancient anxieties engendered by the seemingly intractable struggle with the natural and human environment.

In Neo-Confucian eyes, reforming the world was a near heroic effort, admirable but seemingly doomed. Raising impressionable children to be upright in a moral wilderness partook of some of the same bravado and futility.

BECOMING HUMAN: TENSIONS IN A PHILOSOPHICAL PERSPECTIVE

In the popular religion of the peasants, the world was broken into visible and invisible realms as human minds strained imaginatively to comprehend and cope with powerlessness and defeat. The visible and invisible dimensions of reality interpenetrated each other in a literal way, as the belief in spirit sadism reveals. The peasants had learned to be aware of meanings within meanings; the tangible reality of words, places, parts of their own bodies, all had overlays of taboo, prohibition, caution, grace, good fortune, danger. Daily life was a minefield of hidden considerations.[36] Although much of this unseen world, at least in terms of literal beliefs in spiritual beings, was screened out in the understanding of reality accepted by the followers of the Great Tradition, they also experienced the tensions of a divided consciousness in their daily lives. They lived under the judgment of their moral principles enshrined in ancient ideal legendary sages and classical books, and in the more proximate regulations, rules, and maxims of family, clan, and school that gave these principles everyday meaning. These moral ideals and guidelines defined what it meant to become fully human *(tso jen),* and stood like an archway over the passage from childhood to adulthood.

This tension between moral ideals and daily existence, as it touched upon human development, was muted in the classical philosophical synthesis, especially among those affirming the dominant Mencian view of man. Ideal behavior was believed to be a natural outgrowth of potential within each human being; there were no innate flaws in human nature that obstructed this development. Anyone could become an ideal sage like the mythical emperors Yao, Shun, or Yü, by applying enough will to the task. This argument for a natural morality may be illustrated by the understanding of *hsiao* or "filial piety" which was a centerstone in the arch of moral ideals.

In one classic formulation in the *Classic of Filial Piety (Hsiao ching),* a Han text venerated into the twentieth century, *hsiao* articulated the nature of the first basic relationship of a growing child, that between parents and children. The *Classic of Filial Piety* implies that two early emotions point toward *hsiao:* affection *(ch'in)* and awe or reverence *(yen).* Affection is believed to be a natural admiration of children for parents, while awe or reverence seems to be derivative of this, and learned in practice. The former is related to the mother, the latter to the father, though not exclusively in either case.

> Affection arises during childhood, and reverence grows while supporting the parents [in later life.] Since every man develops a sense of reverence, the sages teach him how and when to show respect; and since he has a natural feeling of affection, they teach him how and when to cultivate it.[37]

The possibility of ethical life is founded upon the spontaneous activity of human nature; this activity both points to natural virtues, such as love and respect, and justifies the teaching of these virtues.

In Sung Neo-Confucian thought, a similar paradigm is found. Fundamental virtues—humaneness, righteousness, propriety, and wisdom—are believed to be inherent in human nature. Ethical impulses are manifested in the Four Beginnings, as understood by Mencius: the sense of commiseration, the sense of shame and dislike, the sense of deference and compliance, the sense of right and wrong. These impulses are developed by practicing the functional virtues, such as *hsiao* and *t'i* (brotherly deference) and *chung* (loyalty); but the higher pursuit of *jen* (humanity) includes these virtues and penetrates these beginnings while being something more: a generative principle reaching out to people and objects and transforming the universe.[38]

The Four Beginnings or innate moral qualities are accessible to introspection and provide the clues to the moral way. They are felt to be as
factual as biological existence, just as the virtues they point to are believed to be part of the frame of the cosmos. In the words of Mencius,

> [A] man without the feelings of commiseration is not a man; a man without the
> feeling of shame and dislike is not a man; a man without the feeling of deference
> and compliance is not a man. The feeling of commiseration is the beginning of
> humanity; the feeling of shame and dislike is the beginning of righteousness; the
> feeling of deference and compliance is the beginning of propriety; and the feeling
> of right and wrong is the beginning of wisdom. Men have these Four Beginnings
> just as they have their four limbs.[39]

Mature virtue represented the proper cultivation of these diffuse emotions. If they were not cultivated, they would "not be sufficient even to
serve one's parents." But when cultivated, they would be like "fire beginning to burn or a spring beginning to shoot forth."[40] Teaching by
parents and tutors was viewed as assistance in the cultivation of these
innate moral beginnings, so that they would form into ethical attitudes
and practices. Underlying the ethical life was thus an assumed covergence of nature, morality, and learning, as expressed at the beginning of
the *Doctrine of the Mean:*

> What heaven (*T'ien,* Nature) imparts to man is called human nature.
> To follow our nature is called the Way (*Tao,* Moral Law).
> Cultivating the Way is called education.[41]

This classical argument of natural covergence, or at least the optimism
about its easy achievement, is called into question by the Neo-Confucian
understanding of what was actually happening during the childhood years.
Darker realities forced themselves upon the minds of reflective Neo-Confucian scholars, just as they had led to a more pessimistic appraisal of
human nature in some circles in classical times.

THE LEGACY OF UNCONTROLLED FEELINGS. Philosophically, the Neo-
Confucians conceived of two components of human nature, the essential
or original nature and the physical nature. The essential nature, embodying the *li** of heaven, is good; but from the moment of birth, the
essential nature is enmeshed in physical nature, which is a specific en-

dowment of material force *(ch'i)*. To varying degrees, this material force obstructs the clear presence of the essential nature. "Nature in man is always good . . . With the existence of physical form, there exists physical nature. If one skillfully returns to the original nature endowed by Heaven and Earth, then it will be preserved. Therefore in physical nature there is that which the superior man denies to be his original nature."[42] This distinction allowed the Neo-Confucians to explain the occasion for evil, or deviation from the mean, as man's physical nature, while preserving the Mencian postulate of essential human goodness.

In developmental terms, childhood was divided into two phases: birth to seven years of age and seven to fourteen, the latter phase being the time for *hsiao hsueh* or elementary learning.[43] Birth initiated the arousal of emotions through the contact with external stimuli. The seven feelings—pleasure, anger, sorrow, joy, love, hate, and desire—ensued and were expressed recklessly without any sense of proportion. The original moral nature was damaged. There was deterioration from the good and deviation from the mean.[44] Studying and learning emerged as the way to reclaim the original nature, the way to harness the unbalanced expression of the feelings. Ch'eng I gives us a concrete description of this process:

> [Man's] original nature is pure and tranquil. Before it is aroused, the five moral principles of his nature, called humanity, righteousness, propriety, wisdom, and faithfulness, are complete. As his physical form appears, it comes into contact with external things and is aroused from within. As it is aroused from within, the seven feelings . . . ensue. As feelings become strong and increasingly reckless, his nature becomes damaged. For this reason the enlightened person controls his feelings so that they will be in accord with the Mean. He rectifies his mind and nourishes his nature. This is therefore called turning the feelings into the [original] nature.[45]

Centering upon the mind as the host of one's nature and the master of the feelings was the way to conquer oneself, to cultivate oneself as a moral being.[46] The mind, through study and investigation, could deepen its knowledge of the moral life and in practice learn to harmonize the feelings so that reactions would be appropriate. Without this conquest of the self, the deterioration would continue, for the feelings were "loose" without control. They could become depraved, fetter the original nature, and destroy it. "This is called turning one's nature into feelings."[47] The second half of childhood was thus a critical stage in an all-out, either/or struggle against losing. In "The Examination of the Self and Things," Chu Hsi makes this clear:

> If the Principle of Nature exists in the human mind, human selfish desires will not, but if human selfish desires win, the Principles of Nature will be destroyed. There has never been a case where both the Principle of Nature and human selfish desires are interwoven and mixed. This is what the student must realize and examine for himself.[48]

This mixed state, however, was the perceived *actual* condition of the child and young student, as they were "not yet developed in knowledge and experience" (*chih-shih wei k'ai*) and did not yet possess the tool of understanding to cope with their environmentally induced "contamination."[49]

WAS MAN UNWORTHY OR INCAPABLE OF HIS NATURE? Despite the truth that "harmony" was achieved by great struggle against undisciplined feelings—a conquest of self perfected only by the sage—few philosophers were tempted to put these feelings at the heart of human nature and call it evil. The "tough-minded" Hsun-tzu (third century B.C.)—sometimes contrasted with the "tender-minded" Mencius—fully acknowledged this dark underside of human existence. He brings us down into the actual evidence and into the murky reality of social life, where humans are caught up in powerful emotions.

> If man gives rein to his nature and follows his passions, he will strive and grab, leading to a breach of order and confounding of reason, and culminating in violence. Only under the restraint of teachers and laws and the guidance of rules of the *li* [propriety] and *yi* [righteousness] does man conform to prudence, observe good manners, and yield to order. From all this, it is evident that the nature of man is evil and that his goodness is acquired. Crooked wood needs to undergo steaming and plumbing; only then can it become straight. Blunt metal needs to undergo grinding and whetting; only then can it become sharp. Now the nature of man is evil; therefore, he needs the teachers and laws so as to be upright; he needs the rules of *li* and *yi* so as to be orderly. Without the teachers and laws men are biased, vicious, and unjust; without *li* and *yi* men are rebellious and disorderly.[50]

Hsun-tzu argued that unethical behavior flowed partly from a natural tendency towards excessive desire for external things, partly from the condition of scarcity. Such behavior made it necessary to institute social distinctions, hierarchical organizations, moral indoctrination, and legal controls backed by the state. He had no trust in individual moral intuition and exhortation in social and political affairs, and vigorously disputed the Mencian doctrine of the innate goodness of man. His influence overshadowed Mencius through the Han period (206 B.C.–A.D. 220), but then receded. Mencius, not he, came to be regarded as in the direct line of transmission from Confucius.[51] Nevertheless, Hsun-tzu continued to be read, for his realism accorded better with the actual world of human institutions, from families and academies to armies and bureaucracies.

Hsun-tzu had recorded loudly and openly a fear that is muted in the mainstream philosophers: the fear that human beings in general are unworthy, or perhaps even incapable, of the virtue that nature had supposedly bestowed upon them; that instead of cultivating the higher "mind of Tao," they will cultivate the lower "mind of man."[52] The potential in man for disorder, for violence, for willful and selfish behavior was a perception that few could suppress, even within their idealistic systems. Mencius with his Four Beginnings had postulated a kind of natural incarnation of virtue within every human being, but this ideal seemed distant and remote from childhoods contested by surging feelings and immature minds. Could all men win that contest? Theoretically yes, argued Ch'eng I.

Question: Since man's nature is originally clear, why is there obscuration?

Answer: This must be investigated and understood . . . There is no nature that is not good. Evil is due to capacity. Man's nature is the same as principle, and principle is the same from the sage-emperors Yao and Shun to the common man in the street. Capacity is an endowment from material force. Material force may be clear or turbid. Men endowed with clear material force are wise, while those endowed with turbid material force are stupid.

Further Question: Can stupidity be changed?

Answer: Yes. Confucius said, "The most intelligent and the most stupid do not change." But in principle they can. Only those who ruin themselves and cast themselves away do not change.

Question: Is it due to their capacity that the most stupid ruin and throw themselves away?

Answer: Certainly. But it cannot be said that they cannot be changed. Since all have the same basic nature, who cannot be changed? Because they ruin and cast themselves away and are not willing to learn, people are unable to change. If they are willing to learn, in principle they can change.[53]

The philosopher Chu Hsi, however, could not simply affirm human moral capacity in the abstract. He recognized through his own experience the multiple sources of distraction, confusion, temptation, and failure, and the powerful effort required to anchor oneself in the midst of this struggle.

[A]lthough man is darkened by material force and degenerates into evil, nature does not cease to be inherent in him. Because of this, man must increase his effort at purification. If one can overcome material force through learning, he will know that this nature is harmonious and unified and from the beginning has never been destroyed.

[T]he cultivation of the essential and the examination of the difference between the Principle of Nature and selfish human desires are things that must not be interrupted for a single moment in the course of our daily activities and movement and rest. If one understands this point clearly, he will naturally not end up drifting into popular ways of success and profit and expedient schemes. I myself did not really see this point until recently. My past defeat of emphasizing fragmentary and isolated details revealed various symptoms from these ways of life. The faults of forgetting the self, chasing after material things, leaving the internal empty, and greedily desiring the external remain the same. Master Ch'eng said, "One must not allow the myriad things in the world to disturb him. When the self is established, one will naturally understand the myriad things in the world." When one does not even know where to anchor his body and mind, he wrongly talks about the kingly way and the despotic way and discusses and studies the task of putting the world in order as if it were a trick. Is that not mistaken?[54]

Becoming a sage, like becoming Christlike, is a task so exquisite in its demands that only those with special gifts or "grace" seem to have a real chance. The sage, Chu Hsi told us, is "good from childhood," and "preserves his heavenly endowment complete."[55] And for the rest? They may learn virtue by study, by hard work and practice. But as Confucius contended, there were still many—"the lowest of the people"—who never learned virtue.[56] The Confucian criterion used to determine the "lowest of the people" was level of moral and rational being. Those who lacked self-control were by definition low on the scale, for they deviated from the mean. Those who pursued the external and neglected the internal were also low on the scale. But the correlation with class was complicated, for the *hsiao jen* or "inferior man" could refer to a highly literate but immoral person. Similarly, an illiterate person could be a *shan jen* or "virtuous person." Some of those with the most filial hearts seem to have appeared among the lower classes, especially among women; but such virtue was often qualified by an ambiguous label *yü-hsiao* which might mean "simple but filial" or "foolishly filial."[57]

Whatever their theoretical affirmations about human potential and natural equality, the scholars and their students were mainly talking to their own kind among the educated males, those who had the chance to study and learn, to acquire self-control by self-cultivation, and to come to know a rich symbolic world of values within which to measure themselves and others. They knew that the lives of common people were dominated by economic survival and second- or third-best choices; without this requisite learning, commoners could not be trusted to act on their inner moral intuition, theory or no theory. As Colonel Tcheng Kitong expressed elite sentiment in 1884 in *The Chinese Painted by Themselves,* the common man was too ignorant, too undisciplined to "put off his nullity" and "to feel himself a spirit, a being, thinking, willing, knowing." He was too inert and "abased by the bad use of his faculties" to "open his eyes to the azure splendor of the illimitable universe."[58] The remoteness of the ethical ideal of the sage was reflected in the dual ethical standards that came to prevail in practice: the ethic of the superior man *(chün-tzu)* and the ethic of the inferior man *(hsiao jen),* the rules of propriety and self-regulation for the educated, and law, indoctrination, and external control for the masses. This dual standard was a concession to reality recognized within Confucianism itself, with the idealistic Mencian wing advocating the way of the superior man as praiseworthy while the realistic wing, drawing upon Hsun-tzu among others, at least tolerated the way of the inferior man as normal.[59]

Young students during the period of elementary learning were viewed as closer to the ways of the inferior man than to the self-disciplined behavior of the superior man. They were, after all, immature and could not yet be trusted to do what was right on their own; as such they required a scaffolding of regulations and rules to guide their behavior within proper bounds until they developed internal means for self-direction. These extra-legal regulations and rules, such as those established by families, clans, and academies, should thus be seen as practical applications of the basic principles that were designed by gentry and scholar-officials for the use of commoners and beginners. Like the *Sacred Edict (Sheng-yü)*, a series of moral maxims devised by the Ch'ing emperors to be read to villagers and students by local officials and gentry, they may be viewed as ideological social controls that represented concessions to the arrested or incomplete moral and rational development of most Chinese, certainly the young but also most uneducated adults as well.[60] Within a Ming academy, for example, these regulations might typically have consisted of three elements: a general statement of principles, such as Chu Hsi's Articles of Instruction at the Pai-lu-tung Academy in Nanchang; a more detailed set of proprietary rules, such as the Rules of Conduct or School Regulations written by Chu Hsi's pupils, Ch'eng Tuan-meng and Tung Shu; and finally a set of study rules. The first and second were often published together and thought of as complementary, joined metaphorically as the "roots and branches" of a sound moral curriculum.[61] Chu Hsi had apparently felt that detailed school regulations were needed only for younger students during the period of elementary learning. Yet youngsters of fourteen years of age or under were undoubtedly the exceptions within academies, as the average age for the attainment of the status of government student or licentiate (the *sheng-yuan* degree) which qualified one to attend a government college or private academy was twenty-four during the Ming-Ch'ing period.[62] Even in these elite settings the time for guided or controlled living and learning seems to have extended well beyond the period of elementary learning, reflecting an ambivalence towards giving behavioral and intellectual scope to growing children and young adults. Confucian idealism about human development thus commonly became translated into detailed rules, prohibitions, and sanctions as well as moral exhortations. This Confucian moral education in practice did instill in young people a tension between ideals and daily life; but it also created an ambivalence within many of them over prescriptive control, protection, and guidance. The New

Learning of the late nineteenth and early twentieth centuries would cast fresh perspectives on both of these traditional areas of tension.

Philosophical conceptions of human development within a culture are problematic pieces of evidence for understanding childhoods and children. They represent formulations by the highly literate segment of the populace and probably have a disproportionate reference to this group over the rest of society. While the mandarin father may worry about his son turning towards his original nature, peasant parents as well as upper-class mothers may worry in other terms about other things, such as successfully overcoming the thirty barriers of childhood and locking the child's soul into this earthly existence. Philosophical evidence also does not describe actual persons in actual situations, which is the kind of evidence one finally requires in order to establish generalizations about human behavior in any time or place.[63] The philosophical conception of the struggle to become fully human during the early years of life, however, offers an important clue to actual happenings in Chinese society. This clue is the adult conception of childhood, at least for boys on the path of learning, as a time of crisis, a time when "a chronic sickness in the roots" can set in, and when life is set on a rotten or firm basis.[64] If there were the all-important turning towards the original nature between seven years of age and fourteen, then one had laid a basis for the adult task of "straightening the inner life" *(cheng-hsin)* and becoming fully human *(ch'eng jen)*. If instead there were an acquiescence in self-centered, unbalanced passions, then one became increasingly arrogant, lazy, aggressive, spoiled, and inconsiderate. Schoolboys as they emerged from these years were thought to be deeply biased towards one or the other of these diverging paths of development, and thus deeply in need of strong and timely encouragement and guidance from parents and teachers to develop their innate goodness before it was too late.

Implicit within this concept of childhood is a view of the earlier period, birth to seven years, as a time when good and evil beginnings flourished indiscriminately. There was an inevitable phase of deterioration and deviation in the human life cycle, except in the case of those "born good." External stimuli aroused strong feelings and desires in the child, desires that an environment of scarcity could not satisfy. Children were not capable of controlling their feelings, nor did they possess the means to concentrate, to discriminate, or to regulate their relationship to the environment. They were victims of their physical nature, immersed temporarily in the state of evil without the inner resources to do anything about it. Children in this state were not expected to be responsible for their own behavior, but were necessarily dependent upon the guidance and protection of others.

The perception of these two periods of childhood as times of critical danger—first in the child's helplessness to resist evil and then in the fateful turning towards or denying of the child's original nature—provided a rationale for parents' strong intervention into the lives of their children. Unlike the rationale about children being weak, vulnerable, and dependent beings who needed to be protected from an indifferent, even hostile, environment, this rationale was based upon an understanding of what was happening inside children over time. The concern was not only to shield children from undesirable external influences, but also to save their moral nature from choking in internal weeds by cultivating a proper orientation towards self and world. The conclusion in both lines of thought was that children needed to be protected, from the environment and from themselves.

In the practical understanding of children, the guiding assumption seems to have been the one that stressed their malleability and susceptibility to evil rather than teachings about their natural goodness and predisposition to virtue. Once again, the teaching of ideals appears as an outcropping of rock in the midst of turbulent waters, a positive hope in a sea of negative possibilities. The Ch'ing educator Chang Po-hsing in a commentary on a passage in Chu Hsi warned explicitly of the consequences of careless neglect in the educating of the young during the period of elementary learning:

> If the father and elder brother do not teach him at the first and a pupil picks up these bad habits when he is a little older, he will become addicted to sensual pleasures as soon as the desire for them arises within him, while he will be infused from without by the vile habits of those with whom he keeps company. Although at this time you may try to restrain him with the proper way, he will already have become overbearing and difficult to control and any attempt to correct him will not make any impression on him. To attempt to refute his arguments in

order to bring him back to purity or to make good his deficiencies in order to make him perfect, how difficult that would be! Fathers and elder brothers should respect and write down these words of Chu Hsi in their entirety.[65]

The environment was not all-powerful, but whatever learning entered the child first was believed to become dominant *(hsien ju wei chu)* and then to bedevil or facilitate the process of moral and intellectual development. Various common expressions underlined this point: "What is formed during childhood appears as though it is innate *(t'ien hsing)*" and "When habits develop, they are like second nature."[66]

Parents and teachers were urged to start early in order to occupy and control that inner space, as if the child were an empty receptacle that could be filled. Chang Po-hsing commented favorably on this passage from Ch'eng I:

[Y]ou should spread out maxims and discussions exemplifying the highest reason before him every day. Although he is not yet capable of perceiving these with understanding, if you cultivate him with them until his ears and belly are full of them, he will practice them readily as though he were born with them. If you do this, he cannot be deluded by other ideas.[67]

Once occupied, Chang Po-hsing believed, the inner space could be securely held, for then "he cannot hear or fill his belly with other ideas."[68] The strategy of education indeed started during the period of elementary learning with the unreasoning practice of conduct and the uncomprehending memorization of texts, so that certain ideas were imprinted on the mind in rhythmic patterns and certain behaviors became natural in the bearing and motion of the body. Subsequently, the major aspiration was to integrate conduct and the conscious knowledge about conduct gained from the classical texts.[69] Eventually, after age fourteen, learning became a more self-sustaining matter of personal choice and self-cultivation, still backed up by family, clan, and academy codes and regulations. Leverage slowly passed out of the hands of parents or teachers, who had done what they could to put their sons on the path towards becoming fully human. Above all, this meant young men coming to measure themselves by the moral standards of the Great Tradition, that archway dividing childhood from adulthood.

So appeared the stakes of childhood to many Chinese philosophers and educators, and presumably to many educated Chinese fathers as well in their role as parents. The early years of parenthood were a crucial time with heavy responsibilities. The exact feeling of how "crucial" or how "heavy" is comprehensible only to one who has experienced childhood— as a parent or child—as such a time of physical and moral crisis, for the particular Chinese assumptions about children and the years of childhood are not universal truths. The children themselves, of course, had little chance to get a critical perspective on what was happening to them, although some of the mischievous ones did indeed perceive that they were being stretched to fit a frame that felt imposed and wrong. As the Chinese cultural world began to break apart in the early twentieth century, some adult educators and reformers began to agree with these dissident children. By the end of the New Culture period (1915–1921), a veritable tide of feeling and arguments against filial upbringing and authoritarian education had swept through coastal and literate China. By then a historic restructuring of the process of growing up had occurred, allowing long latent capabilities for cultural criticism and innovation to surface and ride the waves, if only for a few brief decades.

Boys on exercise field of new-style government school, Chihli, ca. 1900.
Courtesy, Essex Institute, Salem, Mass.

TWO

The Locus of Innovation, 1840–1920

For Lu Hsun and other cultural reformers of the May Fourth era, the traditional child-rearing in family and school made children "more dead than alive." They felt that the prized virtue of *hsiao* or "filial devotion" reversed the proper order of relations between young and old. Instead of emancipating their children into independence, parents required that children "learn from the sages and sacrifice themselves." Instead of guidance, there were orders; instead of understanding, only commands to obey. "Children," Lu Hsun charged in 1918, "are simply material for their parents' happiness, not shoots of future men." [1] These accusations were not based upon a misunderstanding of *hsiao* but rather upon a rejection—often emotional and impetuous—of its assumptions. The filial system had become transparent; no longer held to be natural or enjoined by cosmic order, it had to stand or fall on the basis of critical examination under contemporary criteria.

The intent of training in *hsiao* was indeed to create a dutiful being prepared to act morally in a network of human relationships, not to create an independent-minded individual intent upon pursuing his or her own way in the world. In the supplementary childhood text, *The Twenty-four Examples of Filial Piety,* the child never outgrew the status of son and was expected to live in the original family setting under the shadow of his parents and ancestors. [2] Four of the twenty-four examples are married men; and five are older men, including the tale of Lao Lai Tzu:

Although upwards of seventy years of age, he declared that he was not yet too old, and dressed in gaudy-colored garments, would frisk and cut capers like a child in front of his parents. He would also take up buckets of water and try to carry them into the house, but feigning to slip, would fall to the ground, wailing and crying like a child; and all these things he did in order to divert his parents.[3]

Ideally the son would dedicate his innermost self to the well-being of his parents, and not just satisfy their material needs.

Great filial piety, such as that exemplified by the legendary Emperor Shun, consisted of a steady outpouring of respect, devotion, tolerance, and good will, no matter how great the sacrifice, how unreciprocal the relationship, how undeserving the parents. His father was constantly unprincipled, his stepmother insincere, and his younger half-brother arrogant; but he persevered in his filial obligations despite their wickedness. His perfect sincerity eventually converted his parents and brother and brought his name to the ears of Emperor Yao, who "sent his nine sons to serve him, gave him two of his daughters in marriage, and afterwards resigned to him the imperial dignity."[4] One flaw in Shun's filial performance, in the eyes of some pre-Mencian scholars, was his Job-like grumbling, which suggested that he might have been murmuring in resentment against his parents. In an unusual and strained defense on Shun's behalf, Mencius denied this charge, arguing that Shun was sorrowful because he deplored his own inability to secure the affection and sympathy of his parents.[5] Of course, nobody really knows what Shun felt, for he was supposed to have ruled from 2255 to 2205 B.C., near the beginning of Chinese civilization. The argument is illuminating, however, for the diverse projections into Shun's life story reveal the moralistic sniping that surrounded the concept of *hsiao* and the perfecting of filial obedience.

The injunction to obedience was circumscribed by the right to remonstrate and the expectation of mutuality, as living traditionalists are quick to remind one. In the *Analects* the right to remonstrate is defined as follows:

The master said, in serving his father and mother, a man may gently remonstrate with them. But if he sees that he has failed to change their opinion, he should resume an attitude of deference and not thwart them. He may feel discouraged, but not resentful.[6]

Resentment was an unacceptable emotion, no matter how justified. Remonstrance against unworthy parents was a weak right when weighed on the scales with the duties of obedience and submission. Similarly, mutuality was an expectation; but when it was not forthcoming, there was little that the son could do. Both ethically and legally he had the choice of bending or being bent.

The categories "moral" and "legal" in Ch'ing China were very blurred, for the law contained "a command to obey the dictates of the highest morality (as distinct from customary morality)." Moral lapses, if discovered, had to be punished, although the degree of guilt varied with status and circumstances. The penal law of the official yamen courts was reinforced by clan law *(tsu-kuei)*, which operated in villages and among families with a kind of delegated authority. For example, the "ten big offenses" in the penal law of the empire were sometimes expressly included in the list of offenses punishable by a clan. The essence of these ten crimes was disobedience to constituted authority, whether in the family or the state; one of these ten was the unspecific "lack of filial piety," another, discord within the family. Although lax enforcement and attentiveness to circumstance in reaching decisions worked in general to mitigate the surface harshness and one-sided nature of the legal codes, the Chinese administration of justice overall provided no check against oppression by the constituted authorities: "When the administration was most oppressive, the actual operation of the legal system was at its worst. Nor did it offer protection to the weak against domination by stronger members of groups," nor of weak groups by strong groups.[7] Children were clearly a weak group within the system, although it does not inevitably follow that as a group they were normally and systematically oppressed.

Legal or ethical support aside, children's sense of the right to have, let alone to assert, feelings of their own was underdeveloped. This was partly because they were made to feel overwhelmingly indebted to parents for their very existence. Filial gratitude crowded out many "unfilial" private emotions, or pushed them deep inside. Part of this debt was for the biological gift of life itself; part was for the care that the child received during its early years, a debt created by the perseverance of the parents in the face of the trouble and anxiety caused by the child. As expressed in *The Twenty-four Examples of Filial Piety,* "children should have deep and ardent affection for their parents, who have endured so much anxiety in nourishing them."[8] The expressions of affection were obedience and support, the former implying the yielding of the self, the latter the kind of material support that some have characterized as "social insurance" Chinese-style. The first examples of filial behavior among children seem to have been tales of yielding. In the *San Tzu Ching* (Three character classic), K'ung Jung at age three yielded the bigger pears to his elders and chose only small ones for himself. In *The Twenty-four Examples of Filial Piety,* six-year-old Lu Chin set aside two gift oranges to give his mother. Even the last Ch'ing Emperor, who had a very self-centered childhood, recollected running off to share "the pill of immortality with his mothers, out of a sense of *hsiao.*"[9]

Clearly it was the parents' needs, material as well as psychological, that were in the forefront. The reformers attacked this order of priorities and the underlying rationale of indebtedness because they knew these helped erode the sense of the self as an independent center of action. Hu Shih, for example, wrote in a letter to a friend that his newborn son owed him nothing whatsoever for the gift of life.

> I want my son to know that I only hold a feeling of guilt towards him for causing his birth. Certainly I am not in a state of merit, nor do I display any grace . . . I certainly do not expect my son to return my kindness, for as I have announced already, I have given him nothing that requires gratitude.[10]

By renouncing any state of merit simply for being a parent, Hu Shih was undercutting a key assumption within the filial system, and presumably giving his son more inner space within which to develop his individual perceptions. Trapped within parental perceptions, all children acquire a skewed version of "the way things are"; the spontaneous expression of their own bodily needs and budding thoughts are necessarily secondary to adapting to the cultural world of the surrounding adults.[11] While such adaptation often protects children by encouraging them to develop a healthy sense of reality about their environments, in other guises, such as the inculcating of a heavy sense of indebtedness to adults, this adaptation serves mainly to close off areas of individual experience and exploration.

The reformers also attacked old-style formal education for its deadening impact upon children. Indeed, in retrospect, the traditional approach to educating children from age seven to fourteen was very restrictive in several areas, as one Western study has demonstrated.[12] First, the demands of the classical language and the examination system created the perception that children were incapable of intellectual understanding and self-direction until around age fourteen, and that prior to this age they could only be indoctrinated into right principles and conditioned into right behavior. The child's difficulty in learning a foreign language—as foreign as Latin would be to a native speaker of Italian—was translated into intellectual immaturity. The philosophical and historical texts from which the child was expected to learn also bore little if any relation to the everyday world around it. "Traditional Chinese teaching practice required the pupil to grow intellectually to meet the standards of the literary language and its philosophical and moral content . . . Chinese theories of intellectual maturation are thus in part theories of how the child grows to meet the demands of the Confucian intellectual system."[13] In the sense that capacities were deduced from performance within a very particular learning framework, the observations and the theory based on them were accurate; but they are not universal insights into children or the process of learning.

Second, the scope of "useful" knowledge and the range of "acceptable" behavior were narrow indeed. The curriculum might well have included many indigenous Chinese works, from studies on science and technology to non-Confucian classics and vernacular novels; instead it focused almost exclusively on the Four Books, the Five Classics, and certain commentaries and collections of model prose compositions and poetry.[14] The range of acceptable behavior is suggested by this passage on "speech" from the *T'ung-tzu li* or *Decorum for the Young,* a sixteenth-century text reprinted with commentary in the eighteenth century by Ch'ing official and educator Ch'en Hung-mou. The text provides a set of behavioral prescriptions for the right way to walk, sit, talk, and behave in the presence of teachers and other elders. This, for example, was the specific comment on speech:

> In general the young person should make a habit of keeping his mouth closed and remaining silent. He must not speak out frivolously. If he has something to

say, he should be subdued of voice and manner. He must not chatter noisily. The
matters about which he speaks must be genuine and have a basis in fact. He must
not tell lies nor be overbearing toward others to the point where he lightly criti-
cizes their good and bad points. He should be stopped from using the vulgar
language of the marketplace and from jesting. [15]

The restrictions entered both into what one was told to be ("Be serious,
subdued, cautious, refined") and into what one was told not to be ("Don't
be frivolous, noisy, critical, vulgar, lighthearted"). Besides these explicit
messages there was the implicit message that running, climbing, swim-
ming, ballplaying, playacting, dancing, and many other activities had
no acknowledged place in the world of the educated adult.

The reformers' perception that Chinese children were "more dead than
alive" grew out of an urgent sense of need and an enlarged sense of
possibilities. They were groping towards a new set of assumptions as
well as rejecting an older set. Whatever they were, children were not
just vulnerable, dependent beings that needed to be protected and filled
up with "correct" ideas; and childhood was not just a moral struggle. A
restrictive filial system in child-rearing and schools was not the only
imaginable one; in fact, this system now seemed unwise as well as unnecessary to many reflective Chinese adults who had begun placing a
premium on the cultivation of individual resourcefulness, initiative, and
vitality. Were some of the "dangerous" and "immoral" behaviors detected through traditional eyes on the contrary perhaps something else,
perhaps even desirable personal traits? If so, how could they be encouraged? It had taken a long time to prepare the ground for the very asking
of such questions, let alone for their receiving a wide sympathetic hearing. Much of a world had had to fall into ruins first.

THE CONTEXT FOR INNOVATION, 1840–1910

Times of sharp historical discontinuity remind us that human institutions are precipitates of perceived human needs and purposes, not systems with a reified life of their own. As embodiments of ideas, elite
institutions rest upon the continuing affirmation of the worth of these
underlying ideas by the educated leadership appearing in each generation. If such natural leaders, in large numbers, feel something other

than an affirmation born of intellectual and emotional commitment, then an institutional crisis is being prepared, however long it might take for alternative symbols and structures to crystalize. By 1905 in China the centuries-old civil service examination system had been abolished; by 1912 the monarchy itself was overthrown; and by 1920 the family system—including such venerable ideals as *hsiao*—was coming under attack from a youthful urban counterculture. The battles going on inside the minds of May Fourth reformers like Hu Shih and Lu Hsun reflected an advanced stage of the coming apart of the ideas that had been one integrative force among the educated in China.

The nineteenth century was a time of preparation in the minds of the Chinese elite for widespread institutional changes that were to occur in the early twentieth century. "The great change was in the mental landscape of China's educated. The invisible bars which two or three generations earlier had locked the minds of Chinese scholars in a closed Confucian world had first been made visible and then, after much painful effort, had been pried apart, letting in a whole new universe of ideas, information, and values." [16] The geographical seat of this "new universe" in its modest early form in the 1840s and 1850s was an unimpressive string of treaty ports along China's coasts and rivers, a frontier land where a new maritime civilization was taking form. [17] The cross-cultural contagion between hinterland and frontier fringe during the nineteenth century was very limited because this treaty-port world was economically and culturally marginal, the participation of Chinese in it very selective, and the psychology of the encounter between these two different civilizations grim and manipulative. Yet by 1900 tens of thousands among the educated had made the transition to the era of factories, trains, newspapers, and modern firearms, and to new concepts such as national sovereignty; by 1920 a whole generation of self-conscious youth had enthusiastically committed itself to "modernity." The role of the treaty ports in this transformation was catalytic and hence their marginality was deceptive.

Geographically, the treaty-port order was very peripheral, clinging to a few outposts on the Chinese coast and up the Yangtze river. Most were initially located on the outskirts of an existing Chinese trading center, using land lying between a Chinese city and a river, and often even an island in the river. Four northern provinces (Honan, Shansi, Shensi, and Kansu) and one southern province (Kueichow) had no treaty ports at all. The interior opened up to trade quite slowly beyond Hankow: Changsha became a treaty port only in 1905 and Chungking in 1907; there was no regular steamboat service into Szechwan until 1908. While some treaty ports, notably Shanghai, Tientsin, and the colony of Hong Kong, developed into major urban complexes, many remained small stations with a handful of foreigners; there might be a dock, a customs office, and a tacit or legal foreign residential section.[18] The separate residential area meant that the nineteenth-century foreign merchant community had virtually no contact with Chinese apart from household servants and business agents. Their world was bounded by the anchorage, the bund, the club, the mission station, the cemetery, the consulate, and the racecourse.

The Western merchants' hope for the economic transformation of China, with the treaty ports as the "leading edge," never occurred; for the immense, relatively prosperous, and self-sufficient indigenous economic system frustrated the efforts of Westerners to remake it, and in fact even limited the development of Western systems in the ports themselves. Instead of transforming China economically, the foreign-dominated sector of China remained apart, a separate, urban world, legally encased in extraterritoriality and politically confined. With few exceptions, its innovative economic potential did not spill over into the hinterland.[19] Foreign missionaries, however, secured the right to own land and to proselytize in the interior after 1860, and their street chapels multiplied throughout China. By 1920 the chart of "conquest" could be computed down to the county level.[20] The missionary perception of the Chinese—narrowly as souls to save, broadly as humans with needs to serve—encouraged a more intimate encounter than the merchant perception of the Chinese as producers of tea and silk and consumers of kerosene, cotton yarn, and tobacco. The missionaries were not selective about whose souls they saved, and proselytized directly in the streets among poor people. Missionary pioneering in schools, hospitals, and relief work concentrated their impact upon large groups of Chinese at critical points in their lives: schooling years for the young, and the experiences of coping with disease and disaster.[21] But China was stony ground on which to scatter the seeds of the Gospel, even the social Gospel: Measured by the number of Chinese converts, both Catholic and Protestant, the Christian community in China never exceeded one percent of the population.[22]

Despite this evidence of marginality, the treaty-port order has significance as a set of ideas and institutions in tension and counterpoint with Chinese life and thought. The growing awareness of this fact, first by the "pioneer reformers" and later by virtually the entire group of educated Chinese, meant the internalization of this tension in their own minds. This fringe world was a concentrated presence of alternative ways of thinking, feeling, and organizing life fastened firmly onto the body of China in such a way that it could not be easily absorbed nor cut off and ignored only for so long. Given the weakness of the imperial Ch'ing dynasty, the danger of contagion by this alternative cultural order could not be resolved by force, that is, by noncultural confrontation. The treaty ports, linked as they were to Europe, America, and Japan by a flow of people, goods, and gunboats, could only be influenced by Chinese authorities, not controlled. In the course of the nineteenth century, the new order grew into a separate cultural and political entity beyond the reach—if not the titular sovereignty—of Chinese officialdom. It was a world that Chinese officials disliked but were powerless to contain, let alone eliminate.

As an institutional complex, the treaty ports represented a qualitative change from earlier patterns of contact between Chinese and foreigners. The factory system in Canton under the tributary system, or ecclesiastical missions in Peking such as those the Jesuit order maintained in the sixteenth and seventeenth centuries, or the Russian Orthodox church in the eighteenth and nineteenth centuries, did not represent a transplanted world, complete with family cells and a variety of social, economic, and political institutions. By contrast, the treaty-port order was just such an institutionally complete alternative. In some areas, notably the administration of justice, language, and architecture, and in the pattern of its economic life, this transplanted world was a hybrid of Chinese and Western cultures. Otherwise the treaty ports were already "West" and not China: They were "tiny and isolated islands in an alien Chinese sea . . . they remained foreign in everyone's eyes, clearly distinct from the country as a whole, external, fragile, superficial grafts."[23] When the pioneer reformer Wang T'ao traveled to Europe for twenty-six months in 1867–1870, he only had his previous knowledge of the West deepened and confirmed by this "field experience"; the essential image he had drawn from his contact with Westerners and their institutions in Hong Kong and Shanghai remained intact.[24] Thus the treaty-port order presented a clear conjunction of differences inside China where another cultural entity, the "West," could be observed in concrete detail, if the desire to do so was present.

It is hardly surprising that the dominant attitude toward the treaty-port world among the official "barbarian experts" or "treaty-port mandarins" who were recruited by Ch'ing officials to manage relations with the unwelcome Western powers was negative and manipulative. They "participated" in treaty-port life in order to control and limit an undesirable phenomenon, and "learned" as much as they felt was necessary to achieve this objective. As one scholar noted, "The new specialists in barbarian-taming appear to have been tolerated by their colleagues: they did an odious and distasteful job, like sewer-inspectors . . ."[25] These colleagues, if the lower- and middle-level officials who expressed themselves through *ching-i* or "public opinion" during the 1870s and 1880s are indicative, reinforced this perspective through their conservative and bellicose attitude towards self-strengthening innovations, individual reformers, and any signs of a conciliatory attitude towards the Western powers. For them, the inner experience of this "clear conjunction of differences" was psychological shock, a sense of incredulity that the Chinese state and customs could be and had been violated; it bred a defensive desire to hold on and strike back.[26]

Even a cursory exploration of the nineteenth-century record, however, contains descriptions of other inner responses to this intrusive alien fringe civilization. In some individuals, the sharp comparison caught hold of the imagination and enforced a certain suspension of judgment and enlargement of perspective. The defensive language of shame, manipulation, techniques, warnings, and reaffirmations could give way to surprise and wonder, to an enthusiasm for learning and openness to the unknown. The succinct, uncritical descriptions of the Western countries by the Ch'ing official and geographer Hsu Chi-yü fit into this category, reinforced as they are by his adoption of world geography as a hobby, and by his wide capacity for friendly contacts with foreigners.[27] The frank and open account of English life by the diplomat Kuo Sung-tao also reflects a capacity for inward participation in another culture; his reaction, however, was so out of keeping with the tenor of the times that "public opinion" forced him to retire into self-imposed obscurity.[28] And Wang T'ao was fascinated by modern science and the potentialities of the machine age for inaugurating a more unified world; the diary of his experiences in Europe confirms his openmindedness, both socially and intellectually, to the "alien" world around him.[29]

This opening outward to assimilate unknown and alien phenomena could, and in some cases did, lead to deracination and even expatriation. Among the first category of the uprooted were the "treaty-port Chinese," such men as Ho Kao, Wu T'ing-fang, and Yung Wing, who supported many of the experiments of the pioneer reformers. They were sober-minded men of action with little traditional Chinese learning; often Christian-educated and cosmopolitan in orientation, they had been socially and culturally cut off from their elite counterparts in the hinterland.[30] And the conflict of cultures led to expatriation in the case of five to ten of the original 110–120 young students who went to the United States with the Chinese Educational Mission in the 1870s. They came to prefer the way of life in the United States to that of their native China.[31] This life choice can be seen in the career of one student, Yan Phou Lee, who returned to China only to discover that he wanted a deeper encounter with America. He resigned from a teaching position at the Tientsin Naval Academy, taught in Hong Kong for two years, and then returned to study at Yale. After graduation he stayed in the United States, working in a bank in San Francisco, writing articles, studying medicine in Tennessee, and even running a poultry farm in Delaware.[32]

The extremes of deracination and expatriation were largely limited in the nineteenth century to Chinese with extensive participation in treaty-port life. More important was the reorientation appearing inside China among a tiny minority of the literati and officials, some younger scholars, and the "pioneer reformers" who were residents of the treaty ports. They represented the vanguard of a movement of cultural criticism and institutional reform that was to capture the minds of a whole younger generation of educated Chinese in the early twentieth century. At the heart of this reorientation lay a displacement of perspective touched off by the crisis they perceived was coming for China and often by an empathetic encounter, in spite of themselves, with intriguing alien ways. They came to see their own cultural tradition and institutional solutions from fresh, outside perspectives, and could not affirm the old verities in the old way. Thus the "pioneer reformer" Wang T'ao came to advocate institutional reforms through his assessment of the present situation in China and reassessment of the traditional wisdom. During the decades when he had worked in intimate contact with the elite of Protestant missionaries in Shanghai and Hong Kong, he had come to have a grudging respect for some elements of their civilization. They were not barbarians, he noted, but neither was Confucius their hero. Westerners had achieved fundamental insights into the nature of the Way *(tao)*, too, especially insights into the workings of nature; fundamental learning was not all of Chinese origin. And he felt contemporary Western political practices could be viewed as closer to fulfilling the ancient but universal Chinese political ideals than the late Ch'ing imperial state. The equation between China and civilization had been broken.[33]

This was a momentous change in the inner landscape of an educated Chinese. The cultural orientation that saw China as the perennial homeland of certain universal values broke apart into two perceptions: There was a society of people calling themselves "Chinese" with a border defining an entity called "China," and there was a set of folkways and values practiced there that did not encompass all ideals of civilization. The threat to the former brought the value of national survival or what was "good for China" to the foreground; the loss of universal validity for specific Chinese historical values initiated a search for new values of universal validity, for a new cultural ideal that was "good in itself." The integration of "society" and "culture"—the homeland administered and defended by statecraft, the universal values affirmed by moral philosophy—had become problematic as never before.

The fundamental innovation of this fringe civilization, thus, is not to be found in specific institutional models or striking ideas, however momentous. It is to be found in the perceived comparison between the Chinese scene and this new intrusive order, in the emotional and intellectual restlessness thus engendered in individuals. The sundering of the assumed equation between China and civilization was an expression of this restlessness inside Wang T'ao's mind, a sign that he had become infected with the contagion of cross-cultural comparisons. Such contagion has become part of the structure of the contemporary historical experience in which many peoples in the Third World daily face an induced confrontation between their own traditions and historical forms and an intrusive alien order that supposedly is the blueprint for their modern future.[34] Confrontation, comparison, restlessness, reordering—these define the inner process that ultimately can lead to the more or less planned and deliberate transformation of social forms. Wang T'ao (1828–1897), K'ang Yu-wei (1858–1927), and Mao Tse-tung (1893–1976), despite the differences in the timing and the depth of their exposure, all stood in this whirling land of overlapping cultures which demanded that a "new universe" be created. They differed from many in that they could imagine such a synthesis and had the energy and capability to work to bring it into existence, without succumbing to rootlessness and anomie. They became not only cultural critics but also reformers and revolutionaries.

The fires of restless discontent in China did not require foreign brands to be kindled, even though they burned more brightly and fiercely when ideas like national sovereignty, women's rights, evolutionary struggle, and industrial democracy were thrown into the flames. But the spreading of these fires did indeed depend upon their beginning to burn in the right places, not among treaty-port types or barbarian officials, but within the minds of the traditional educated elite, within the circle of the inherited philosophical and social concerns. The inner journey of one young traditional scholar, K'ang Yu-wei (b. 1858), illustrates the supplementary role that foreign learning played in the impulse to reform, while at the same time underscoring how the intellectual, social, and political landscape had changed by 1900 through the Western catalyst. The insights K'ang achieved by the 1890s became starting points for those educated youth born in that decade; if their thoughts evolved more rapidly and in an iconoclastic direction, it was because they confronted the New Learning at earlier ages, in more concentrated forms, and within an international context of greater peril for China.

The young K'ang Yu-wei grew up in that part of South China with

the longest traditions of Sino-Western contact, but he had had no contact with foreigners before he journeyed to Hong Kong in 1879 at age
twenty-one. On that trip he corrected the image, probably picked up in
the strong anti-foreign currents among the local gentry in Canton, that
Westerners were like the barbarians of old. On several trips to the treaty-
port fringe, he was struck by the elegance of the buildings, the cleanli-
ness of the streets, the orderliness of administration, and what he considered a high level of political morality. He purchased maps and books
on the "Western learning" available from the missionary press as well as
from Chinese self-strengthening institutions like the T'ung-wen kuan
(Translation College) and the Kiangnan Arsenal. His reading in Western
materials ranged over the fields of acoustics, optics, chemistry, electric-
ity, mechanics, mathematics, astronomy, medicine, and histories of individual nations; he picked up a fund of new concepts, principles, and
values which he was to use extensively in formulating his own philosophy.[35]

The Western Learning that K'ang acquired on this trip and after a
second trip to Shanghai in 1882 was grist for fulfilling his ambition of
becoming a sage and savior of humankind. This goal had already separated young K'ang from the values and goals of most of his fellow students and contemporaries. At age eleven he had assumed an air of superiority, fancying himself to be an equal to the great men of the past.
At age seventeen he had felt himself to be beyond the required eight-
legged literary essay and conventional aspirations for wealth and high
office. "I then believed that it was possible for me to be a sage, that it
was possible for me to read all the books before I was thirty, that I alone
could establish myself in life, and that I could remake the world . . .
I stood towering and lofty, above the common people, associating myself
with the great and good men of the past." At nineteen he had tired of
book learning, left the academy where he was studying, and turned to
contemplation, taking up for a time the life of a Taoist hermit. He
emerged from this experience in 1879 dedicated to the active mission of
setting in order all under heaven.[36] His explorations in Western Learning were thus part of a survey he was undertaking of the whole range of
Chinese learning in preparation for the self-adopted and traditional roles
of sage and savior.

In the face of charges that he was wrongheaded and intellectually arrogant, the young K'ang persisted in re-evaluating the worthies of the past, stood up to the judgments of his teacher, and undertook to revise the Imperial Confucianism of his day. Coming to believe in his mid twenties that understanding was proportional to the scope of one's love, he concluded that Confucian learning needed to be supplemented by that of Mo Ti and Buddha. The virtue of righteousness *(yi)*, with its exclusive, judgmental air, was a lesser virtue when compared with humaneness *(jen)*, which broke through such distinctions as the worthy and the worthless. He came to question the hierarchy of relationships between ruler and subject, elder and younger, male and female as unequal and oppressive, and on the basis of sympathy for the position of women in his own household began to perceive filial piety as a "hollow ideal."[37] K'ang Yu-wei became a cultural critic and reformer through personal family experiences and through reflection on the full range of perspectives in the Chinese corpus of learning.

K'ang's critical insights into the Confucian tradition were generalized into "universal truths" on the model of axioms in geometry and presented in his work *Universal Principles of Mankind* in 1887. During its gestation period from 1880 to 1885, his encounter with Western Learning had both intensified and broadened his search for intellectual synthesis. As described by Kung-ch'uan Hsiao, K'ang groped excitedly among heterogeneous notions before managing to order the chaos brought about by "the collision of two worlds in one mind."[38] The nature of the one world of his synthesis, the world within which the sage found his mission, had been undeniably altered by his exploration in Western science and thought. Observing objects through the microscope and telescope heightened his awareness of the relativities of size, including that of the Middle Kingdom: "[I]f [such a being] were to see among all the star clusters and nebulae of our own heaven just the one sun, and within this sun [system] just the one [planet] Earth, and on this Earth just the one eighty-third part of it which is China, would there be any calculations complex and ingenious enough for him to establish its infinitesimal minuteness! This being the case, is not China of even less consequence than some other supposedly 'vast' realms, like that of the ant-king of Nan-k'o!"[39] Western notions of nationalism came to penetrate K'ang's thinking by the early 1890s. Certain ideals, notably economic and sexual equality and a federation of nations, became part of his vision of Great Unity *(ta-t'ung);* they at least coincided with Western ideals he had encountered in Chinese translations, if they were not more directly inspired by them. Many specific practices in the West, K'ang felt, were worth not only admiration but emulation. Constitutional monarchy was the political form that impressed him the most; it became part of his reform platform, as did almost all of the economic reforms urged by the Western missionary Timothy Richards.[40]

To achieve realization, the mission of the sage to express compassion and alleviate suffering had to crystallize into specific, historically appropriate formulations. The most urgent task in the 1890s was to devise means of protecting China, its land and people and traditions, against foreign aggression, not to draw up a vision of the ideal society of the future transcending the nation state form. Yet K'ang Yu-wei undertook both the task of protecting China and reformulating the vision of the good society. The latter goal was most fully expressed in the *Ta-t'ung shu* (The book of universal commonwealth) of 1902, the former in his reform proposals of 1895 and 1898. For K'ang Yu-wei the two tasks were interrelated, both in the present and in the future. In the present, he sought to incorporate his scheme of universal values, including the ideal of progress, into the "true" Confucian tradition in order to justify his reforms; and for the future he argued the practical necessity for China to survive in order that this true Confucianism might have a territorial base for its future propagation and the eventual fulfillment of his ideal vision.[41]

K'ang Yu-wei was not an exclusive nationalist, viewing the Chinese nation state as an end in itself; his nationalism was a "provisional expedient" in the present, a "preliminary step" towards an ideal non-Chinese world commonwealth. The overall problem K'ang was trying to solve was human suffering;[42] those who followed after him were less steeped in traditional philosophical concerns and more exclusively nationalistic. The practical imperative for a strong Chinese state to counter Western pressure had by 1900 framed the historical situation; the task for intellectual leadership was to arouse a weak and tradition-encased state and society.[43] Western and Japanese imperialism had become a formidable structure of power, casting ever larger shadows over China from the treaty-port rim; this problem had to be faced. Foremost, Chinese patriots had to discover the contemporary secrets of wealth and power, not the first principles of moral action. The catalytic role of the West thus lay in structuring a specific and unavoidable historical predicament, which in turn created a need for unconventional solutions, a wider receptivity to change among the educated, and an ever swelling flow of Western Learning into China.

By the 1890s foreign learning per se was no longer anathema to a growing segment of the Chinese upper strata. The attractiveness of something alien and new, whether this was an idea like constitutional monarchy or an object like a telescope or a railroad, can be traced to a variety of variables for any individual, including the question of who is advocating its adoption.[44] In China this question of advocacy was crucial because of the presumption, based upon centuries of confirming experience in East Asia, that foreign meant inferior. The resistance of the Chinese gentry, both in its diffuse local "large family" form and in its concentrated bureaucratic form, virtually sealed off the "contagion" of foreign influence. Unless this stronghold of resistance could be penetrated, the social and geographical spread of new ideas and ways would be limited to marginal individuals in the treaty ports and Christian mission stations. The peasantry was not an autonomous base for innovation, as traditionally they had either looked inward for guidance to their own regional and ethnic folk customs or aspired upward to the pattern of gentry life, which was the only alternative pattern they knew. Outsiders in the treaty ports could hardly be models because they lacked legitimacy as arbiters of Chinese values and norms. K'ang Yu-wei and other "pioneers of the hinterland" broke this social barrier. They were insiders with impeccable credentials secured through the imperial examination system, not outsiders of dubious standing. They were the first spans to bridge the antagonistic gap between innovation and power in nineteenth-century China.[45]

That gap closed rapidly after the Chinese defeat in the Sino-Japanese War of 1894–1895. The pillage of Peking in 1900 in the wake of the Boxer Uprising had further exposed the weakness of China in an unmistakable fashion, and seemed to pose a harsh choice: national extinction or wholesale transformation. A sharpened consciousness of national sovereignty and a determination both to arrest the imperialist advance and to build up a strong, centralized state—the main elements in early Chinese "nationalism"—marked the transition and shaped the response.[46] In this fluid historical situation the treaty ports figured in a complex way that forces us to give up the concept of a single treaty-port model for China's development being spread by treaty-port men, whether Westerners or Chinese. The social and geographical isolation of the treaty-port cities was ending.

Many traditional gentry families, which had long scorned the foreign ports and all they represented, began to transform themselves economically and ideologically. They started to diversify their economic base from landholding (and occasional clan-based merchant enterprises) to commercial and industrial undertakings. Merchant merger with the gentry became so extensive in some areas that a new compound, the *shang-shen* or "merchant-gentry," appeared in the language.[47] Gentry elders were ready to broaden their ideological base by embracing "modern" ways and by releasing their sons into new hitherto suspect career possibilities. The term *Western Learning (hsi-hsueh)* was being replaced by the more approving term *New Learning (hsin-hsueh)*. A Szechwan family that in 1896 could still reject the Western Learning for its corrupting moral impact had turned around by 1902 and was now sending its sons to Japan to study teaching, to Europe to study railway engineering, and to Chengdu to learn the new military science.[48] In the nineteenth century, the compradors in the treaty ports were almost alone in reorienting their lives and those of their sons towards the opportunities of the maritime fringe world.[49] After 1895, for the first time, those hastening to be transformed included not only the limited treaty-port clientele, but large segments of the traditional gentry elite throughout China. Foreign objects quickly became symbols of fashion and prestige, from oil lamps and cigarettes to Japanese diplomas.

The innovative order of the treaty-port world could no longer be said to be confined there, even though it was still most heavily concentrated in the port cities. Other cities without treaty-port status were becoming innovative centers, and gentry groups were initiating reforms themselves *in situ* in the provinces.[50] The voluntary study associations *(hsueh-hui)* that mushroomed between 1895 and 1898 mainly under gentry-literati leadership were not concentrated in the large coastal cities but rather spread out among ten provinces and thirty-one different cities, twenty-five of which were inland. During the same period about sixty new newspapers came into existence, many of them outside the treaty ports; reformist in tone and national in distribution, these newspapers, along with the study associations and the new schools, marked the beginning of a modern public opinion throughout China.[51] Not only did the treaty ports lose their internal monopoly as centers of reform, but they were also being rapidly displaced as an almost exclusive channel to Western values and institutions. The treaty-port West, symbolized by the commercial firm, the mission compound, gunboats, and a colonial mentality, now appeared less representative to those Chinese officials, students, and businessmen who began to have direct contacts with Europe and America or indirect ones via Japan. The meaning of the West was enlarged and complicated by exposure to Japan and to Western home bases in their original complexity.

By 1910 the context for innovation had changed decisively. Change was now actively anticipated and even desired by the politically conscious leadership, whether revolutionaries, reformers, or Ch'ing officials. The traditional gentry elite had formed itself into a leading edge in reverse; it was undertaking the transformation of China itself in order to counter foreign pressure and full colonization. The monopoly on the definition and forms of "modernization" held by the treaty ports was shattered when the traditional indigenous leadership began to assert itself; only through the indifference and hostility of this group to anything more than limited, defensive changes had the treaty ports, in splendid isolation, enjoyed that earlier monopoly. Modernization Chinese-style had come to include innovative resistance to foreign control and privilege in China; the pupil was learning its lessons all too well.[52]

There was much excluded or unperceived in this new gentry-merchant understanding of modernization. No fundamental flaws were detected in the social structure, nor in the old personal and family morality.[53] Few peasants were drawn into the new politically conscious leadership, although some young peasants, like ten-year-old Mao Tse-tung in 1903, ran away from school and home and discovered the city for themselves. A strong argument has been made by Chūzō Ichiko, in fact, that the reforms of these years, both those by the Ch'ing government at the center and by the Chinese governors-general and the gentry-literati in the provinces, were holding actions by these groups in an attempt to maintain their privileged positions within a changing context.[54] But the revolution—the term that best describes the internal perception of what was happening in China—was after all still in an early phase in 1910; and the next four decades would reveal unexpected developments to many participants, from Manchu nobles and officials to rural gentry. Some of these surprises centered on the roles to be played in future events by the small, emergent social groups appearing in the new urban settings: intellectuals, women, educated youth, overseas Chinese, industrial and transport workers, and a burgeoning sub-proletariat. In particular, we want to look at what was happening to those Chinese children whose family backgrounds and schooling marked them for membership in the first generation of educated youth.

THE GENESIS OF EDUCATED YOUTH AS A COUNTERCULTURE, 1905–1920

Children and youth are significant for innovation inside a society because as a group they are relatively indifferent to the prevailing customs and ideals. In the words of H. G. Barnett, children "have to be domesticated; and until they are habituated by this process, the vagaries of their own imaginations and those of their wild relatives are as appealing as the arbitrary standards of their elders."[55] A bonding to a culture takes place through years of learning and indoctrination. Chinese parents and educators intervened early and forcefully into the lives of children to attempt to ensure that this bonding would take place, and that the child's self-understanding and social roles would be shaped by its elders. But this outcome could never be guaranteed.

Intergenerational tensions are inherent in the very process of growing up, a process described gently by some as initiation into the adult world, less gently by others as a breaking-in to the demands of maturity. During relatively peaceful times in China, these normal tensions could be held within manageable limits as the elder generation transmitted its values and skills to the younger one with slight modification. The elders for their part monopolized control of family, school, and village, and guided the process of domestication, confident in the rightness of their authority and judgment; and most children probably felt fulfilled in a self-evident pattern of life that linked them with the ancient ways of the community and their ancestors. Those young people, women, and misfits who chafed badly under the prerogatives of elders and males, and who resented that options in marriage and work were family and not personal decisions, had little ethical recourse short of leaving society, for example by retreating into a religious order, becoming homeless wanderers, or committing suicide.

With the particular generation of young Chinese born in the 1890s, the tensions inherent in the slow domestication process of becoming a Chinese adult no longer had to be resolved within the confines of the same parent-child, elder-younger relationships that had prevailed for centuries. Under the post-1904 school system, it became commonplace for gentry families to send children away from home for further schooling at an earlier age; and although they were theoretically under the watchful eye of relatives and sponsors and authorities *in loco parentis,* they were actually being released into a peer group in an untraditional urban setting. Parental control of their children's ideas, physical mobility, and personal contacts was greatly weakened, although money and ties of sentiment still worked as levers of influence. The provincial capitals and the coastal strip also had become alluring magnets for those curious enough, or desperate enough, simply to run away from families and villages. The existence of the coastal strip provided a sanctuary, a place of relative security to explore new possibilities and to be confirmed in a style of life that was alien and unwelcome almost everywhere in the vast Chinese hinterland.

The setting for this type of peer group experience had seldom, if ever, existed in earlier periods of Chinese history, because the grip of gentry parents and families upon their children and youth had been effectively institutionalized. Elementary education had always been a family or local undertaking, conducted in private tutorials or in a clan school, charity school, or village school. Pupils being close to home, and in wealthier families often inside the family compound, meant that parental control of this early education was greater, although by no means complete. Even after some sons in their late teens or early twenties had passed the first step in the examination ladder and were able to enroll as boarders in an official or private academy, the connection with family remained close. In the case of wealthier students, family servants might accompany them into the academy. And as sons were often engaged, if not already married, by their late teens, they left wives and even children of their own behind them as they pursued the examination route; this circumstance made them ever mindful of their kinship obligations and the need for gratefulness to the larger family for its assistance and support. In the regulations of one private Ming academy, the argument of indebtedness was explicit:

> Students leave their fathers, mothers, brothers, wives, and children to come to the academy to study. They must use their time fully to redeem the wrong of leaving. If they pass their days idly, the wrong becomes extreme.

Many students appear to have lived at home rather than boarded at the academies. For example, at the Pai-lu-tung Academy near Nanchang around 1500, there were only sixty residential study cells for five hundred students. The frequent back-and-forth pattern between academy and family, reinforced as it was ideologically by the hope that moral learning within the academy would bear fruit within family relationships, served to restrict the development of peer relationships.[56] No such ideological controls through schooling existed among peasant sons and poor urban youngsters, who were much freer to form peer groups of cow boys and street mates; these peer groups, however enhancing they were to the development of a sense of autonomy and initiative (a theme we shall take up in Chapter Three), did not seem to undermine families and traditional values, and hence were tolerated traditional outlets for boys from poor rural and urban families.

The prospects for smooth management of the process of domestication were profoundly altered as educated youth began to emerge as a separate, self-conscious, countercultural group in society. The tensions of growing up began to be played out on a much larger stage than the household, tutorial school, and academy. The time of youth was in fact being torn out of the traditional life cycle and family context and given an identity and purposes of its own. Unlike earlier situations in which young dissidents were contained and assimilated or opted for personal solutions that led away from society, this generation of students was propelled by its progressive self-image and its insiders' credentials to act in society; these educated youth sought to find or create institutions within which to live their new ideals, and thus bring inner selves and outer society once more into correspondence. New-style schools, study groups, journals, political associations, and other student-dominated organizations provided the structures for this counterculture. *Ch'ing-nien* or "youth"—a very restricted term before—came to mean a distinct group of young persons, aged sixteen to thirty or older, who were studying the New Learning and setting out to secure reforms in China's family and political life.[57]

The basis for a self-conscious student group developed rapidly in the years after 1905. The final phasing out of the old examination system in that year saw many communities converting temples, examination halls, and academies *(shu-yuan)* into "modern-style schools" *(yang hsueh-t'ang)*. Before this the New Learning had been promoted by private patrons or foreign missionaries, and had achieved a limited presence primarily in the treaty-port cities and in certain provincial capitals and prefectural cities. After 1905, the New Learning penetrated down to the district and departmental towns; and even on the outer reaches of the empire, from Lanchow to Kunming, the new schools were taking root and thousands of young lives being reoriented towards futures that their elders could hardly anticipate, let alone control.[58] The extent of ambitions for this late-Ch'ing educational reform may be glimpsed in the chart for the new educational bureaucracy, recorded by two Russian student-interpreters in Peking just before the 1911 Revolution. They document the effort of the government to organize "a net of schools, where the younger generation may study science as in Europe, America, and Japan." Lower primary schools were to be established in all cities, market towns, and villages. Department and district towns were to be required to have both upper and lower primary schools for men and women. Prefectural cities were to be obliged to set up middle schools. The system in provincial capitals was to include higher normal schools, univer-

sity preparatory schools, and a wide range of professional schools (agriculture, industry, and trade), model schools (attached to normal schools),
and special schools.[59]

The appearance of such modern-style schools, although sometimes remembered in diaries and memoirs as shallow, hybrid institutions worth
only a laugh or a contemptuous dismissal, meant a pervasive change in
the socialization of the new intelligentsia.[60] The subjects taught—world
history, geography, mathematics, natural sciences, foreign languages,
physical education—were different, at least at the middle school level;
and the way they were taught sometimes contrasted sharply with the
strict decorum and book memorization of the traditional tutorial school.
One man from a scholarly family reflected upon his entry into an upper
primary school in Soochow in 1906:

> The moment I entered I found myself in an entirely new world . . . The teacher
> of history took us to view famous places and ancient remains . . . Our teacher
> of science accompanied us in search of zoological and botanical specimens—all of
> which we had to write up in the form of travel essays for our teacher of literature
> or reproduce from memory for our teacher of drawing. I feel this very interesting
> form of physical exercise and the connection established between the materials of
> the different branches of knowledge to be the most congenial teaching which I
> received.[61]

The textbooks prepared between 1903 and 1906 for the new school system preached the importance of racial competition and the virtues of
military valor and nationalism, stressing China's recent history of loss
and humiliation before the Western powers. By 1909, a million-and-a-
half students were being nurtured on this potent fare.[62]

Perhaps more important than the teaching curricula, methods, and
materials, were the behaviors that the basic learning situation encouraged. Being physically separated from the kinship matrix and often living among peers, students felt encouraged to live beyond traditional
conventions and restraints, and to explore some of the potential of the
unattached self. The "natural" *(tzu-jan)* and "bohemian" *(feng-liu)* life
styles of writers such as Su Man-shu (1884–1918) and the "modern"
(mo-teng) style of some returned students from Japan offered living models
for students to emulate in their language, clothing, hair styles, tastes,
opinions, and prejudices.[63] A self-assertive, self-expressive posture towards

the world was prized, and possible; and the careers open to the new intelligentsia—as writers, journalists, teachers of modern subjects, new-style bureaucrats, professional revolutionaries, and organizers—meant it was now possible to earn a living while pursuing reformist goals.

The number of those exposed to some extent to the New Learning in the new-style schools shot up, in one estimate, from several hundred thousand in 1905 to about ten million at the start of the New Culture movement in 1917.[64] In giving cohesiveness to the group, sheer numbers and concentration in the large cities were probably less important than were the mentors who articulated the students' ideals and fears and gave initial shape to their critique of China's traditional culture and politics. Liang Ch'i-ch'ao (1873–1929) stands out as the most stirring individual figure prior to the founding of the *New Youth* journal by Ch'en Tu-hsiu (1880?–1942) in 1915. During his fourteen years in exile in Japan (1898–1912), particularly as a revolutionary publicist from 1899 to 1903, Liang moved Chinese youth with his expressive literary style and sharp attacks on tradition. His mind had grown dissatisfied with "provincial" fare; and he feasted abroad on new thoughts, which he shared generously with his younger readers. As an intellectual barnstormer, Liang influenced many young people coming of age in the 1900s, from the future liberals of the New Culture movement to later Marxists. One unpublished memoir by the Chinese animal behaviorist Kuo Jen-yuan (b. 1898), explained Liang's impact this way:

As his intellectual interests were almost unlimited, the range of his reading of European books was extremely wide, so much so that a few years before Liang's death in 1929 this writer, a young upstart then, nicknamed him "the twentieth century Aristotle" and in his characteristic way, Liang replied that he was really only a "jack of all trades but master of none." And it was this master of none that made him so successful in stirring the minds of youth. Each time he read a book, be it Charles Darwin's *Origin of Species* or Immanuel Kant's *Critique of Pure Reason,* he thought it was so important that he had to share it with his Chinese readers. And in a few days there appeared in the journal which he was editing in Japan, an excellent and most readable Chinese article, with his own comments on Darwinism or Kantian philosophy. In the next issue the reader would find Liang's article on Jean Rousseau or Adam Smith. During Liang's exile in Japan there had been a small number of European philosophical and scientific books translated into Chinese, but all of them were done in the old classical style and were rather hard to read. At any rate they were far from attractive and failed to stimulate young readers. Liang's articles, on the other hand, were clear and lucid, and were eagerly awaited by young people. Liang created a style never before seen in the history of Chinese literature, a style which was vivid, fluent, simple, and yet expressive. He was the first man . . . to put feeling and passion into writing. This is the main reason why Liang's gifted pen became a most powerful weapon for turning Chinese youth into revolutionaries, both in politics and in intellectual life. His intellectual liberalism was another major factor which influenced Chinese youth and caused them to question Chinese intellectual traditions. He was the first and only man in Chinese history to cite, with a feeling of shame, Confucius' execution of his intellectual rival Shao Chen-mao.[65]

Liang Ch'i-ch'ao's thought during this period of exile assumed an amoral evolutionary struggle of nation states, with victory going to the vital and defeat to the stagnant. In order to avoid defeat, subjection, and even extermination, China had to shed anachronistic fantasies and embark upon new ways. In this process of revitalization, Liang was a self-styled Luther or Bacon or Descartes, liberating his contemporaries out of a corrupting orthodoxy; the process itself he believed was the same one that the West had undergone four hundred years earlier when it had thrown off the confines of the "Jesus system."[66] Liang had furthermore initially believed that liberalism, represented in Anglo-Saxon institutions of constitutional and representative government, was essential to this revitalization; new citizens, imbued with the spirit of independence and self-respect, would assert their rights through democratic participation and make the nation strong, thus making China fit to survive in an era of ruthless, expansive powers. But after his journey to Canada and America in 1903, Liang became convinced that his call to shed the "slavish spirit" of the past in favor of modern liberalism was too idealistic and that China was not ready for democracy. Only mature nations were capable of liberal democracy; immature China required an enlightened despotism to survive as a sovereign nation in the current, perilous, international scene. This shift in Liang's thought had by 1906 put him out of touch with many progressive young people who had come to share the anti-Manchu nationalism and republicanism of Sun Yat-sen and his newly created United League (T'ung-meng hui). As Philip C. Huang has pointed out, however, Liang's basic assumptions—that the Western threat represented a root-and-branch challenge to China, that imperialism was an agency for the spread of modern civilization, that modernization was not only necessary but desirable—had become commonplace by the time of the May Fourth intellectual revolution.[67]

Yen Fu's annotated rendering of T. H. Huxley's evolutionary theories, originally published in 1898 and reprinted in a larger edition in 1905, was wildly received among schoolboys during the prerevolutionary decade. For many young minds freshly awakened to China's plight as a weak and threatened culture and polity and no longer convinced by Confucian moral explanations for that plight, the competitive world view of Social Darwinism helped make events comprehensible, and justified, even demanded, a personal liberator role. In the writing of Ch'en Tu-hsiu in the *New Youth* magazine in 1915, this Darwinian language of struggling races, nations, and groups still survived; but "youth" as a group in society and the time of youth as a segment of the life cycle were given particular value and social function.

> Youth is like early spring, like the rising sun, like trees and grass in bud, like a newly sharpened blade. It is the most valuable period of life. The function of youth in society is the same as that of a fresh and vital cell in a human body. In the process of metabolism, the old and the rotten are incessantly eliminated to be replaced by the fresh and living . . . If metabolism functions properly in a human body, the person will be healthy; if the old and rotten cells accumulate and fill the body, the person will die. If metabolism functions properly in a society, it will flourish; if old and rotten elements fill society, then it will cease to exist.
>
> According to this standard, then, is the society of our nation flourishing, or is it about to perish? I cannot bear to answer. As for those old and rotten elements, I shall leave them to the process of natural selection. I do not wish to waste my fleeting time in arguing with them on this and that and hoping for them to be reborn and thoroughly remolded. I merely with tears, place my plea before the fresh and vital youth, in the hope that they will achieve self-awareness, and begin to struggle.[68]

In sharply distinguishing the "fresh and vital youth" from the "old and rotten elements," Ch'en wanted young people first to straighten out in their own minds who they were, cutting themselves resolutely off from any contaminating influence. Having attained clarity in first principles, which included a set of model personality traits, they could then attack conservative and decaying traditions with decisiveness, as "a sharp knife cuts hemp."

But first they had to apply the knife to themselves, and Ch'en had no illusions about the immensity of this task.

> I have seen that out of every ten youths who are young in age, five are old in physique; and out of every ten who are young in both age and physique, nine are old in mentality. Those with shining hair, smooth countenance, a straight back and a wide chest are indeed magnificent youths! Yet if you ask what thoughts and aims are entertained in their heads, then they all turn out to be the same as the old and rotten, like moles from the same hill.[69]

What are these thoughts and aims still entertained in their heads? The list is formidable and echoes many of the critical comments made by Liang Ch'i-ch'ao over ten years earlier: depending on the slavish morality of loyalty, filial piety, chastity, and righteousness, and blindly following others; revering only the history of the twenty-four dynasties and making no plans for progress and improvement; weakly desiring to retire and shrink before difficulties and evils, while feigning superiority to a vulgar world; being pessimistic and not wanting to compete with the rest of the world; having ritualized expectations based on "the agelong precepts of ethical convention" and "empty formalism" that excluded questions of practical usefulness; displaying a way of thinking that leaped over objective phenomena and disregarded reason to construct imaginative hypotheses out of thin air without recourse to facts. The "gentry tail" was indeed long, and few in this generation of Chinese youth could shake it off completely.[70]

Having discovered the ambiguities of the word "young" when applied to his contemporaries, Ch'en's task now was to project an image of youth that would integrate mind and body and harness the vitality and energy of this time of life to the great work of national renovation. Over against the negative traditional mentality stood the modern self-image: independent, progressive, active and competitive, optimistic, alive to practical benefits and characterized by demonstrative inductive thinking. In urging self-reflection and offering these standards as yardsticks for the self, Ch'en helped to give further definition to "youth" as a group in society with its own identity and mission. The next step was national organization, which came with the May Fourth movement of 1919. By then a dialectic based on the contradiction between the young (fresh and vital) and the old (decaying and stagnant) had become the rationale for a wide-ranging cultural critique. In the course of the movement in the 1920s, however, the age dialectic—so loose and unprogrammatic in form—was subsumed into a theory at once more comprehensive and specific: the dialectic of socio-economic class struggle in the Age of Imperialism.

Just as the age dialectic was made subordinate to the dialectic of socio-economic class struggle, so the youth counterculture was absorbed into a larger configuration of contending forces. Youth's moment on the stage as chief protagonist was over; and other figures—striking workers, party cadres, Comintern agents, angry peasants, militiamen and soldiers—began to come to the forefront. During the May Fourth period, educated youth had been a revolutionary vanguard reaching out to workers and merchants and even to peasants to bring them into a revolutionary orbit. In the 1920s, 1930s, and 1940s the student movement and student nationalism continued to play a role, but it was increasingly an ancillary and dependent role. Students could dramatize the nation's precarious fate and arouse indignation and concern at critical moments, but the long-term leadership lay in the hands of adult professionals in the Kuomintang (KMT) and Chinese Communist Party (CCP), who sought to recruit youth into their orbits.[71] Youth was a reservoir of energy and idealism to be drawn upon, not an independent wellspring of political, social, or cultural wisdom. Educated youth, along with the rest of the modern intelligentsia, found that intellectual autonomy had to be paid for at the high price of estrangement from the political center. So it had been at the turn of the century; so it was under KMT and CCP rule.[72]

In 1966 many Red Guards believed that they were playing an analogous role to the students of the May Fourth period, as spearheads of the action. Designated as "revolutionary successors," they had been told by Mao that they were "the most active and vital force in society, the most eager to learn and the least conservative in their thinking," that they were "in the bloom of life, like the sun at eight or nine in the morning. Our hope is placed in you . . . the world belongs to you. China's future belongs to you." The echoes of Ch'en Tu-hsiu in 1915 in *New Youth* are unmistakable; but except for the similarity in rhetoric, the analogy failed. Whereas youth in the May Fourth movement had played an independent, leading role, in 1966 they were warned by adult party leaders that they were "on trial" and given cues about what criteria would be important in evaluating their political performance. Whereas May Fourth youth actively went out into society to seek allies for the cause of national salvation, millions of Red Guards in their faction-ridden movement were "integrated" with the masses in 1969 by being sent down into the countryside for productive labor. In retrospect, it is hardly surprising that many former Red Guards being interviewed in Hong Kong felt used and manipulated by the Mao group in the course of the Cultural Revolution. David Raddock has argued that it was perhaps the genius of the Cultural Revolution leadership group to have manipulated, through political channels, what they knew to be the psychological strengths and vulnerabilities of Chinese adolescents.[73]

For the first two decades of the twentieth century, educated youth in China had been part of an unprecedented cultural movement pressing from within on the boundaries of the existing polity and civilization.[74] As the New Learning caught hold and spread its influence via new schools, study associations, newspapers, and journals, it helped generate pressure both for the reform and the demise of the imperial monarchy. During this period, Frederic Wakeman, Jr., has argued, a new ideology of association had come into being, one that allowed "scholars of resolve" to express a corporate interest and solidarity apart from governmentally sanctioned views. This new ideology was particularly evident in the type of adult study societies that began to appear in 1906–1908: voluntary associations that were issue-oriented (railroad and mining rights), intent upon organizational outreach among local provincial gentry and commoners, and run by elected officers controlled by the membership.[75] These new possibilities for disciplined group assertiveness unintentionally found expression within late-Ch'ing schools, where strikes and protests by students became frequent occurrences. Such collective action differed sharply from the emphasis upon individual attainment and family success encouraged by the old examination system or from the traditional recourse to conscientious individual action (withdrawal, passive resistance) by scholar-officials in the face of immoral situations.[76] The vague and emergent ideology of nationalism itself, whether in the anti-imperialist formulation of the Ch'ing officials or the anti-Manchu views of the United League revolutionaries in Japan, taught young Chinese to think of themselves collectively as citizens of a young nation, a role and responsibility that was not illuminated in the classical literature. A new loyalty to the nation-state, expressing itself through the organs of an independent "public opinion," had intruded into the old personal obligations to rulers, family members, and friends.

But new political banners, and even a consciously redesigned self-image, did not spare educated young people from intensified problems of self-definition in a world coming apart. The old negative self-image—that part within themselves that they rejected—shadowed their individual struggles, just as old political habits and instincts bedeviled the new republic. As individuals they mirrored the social and intellectual fragmentation occurring around them, sometimes rising above it with clarifying syntheses, sometimes falling victim to it, drifting and fixating on parts when wholes were too elusive. Their ability to ride out the storms of personal, cultural, and political change depended in part upon how successfully they had been able, and enabled, to establish themselves during the two halves of childhood.

PART TWO
Establishing the Self

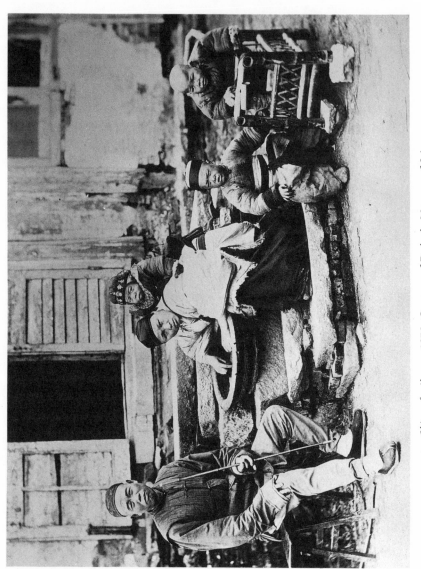

Chinese family, ca. 1875. Courtesy of Peabody Museum of Salem

THREE

Mischievous Sons: Perfectly Human, Imperfectly Chinese

The analysis of inherited understandings, affirmations, and situations can take us only so far. In the first chapter we saw a perception of the child and childhood as part of larger ideas about the environment and becoming human, ideas so reinforced by daily experience that they were opaque, thick as stone walls, as unquestionable as trees and mountains and rivers. In the second chapter we traced the historical moment that brought two civilizations together, creating a crucible for innovation in which objects, people, ideas, institutions were newly mixed and tumbled, fused and transformed. These were important pieces of the setting of most children born in China in the 1890s, but they were especially fateful pieces for that minority of children who grew up to be the educated youth of the early twentieth century. But how does setting become consciousness? Are we human beings reflections of our environments, our minds mirroring what is outside them or soaking up an imprint like a blotter? The inadequacy of such conceptions underscores the problem: The description of outer environment cannot be assumed to provide the content of inner realities, for the mind has independent laws of its own.

In becoming human, this particular animal *Homo sapiens* develops an ego not bound by rigid instinct or present time. This ego, a center of conscious awareness, creates an identity around an "I" with a specific name, and learns, already in early childhood, to discriminate among the people and things in its environment and to separate time into past, present, and future. *I am Wang Tzu-chen, third son of Magistrate Wang. I*

*live in a yamen near the river with my grandfather. Before, we used to live far
away from here.* As the child encounters ever more of the world in space
and time and dreams—some of it painful or threatening, some of it
warm or exciting—the ego begins to build up expectations based on
prior experience. *I fell in the river once. My body couldn't breathe and my
eyes got black. My mother found me and said some hungry ghost was trying to
catch my soul. I don't go near the river anymore.* The ego begins to protect
the whole organism, body and mind together, from future threatening
experiences by labeling things dangerous or scary or bad or unworthy.
The labels begin to constrict and limit what children allow themselves
to feel comfortable in doing, and thinking, and feeling. *Grandpa calls
me Young Master Wang and says I should study hard to become an official some
day like my father. He doesn't want me climbing trees and playing with the
village kids. I guess I don't mind.* In this process, reality is personalized
and distorted by the ego's work in innoculating the person against anxiety, distress, and pain, especially the pain of displeasing important adults.[1]
If we want to explain human behavior in the past or present, we must
immerse ourselves in this learning process and experience it from the
inside looking out. We must posit not the mind as *tabula rasa* but the
world as *tabula rasa,* and see it through the eyes and emotions of a
developing child.[2] We must go beyond environmental approaches to
visualize ourselves, as children and adults, helping create the scaffolding
of our own uniquely shaped and furnished inner dwellings.

The presence of this screening, coping, protecting individual ego—a
"psychological organ" as important to the human organism as the heart
or liver—impresses itself upon us all the more when the norms and
institutions that lend social life its apparent solidarity are collapsing.
This collapse of outer structures tests individual inner strengths and vulnerabilities; personal capacities become more marked and visible in extreme situations in which the old reference points of status and role are
radically redefined.[3] An amorphous present and future require meaning
and form; continuity and direction become problematic and must be
achieved through inner struggle. During the twentieth century in China,
individual adult capacity to endure chaos and brokenness, to understand
what was happening, let alone to create new meanings or build new
institutional forms, was sorely tested. Many were unable to make the

transition: They saw only a wrenching process that was mindless, victimizing, random, beyond their control, and settled for partial views that excluded the unpleasant, the ugly, the painful. Han Suyin commented on an old friend:

> How many are like her, I do not know. Perhaps they cannot do otherwise then choose to remain with their familiar childhood held close to them . . . Perhaps they cannot reassemble, make a continuity where there appears to be only cleavage. But I had to do it, to live with myself, to be myself, and to continue growing, where others have stopped. I would not be a crippled tree marring the landscape with its own malady. At least I would greet the tomorrow I had not made, even if it killed me.
>
> Indeed it is suffering to go on growing, to hold to what is, to try to understand, to knock down one's own preconceptions. To find one's memories ravaged by time and revolution, one's intimate illusions ripped up, laughter for one's own private desolation the only answer; to realize how difficult, agonizing, is the process of understanding, and how long it takes.[4]

At such historical junctures, the narrow channel of childhood, through which each generation transmits its beliefs, attitudes and skills on to the next, becomes very important for cultural change. In stabler eras, the dominant elements in the culture pass through almost unquestioned; but in times of rapid historical change, new pressures and opportunities induce parents and children to choose and act differently, leading over time to the adaptation or even abandonment of some cultural practices and to the adoption of new ones. Children are relatively indifferent to the ideas they are exposed to; it matters little to them, initially, whether a given practice is inherited, traditional, or new. They can abandon or adopt a given practice with more alacrity than their parents; and when they themselves are parents, either it will have ceased to be an effective reality for them, or, in the case of a new practice, it will have been incorporated more fully into their lives.[5]

But this general case has some important qualifications. In complex, historical civilizations like China, India, or Europe, cultural change was always occurring by a process called "cultural drift," which is change initiated by individuals who exploit the range of permitted variation within institutions to become catalysts for slow, cumulative change within a culture.[6] Many thinkers, for example, enlarged Confucianism with their reinterpretations of certain words and concepts, and tens of thousands of others developed new forms and techniques in agriculture, medicine, the culinary arts, technology, and administration. But specifying a range of permitted variation still does not tell us who was prepared to take advantage of it, to exploit the loopholes within an institution, to press for new ways of thinking and doing things. The technical term "personality-induced change," in positing differences among adults that lead to cultural innovation, elicits further questions. Are there also differences among children in their ability to anticipate and grasp the opportunity for change? Does personality-induced change accelerate in eras when institution constraints are greatly weakened and the range of behavior, permitted or not, suddenly expands? Some children, like some adults, appear to be readier than others to grow into "the tomorrow [they] had not made," and even to try to make that tomorrow themselves.

What is it that enables or compels some people to define chaotic, open, less defined situations as opportunities, while others feel helpless, paralyzed, trapped? There is no easily named, single cause for this difference; but on the basis of some developmental theories and a variety of life histories, village and family studies, we can begin an answer. Part of the answer is negative: Lives mired in dependency or parasitism are not going to enable persons to deal with social and historical crisis in a creative fashion. A sturdy self, anchored in trust and hope, possessing a sense of autonomy and competence and understanding, appears necessary. I have found the human development perspective of Erik Erikson helpful, but not definitive, in framing the evolution of such a "sturdy self" with its associated virtues. In Part Two we shall be exploring the emergence of children with such character traits within the interstices of the traditional family system and the altered structure for growing up in early twentieth-century China. We shall begin with one of the earliest crises: the child's struggle to establish a rudimentary sense of autonomy.

EARLY CHILDHOOD AND THE THREATS TO AUTONOMY

The two traditional Chinese categories for the childhood years are the *ying-erh shih-ch'i* and the *yu-nien shih-ch'i,* the former being the "infancy period," and the latter, in a free translation, the "immaturity period."

The *ying-erh* period had a variable length, from birth up to four years; the following *yu-nien* period lasted to about age fifteen. The contrasting style of parental treatment during these two periods has commonly been cited as significant: the *ying-erh* period characterized by mild discipline, relative freedom, and security; the *yu-nien* period by quickening discipline and training, when the full brunt of cultural learning began to descend upon the child, especially with the beginning of formal schooling around age six or seven.[7] The *ying-erh* period and the early *yu-nien* periods overlap with several critical steps in Erik Erikson's theory about human development: the struggle over basic trust and mistrust during infancy, and the struggle over a sense of autonomous will during the toddler stage.

The sense of autonomy manifests itself in the child as the first efforts at emancipation from the helpless dependency inherent in the months of life as an infant; it is triggered by the increasing ability to verbalize and particularly by the new possibilities of muscular coordination. The toddler is capable of standing firmly on its own feet and delineating "I" and "you" and a sphere of "me" and "mine." In stubborn and often violent assertions of will, the child experiments with a sense of autonomous power within and asserts its rights to an independent sphere of action, to hold and let go of things freely.[8] As one Chinese youth wrote, reflecting back on his earliest remembered emotion: "I did not merely wish: I willed. I had one capacity, and one only—to be and to possess."[9] According to Erikson's epigenetic theory, however, such a robust recollected desire to move beyond dependency reflected a sound base of strength imparted through the earliest nurturance and care of infancy.

Western understanding of the early bonding process between parent and child has centered on the nuclear family and the strong mother-child tie, with the implication that this lengthy one-on-one dependency creates the basis for a strong individuality in the child. Theories have begun to factor in plural mothering and extended family situations, such as those commonly existing in both traditional and contemporary China. In China the newborn has been a member of a group, with little emphasis upon nurturing a self-centered I as the core element of a budding personality. The infant internalizes a more group-oriented, group-centered world. There is no good reason to suppose that this approach of plural mothering does not indeed provide that necessary foundation of trust and hope in the world that an infant needs, provided, of course, the infant's basic nutritional and medical needs are also met.[10] We can begin to see, however, that the rudimentary sense of a separate identity that begins to emerge with the toddler stage was and is going to have different emphasis and meaning in China. Most important, perhaps, the emergent capacities for self-expression were not nurtured by parental stimulation during these years, and, in fact, were often greeted by harsh rejection.

The expression of autonomy is both a partial emancipation from the earlier period of infancy and a further development from the base of strength imparted through early nurturance and care. But conversely the capacity for expressing autonomy can also be jeopardized in two ways: by the prolongation of the initial dependency of infancy or by a poor foundation for trust and hope in these preceding years. There is some evidence that both these undermining influences occurred regularly in traditional Chinese child-rearing. The practice of protective restraint often prolonged the period of dependency well past the first year of life; and, despite the positive effects of group care, many Chinese infants experienced a world of scarcity and disease. Some children's ability to express autonomy was, therefore, jeopardized early on.

The period of infancy in China is usually portrayed as a time of great parental responsiveness, if not outright indulgence, towards the welcomed infant, the Omnipotent One.[11] This responsiveness, however, was not an empathetic approach to the infant and the young child as an individual with its own independent needs. As we have seen in Chapter One, the child was felt to be passive and vulnerable, with physical needs for nourishment and rest, but little capability or need for stimulation or learning. In their child-rearing, parents were responding to this image of the child's basic nature by keeping it out of harm's way during the earliest years and then preparing it for future adult roles. "There was no idea of helping children to develop as children, each with his or her individual personality," commented Francis L. K. Hsu on the educational goals of villagers he studied in Yunnan province. "Attention was directed only to preparing children to assume their traditionally prescribed roles in adult life as soon as possible."[12] For a son the traditionally prescribed roles meant the ceremonial and economic functions of filial sons within the family: serving his parents by providing descendants, supporting his parents materially in old age and ritually after their deaths, and honoring his forebears through his acts and achievements. The first task of parents was thus to ensure the infant's physical survival and, when this was secured, to prepare the child to become a loyal and productive member of the family.

The completely dependent infant was held, fed on demand, smiled at, buzzed over, and its needs anticipated insofar as the parents had the means, time, and energy to welcome another "mouth" into the family. From the age of two or three months, the infant began to experience a multiple parenting; besides mother or nurse, it was attended by older siblings, grandparents, or even neighbors.[13] The crying of children was dreaded, and everything was done to prevent it; one social commentator noted that there was at least equality of the sexes in the determination to stop this most visible sign of pain and distress.[14] Nursing ended when a younger sibling arrived, and without a younger brother or sister nursing might be prolonged until age two, three or even longer. This arrival of a younger sibling usually signaled the end of the *ying-erh* period, hence giving this period a variable length.[15]

The governing desire of parents to protect the child from bodily harm was often active beyond the age of helpless dependency. At the walking stage, constant tending and anticipation of needs could begin to constrain the child's exercise of its own powers. Various clues testify to this lingering practice of protective restraint: the carrying of children, especially sons, long past the age of walking; the spatial confinement of children; the effort to prevent "wild games" and "dangerous play"; an exaggerated fear of unknown beetles and plants; and finally, the burying of sleeping children under mounds of bedding, which one man speculated was the cause of his childhood insomnia.[16] This protective restraint characterizing the late *ying-erh* and early *yu-nien* years was not marked by any severe discipline or training; rather, certain areas of exploration were simply not opened and developing motor and mental skills remained untested in doses and forms possible for the child at this age.[17] Such restraint prolonged the time of dependency and non-autonomy, permitting a direct transition from a state of dependency upon nurturing and protecting elders during infancy to a training in dependency upon the family network during the *yu-nien* years. In this pattern many children, by default, were effectively prevented from establishing a strong sense of themselves as centers of independent action.

The desire to protect the child must be seen against the stark backdrop of scarcity, death, and danger. The statistics on infant mortality are impressionistic and speculative, but the death of one out of three children before the age of five is a plausible estimate for the early twentieth century. "One son is no son, two sons are an undependable son, and only three sons can be counted as a real son," says a Chinese proverb.[18] The years of infancy, especially birth to three, were believed to be the time of greatest crisis; only after ten was a child thought to be beyond danger.[19] Numerous memoirs of the early years accent childhood illnesses and the heart-rending efforts of mothers to cure and protect their sons.[20] The ability of mothers to nourish their children was often uncertain. Poor diets and disease could affect the supply of mother's milk; and when it dried up, one had to resort to cow's milk or rice gruel fed by spoon or finger. Village lore recognized that mothers with little milk had poor survival records. Wet nurses for gentry children of course had to shift priority from their own children, who got what was left. Beginnings marked by poor nurturance could easily lead to persistent fears of "being left empty" and being "starved of stimulation"; such beginnings hardly laid a foundation for hope and trust, those vital strengths imparted through the earliest bonding relationships.[21]

The parents in peasant families controlled the consumption of food and use of physical objects with minute attention, a control that would be incomprehensible without considering the material context of life. Fei Hsiao-t'ung describes the process in some detail for a village on the Yangtze River in Eastern China in the 1930s.

> The relation between a child and the objects that satisfy his need is through his parents. At the beginning he cannot use anything without the consent of his parents. For instance, the basic need of nutrition is dependent on the consent of his mother. Indeed, this consent is to a certain extent guaranteed by human sentiment and social rules, but even this is not always secured. In case the child is not welcomed to the house, he may be killed by the refusal of milk. As he grows up, the objects allotted for his use increase. But he has no free access to

these things. The clothes he wears are put on him or taken off according to the will of his mother. Food is put before him. He cannot take things without the permission of his mother. The gifts given by his relatives are kept by his mother . . . When the child knows how to take care of itself and learns the proper use of objects, the control diminishes. As technical knowledge increases and he participates in productive work, the child gradually acquires the right use over objects that belong to the *Chia* (household). But there are very few objects exclusively and freely used by him. The type and amount of goods he consumes are also always under the control of his elders.[22]

The lesson children learned though this control was that the world offered only limited gratification, and then only if one complied with the rules, and that there was very little that was exclusively "mine." What there was depended upon outside forces and persons, not personal initiative and desire.[23] Only during the periodic festival days on the rural calendar were the controls "let go" for moments of feasting and joyous sharing.[24] At these times, too, more "mischief" was tolerated in children.

The children who lived daily with such restraints throughout childhood acquired an attitude of expectant dependence upon those who had the power to give and withhold. In this they were like their economy-conscious parents. In the practice of protective restraint and in the careful dispensing of the means to life and growth, parents were conveying their own inner sense of precariousness, frustration, and fragile hopefulness. "In the last analysis," Erik Erikson has observed, "the kind and degree of a sense of autonomy which parents are able to grant their small children depends upon the dignity and sense of personal independence they derive from their own lives . . . The sense of autonomy is a reflection of the parent's dignity as autonomous beings."[25]

In all societies, through some combination of intrinsic wisdom, unconscious planning, and superstition, child-rearing practices tend to induce behaviors in children that are consistent with adult values and cultural norms. Too much autonomous will and initiative, too strong a sense of separate identity were clearly not desired by parents in late Ch'ing China. But let us be cautious here. The Western notion of the isolated, assertive, and self-conscious individual may reasonably be regarded as an exaggerated belief in the power and importance of the individual.[26] It is a prejudicial standard for measuring a sense of individual autonomy. Post-Sung China, as a complex civilization with many specialized activities and institutions and a concomitantly wide range of human types, produced many assertive, introspective, and even eccentric individuals. But the contemporary concept of individualism in the West, whether manifest in guaranteed individual freedoms and rights or in extreme forms of subjectivism and alienation, failed for whatever reason to develop in China.[27] What did develop was a high degree of awareness of the self as within but still distinct from the group. A self constantly monitoring its interactions with others may to some Westerners seem like a novel perspective in social psychology, but in China such monitoring was often a natural outcome of growing up in the complex behavioral environment of a Chinese family.[28] The prescriptive quality of rules for interaction based on generation, age, and sex made it very difficult for a young person to weave spontaneous feelings, hopes, wishes, and decisions into the desires of those in authority; building up an active, private inner life, therefore, was a compensation for non-negotiable group restrictions imposed on the outer behavior of *yu-nien* children. A "real self" inside split off from the social self that others saw; and this inner self was engaged in constant monitoring, evaluating, and decision-making. Once the undifferentiated response of a tantrum was outgrown, action depended upon many considerations: the overt deeds and words of others, the underlying motives and needs that these words and deeds seemed to convey, the ideal action enjoined by group harmony, the personal need for self-respect, filial obligations to siblings and parents, and the decision on how much to disclose overtly and how much to withhold and deal with internally.[29]

In analyzing Chinese behavior, Erikson's phrase "the courage to be an independent person" must be evaluated in terms of questions not usually raised in our own cultural context. Does it take more courage in a difficult social situation to make a fuss and risk "losing it" as we might say (or "losing face" as Chinese might say) or to remain in control and be temperate? Is it impossible to be "independent" and at the same time act in accord with what group solidarity seems to require? Must independence always be reflected in overt behavior, or is independence a quality of mind that can have various expressions, sometimes invisible in outer behavior? Does external compliance imply lack of ego autonomy and a self-doubting personality? How much ego strength is involved in successfully detaching sentiment from action, individual feelings from social performance? Learning to act responsibly within the Chinese group involved much more than taking orders or following dictates; it meant a perpetual dialogue, within the self and with various others, a continuing exploration of boundaries for self-expression in feelings, thoughts, speech, and deeds. There may indeed have been special forms of autonomous behavior inculcated in young persons through growing up within the Chinese family system and through succeeding in the old-style classical education, forms that outsiders have not yet learned to appreciate.

The sharp break in treatment between the *ying-erh* and *yu-nien* years seems to have had much to do with inducing this heightened awareness of the self within the group along with the need for careful discrimination of the boundaries between inner feelings and thoughts and outer words and actions. Richard H. Solomon has traced several enduring contradictions within the filial pattern to this break in the two halves of childhood. He claims that the harshness of the discipline during the *yu-nien* years, if not balanced with a minimum level of support and justice from elders, created deep resentment and anxiety about authority. And since self-assertion, hostility, and willfulness against elders were sharply discouraged, the child could only "hold in" or swallow these emotions and mask their expression in other relationships, such as those with younger siblings. The promising start towards a strong sense of self-worth that had begun as a "indulged infant" was aborted, leaving the individual with a deep longing to recapture the sense of power and security known early in life. The legacy was ambivalence about authority, an explosive cultural fixation with emotional control, and an arrested development of self-esteem.[30]

I find little to quarrel with on this general level of argument in Solomon's essay on traditional Chinese socialization. The two halves of childhood often did conspire to hinder the possibility of strong individuality in the growing child; and children did come to understand their experience as a security pact in which sacrifices in a sense of autonomy and initiative in social matters were balanced by a measure of safety and worth within the group. In many cases the sense of sacrifice itself would be muted, if lived experience approached the ideals of human relations:

interdependence, mutuality, and reciprocity among people of different statuses.[31] The basic moral teaching that becoming a human being worthy of the name *(tso jen)* took precedence over "selfish" individual striving was hard to counter from within the system. Yet, if the life situation of many small Chinese children seemed to bias their development towards dependency or interdependence instead of towards a separate more autonomous identity, it is with heightened interest that we turn to wrestle with a contrasting figure: the *t'ao-ch'i* or "mischievous" child. He is abundantly visible in the autobiographies, and was noted by astute observers of long ago, although he seems to have fallen through Solomon's conceptual net. Isaac Headland, an American missionary, wrote in *The Chinese Boy and Girl* in 1901 that the identifying trait of Chinese children was none other than *t'ao-ch'i.*[32] This quality was indeed common, and we must inquire into its appearance and meaning.

THE T'AO-CH'I CHILD AND PATERNAL ANXIETIES

T'ao-ch'i. adj. Disobedient, undisciplined, annoying, willful, obstinate, intrusive, assertive, boisterous.

The various meanings attached to *t'ao-ch'i* (lit., "taxing the breath") and to related words, such as *t'iao-p'i* (lit., "irritable skin") and *wan-p'i* (lit., "tough skin"), express precisely the traits that many contemporary Western parents would associate with young children struggling to emancipate themselves from dependency, trying to be a "self" and to possess a personal sphere. They describe the opposite traits of that model *kuai hai-tzu* or good Chinese child, who, as Lu Hsun noted as late as 1934, was obedient, composed, self-effacing, respectful, and industrious.[33] By contemporary standards of considerate parenthood, the mischievous child would be accepted by its parents as a normal child caught up in the serious play of testing its powers in all directions towards people as well as things; such parents would be disturbed if their children aged two to six, acted like the *kuai hai-tzu,* or as adults matured before their time.[34] But most Chinese parents in late Imperial times—and indeed many nineteenth-century parents in Western countries as well—had little tolerance for such "mischievous" or naughty behavior. As the child grew into the stage that enabled it biologically and required it spiritually to express a sense of autonomy and initiative, parents were prepared to see mainly willfulness, selfishness, and a "childish" display of wasted energy. Parents contested and sought to stamp out these undesirable traits, which were to them improper, even dangerous and criminal. The child, in its own inner life, had to confront this onslaught. The offenses of the *t'ao-ch'i* child, particularly in the eyes of gentry elders, indicated a sensitivity to deviation that is almost incomprehensible to contemporary outsiders. How are we to understand this parental sensitivity?

One way of answering this question is to view the traditional Chinese gentry family as a large, complex, awkward institution that required strict adherence to established patterns of behavior if it were to retain stability and guarantee its own continuity.[35] Such families provided models for inspiration and imitation throughout Chinese society, although most families had three generations and not the ideal five living under one roof. All families at least nodded to the principles of adult, male, and generational precedence, which made the line from father to son to grandson the central axis around which all other relationships were hierarchically arranged. The gentry family was, as Marion J. Levy, Jr., has argued, a particular kind of institutionalized living system. The need to buttress the solidarity of a large group made up of many married couples and their offspring was met by several ancient devices, including adherence to prescribed patterns of interaction (the *li*) that minimized the possibility of conflict and the need for words and the actual division of households under one roof.[36] But one of the secrets surely was the pervasive preference for respect and avoidance over affection and intimacy, as Levy has noted.

> [F]ather-son solidarity has to be such that its extreme strength and intensity could combine with a structure which placed the emphasis not on the interests of any one individual in the family but upon the family group as a whole. Respect is the affect best suited to such purpose. It permits a high intensity in the relationship and forges a strong positive bond between the individuals concerned, but it does not commit them to any primacy of concern for any individual's personal interests, as would be the case with a bond based on "love." Respect in the nature

of the case is more easily preserved and fostered by avoidance than by intimacy. It is perhaps too much to agree with the cynical view that familiarity breeds contempt, but, if the basis for contempt or for challenging respect is present, intimacy is more likely to make it obvious and inescapable than is avoidance.[37]

In some relationships, affection and intimacy were permitted, for instance, between parents and children during infancy, husband and wife in the privacy of the inner room, and the minor relationships of mother-son, brother-sister, and grandparent-grandson. But for parents and children during the middle and late *yu-nien* years, for teachers and pupils at school, for husbands and wives in their visible family and public life, and for a variety of other relationships in the family, undemonstrative, reserved expressions reigned on all faces.[38]

The undemonstrative facial mask eased strains within the large family; and the inner ability to yield, to flow around situations, to accommodate to others made conflicts less likely. Cultivating this ability was stressed in the practical wisdom passed on within families. Ch'en Ch'i-t'ien (b. 1893), for example, recalled these early family lessons:

> In his work, my father was willing to suffer hardship [lit., "eat bitterness" *ch'ih k'u*] and in relating to people, he was willing to sacrifice [lit., "eat losses" *ch'ih k'uei*]. My mother was more inclined to seize on the important duties of life than to engage in idle talk. She simply toiled and helped in the management of the household. My mother and father taught [by example] and without words *(pu yen chih chiao)*.[39]

The *Family Instructions for the Yen Clan* by Yen Chih-t'ui (531–591), a standard model for this genre of writing right into the twentieth century, contains practical advice on managing a large family and teaching the oncoming generation. The family head, he stressed, must be magnanimous and aloof and never show anger, even though he may feel, correctly, that the large family is like a house being eaten away and undermined by vermin, wind, and rain—Yen's metaphors for servants, concubines, sons, wives, and in-laws. Intimacy was to be avoided because it produced resentment; similarly, familiarity between parents and sons led to carelessness and disrespect.[40]

In this difficult living arrangement, the father-son relationship, that central focus for family continuity and harmony, was unusually burdened. How could the father guarantee that his son would be capable of the administrative expertise required of a family head? How could he impart to him that sense of primary duty to the family, whose fortunes he would inherit and pass on to his own sons and grandchildren? How could he prolong his own control, before the rising competence of his sons and the inevitable transfer of power to the next generation? He could not guarantee these results, but he could read the portents of danger and disaster in the deviant behavior of his son. When the father saw the beginning of strong individuality and unconventional indepen- dence in his *t'ao-ch'i* son, he could envision this force disrupting and tearing apart the delicate network of the family in the name of "selfish" personal indulgence. When he thought of strong bonds of horizontal intimacy between mother and son or wife and husband, he saw them as potential threats to the vertical lines of precedence, filiality, loyalty, and respect upon which family continuity and his own continuing authority rested. The result was the virtual disappearance of open affection in the family after the early *yu-nien* years, and the onset of an intense training regimen that only let up after age fifteen, when marriage and responsi- bility locked the son, particularly the eldest son, into the family for good.

This training regimen concentrated foremost on *character* formation: the learning of precedence and respect, the importance of toleration and patience, the necessity of obedience and mature behavior.[41] It was the father himself who had to take over final responsibility for the education of his sons. As he moved in to make demands and refuse desires, to punish and review conduct, the relationship between father and son be- came strained and rigid. For the son, the father became a distant, im- personal figure—"the terrible one"—to be avoided out of fear. He could scarcely be loved, and was sometimes openly hated; but most often the perception of underlying good will allowed their relationship to settle on that in-between affect of respect.

THE TESTIMONY OF YAN PHOU LEE. An unusually clear account of the attitudes and emotions with which parents and children regarded each other is found in the memoir of Yan Phou Lee. Lee, who in 1873 at the age of twelve left a gentry family in Kwangtung to come to the United States with the Chinese Educational Mission, wrote this account in English while an undergraduate at Yale, where he earned his way by "tutoring and lecturing on Chinese manners and customs."[42]

> Babyhood is the most enjoyable stage in the life of an Oriental. It is the only period when his wishes are regarded and when demonstrations of affection are shown to him. The family regulations in China are such that as soon as a child begins to understand, he is not only taught to obey, but also loses his freedom of action; nor does he fully recover it till he is old and past the brief season of youthful enjoyment.
>
> Every person in China is in strict subjection to somebody. The child is subject to his parents or guardian. They, in turn, are subject to their parents who are liable to be called to account by the elders of the clan. The magistrate is considered the father of the people he rules over; and the Emperor stands in the same relation to his subjects as the father to his children. Women are subject to their fathers or husbands . . .
>
> Accordingly, obedience and respect, rather than affection, are required of the Chinese child. His homelife . . . is constrained, sober, and dull. The boy attains to the ideal character only when he habitually checks his affectionate impulses, suppresses his emotions, and is uniformly dignified with his inferiors. Therefore the child is early taught to walk respectfully behind his superiors, to sit only when he is bidden, to speak only when questions are asked him, and to salute his superiors by the correct designations. It would be the height of impropriety for him to mention his father's name, or call his uncles and elder brothers by their names . . . He must rise from his seat when they approach him. If he is taken to task for anything he has done, he must never contradict, never seek to explain. Such an offense is not easily forgiven and double punishment is likely to immediately overtake the offender. How often have I rued my imprudence in contradicting my parents, uncles, or teachers! Often I was simply trying to give the explanation of seemingly bad conduct. But the Chinese take no explanations from those subject to them. It is better for an accused son, pupil, or servant to suffer punishment in silence although he may be conscious of no wrong doing. This seems very unreasonable; and, in fact, it does foster sullenness and a spirit of rebellion which fear alone keeps under. But the Chinese deem this method absolutely necessary for the preservation of authority. In every household the rattan stick is always ready to the hand of the majestic wrath of outraged family law. It is not my intention to represent the Chinese as naturally cruel. They are not. They simply maintain family discipline by customs handed down from one generation to another. Fathers and teachers have undergone the same training. The customs of their ancestors enjoin it, the teachings of Confucius prescribe it, and the laws of the empire arm it with authority.
>
> . . . [T]he regulations and government of my family were as rigorous as possible. I lived the years of my childhood in a shrinking condition of mind. Like all youngsters, I wanted to shout, jump, run about, show my resentments and

my affections, give my animal spirits and affectionate impulses full play. But like
a colt in training for the harness I was checked and curbed, my tongue was
bridled, and my feet clogged, by fear of my elders. My father was a stern man as
was his father before him. I remembered him vividly by the beatings I got from
him.

Yet he was truly good and kind.[43]

A striking aspect of young Lee's commentary is how unsuccessful the
system was in breaking him in. "How often have I rued my imprudence
in contradicting my parents, uncles, or teachers!" And this imprudent
lad admits to no more than external conformity, while implying that
inside he was sullen and nursed "a spirit of rebellion." His testimony,
and that of many others, raises the question of how thoroughly internalized these cultural norms in fact were. To what extent did filial sons
come to want to be what they were told they had to be? Scholarly studies looking for a "national character" or a "modal personality" within a
given culture often postulate that dominant cultural norms are internalized half-knowingly by all children and thereafter remain stubbornly
lodged in the superego or conscience; thus children come to value, not
just acknowledge, what adults teach them by word and example. But
such approaches have blunted the exploration of permanent and unresolved areas of conflict between individuals and institutions like the family. And this in turn has obscured the actual variety of experience, behavior, and individual personalities found within families and society.[44]
There were undoubtedly Chinese lads who internalized the filial norms
exquisitely into their being; but many others were "filial sons by default," held in this role not so much by the voice of the superego as by
the overwhelmingness of the concrete situation which offered them only
disastrous alternatives. Let us look at four permanent cracks in that Chinese
establishment called the Totalistic Family and the Despotic Father, cracks
that allowed the *t'ao-ch'i* boy (and occasionally girl) to emerge and even
thrive inside the filial system. These cracks, documented in evidence
derived from actual families and villages, compel us to recognize that
late Ch'ing society contained within it a considerable variety of childhood experiences and hence character tendencies.[45]

I. THE TARDY IMPACT OF PATERNAL DISCIPLINING. Paternal discipline,
the linchpin in the training of sons, was not evenly applied through

childhood. During infancy, little effort was made to discipline children, except for mild scolding by mother or nurse. The father began actively to supervise the training of his son only towards the end of the *ying-erh* years (ages two to four, and sometimes later).[46] In any case the source of authority must be distinguished from the actual disciplining agent, as described for a village in Yunnan province:

> The father has the final authority in punishing at all times, but the mother deals with children of both sexes before they are ten or a little older. Up till then the father comes into the picture infrequently. When the youngsters are more than ten, the father will discipline the male children and the mother the female children. Older brothers can also discipline their younger brothers and in the absence of the father, occasionally their younger sisters.[47]

In another village in Shantung province, a similar practice was observed. Before age ten, the mother sanctioned a boy's behavior in the father's absence. Between age ten and fifteen, the father was the boy's sole disciplinarian, in theory and fact, with the mother in the background as refuge and comfort. After age fifteen, the father was not expected to beat or scold his son and would create resentment in the son and criticism from neighbors if he did. Indeed, beyond age ten, disciplining, if required, was to be done privately with only the parents present.[48]

The pattern in these two villages reveals the late emergence of the Terrible One into a dominating child-rearing role. Only for a period of about five years, from age ten to fifteen, was he solely responsible. Before this, the son was under the joint supervision of father, mother, nurse, servants, grandparents (if present), elder brothers, and teacher or master. The practical effect of this joint supervision was often to undermine or counterbalance the negative stance of the father. Only when he was present and solely in charge could his "majestic wrath" be fully manifested and inconsistencies minimized.

What is the significance of this pattern for the *t'ao-ch'i* child? It offered him a chance to join the two halves of childhood in unconventional ways, and hence to avoid the crimping of the sense of autonomy and competence that marked the passage of many Chinese children. In the years prior to schooling, some children developed a strong sense of their own power in a nurturing setting. If the protective restraint of child-tenders was not too rigid, and if a boy had generous access to the objects in the household around him, he was able to reach out and explore beyond the safe and familiar maternal world that anchored him. This was especially true for the Young Masters of the upper class. One of them describes his preschool play.

> After my father left [for Honan], I occupied the reception room and study by myself. There was no wall between these rooms, only four wooden chairs and two small tea tables to serve as a partition. The reception room had four more of these chairs and two more tea tables, placed opposite the other chairs and tables. I fingered through books and climbed up and down [on the chairs], amusing myself at will. When I tired of playing in the study and reception room, I went to the opposite side [of the courtyard] to admire the sedan chairs, resting at an angle [against the wall]. The male servants had been released by Father when he returned to Honan. My elder brother was away at school during the day. I played freely by myself in these seven or eight large rooms. Running about, sitting astride the stone drum, singing and chanting, I told stories to myself. But then I had enough of solitude. Sometimes I would push open the middle door facing the corridor, call out strange sounds and listen to the echoes. Sometimes I could suddenly become afraid, scared of demons and snakes, and with one burst I would run north past the innermost door screen, walk to mother's chamber, and look for "Niang" [name for mother]. As soon as I saw her, all my fears vanished like drifting smoke or scattering clouds.[49]

The years from four to six or seven, after the dependency of the *ying-erh* period and before the advent of schooling, were years of some informal learning of characters and numbers; but mostly it was a time for playing with brothers, sisters, and cousins, hearing stories from elders and servants, especially the milk-mother *(nai-ma)*, and exploring nature by oneself. If the curiosity and self-confidence generated during this play period were not smothered entirely by the schooling regimen, some of these children stood a reasonable chance of outlasting their fathers during the harshest years of paternal disciplining (ages eight to twelve) and becoming, in Yen Chih-t'ui's highly partial view, "scoundrels." There was a certain age beyond which angry displays and physical punishment were counterproductive, as was recognized in the *Family Instructions for the Yen Clan:*

> After a child has formed proud and arrogant habits, they [the parents] begin to control him. But whipping the child even to death will not lead him to repen-

tance, while the growing anger of the parents will only increase his resentment. After he grows up, such a child becomes at last nothing but a scoundrel.[50]

For some young boys that point of no return passed by unnoticed.

II. THE DELEGATION OF AUTHORITY TO TEACHERS. Precisely when the son's training was to quicken, an outside authority came to have a central disciplinary role. Passing this duty along to teachers was an obvious way of lessening the strain between father and son. Since the time of Mencius, it had been recognized that a father should not instruct his own son. Making a son in the orthodox mold required admonition and reproof, and hence the possibility of anger, hypocrisy, mutual ill-feeling, and loss of respect.

> Kung-sun Ch'ou said, "Why is it that the superior man does not teach his son himself?" Mencius said, "The circumstance is such that it cannot be done. To teach is necessarily to inculcate correct principles. When these correct principles are not practiced, anger will follow. As anger follows, feelings will be hurt." [The son would say,] "My master teaches me the correct principles but himself does not proceed according to correct principles." This means that the father and son hurt each others feelings; it is bad . . . Between father and son there should be no reproving admonition to what is good. Such reproofs lead to alienation, and nothing is more inauspicious than alienation.[51]

The task of "inculcating correct principles" was thus given over to an outside master, who *in loco parentis* would attempt to make his charges into virtuous and literate representatives of the gentlemanly tradition.

Learning and moral cultivation were viewed as the process of acquiring control over the undisciplined feelings let loose during infancy and the early *yu-nien* period. The schoolroom was the place where the "crooked wood" (Hsun-tzu's metaphor for premoral human nature) was steamed and bent into shape. It was the place where *t'ao-ch'i* sons were supposedly brought into harness or tethered by a nose-ring. As a popular saying in Hunan put it, "Boys are brought into submission in the schoolroom [by the teacher], girls by marrying [and coming under the mother-in-law]" *(Nan fu hsueh-t'ang, nü fu chia).*[52] In breaking in mischievous youngsters, the forms of traditional teaching methods were all-important. Pupils were required to sit for long hours on hard wooden benches or stools, put to memorizing the sounds of texts they did not understand, forced to recite flawlessly before the teacher, and made to copy hundreds of characters within lined squares. There were no recesses and no weekends, and only occasional holidays for the Ch'ing-ming festival to visit ancestral graves, the Dragon Boat festival in the spring, the Mid-Autumn festival, the fifteen day New Year celebration, and the birthdays of the Emperor, Confucius, and the students' own parents.[53] And the discipline was strict. Even slight mistakes in recitation, not to mention insubordination, could bring the ferrule down on the head or palm.[54] The message to pupils was clear: Box in your emotions, suppress your frustrations, and be diligent in study. Their chief consolation lay in fantasies about the future; for all students were apprentice officials, and embarked on the orthodox path to status and wealth.

From the perspective of the *t'ao-ch'i* child, this system organized around the delegation of authority to teachers had at least two weak points: the possibility of truancy and the vulnerability of many teachers in the role of moral exemplar. Truancy was a possibility created by the separation of the schoolroom from the household, a situation that the well-to-do were usually able to avoid by employing a tutor who resided with the family or an outside tutor who was a relative. The resourcefulness of a child bent on opposing the regimen of schooling is vividly revealed in the story of Tien-sze, whose poor but ambitious mother sacrificed much in order that he might study.

But Tien-sze did not like school, and he refused to go. At first, the mother tried to overcome the boy's objections by persuasion. She gave him good food, candy, and interesting things to play with, but these methods were not effective; the boy still did not want to go. Then harder measures were tried. The boy started to attend school again, but only three days out of five. The other two days Tien-sze spent neither at home nor at school. On the way from his home to the schoolhouse there was an empty house that belonged to a neighboring family. In the house there was a huge empty basket. Tien-sze would leave home shortly after his brothers had gone and would proceed to the empty house. Here he turned over the basket and crept under it. After about two hours, when his brothers and the other boys passed by the house on the way home to dinner, he would come out of his hiding place and run home behind them. His parents supposed that he went to school; his brothers thought that he was permitted to stay at home, and so his hiding place was not suspected. But he was finally caught by his brothers, and his parents discovered what he had been doing. Tien-sze was severely punished. Depressed and ashamed he went to school again for a few days, and then

he began to hide in a neighbor's vegetable garden. It was not long before he was
discovered and he got another beating. This put an end to his truancy. He went
to school regularly, but made no attempt to study. He would fall asleep even
when the teacher was present, but when the teacher was absent, he was the most
mischievous of all the pupils. Gradually both the teacher and his parents came to
the conclusion that it was useless to compel the child to study. When the school
year ended, Tien-sze's schooling was also over, at least for the time being.[55]

Once the truant had won his case against schooling, he was pulled back
into the family setting and given disciplining tasks, usually field work,
but sometimes, as in the case of Tien-sze, the humiliating "girl's work"
of caring for the younger children. The manual labor of young farm
boys, however, often proved quite liberating, for it released them beyond the control of elders. At age eight or nine, Tien-sze assisted his
older brother in taking the cow to the fields to graze.

> Tien-sze liked this job. He could run in the fields, over the hills and down the
> valleys, he could catch fish in the streams, collect flowers, hunt eggs or young
> birds in their nests underneath the bushes or in the trees. He would dig out the
> clay from the holes in the weatherbeaten rocks at the foot of South Hill and from
> it, fashion toys and other objects to give to his sister and her friends.
>
> Nobody expected the boys who took the cows to the fields to behave like
> adults. They raced along the road or the edges of the fields, and fought among
> themselves . . . They roasted birds they had caught, or peas, beans, peanuts,
> and sweet potatoes that they picked up in the fields. Swearing, teasing the smaller
> boys, and plotting against a villager they did not like, were frequent activities of
> the cow-boys. Tien-sze always got very excited in these adventures. He was a
> mischievous and stubborn child, but he was intelligent and full of wit. Although
> he was still young, his tricks were highly appreciated by the older boys who
> therefore forgave him his age somewhat.[56]

In these free acts, Tien-sze was weaving his own designs and meanings
into the world of things, which is the basic process of art and a distinctive capacity and need of human beings.[57] The aim of others, at home
and school, was to fit him into meanings predetermined by cultural
beliefs, patterns, and economic necessities.

In schooling and work experiences away from home, however short-
lived, the *t'ao-ch'i* child found truancy-mates and work-mates to support
his needs and give him a sense of belonging. The peer group provided a
sphere for free and open-ended action that contrasted sharply with the

well-defined expectations and relationships at home. Among boys from poor families who never knew the schoolroom, activities with age mates away from the family may well have been more prolonged and important as a peer group experience than it was for those in school; but too little is known to make a claim that these activities constituted a permanent adolescent subculture. A different ethic did prevail on the grazing fields and city streets, where strength, cleverness, and companionship outstripped virtue, book skills, and proper demeanor; an outside perspective on conventional family norms, whether elite or folk, was certainly accessible to participants in such peer group activities. The city boy Sheng Cheng, for example, became "commander-in-chief" of an "army" of 120 children (ages six to fourteen), which, around the years of the Republican Revolution of 1911, clashed between the gates of the city of Nanking with another children's army of 400. He received the post for the feat of stealing a vase and lances from the Hunan Club. These clashes were earnestly undertaken; and after one defeat, the young lad threw himself into the study of military strategy and terrain in order to fashion a victory and recover his honor.[58] Parents could not condone these activities openly, especially when they involved immoral behavior. Lying and stealing were wrong and had to be punished; still many parents were probably secretly pleased with the unconventional vigor and intelligence of their children. But whether pleased or not, poor parents could do little to prevent a determined son from joining these unorthodox adventures.

In theory, the teacher in the traditional private school *(ssu-shu)* was the firm right hand of the father, a model of virtue, and a staunch disciplinarian. But once again, from the perspective of the *t'ao-ch'i* child, teachers were considerably more vulnerable figures than the theory suggests. Many were poor, frustrated scholars who had failed in the examination system, and there may have been a considerable component of sadism in their treatment of their pupils. Such men could hardly convey the impression to young boys that they were "models of virtue." Hypocrisy bred disrespect and even contempt, just as it would have between father and son. Other teachers struck pupils as somewhat ridiculous and ignorant figures. The local "scholar" in one mountain village was a near-sighted old man who had to press his drippy nose into his

pupils' books in order to read what they were reciting. After each recitation the pages were stained with mucus, and inevitably he acquired
the nickname "The Filthy Blind One."[59] There was rarely a teacher who
was not the target of humor and pranks, at least among some of his
pupils.

The ignorance or narrowness of a teacher could become painfully obvious if there were outside standards of comparison. After 1905, the
flood of ideas created by the New Learning undermined the old standards of evaluation and swamped many classical teachers and scholars. A
teacher who did not know the elementary facts of geography, history,
and arithmetic, let alone the natural sciences, lost respect as the "complete man of knowledge" in the eyes of his pupils. Young students exposed to the New Learning by brothers, friends, or teachers who had
been abroad perceived the world differently; and there was no going
back. The rapid turnover of teachers and schools introduced them to a
variety of personalities and competencies and gave them the leverage of
perspective on the learning situation. This divergence of ways can be
seen in the case of young Li Tung-fang confronting Tutor Ku. Having
spent two years in a new-style primary school, young Li held ideas that
were incompatible with those of his old-style tutor. Tutor Ku equated
freedom with the denial of superiors *(wu-chün)* and equality with the
denial of fathers *(wu-fu);* he was suspicious of this pupil who has been
to a "foreign-style school" and picked up "evil habits." Young Li recip-
rocated with contempt.[60]

The derivative nature of the teacher's authority, most evident in his
financial dependence upon a family or group of families, is visible in
other ways as well. Sometimes this "right hand of the father" was vulnerable to special pleading. Formal authority to "beat and scold as necessary" might be weakened by pleas from nurse or mother. In one case,
a "milk mother" *(nai-ma)* implored the tutor's wife to intervene in any
disciplinary action against her boy.[61] Sometimes the books to be taught
were specified by a brother or father or grandfather, and the tutor was
almost a substitute pair of ears and eyes, a mere menial and not a contributing mind. Shen Kang-poh (b. 1897), for example, had been taught
by his grandfather for two years, from age three to five, and then he was
turned over part-time to a tutor.

At age five I began formal study and started to write characters. Each morning my grandfather would punctuate the sentences in the texts and read them to me. After reading them, he paid no more attention, for my study, recitation, and writing were supervised by a family tutor whose surname was Tung . . . Tutor Tung at that time was already approaching forty. Formerly he had been one of my grandfather's least successful students. He had taken the first exam tens of times, but never received a *hsiu-ts'ai* degree. Towards me, however, he was extremely friendly. When reciting, I would often take the chance to tug at his beard, play with his pipe pouch, or sometimes even tie his queue to the back of the chair or put a small insect inside his collar. He always laughed about these things, and never once reprimanded me.[62]

A final comment on the relative impact of teachers as disciplinarians is a passage in the preface to the *Family Instructions for the Yen Clan* by Yen Chih-t'ui:

> In checking the mischief of children, the warnings of teachers and friends are not as effective as the commands of nurse or maidservant; in stopping quarrels and fights between coarse brothers, the doctrines of Yao and Shun are not as influential as the instructions of a widowed mother. I hope this book will be for you boys something a little better than the words of nurses and widows.[63]

But were the father's intermittent instructions enough to check the spread of mischief?

III. THE INTERVENTIONIST SYLE OF THE FATHER. The father's calling was not to praise, encourage, and reward, but to embody the sanctioning spirit—criticizing, scolding, and beating when necessary—that remained the backstop for the process of correct learning. To the son he was a distant figure of awe, fear, knowledge, power, and respect who could emerge suddenly from the background with anger and decisiveness, and sometimes mercy, but almost never understanding. Conforming behavior seemed to be the only way of keeping the Terrible One at bay, short of the drastic alternatives of running away or attempting suicide. These alternatives, although drastic indeed, offered the child some leverage in the process of accommodating his desires to parental demands. Young Mao Tse-tung resorted to both alternatives, and discovered their tactical value as threats in securing better treatment from his domineering father.[64] Hsieh Ping-ying, a "girl rebel" whose future schooling was being blocked by her strong-willed mother, contemplated suicide by all the locally known methods before settling upon starvation; a three-day fast secured the grudging retreat of her mother.[65] In these unequal confrontations, established power met the power of desperation; an accommodation of demands might result, but there was seldom an inner catharsis or mutual understanding.

The direct confrontation, however, was less common in the large gentry family which lived by the code of quiet diplomacy and the avoidance of conflict. In contrast to the simpler constellation of the nuclear family in the West, this Chinese family was an intricate network of people, both living and dead, which held its individual members in place. It was a complex of relationships, "a pyramid of authority, not only of people, but of rooms and courtyards, trees and flowers, servants and sedan chairs."

> In this peopled, furnished domain, kin and clan dovetail finely as fine woodwork; not beings in themselves, but beings in relation to the common structure to which we belonged, which we owned and which owned us.[66]

In this kind of family setting, many people could provide support and discipline for children, so that the absence of one or two individuals—even the father—was not perceived as catastrophic. When required by work or study to leave their families for periods of months and even years, fathers could do so without great anxiety, knowing that the "paternal mode" would not be completely missing because of their physical absence.

The Chinese father relied greatly on the family network and teachers to care for and train his children for him. His was the final authority and responsibility, but he exercised it by intervening periodically in the lives of his children and alarming them with his large presence, not by close day-to-day sharing of their frustrations, successes, and failures. I recorded in my Taiwan notebook the following description of a father and his sons in a wealthy official family during the *yu-nien* years:

> They lived in a yamen, up river from Shanghai. His father was the magistrate, and a severe man indeed with his children. After he and his elder brother (three years older) started to study with Tutor Liao at about the age of four or five (ca. 1908), their life was very separate from the rest of the family. Their rooms were

close to the tutor's quarters, which consisted of bedroom, study, and classroom;
and they ate three meals with him and served him in the morning with hot water
in a copper pail, waking him at dawn for the start of classes. Only every few
months would the father summon them before him, and ask them to cite this or
that passage in the *Odes* or *Tso chuan,* or ask them how often they had been beaten
on the palm, as every lapse of memory or wrong intonation was so punished by
the tutor several times each day. It went on like this for about two years, when
one night his father summoned them and said that the times were changing, and
that they should learn a foreign language: Latin. He had engaged an Episcopal
priest to instruct them; and after a year and a half, they had learned some Latin
but still no [useful] English. This tutoring went on in the evenings, for the priest
did not live in, as no contact of the two tutors was desired. When the priest had
to leave, a student returned from Japan was hired to teach them English, as his
elder brother had finally gotten up the courage to ask the father. They loved this
student, who was more informal and vivacious than old Liao. Yet one day they
discovered that his queue was false; and after ten days of agony, they finally told
a servant who told the father. The young tutor was "liquidated" or so a servant
said. They did not know what became of him.[67]

This account illustrates the interventionist style of the father. The sons
were bound by his dictates and whims, such as the study of Latin, and
also by his values, which led them to expose their favorite tutor. From
a distance, the father could control their environment and channel their
energies, but he remained out of contact with the inner lives of his sons.
The structures of respect crowded out the possibility of intimacy in the
father-son relationship.[68] In one apt formulation, the father was *the one
whose presence killed all laughter.*[69] But laughter itself—a true sign of intimacy—did not disappear from the Chinese household.

*IV. THE SUPPORTING NETWORK: MOTHERS, NURSES, GRANDPARENTS,
SISTERS, AND KINDLY MALES.* With the exception of the grandparents,
all members of a household were subject to the father's authority; and
any support they offered a child could be overruled by him during a
confrontation. But the paternal vetoing power did not prevent relatives
and servants from providing general nurture and support to a son (or a
younger brother, or a grandson), thus providing him with elders who
shared his inner life to some extent. Nurses were able to exert their
power directly and indirectly in areas that overlapped with parental prerogatives, especially the dispensing of physical punishment. Sheng Cheng's

nurse, Mama Wan, who was with him until age ten, reacted strongly
whenever he was punished:

> If my father punished my brother or me, she would grumble all the rest of the
> day. She would say: "Teaching does not mean punishing. It means guiding, not
> forcing." When I was bad—which happened often—she would scold me and give
> me good examples to follow.

Li Tung-fang's nurse disputed with his mother and even threatened to
leave to make her point; as a result, he was never punished physically
by his mother.[70]

And should events come to an impasse, the supporting persons were
not without resources and courage, as the following interplay reveals.
The *t'ao-ch'i* son Tien-sze, who had lost a knife belonging to a preacher,
was accused of having stolen it.

> The preacher told his parents about it, and the father became very angry and
> shouted, "What's the use of his going to school if he learns to do such shameful
> things?" The mother also was quite astonished . . . They both felt they had to
> punish him severely or the preacher would think they were lax. The father thought
> he should beat his son, but the mother objected on the ground that he was already
> more than ten years old and reputedly a good student. Tien-sze's sister kept her
> brother in her room when the time for the punishment came. The father scolded
> the boy through the closed door and while the mother also complained that the
> family's reputation had been ruined by his misbehavior, she secretly blocked the
> father's path to the boy. Finally it ended with only scolding and complaining.[71]

Support at crucial times might also come from beyond the immediate
household: uncles, neighbors, friends of the father. In the case of Tien-
sze, a coalition of voices formed to balance and finally outweigh the
father's objections to his future schooling. His first elder brother (who
had acquired some New Learning in the market town and sought for his
brother what he could no longer undertake himself), his mother, his
older sister, several older cousins, a distant uncle (who had noticed his
talents), and a member of the neighboring, wealthy P'an family (who
had observed his fine intellect and the brightness of his eyes), all exerted
influence in his favor. Such coalitions existed in almost every family;
rarely was a growing son, however mischievous, completely isolated.
The size of the family was an important variable, however; for in small
conjugal families, as were common among the peasantry, there was less

room for indirection and avoidance. The strains behind the loose factions in a gentry family might well manifest themselves as warring parties in a peasant family. Mao's family, as he told Edgar Snow in consciously political imagery, consisted of his father as Ruling Power and his mother, himself, his brother, and sometimes the laborer as Opposition.[72]

Childhoods that were organized around these nurturing relationships favored the emergence of autonomy and a strong sense of self-worth in the child. These alternative constellations became more dominant, of course, if the father were weak or absent during the *yu-nien* years owing to death or work. Kuo Jen-yuan [Zing Yang Kuo], whose father was physically ill and weak, had virtually reversed roles with his father by age twelve, and was managing the family finances. His father was "weak" in two senses. First, he was suffering from tuberculosis, which made him "a sick, feeble old man . . . coughing and spitting blood every day." Second, he was less competent in management than his wife and his son, so that his dominant status position was eroded by his dependence upon them. The son's relationship with his educated and strong-willed mother was the anchor for the first ten years of his life, until she died in a plague. She supported him in his inner interests, as the following passage makes clear:

> I began to raise pigeons and dogs when I was six years old . . . As I was too young to build pigeon coops myself, my mother ordered a carpenter to put them up for me. Two years later I was able to make partitions from wooden kerosene cases. Mother was always on hand to help and advise me on these matters; but Father's dislike for the pigeons was so strong that once in an angry mood he tried to destroy my pigeon house to prevent me from spending so much time with the birds. Mother immediately appeared on the scene and told Father to leave me alone, and with her help I salvaged the fallen birdhouses.[73]

After her death he was old enough to manage without her help.

In such situations of weak or absent fathers, mothers had to be both mother and father to their sons; but if they were competent, disciplined yet loving persons, they could fuse the maternal and paternal modes in one person. Authority, instead of being distant and unresponsive, became concrete and near, and was more likely to be understanding; it asked and demanded out of love and hope and not simply to maintain obedience, respect, and propriety. For sons who grew up in such supportive settings under maternal guidance, the gap between home life and normal society—the latter so dominated by paternal disciplining modes—could be great. It is a plausible hypothesis that as a group, they would be more inclined to try to remake society in their own image than to accept prevailing cultural patterns.[74]

THE MATERNAL LEGACY

The explicit recognition of the kindred feelings that find their archetypal expression in a warm, early mother-child relationship—that is, affection, compassion, trust, optimism, a sense of unity and fullness—is often derogatorily labeled in the West as "sentimentality." Educated Chinese men seem to have fewer inhibitions in talking about their mothers and acknowledging this early debt. Paul Valery comments in his 1930 introduction to Sheng Cheng's *A Son of China,* "If the author had known us better, if he had become more occidentalized, perhaps he would never have had the idea of appealing to his mother to help him, would never have thought of converting us to the doctrine of universal love by the indirect approach of maternal affection."[75] The maternal matrix of strength was, in fact, seen by many Chinese as a natural source of later ideals that are meant to enclose, nurture, and transform humankind. Sheng Cheng, a May Fourth organizer, grew up with his nurse and mother forming the underpinning of his childhood and youth. He acknowledges this central truth in his autobiography, and links his faith in human unity, his hope in future generations, his belief in solidarity and patient idealism with their teaching and example.[76] His tale is a needed reminder that the vision and motivation of young rebels and reformers originates in the invisible experience of maternal strength as well as in the visible struggles against paternal power and authority.

All Chinese children faced a continuum of possible treatment during the childhood years, stretching from a maternal style to a paternal style. In the maternal style, the face of authority was kindly: it nurtured the inner life, guided by example, persuaded with words, and exhorted out of love. In the paternal style, the face of authority was severe: it commanded, scolded, threatened, and beat palms, heads, and bodies. If a son were to emerge from the childhood years with a strong sense of autonomy, initiative, and self-worth, he would have to have a generous early experience of the maternal style. And, in addition, he would have to outlast the deadening impact of the paternal style, encountered most often—and in its pristine state—in fathers and teachers. The *t'ao-ch'i* youngster was one kind of son who had a good chance of doing so. His healthy vigor indicated that there had been no severe emotional or nutritional deprivations; his ability to explore the world around him independently during the early *yu-nien* years was built upon a strong attachment bond formed during infancy. Now, if he could thread his way through openings within the filial system during the later *yu-nien* years of schooling, he could keep his sense of autonomy intact. Ideally, seen through the eyes of theorists like Yen Chih-t'ui, these openings would have been closed by alert parents and teachers, in order to harness the son's strong and threatening independence. But in actual practice, the openings were permanent irregularities that continued to generate a stream of unusual or atypical children inside the traditional filial system.

Visible mischievousness was one major way for some sons to resolve the autonomy crisis in a positive fashion. Other sons, building on a similar, strong maternal base, adapted to the paternal mode by keeping their feelings and thoughts to themselves. Outwardly they might appear obedient, industrious, and passive, in the mold of the "good child" (*kuai hai-tzu*), but inwardly their minds were active and independent. Their minds, after all, had had plenty of stimulation in learning how to be skillful social beings within the complex behavioral world of the Chinese family, and through memorizing significant portions of the Chinese literary heritage written in a difficult, unspoken classical language. Both positive resolutions of the autonomy crisis, whether through visible mischievousness or invisible inner resistance, were still only one long and important step towards an independent, self-reliant youth and adulthood. There were other crises, both developmental and historical, to be confronted along the way, new and subtle means by which the culture and the era threw up barriers in their paths.

Child carrying a baby, Chihli, ca. 1900. Courtesy, Essex Institute, Salem, Mass.

FOUR

Culture Triumphant: The Making of Social Selves

Lu Hsun remarked in an essay on "Shanghai Children" that Chinese parents seemed to have two ways of bringing up children: Either they let them run wild without control, so that they became incompetent and aggressive like spiders without webs; or they treated them with invariable harshness, so that the child became a slave or marionette. He found these two images confirmed in picture books in which Chinese children were portrayed either as savage or stupid.[1] For Lu Hsun these children represented human failures in Chinese dress. They were testimony to the continuing power of the family in China to determine the next generation, whether through its ability to create well socialized children in its own image or through its squandering of the talents of children by spoiling them. To Lu Hsun neither dominant pattern boded well for China, which needed children who would be the roots of "real human beings"—that is, active, independent, rational, high-spirited, mischievous, lively, fearless, stubborn, and healthy children.[2] He was not optimistic: The encompassing force of the traditional culture victimized parents as well as children.

The triumph of culture, whether a despised one or not, is a fundamental dilemma in humanization itself. Individual children need to acquire a cultural pattern through social learning in order to become human. Without group-transmitted cultural patterns, humans would be, as Clifford Geertz has noted, "unworkable monstrosities with very few useful instincts, fewer recognizable sentiments, and no intellect." Of all animals, humans most depend upon extragenetic, outside-the-skin, cultural controls for ordering their behavior.[3] Yet in developing from a not-yet-human creature into a fully human social being, children pay a heavy cost: They lose aegis over themselves in undergoing a confusing, frustrating transformation. At first the infant is only a body, with a very meager ego. It may be able to bask in the mother's warmth and nourishment throughout infancy, but then she and others begin to block the child's actions and make demands. Because even small children are self-reflexive beings—"I can think of me"—they respond to the blockage by pausing, delaying action, and considering from the perspective of others what the blockage and frustration mean. By age six the child has learned to think of itself in the symbolic ways of the culture. The very sense of self has been a social construction, built from the outside in on terms that are meaningful to others, principally the language of the culture and the values of the immediate family that surround and dwarf the child during the early years of life.[4]

There is little choice about this process.[5] Since human young undergo a long period of dependence upon older members of the group, inequality is built into the human life cycle. During long years of apprenticeship in "becoming human" by adult cultural standards, children are initiated, harshly or gently, into the ways of the group. They are drawn along or levered into ever higher stages of social interaction and environmental mastery, initially by the desire to keep the love and meet the demands of the mother or nurturing adult. In his autobiography, Hu Shih has given us a vivid glimpse of these universal elements—the mother's love and demands and the child's dependence and intense emotional participation in the process of learning.

> Every day just before dawn, my mother would call me to wake up, tell me to put my clothing around my shoulders. I never knew how long she herself had been up and sitting [there on my bed]. When she saw that I was clearly awake, then she would tell me what I had done wrong and said wrong the day before, and that she wanted me to study diligently. Some days she would tell me each of my father's good points, saying "You should always follow in your father's footsteps. He was the only complete man that I have known in my life. You want to emulate him, not cause him to lose face." When she talked about things that hurt her, she always began to cry. When it was broad daylight she would dress me and urge me off to my early studies . . . My mother disciplined me very

strictly. She was a mother who doubled as a father. But she never scolded me in front of anyone else, nor hit me physically. When I did something wrong, she would only give me a look. When I saw the reproach shining in her eyes, I was struck still. If the misdeed was small, she would wait until early the next morning to admonish me. If the misdeed was great, she would wait until evening when people had settled down. She would close the door, first reprove me and then punish me, sometimes by making me kneel or by pinching and twisting my skin. No matter what kind of heavy punishment she gave me, she never permitted me to cry out loud. Her discipline of her son was not a way of using him as a target for the display of her own emotions.[6]

Slowly children learn how to live within ever larger and more complicated groups, and how to monitor their own behavior at the same time. In the process of differentiating the world of objects "outside" and coming to discover the self at the same time, they are controlled and pressured by the external environment until they can function autonomously via self-control and self-regulation. A child learns to act autonomously by discovering the operative values of the nurturing adult, then of the family and larger society, and finally by internalizing these values as his own guidelines for surviving, navigating, or thriving within the given settings.[7] It matters little whether, at this early stage, self-control and self-regulation are half-truths; the child may appear more like a social puppet than an actor with honest, inner control, but he has become a social being with a symbolic world view.[8]

The learning in these early years has a certain fatedness about it; for given the basic inequality in childhood, children are more acted upon than the authors of their own dramas. One consequence of this fatedness is that the first world of childhood has a massive, indubitable reality. The persons with whom the child identifies are given; the identification is semi-automatic, just as the internalization of their notions of reality is also almost inevitable.

The child does not internalize the world of his significant others as one of many possible worlds. He internalizes it as *the* world, the world *tout court*. It is for this reason that the world internalized in primary socialization is so much more firmly entrenched in consciousness than worlds internalized in secondary socializations. However much the original sense of inevitability may be weakened in subsequent disenchantments, the recollection of a never-to-be-repeated certainty—the certainty of the first dawn of reality—still adheres to the first world of childhood. Primary socialization thus accomplishes what (in hindsight, of course) may be seen as the most important confidence trick that society plays on the individual—to make appear as necessity what is in fact a bundle of contingencies, and thus to make meaningful the accident of birth.[9]

The actual contents of this first world are enormously variable, but the language of the culture with its motivational and interpretive schemes is one of the most basic acquisitions.

THE INEVITABLE FIRST WORLD OF A CHINESE CHILDHOOD

Let us turn to the first world of Chinese childhoods, to a consideration of some persistent emphases in defining what it meant to be a member of Chinese society, a member of a Chinese family. The language of *lien* or "face" defined, and still defines, social existence within Chinese society. Understanding how it describes the fit between the individual self and the group permits us to perceive the normative moral order that embraces all the members of the group. In interpreting the outer social world to the self, the language of *lien* gives the individual a set of coordinates by which to measure his behavior. More than an interpretation, it poses the very nature of social existence. Loss of face, for example, is not viewed as a punishment inflicted from the outside; it is a state of being, intelligible through a shared vocabulary of what constitutes decency.[10] *Lien* is a quality so basic that it is noted primarily in its absence. Its most common formulations are negative: loss of face *(tiu lien), to have no lien (mei yu lien),* not to want *lien (pu yao lien).* In these expressions, the fall from decency is marked by degrees, with each category implying greater humiliation and social isolation. Loss of face *(tiu lien)* was a temporary condition; it could be redeemed in most instances, and face thus regained. Not having *lien* was a kind of consistent obtuseness towards group values, a more serious shortcoming in an individual because it indicated a failure to have internalized conventional norms for social behavior. Not wanting *lien* was the most serious shortcoming, a category reserved for criminals and foreigners; more than having no feeling for *lien,* this shortcoming implied a willful rejection of its claims. Such persons were shameless or unpredictable, unsocialized by Chinese standards.

In contrast, to possess *lien* is simply to be a "decent human being," a man who has respect in his own eyes as well as in the eyes of others. It implies moral credibility—that is, first of all, the ability to perform dependably in conventional roles. Particularly important in late imperial China were the "five primary relationships" *(wu-lun)*: ruler-subject, father-son, husband-wife, elder brother-younger brother, and friend-friend. Failures in these roles were more corrosive to one's social standing than lapses in minor relationships. Besides role performance, the ability to make an accurate estimate of one's own power and station in life counted, that is, an ability to avoid being either boastful or overly self-effacing. *Lien* is a quality which the poorest person of the lowest status may have and which even the wealthiest official must have if he is to be respected in the moral eyes of the community. Unlike its counterpart term *mien-tzu,* which refers to an external accumulation of prestige, influence, power, position, and wealth, *lien* points to an inner sense of worth that is maintained or lost as a whole. It is an "indivisible entity as experienced by ego, although felt more or less strongly."[11]

The emotional impact of the loss of *lien* could "come to constitute a real dread affecting the nervous system of ego more strongly than physical fear."

> A single lapse is punished by ridicule and comments on loss of face; repeated offenses arouse strong disapproval and cause the withdrawal, psychologically speaking, of the community from ego. The consciousness that 'loss of face' means that the confidence of society in his character is impaired, and places him in danger of being despised and isolated, usually acts as a strong deterrent in the individual.[12]

Learning to be Chinese in part meant acquiring this emotional sensitivity to *lien* and the regard of others. Our words *shame* and *guilt* are inadequate to express the inner feel of the emotional state involved; for neither the anxiety of being "out" or "wrong" or "exposed," nor the comforts of being "in" and "right" find exact counterparts in English. This sensitivity was acquired by a dual process of overt training in group ideals of loyalty and unity and by using shaming techniques to inculate a high moral anxiety if the groups norms were violated. In a 1970 study of grade school children on Taiwan, parents and teachers were found to provide children with an individual identity defined in terms of the

group as family, school, and nation. Children came to think of themselves as "we children" and "we Chinese," linking their individual self-
esteem with a collective consciousness. Negatively, the fear of being
isolated, exposed, or left out was heightened by generous use of punishing techniques that conveyed rejection, ostracism, and the withdrawal
of love.[13] The parents did not want to be exposed either. The prospect
of unsocialized children, and with it wagging tongues and social ostracism, prodded Chinese parents into exercising "great vigor and wit" in
shaming their children:

> The parent is horrified at the prospect of his child ever becoming shameless.
> To be shameless is to be uncontrollable, and hence an outcast from both the
> family and the culture. When the Chinese child experiences shame and humilia-
> tion, he wants to disappear from sight, to fall through the floor, to shrivel up
> and be inconspicuous, to hide his face, indeed, to feel the loss of his face.[14]

The concept of *lien* provided one of the basic orientations of the self
within the Chinese behavioral environment. As something common to
all classes, the constant need to consider *lien* was a unifying force in
society; but class affected the way *lien* was understood and the behavior
demanded to maintain it. Illiterate peasants lived within the emotional
and moral vocabulary of sin and guilt before supernatural agencies, which
included a population of demons and gods. In the *shan-shu* or "popular
religious books," 38,000 gods watched day and night for transgressions
and violations. The sense of wrongdoing and remorse was presumably
widespread among the lower, non-privileged stratum of the literate who
read these books and among the illiterate who came to comprehend such
texts through their circulation in oral mediums. Among the educated,
this world of sinfulness was left behind; there were instead crimes against
the natural cosmic order, and failures to live up to the code of honor
and *noblesse oblige* by which they had learned to measure themselves.[15]

Becoming conscious of the family as a natural unit with whom and
through whom the self existed was also a major substantive reality in
that small first world of Chinese children. The starting point was different from our own: not separate individuals linked together, but related
persons developing individuality within the group.[16] The borders of the
family as human "group" are as selective as the internal cultural vision

of how the self is related to others in time and space.[17] This Chinese kinship group differed sharply from the contemporary Western one in including a wider range of "significant others" in the extended family (gentry) and the stem family (peasants), and in reaching beyond the living to incorporate dead ancestors, especially those in the paternal genealogy. Biological continuity between father and son, ancestors and self, the dead and the living were cultural emphases. "I am of the 81st generation," announced Alfred Sze, as the natural observation with which to begin his life history.[18] Hu Shih, asked to write his credo, found it natural to begin with his father: "My father, Hu Ch'uan, was a scholar and a man of strong will and administrative ability." He alone among the contributors to a volume of credos by famous persons around the world felt the inherent appropriateness of this as a beginning point.[19]

A growing child was made to embrace figures—ancestors, gods, and spirits—whose presence was largely fictional, known and made real only through the words and interpretations of others. This dialogue with the dead, as constructed by the living, was one source of leverage for placing the child under judgment and making it self-conscious in relation to the record of the past. The ancestors embodied a past glory that family members should live up to, whose accumulated face (*mien-tzu*) or merits they must preserve and extend by commensurate achievement and proper behavior. They were idealized examples to the younger generations of what it meant to *tso jen*. Sometimes ancestors could be concretely present in the form of written wills and instructions and loom as giants governing the moves of parents and children alike.[20] When fatherless, thirteen-year-old Chiang Kai-shek first left his native village, he was admonished by his mother to "maintain the reputation of the ancestors." Her meaning, as Robert Payne notes, was not restricted to the farmers and salt merchants among his paternal ancestors, but referred to a family tradition that linked the Chiangs with Tan, Duke of Chou, the great innovator who founded the Chou dynasty in the twelfth century B.C. It mattered little to a young lad that hundreds of thousands might claim the same ancestors or that genealogical accuracy was fanciful over such a long time; his dreams and ambitions were linked with the ghostly presence of this ancient giant, whose virtue and energy he felt to be his inheritance.[21]

But the Duke of Chou and other past heroes in history and literature were primarily supplementary to the image of a respectful adulthood, which for a son came particularly from the father or grandfather. However aloof and awe-inspiring he might be, the father was a model for the son's future, an image of an honorable place in society. The son was told this at the age (around five or six) when he could "understand things" *(tung-shih)*; he came to sense it in his own search for the connectedness of his pains and joys, the reasons for the prohibitions and exhortations, the logic behind the beating and the loving. *Obey, learn self-control,* he reasoned to himself, *conform to the ways of the group, and you shall in time have your position of respect, a sense of belonging, the chance to lead and teach others. You shall one day be as your father is, if you learn to live as your father lives and think as your father thinks.*

This inducement to conform and adopt the values of the adults draws its power from the anxiety of not belonging, of losing respect in the eyes of others, of being inconsequential and even ostracized. How can a small child bear this prospect?[22] A son could not know that his parents' words described reality as they felt it and wished it to be, not as it actually was. He could not yet reach an outside perspective on the parents' values or strip away the layers of interpretation surrounding the "realities" he came to learn. He had little defense before a plea that could bring to bear all the leverage of a mother's love and a son's obligation.

> Your father is dead; you live for him. You are bone of his bone, flesh of his flesh, blood of his blood, soul of his soul. If he is the bud, you are the flower. If he is the cocoon, you are the butterfly. My terrible fear is that you shall not grow to be men, and that all my sacrifices will be crowned only with pitiless disappointment and irremediable despair. I am afraid of being false to my duty as a mother, and thereby unworthy of your father. If you need me, take me wholly.[23]

The intensity of this specific plea is rooted in the suffering of a mother bringing up her sons alone in her in-laws' extended family. But the meanings expressed here—biological continuity, the obligation to past family members, the need to achieve a standard of worthy adulthood within the human group *(tso jen)*—are not idiosyncratic; they reflect the earliest fusions of emotion and idea, of feelings and words for Chinese children learning to orient themselves in the world.

THE APPRENTICESHIP IN CULTURAL COMPETENCE

The harnessing or restraint of self was implied in giving primacy to group values based on the concept of *lien* and family respectability. It was an understandable trade-off: In exchange for accepting group values and applying energy to conventional tasks, the child could enter into a serious apprenticeship in adult cultural knowledge and skills in field and shop and school. When the child was ready for this experience in productive cooperation, he was ready to go beyond the restless assertion of his own will. Erikson identifies the crucial development of the age from five to ten as the achievement of a sense of competence through participation in serious tasks. "The advancing child forgets or rather quietly 'sublimates'—that is, applies to concrete pursuits and approved goals—the drives which have made him dream and play."[24] The child is ready to become an "eager and absorbed unit in a productive situation." He is ready to cooperate and identify with those who know things and know how to do things—"good" teachers and parents who "mildly and firmly [coerce children] into the adventure of finding out that one can learn to accomplish things . . . that are not the product of play and fantasy but the product of reality, practicality, and logic."[25] At the same time that he is learning to share and work with others, he is perfecting his ability to focus in a concentrated way on objects in the nonpersonal world around him, be they books, tools, weapons, or abacus; by this means he is also led beyond wishing and wanting to a larger grasp of reality.[26]

The failure to achieve this sense of competence, aptly summarized as "the free exercise of dexterity and intelligence," could result from two kinds of crippling developmental experiences. The first was the premature extension into these years of a "grim adulthood," emphasizing self-denial, absolute duties, and strict dependence upon elders for cues to behavior. This undermined the sense of cooperative participation, and reinforced the sense of the self as dependent and inferior. The second was the prolonged extension into these years of the natural childhood tendency to find out by playing—doing only what one "likes to do." The undoing in this case came not from the imposition of duties and authority, but from failure to discipline and channel the energies of children (often spoiled or mischievous children) into some serious activities. Children in this latter situation became social parasites, and never made a smooth transition beyond fantasy and play to the experience of concrete mastery and achievement within group-defined tasks.[27] It is these experiences respectively, that might be thought of as helping create children who acted like "marionettes on strings" or "spiders without webs," Lu Hsun's metaphors for Chinese children who were too well socialized or undersocialized.

THE STRUGGLE WITH DEPENDENCY. The most marionettelike children were, of course, those who never surmounted the earlier crisis of autonomy, whose sense of an independent self was squeezed out by parental handling during the earliest years of life. They experienced that transition from the dependency of infancy to training in dependency upon the family network that we spoke of in Chapter Three. They did not come to "dream and play" like the restless *t'ao-ch'i* children; nor did they come to have confidence in the efficacy of "wishing and wanting," for what they had was due to the decisions of others and came as a reward for obedience and self-denial. Their restlessness did not have to be disciplined and channeled, for it had been curbed at its first stirring. They represented the extreme end of a dependency continuum.

The strength of habits of passivity and self-denial depended very much upon how early and how rigorously "grim adulthood" had reached into the child's life. If it started right after infancy, these habits would become deeply rooted in the child, thwarting the growth of a self that felt a sense of legitimate autonomy in relation to others. If it started only later, as was the case for mischievous children, these habits would become less ingrained. Instead of being hooks fastened deep within, demands for obedience were strings pulling at them from the outside. They could be perceived as external manipulating forces, and hence were more vulnerable to countermanipulation than controls built into the inner life of the person. These mischievous children had a more expansive self-image, a greater sense of access to people and things, a less suffocating view of their obligations to others, and a greater confidence that they had the ability and right to act in the world. Such Chinese children had been imperfectly socialized into the filial system, and had learned how to cope inwardly with its demands.

This inward coping assumed different forms and strategies. Only rarely was it possible for children to give direct expression to their own frustrations, needs, and viewpoints, either through open confrontation and anger or through constructive debate over issues with elders. The common alternatives were indirect defiance and inner resistance. We have seen instances of this indirect defiance in the inventive truancy of mischievous children. The inner resistance was predicated upon splitting the self into an inner secret self and an outer public one. In one revealing autobiographical essay entitled "My Secret Self," a young woman of high class background during the Republican era reconstructed this inner division of her childhood years while a participant in a seminar on Chinese culture at Columbia University during the late 1940s.[28] Her inner/outer split occurred at age eight over an apparently insignificant incident with her grandmother, when the trust that she could speak freely to her grandmother and be accepted as she was, was found to be misplaced.

She experienced this misplaced trust indirectly via her father's anger towards her for being so open and "disrespectful." Thereafter, she no longer expressed her inner feelings to adults but kept them inside in an internal dialogue. She was acutely aware of acting outwardly in certain conventional ways while maintaining her own secret understanding of the "true" situation. She found support for this position in such maxims as "The sage looks [like] a fool," meaning that the external appearance is deceptive and she must have the inner confidence to tolerate the discrepency. This inner awareness of two selves was a permanent feature of her childhood in China; it did not disappear until she went to the United States for study and felt she could once more speak and act outwardly as she felt inwardly. Her secret self was no longer necessary as a psychological defense. Through such mechanisms of inner resistance, many children maintained an appearance of conventional filiality while salvaging a sense of integrity and self-respect.

The grip of these controlling strings, whether superficial or fastened deep within an individual, was thus highly variable. In extreme cases, the individual could cease to be an independent center of decision and action, awaiting cues from others, particularly superior authority figures, about what to do and not to do. This relationship of inferior to superior was not a normal modeling relationship, in which the inferior sought to

emulate the behavior of another whom he accepted as an example. Instead, the inferior relied upon the dictates of the specific individuals who
had brought him along to maturity, in most cases father or teachers.
This kind of relationship provided the security such children needed to
order their lives, for through denial of opportunities they had not learned
to control themselves or assume responsibility for their own actions.[29]
In more normal cases, children learned how to control themselves by
internalizing abstract principles to guide social behavior. Such internalized maxims varied from family to family, from child to child. Examples
might be, "The *wu-lun* [five primary relationships] take precedence over
other relationships"; "Outer conformity to parental demands is enough";
"With grandparents and sisters I can do this, with my father only this";
or "If I do my schoolwork well, I will be permitted more liberties."
These expectations about oneself and others applied to general situations
and relationships, and were not rooted in reliance upon specific individuals.

While this phenomenon of reliance upon specific individuals seems to
have been an uncommon form of dependence, there were few children
who did not have to struggle to free themselves from anxieties about
their own capacity for self-control or their competence as freewheeling,
individual actors. It is hard to believe in your own capacity for self-
control if others have consistently sought to deny you that experience
through protective restraint. It is difficult to feel yourself to be a competent, independent person if you are not given space for the free exercise of your powers and must create your own inner space and hidden
self to maintain self-respect. A sense of individual identity that could
come from the exploration of one's own urges and the formation of one's
own meanings in opposition to others was denied by the narrow range
of legitimate behavior set by elders. Such exploration was viewed as
stubbornness or willfulness, traits that were improper, that had to be
suppressed by parents and repressed by the children themselves. The
result was that most individuals were free from inhibitions and self-doubts
only when acting within the ritualized, conventional patterns prescribed
by the language of *lien*. When confronting unfamiliar, open situations,
multiple anxieties came out to haunt the actor. As Lu Hsun lamented,
too many Chinese children were driven into themselves by their parents,

so that, when they were let out into the world, they were like "small birds freed for a moment from a cage who could neither fly, sing, nor hop."[30]

THE COSTS OF OVERINDULGENCE. Extreme self-doubt and inhibition were not the case, as we know, with mischievous children. But however well those children might have salvaged a sense of autonomous power, other developmental traps awaited them as they grew into social beings. A failure common among mischievous children was not snuffed autonomy but unharnessed restlessness. The qualities of assertiveness, stubbornness, and pride that we have associated with the mischievous Chinese child during the years from two to six contained different developmental possibilities. They could be the harbingers of lives of dissipation and social parasitism or the seeds of creative and vital lives. A precipitating cause of these different evolutions seems to have been the development of a sense of competence during the succeeding period of childhood. It is perhaps an irony of humanization that not enough blockage, frustration, and resistance from adults can be as harmful to a child as too much. If too much creates a child whose self is heavily burdened by the priority of cultural symbols and conventions, too little can lead to a child whose self does not know the limits or potentials of his own power and does not respect the rights of others. Neither child is able to be his own master, moving under his own aegis within society: The overly restricted child is a minor player in a rigid drama dominated by others and the overly indulged child lives the illusion that he is alone on the stage.[31]

The early life of the last Ch'ing emperor, P'u Yi (b. 1906), provides a vivid, if unrepresentative, illustration of the overindulged child. Indeed, today in China the often spoiled children in one-child families are called little emperors and empresses.[32] Whether the little emperors of today, the Young Masters of the old scholar-official class, or an actual emperor, all were regarded, by themselves and others, as "different from ordinary people." Therein lay their potential downfall on the slope leading to dissipation and social parasitism.

P'u Yi's early life represented the prolonged extension into the years from age five to ten of the natural childhood tendency to find out by playing—doing only what one "likes to do." His relationship to the things and people in his environment remained a trifling one that never developed into a "cooperative participation" involving sharing, discipline, and performance. As His Imperial Majesty, he was able to manipulate and command all around him by whim, with the exception of the ghosts that inhabited the Forbidden City, his wet nurse, and for a short time, the high consort Tuan Kang.[33] Although omnipotent in his small world, he was denied the chance to become competent, which left him feeling empty and resentful in the midst of incredible splendor and power, and eventually convinced him that his palace was a prison.

He began studying in the palace at age five, but his early learning was undermined by his own capriciousness and by the unresponsiveness of his tutors. As his fascination with the living creatures in the courtyards and his keenness for writing showed, he had the capacity to be absorbed; but nothing in his surroundings helped him develop these interests and talents. They remained secret, almost idle diversions from a tiresome, boring routine.

> I was not in the least conscientious [about reading the classics]. Apart from using minor illnesses as pretexts, I would sometimes tell a eunuch to inform my tutors that they were to take a day's holiday if I was not feeling like studying and had no better excuse. Up to the age of ten I was far more interested in a big cypress tree that grew outside the Yu Ching Palace than in my books. In summer there were always ants crawling up and down this tree. I got very interested in them and would often squat by their tree so absorbed in watching them or feeding them crumbs of cake and helping them to move their food that I would forget my own meals . . .
>
> [M]y tutors did not make me memorize my texts, being content with making me read them through a few times . . . Nobody was interested in how much I remembered or in whether I wanted to remember it or not.
>
> My teachers never examined me on my work and set me no compositions to write. I remember that I wrote some couplets and verses but the tutors would never comment on them, let alone correct them. Yet I was very keen on writing things when I was a child. As the tutors did not think much of such trifles, I wrote them secretly for my own amusement.[34]

The deference of his tutors made it impossible to discipline his "naughtiness," and introduce him "mildly but firmly" to an adventure that might have become a self-generating interest. The teachers after all were his subjects and the pupil was the sovereign. His teachers could only reprove him indirectly by scolding, as a substitute, one of the three fellow students who joined him when he was eight.

Except for the early experience of protective restraint, what P'u Yi did was a direct expression of what he felt; for there were no adult "authority" figures around as persistent realities who could regulate and check his behavior.[35] His real mother and grandmother were not part of his life from age three to ten; his father was weak and stammered during his infrequent audiences with his son; his consort "mothers" paid him scant attention. The ethical restraints on his behavior that his tutors taught him weighed lightly on the scales, for "at the same time they acknowledged my authority and [they] taught me about that authority. No matter how many stories they told me about illustrious sovereigns and sage rulers of history, I still remained the emperor and 'different from ordinary people,' so that the advice had little effect."[36]

The only person capable of restraining him was his nurse, Mrs. Wang: "Although she was completely illiterate and incapable of talking about the 'way of compassion and benevolence' . . . I could not disregard the advice she gave me."[37] Her hold over him was rooted in the strong emotional ties built up between child and nurturing adult, ties which did not characterize his relationship with anyone else, certainly not his nominal parents.

> I grew up in my nurse's bosom being suckled by her until I was eight, and until then I was as inseparable from her as a baby from its mother. When I was eight, the High Consorts had her sent away without my knowledge. I would gladly have kept her in exchange for all four of my mothers in the palace, but no matter how I howled, they would not bring her back.[38]

Mrs. Wang's words had some effect in restraining his cruelty towards the palace eunuchs, who were at once his constant companions, slaves, and earliest teachers. He displaced his own emotional tensions onto them, for he had no need to come to grips introspectively with his own feelings or to learn to live and do things with others in a cooperative fashion.

> Whenever I was in a bad temper or feeling depressed the eunuchs would be in for trouble; and their luck was also out if I was in high spirits and wanted some sort of amusement. In my childhood . . . I took the greatest delight in

playing unkind tricks on people. Before long I learned how to make the Administration Bureau beat people. Many a eunuch came to grief through my practical
jokes.

Growing up as I did, with people pandering to my every whim and being
completely obedient to me, I developed this taste for cruelty . . . My nurse was
the only person who ever told me that other people were just as human as myself
. . . Other people had feelings; other people would feel the same pain as I would
if they were hit by air-gun pellets. This was all common knowledge, which I
knew as well as anybody; but in that environment I found it rather hard to
remember it as I never would consider others, let alone think of them in the same
terms as myself.[39]

P'u Yi's exaggerated sense of self-importance was never tempered by
shared effort in serious tasks that were a foretaste of adult life and work;
he grew up vain, capricious, extravagant, incompetent. His status and
his whole environment combined to prevent him from going beyond the
play world of wishing and wanting into a serious engagement with people and objects, through which he might have come to know himself as
a contributing member in the productive life of the group.

P'u Yi's account should not be taken as an isolated phenomenon.
Francis L. K. Hsu has postulated that the principle of two-way identification between fathers and sons not only allowed the families of the
rich and powerful to incubate extravagant, vain behavior in their sons,
but positively encouraged it. The style of the children's lives reflected
the status attainment of the parents, and indeed was a sign of it. Being
overindulged and underrestrained, the children grew into adults who
were likely to be "vain, excessively touchy about prestige, unsympa-
thetic, licentious, impulsive, *unrealistic, lack*[ing] *in economic and common
sense,* extravagant, carefree, insincere, and boastful."[40] This suggestive
inventory of vices implies both the rejection of conventional standards of
behavior as defined in the language of *lien* and general incompetence.
While this might have been a common correlation, it was not a necessary one; and in fact it conceals an important early forking in the lives
of mischievous children. The mischievous child, without the added experience of cultural competence through participation with others in serious tasks, could become a parasitic adult; with that experience of competence, it could become a leading member of the society. One way or

the other this child/adult was always somewhat in tension, creative or otherwise, with the dominant group and its mores.

In the short sketches of various gentry leaders collected by Chow Yung-teh in Yunnan province between 1943 and 1946, one finds that the future military commander, bureaucrat, gangster, and reformer in varying degrees all had similar childhood traits attributed to them: headstrong, clever, stubborn, courageous, bold, full of wit, domineering, self-centered.[41] The bureaucrat and reformer were also characterized as having been "overprotected and spoiled," although they ended up as able and competent leaders, even if the former retained proud, cold, and snobbish airs. There are also several sketches in which the spoiled child led straight to the dissipating, incompetent adult.[42] Like Francis L. K. Hsu's inventory of vices, Chow Yung-teh's correlation of childhood traits with future adult types points towards the reality of this forking point for mischievous children; more importantly, it identifies the group of disciplined, mischievous children as a key source of potential leadership in a society where individuals could no longer take their cues for action from an old, established script.

BECOMING ONE'S OWN MASTER

If willfulness was a danger sign to Chinese parents, will power in a child was a hopeful, even necessary quality. Will power as the desire to act correctly and to achieve goals that elders and other authorities had defined was distinguished from willfulness as an unreasonable, unruly persistence in asserting a mind of one's own.[43] Parents felt it was essential for their children to learn to act morally by group standards, to set purposeful goals, and to work diligently to achieve them. But where was this will power to come from? External restrictions and controls channeled more than motivated behavior. Common notions of children did not express much confidence that they had self-generating interests and powers; they were viewed as highly impressionable and passive, picking up habits from the environment as a blotter absorbs ink. Left alone, a child would be weak, drifting, lost, an easy prey to temptation and outside influences.

The key to motivating the *yu-nien* child in the minds of many parents seems to have been the use of compelling models or examples, both heroic ones to emulate and identify with and disgusting ones to condemn and separate oneself from. These were believed to have a magnetic power to draw children along the proper path, and support their will to do right. Although wanting to be good was believed to be the "natural" desire of the child, the controlled environment, language of *lien,* strict discipline, and frequent touting of exemplary models all emphasized outward cues as seemingly necessary for good behavior; these acknowledged in practice how little confidence parents and superiors placed in their children's inclination to seek the goals and accept the values they desired for them. Yet often the child's own inspiring, sanctioning conscience—that socially implanted expectation that he or she must be a moral, purposeful being—became the driving force for action. The vision of *tso jen* pulled one forward; the fear of failure, shame, and humiliation for oneself and others pushed from behind.

Once a boy reached fourteen years, or the age for "adult learning," motivation was expected to become fully self-sustaining. No longer just a target for environmental training and conditioning, a young man on the path of learning was now expected to cultivate himself through introspective self-examination. Self-cultivation *(tzu-hsiu)* was a matter of personal decision, a matter of having the will power to create oneself in a certain image on the basis of a conscious desire for self-improvement. Such self-sculpting was what distinguished the superior man from the inferior man. The content of this desired self-improvement was not open to subjective determination but was prescribed on the basis of traditional wisdom. The individual task was to straighten the internal life and to square the external life, or as sometimes expressed, to strive for sageliness within and kingliness without. To attain purity and virtue in actions and feelings so that one naturally felt and did what was good was viewed as a lifelong task. In the *Analects,* Confucius is reported to have measured his own virtue by his progress over decades in overcoming this inner/outer disharmony; it may have been some solace to his late-Ch'ing followers that Confucius himself was seventy years old before he claimed to be able to do the right thing with natural ease.[44]

The typical conceptual framework for self-improvement may be illuminated by a specific example contained in *Jen-p'u* (Treatise on man), a work by the Ming Confucian scholar Liu Tsung-chou (1578–1645), a follower of the School of Chu Hsi, who emphasized meditation and self-cultivation. Liu identified six categories of faults *(kuo)*, in ascending order of severity, that provide a standard for moral self-evaluation:

1. *Indiscernible faults,* which are known only to the individual, such as "innate moral weakness."
2. *Hidden faults,* which are emotional excesses in the mind but not necessarily in behavior. The lack of control over the "seven emotions" is cited (for example, the displacement of anger or excessive fearfulness).
3. *Manifest faults,* which are expressed in manner or bearing. The seven emotions are visibly exposed, coming out in such behavior as cursing, shaking one's head, blocking the doorway, or ridiculing someone.
4. *Major faults,* which are like manifest faults but occur within the context of the *wu-lun* (for example, expressing anger at one's father).
5. *General faults,* which are nonobservance of the requirements of the *wu-lun,* such as lack of diligence, disrespect, drinking, marrying for gain, frequenting singing girls, composing love poems, shouting at birds, cutting vegetables for no reason, or wearing luxurious clothes.
6. *Developed faults,* which are evil acts, such as theft, punishable by law.[45]

Correction of the first two categories requires straightening the internal life, that additional task which the educated set for themselves beyond achieving external conformity with the categories of *lien* or "face." The third and fourth categories describe actions that may cause one to lose face among others, but are temporary excesses that can be corrected. The fifth appears similar to "not considering *lien*" (although with a puritanical bent); the faults are signs of a general failure to act dependably as the obedient subject, the filial son, the benevolent husband, the solicitous older brother, the faithful friend. Overt behavior reveals a frivolous, disrespectful attitude towards people, nature, and resources, and hence casts a bad light on one's family and associates. The sixth marks the fall into the ultimate disrepute of being a shameless social outcast, "having no feeling for *lien.*" Self-cultivation thus proceeded within the basic framework provided by the language of *lien,* with a similar emphasis upon the centrality of the *wu-lun* or "five primary relationships." Instead of a scheme describing a "fit" between self and others, however, it is an agenda for a lifetime of moral striving to attain the perfection of a sage. To a fourteen-year-old just emerging from childhood, the notion that he was now to be his own moral doctor, diagnosing and treating himself, must have posed a frightening responsibility. Perplexities lay on every side, and his feet, as Confucius had observed in the *Analects,* would not likely be planted firmly upon the ground until he reached age thirty.

THE CASE OF WANG MING-TAO: OPERATION MORAL BOOTSTRAPS. The complexity and difficulty of the struggle to become one's own master, so aggravated by the sharp normative distinction between willfulness and will power, is illustrated in the early life of the Christian evangelist Wang Ming-tao (b. 1900). Young Wang displayed the marks of a *t'ao-ch'i* child; he was headstrong, spirited, and unafraid of asserting his own viewpoint in the face of resistance, even though he was small and weak in body. In part, his mischievousness may be traced to his family situation. His father, a medical technician in a Peking missionary hospital, had committed suicide to avoid Boxer persecution just shortly before Wang's birth. Thus the boy grew up in a fatherless family without experiencing the "paternal style" of childhood discipline. As the younger child and only son, he was also highly valued by his mother, who declined to discipline him or his elder sister.

> A mother widowed in middle age with only us two—a son and a daughter—
> naturally valued us like two pearls. [She] was not inclined to instruct us or punish
> us. In this way, we were left to become unusually wild and arrogant. When she
> heard that we were doing extremely well in school, she was pleased and happy,
> and even less inclined to instruct us.[46]

His early years were lived amid many different kinds of people, for his mother was forced to let out rooms in their house to renters. More than thirty people, a cross section of lower-class urban workers in Peking, were crowded together in eleven rooms. Bad feelings and friction were common.

[The neighbors] knew that our entire family lacked influence, and had no adult male. So they often exploited us or didn't give us the rent or had gambling parties or went wild cursing in the streets or would engage in dark illegal affairs. If my mother did nothing, she was held responsible as the landlord. If she intervened and said something, no one paid any attention to her. Mother's nature was extremely explosive, and when she argued about something with the neighbors, she would become very excited after a few words. As a result, the only thing she could do was to restrain her anger and swallow her words. If something bad happened, she would just take it; and if she couldn't take it, she would blow up and become sick with anger.[47]

Young Wang knew hunger during those early years as well as friction, for his mother disliked cooking and often left the children to fend for themselves. He knew cold, too, and remembered the numbness in his hands as he picked up broken bits of charcoal off winter streets to bring home for use as fuel. He knew the harshness of life, and his youthful mind often turned to the question of the meaning of death, seeking consolation with fantasies of immortality.

His inner spirit carried him forward, however, in enjoyment as well as adversity. He learned to read largely through his own initiative and desire:

I often would take a book and ask mother how to read this character or how to pronounce that character. My mother didn't really teach me to read very much, but I kept asking her questions. I learned to read ordinary books through this kind of roundabout questioning.[48]

He composed his own pictorial magazine: "I would take a piece of paper, draw a few people, and then announce an item of news." And in the lanes around the house, he moved freely, whether somersaulting in the dirt or seeing a play performed at the nearby marketplace. "Coming back [from the marketplace], I would smear some red or black coloring on my face and, holding a wooden knife, shout and jump wildly in the alleyway."[49]

When he entered the London Missionary Society school at nine, he did extremely well for the first year; then his diligence for studying flagged, and it was necessary for the teacher to call in his mother and apply great pressure to get him back to the sedentary regimen of poring over classical books. Later in the upper primary boarding school with thirty or forty older classmates, he was the youngest and smallest student and received a lot of harassment. Although things could be done to him and pressures applied, he never submitted to harassment in his heart, and often fought back with words. He kept his independent spirit intact: "Ever since I was little, I have had a special trait of not wanting to submit to other people. No matter what it is, if I don't see the sense of it clearly, I won't follow others and do it. But if I see something clearly, others cannot oppose me successfully."[50]

Qualities of initiative, independence, curiosity, and quick intelligence young Wang shared with other mischievous children; but like others, he was also unable then or later to accept these traits as good in themselves. In his memoirs he expressed the common retrospective judgment that he was arrogant and erring when he was not devoting his energy to those things his elders valued. "Arrogance" was the code word for willful, illegitimate behavior. The mature Wang Ming-tao was also inclined to see his early environment as entirely negative and unpromising: "[Encountering] these [immoral] neighbors in the courtyard, and often the same kind of people in the alleyway, [having] a mother unable to guide us and not caring to guide us because she had to be inside sewing, washing, and doing household chores, a mother happy to tell us to go outside to play and negligent in giving us a direction in life, what can you hope for from a child who grew up in this kind of dirty, debasing environment?"[51] Although he experienced considerable freedom of movement during his early years—a characteristic of what could be called a Huck Finn childhood—he was unable to appreciate this as something valuable. He felt instead a void inside and an aimlessness to his existence. He needed someone else to complete him, to provide answers. At home and at school, no one was instructing him how to *tso jen*.

> Until the fall of my fourteenth year, I lived a drifting, confused existence, without beliefs, without goals, without hope, without seizing the Way. Although I had thoughts and was looking for a way, I still was utterly unable to find a worthy path and there was no leader to bring me to one. Except for my very good performance in school and my stubborn disposition, I was no different from others. I had held every bad view and I had spoken all manner of foul words. If I actually had not committed any great misdeed, it was due to my young age, or

to my timidity in not wanting to stir up any trouble. I was also thinskinned, and was most afraid of losing face. My poor family background was one of my best advantages, because it prevented me from committing those sins that required spending money.[52]

His mother's problem in managing the house and young Wang's difficulty in managing himself had a common root: the lack of respect accorded a "weak" woman, not only by the renters but by her own son. Her presence and purposes did not sufficiently order his life. He could not model himself on her; although she took him to church every Sunday, he came to regard church affairs as a nuisance.

In his fourteenth year, on the threshold of young adulthood, his life was transformed through contact with a sympathetic, older, male student whom he had been admiring from a distance for some time. This encounter filled the void that he had felt, and gave him some fixed points of reference for his life.

First [the student] led me to recognize God, and taught me how to respect God, taught me how to pray and read the Bible, taught me to examine myself daily, and write a diary . . . In that month my inner world and life changed greatly. I began to understand the meaning of life, the responsibility of life. I began to hate all forms of evil and understand righteousness. I began to desire the pure, holy, virtuous life . . . I was dissatisfied with my own drifting, aimless existence. I began to despise the foul words and acts of my fellow classmates. I began voluntarily to join the meetings in the church. At Easter I was baptised as a member of the London Missionary Society.[53]

The continuing problem, however, was how to sustain himself in his new life. At first, the student friend provided the structure he seemed to need. "[He] reprimanded me very strictly every time he saw me doing something wrong. Because of this I loved him very much, and at the same time feared him very much." But alone by himself he felt torn by warring forces. His conscience was activated, but his will power was not adequate to the task.

Every time I did something bad my heart hurt and I blamed myself. Often in the quiet of the night I would walk to a place in the back courtyard where there were no people, unfasten my clothes, and beat my chest with my fists until it hurt. Only then did my heart feel better . . . I knew I was not good, but I wanted to be good. I wanted to be good, but I was unable to be good. This was

a very bitter experience. In one perspective, beginning with that year I had beliefs, the intention to *tso jen,* the determination to strive upwards, and it was
good no longer to be living an aimless existence. In another perspective, my inner
world was now a daily battleground of good and evil forces and this was really
very painful. Still it seems I felt somewhat better than when I was living a
meaningless existence.[54]

During this period, the only way he would win on that battleground
was to have others supplement his will, to the extent of directing his
life and squeezing out any alternative beliefs or behavior.

While the student who had led me to believe in the Lord was still in the school,
he always supervised me, guided and controlled me [*kuan-shu*]. He did not let
me say bad things or do improper things, and I happily received his supervision
and control. But after he graduated and left school, my situation was different.
In my heart I wanted to be a pure holy person, but I could not control myself.
Although I often hated myself and punished myself, it still was not very effective.
I did not want to ask my friend to come again to control me, and anyway this
wasn't possible. Praise the Lord, for He completed me and sent other people to
supervise and control me. These people were not my friends, but those who hated
me and were my enemies . . . To have enemies on all sides was naturally painful.
Who could expect that God would send these enemies to control me and keep
me straight as a pen.[55]

The frank admission of needs makes this account by Wang Ming-tao
a small classic in Chinese autobiographical literature. It would be wrong
to discount it because of the admixture of Christian elements. The need
to become moral, purposeful beings was imparted generally to Chinese
children, although parental understanding of the content and motivation
for this kind of life might vary. The need for a source of power and
direction outside oneself was also strongly felt. This need was intensified
by a fencing-in of the child that closed off many areas for free exploration and development, and by labeling many behavioral expressions as
immoral, illegitimate, unworthy of humans. Hobbled by inner/outer
tensions and hounded by conscience, the child often could not work out
problems alone and found it comforting to rely more on others to guide
behavior, whether this was the family network, some chosen models
(parents, teachers, others), a peer organization, or in Wang's case, the
ultimate support of a never-failing, hidden God who sent enemies to
keep him in line. Given this tendency to be dependent, the values of

self-cultivation and self-direction that were culturally esteemed during the *ta-hsueh* period were very difficult to realize in practice; for they required coming individually to grips with the unresolved resentments and frustrations that had accrued during the early years.

THE BURDEN OF MORAL DIDACTICISM. Moral training being so pervasive in the socialization of Chinese children and youth, it is hardly surprising that later many came to feel the need for a touch of philosophical Taoism to make life somewhat easier to bear; to provide a rationale for inaction, relaxation, enjoyment; to offer respite from moral striving and purposeful living. One man looking back over his early years from 1907 to 1923 cited three important models who came to shape his perspective on a meaningful and complete life. Together they describe an arc of meanings in tension: from the duty to live a moral, purposeful life, to the need to find inner peace and accept one's own limitations and failures. The first was Tseng Kuo-fan, the late-Ch'ing Confucian scholar-official, who became the dominant model in the boy's early studies from age eight to fifteen. He admired the "thickness" of the man: his wisdom and living example of what it meant to "be human" *(tso jen)*. Next he discovered Liang Ch'i-ch'ao, who, with his critical scholarship and acute assessment of China's contemporary historical situation, became a model of an activist and thinker. And thirdly he came to love the poet T'ao Yuan-ming, whose generous, relaxed, open approach to life helped him to acquire perspective on himself and his moral striving. When he was plagued by problems in 1923, T'ao Yuan-ming's poems consoled him and provided some ultimate reference for understanding human "honor," "fame," "dignity," and "shame." They tempered the moral didacticism that came through so strongly from parental attitudes and early school experiences.[56]

An anecdote with a similar point was related to me by a middle-aged Chinese scholar who had lived in the United States since the 1940s. He had had a rich exposure to Confucian thought as a young person, but had been continually frustrated in his efforts to apply its insights to life in his adopted country. When the elderly Chinese historian Ch'ien Mu gave a lecture tour in the United States in 1963, this scholar went to see him about this decades-old personal problem. Ch'ien Mu paced the floor silently for a few moments, then looked up suddenly and said, "There's still Lao-tzu and Chuang-tzu." Confucian moralism, in other words, needed to be supplemented by the "heterodox" schools of Chinese thought, in this case philosophical Taoism, which acted as a counterweight to its unrelenting demands.[57] The philosophical interplay of Confucian and Taoist thought, as weight and counterweight within the Chinese Great Tradition, had a psychological basis. Moral idealism, when inflicted upon the young with relentless vigor, could easily descend into the tyranny, or banality, of moralistic righteousness. At its highest levels, perhaps, the Confucian moral vision could tap the full potential of the individual mind and conscience, but how many children and adults, even among the educated, were trapped in the lowlands of conformity to conventions, loyalty to superiors, obedience to elders. To lead a more complete life, ironically, they needed release from the judgment that human life was a moral quest. Taoist thought, with its asocial emphasis, its suspicion of words and arguments, its mockery of Confucian moralism, its delight in nature and bodily pleasures, embodied an alternative that many earnest learners yearned to hear. And young people found that message, secretly read in forbidden novels and books that were sometimes literally inserted within the covers of an orthodox classic.

PART THREE
Discovering Realities

Barefoot boy at Hai-ning, Chekiang, ca. 1900. Courtesy, Essex Institute, Salem, Mass.

FIVE

Adversity

At age fourteen, young Shu-jen became intimately familiar with the interior of pawnshops. He trekked in and out of them almost daily, dwarfed by the high counter, trading his family's possessions for medicine money and contemptuous looks. All in vain, for his family's decline continued unabated.

At age fifteen, Ch'iu-pai was forced by mounting family debts to leave middle school before graduating and take up work as a teacher to become self-supporting. He watched his mother become more and more desperate in her struggles to keep a father-abandoned family afloat.

At age twelve, in the wake of the Revolution of 1911, Cheng came home queueless, in an army uniform, and full of heretical ideas. His horrified grandmother wished for his extermination as a young Chinese disciple of foreign devils.

At age twelve, Ting-k'ai's three precious years of schooling ended during the "hungry month" of June. His father refused to support his continued schooling in the face of his stepmother's demands that he, like his elder sister, should cut grass in the mountains in order to exchange it for rice to eat.

These dramatic junctures in boys' lives hint at the kinds of struggles they faced in society in becoming young adults. Forget, for a moment, that these boys all succeeded and grew up to become well-known figures. Leave out, temporarily, the dates and places and larger events that distract us from sensing the universal experience of individuals. The end of childhood was often a terrifying time of assuming responsibilities, chosen or not, and making choices. This is what "independence" came to mean in practice in Chinese society: managing to secure some of your own wishes while still acting responsibly in society. The world of others, and the burden of indebtedness, was never far away: Mothers had chosen to give them life rather than turn faces into the mud; many caretakers had nurtured them through the earliest years of dependency; household members and neighbors had trained them in the values and skills of living together in complex hierarchies; teachers and fathers had filled their heads with moral education and instilled the ancient obligation of becoming human. Now they were half on their own, trying to find out where society ended and their individual selves began.

The young men discussed in this chapter were all sturdy individuals, not dependent puppets or asocial spiders. They were up to the task of asserting themselves and finding a way out of difficult situations as well as a way into the new emergent counterculture of modern, educated youth. Their sturdiness had accrued not only through the kinds of positive experiences of hope, autonomy, initiative and competence discussed in Part Two, but also in part through overcoming the experiences of poverty and suffering. Such tempering in adversity in late imperial Chinese society carried heavy overtones of class: these were not the Young Masters of well-established, upper-class families. They had all been born into families that knew hardship, from falling gentry families to common peasant families. The conditions within these families, disrupted by age-old pressures as well as current history, worked against ideal upbringings and the creation of well-socialized children. Diversity flourished in the understrata of Chinese society, especially at the peasant level, where strong women abounded and wild, coarse *(ts'u yeh)* behavior was not uncommon in boys. More openings existed for creating the sturdy youngsters who could summon the strength, in partnership with others or out of their own emotional depths, to come through adversity, though not without being scarred in the process. Within their tales can be sensed the small contingencies of intellect, will, and circumstance that allowed some to make it, while vast numbers of others were silenced by defeat, their stories unknown to us.

PATTERNS OF DECAY AND DISASTER AMONG GENTRY FAMILIES

In late Ch'ing China, an educated family was "a house that for generations had been fragrant with the scent of books" *(shu-hsiang shih chia)*.
In such houses, a child came to know books as other children might
know the tools of field or kitchen or shop. Even the girls, for whom
serious education was thought superfluous, were sometimes taught poetry and might read the classics of womanhood on their father's knees.[1]
These libraries and uncommon practices rested on a base of material and
social power, usually landowning and its counterpart official service; for
there was a close correlation between social power and prestige, the attainment of learning, and the prosperity and security of the family clan.
The negative correlation—no pursuit of learning, no hope for security
and power—can be seen in the oft-told tale of Mencius' mother, which
every schoolboy came to know. When her son would not learn, she
broke the shuttle from her loom to dramatize the disastrous effects of
discontinuity of learning, revealing at the same time how much her own
despair and hopes were connected with his progress and success.[2]

Boys knew that a permanent place in the memory of future generations could be won by raising the prestige and power of the family and
ensuring its livelihood through educational success. The basic primer,
the *San tzu ching* (Three character classic), stressed this consideration
along with the more pure Neo-Confucian argument that education was
necessary to complete one's human nature.

> If foolishly you do not study, how can you become men? The silkworm produces
> silk; the bee makes honey. If a man does not learn, he is not equal to the brutes.
> Learn while young, and when grown up apply what you have learned, influencing
> the sovereign above and benefitting the people below. Make a name for your-
> selves, and glorify your father and mother. Shed luster on your ancestors and
> enrich your posterity.[3]

The prominence of ancestors who had earned success as scholar-officials
was carefully noted in the family or clan genealogy. One interviewee,
whose family attained prominence through a *chin-shih* degree in his father's generation, described his ancestors as an "unesteemed list" except
for one ancestor over ten generations back who had a scholarly reputation. While outlining his genealogy for me, he slashed with his pen

through the intervening generations to draw a line between this ancestor and his father's generation.[4]

It was, however, one thing to know that education and prosperity, prestige and power, were interlocking, another thing to maintain a grip on all of them over a long period of time. The examination route was narrow and difficult, and each generation had to qualify alone in a private cell in a vast hall with thousands of competitors.[5] Intelligence and perserverance could not be magically transmitted from fathers to sons to grandsons. In fact, as we have seen in Chapter Four, the wealth and power of the older generation often led to the indulgence and decadence of the sons; living dependently under the patriarch of the household, and encouraged by their fathers and by the surrounding community to consume conspicuously and carelessly, these sons in wealthy families often had little encouragement to become independent and competent. There were few internal or external restraints upon them. Even financial limitations represented little restraint in the case of official families, for political power could be used to generate wealth by a variety of means, making "income" an elastic rather than a fixed amount.[6]

There were some efforts among the powerful, especially in scholarly families with a tradition of Confucian austerity, to stem this process by strict and proper home education. One example can be seen in the autobiography of Tseng Ch'i-fen (1851–1943), the youngest daughter of Tseng Kuo-fan, the man often described as the last great Confucian. She records her father's efforts to head off corrupting habits and to train his children to live disciplined, simple lives; he was strict about their spending, studying, and work habits, and tireless in his personal supervision. When she was sixteen years old, he announced a work schedule for all the young members of the household, beginning with the girls.

> After breakfast: prepare vegetables, sweets, and related kitchen work. Nine A.M. to 1 P.M.: spin cotton or twist threads. After the noon meal: do fine needlework and embroidery. Five P.M. to 7 P.M., and 9 P.M. to 11 P.M.: make men's and women's shoes or sew. The young men in my household shall read, study, practice calligraphy, and write essays; they must not be deficient in any of these things. The women shall work at cooking, threadwork, fine needlework, and coarse needlework; they must not be deficient in any of these four things. I have already instructed you for many years, but have never set up definite rules. After this, each day shall have a set work schedule. I will personally inspect the work.

Kitchen work will be inspected once a day. Threadwork once every three days
. . . fine needlework once every five days, rough work once a month. Each month
one should make one pair of men's adult shoes. Women's shoes will not be inspected.[7]

This traditional counter-strategy, as well as the long-term pattern of
decline, is reflected in the tale of three generations in a Foochow family
recounted by the grandson in an interview. The grandfather had built a
fortune on high-risk shipping in the last half of the nineteenth century.
His eldest son (father to the interviewee) ran the firm after the grandfather's death in 1907, but took to drinking and concubines; his half-
hearted classical education had poorly prepared him to manage a shipping firm. The second son (uncle to the interviewee) spent lavishly while
leaving debts for the embarrassed family head to pick up. The family
was forced to move to a smaller house and contract the scale of the firm.
Even though contraction was necessary, there was enough left over to
finance the grandson's education abroad. That the pattern of dissipation
did not repeat itself in the third generation, the grandson attributed to
the strict personal supervision of his grandmother and mother.[8]

Causes other than internal decay and unworthy sons brought gentry
families into decline and even ruin. The equal division of family property among the sons coupled with an increase in family members over
time continually broke up large holdings; the ideal of numerous progeny
and concentrated land holdings was almost impossible to realize over
many generations. Unexpected calamities, such as the illness or death of
a key family member, the expense of funerals and trials, the denial of
official patronage, business and property losses or outright confiscation
could also set back the efforts of families whose members were competent and hardworking; Chow Yung-teh maintains, however, that in the
longer history of families such chance occurrences were "too slight to
figure as more than aberrations." The behavior of the family before and
after such crises seems to be a more significant long-term variable.[9]

THE CHILD AND THE TRAUMAS OF DECLINE. Whatever the causes of
downward mobility, decline riveted a gentry family once more to the
problems of basic survival rather than conspicuous public display. And
it left marks on the memories of the children caught up in the process.

The pawnshop became not just a place but an experience, an exposure to a world where anxiety, necessity, and humiliation were facts of life for millions, yet barely sensed by those accustomed to dominance, superiority, and material security. The writer Chou Shu-jen (b. 1881), better known as Lu Hsun, was born into such a falling gentry family, and remembered the stages of decline vividly, from pawnshop to "foreign studies."

> For four years I once went in and out of pawnshops every day, or almost every day. I have forgotten my age then, but I remember the counter at the herb shop was exactly as tall as I was, and the one at the pawnshop was twice my height. From below this tall counter, I passed up clothing and jewelry and received back money along with contemptuous looks. Then I would go to the counter exactly my height to buy herb medicine for my chronically ill father. After coming home it was also necessary to put aside other things, because the doctor who wrote the prescriptions was the most famous one around, and for this reason his ingredients were distinctive: winter reed roots, sugar cane that had passed through three years of frost, a pair of crickets, knots of ardisia . . . all were difficult things to find. But my father ended up worse and worse each day and finally died.
>
> I feel that one who comes from a prospering family that has fallen onto dark days probably can see the true face of men along this road of decline. I wanted to go to N[anking] to enter the K[iangnan Naval Academy]. It seems as though I was thinking of traveling a different road, of escaping to new places to seek out other kinds of people. My mother had no choice; she scraped up eight dollars for traveling expenses and said I could do as I pleased. Afterwards she cried, which was a natural thing to do, because at that time the proper path was to study the classics and take the state examinations. Studying so-called foreign things was in society's view only something a desperate man could do, selling his soul to the foreigners, facing both ridicule and ostracism. Moreover, she wouldn't be able to see her son. I could not consider all these things, however, and ended up going to N to enter the K academy.[10]

The decline in the Chou family had begun years before Lu Hsun's father's illness. Grandfather Chou, the first scholar of distinction in the family for generations, was the one bright spot for vitality and achievement. Otherwise the ambience in the family compound was failure, gloom and unfulfilled lives. Chou Tso-jen, Lu Hsun's younger brother, remembered no strong males with moral fiber during their childhoods, only kindly old pedants, skeletal opium addicts, and unstable failed scholars, like his and Lu Hsun's own father. Grandfather Chou had in fact once pondered the problem of familial decline and become convinced that his sons would be able to make something of themselves only if they were reduced to hard work in a lowly beancurd shop. Precipitous decline threatened after Grandfather Chou was arrested in 1893 for an attempted bribe of an examination official, a daring if foolish act in part inspired by a need to bolster the family's coffers. He was imprisoned in Hangchow; and for one year, in order to escape possible recriminations against male members of the family, the young Lu Hsun was sent to live with a maternal aunt, and remembered insinuations of being a beggar. For seven years the family made annual autumn trips to Hangchow to solicit the Board of Punishment not to execute the family patriarch. These costly maneuvers quickly dissipated the family inheritance.[11] Trips to the pawnshop became common after the father's illness began in 1894, ending in his death several years later.

Such a family disaster did not broaden choices for a young person, as the obligations of status incumbent upon one of the gentry class in Shaohsing—young and old, rich and poor alike—closed off many possibilities. According to their group traditions, for those who could not afford to be idle, living off rent or interest, there were only three respectable ways of making a livelihood. The first way was via the examination system, qualifying for a higher degree as a *chü-jen* or *chin-shih,* and being appointed as an official. The second way was to study to become a private secretary, a path for those who failed to get higher than the first *sheng-yuan* degree. The third was to go into business; but this was limited to operating pawnshops, a savings and loan shop, or a silk goods store, in that order. If one did not have the intelligence or ability for any of these, he could only "sit at home eating up his resources" *(tso ch'ih shan k'ung),* until he was forced to pass through the Respected Gates that identified each gentry household and disappear into the mass of common folk. Beyond these possibilities, as Ts'ao Chü-jen comments, the local gentry had few talents and little imagination, and were the prisoners of their own longstanding habits.[12]

Lu Hsun's decision to enter upon foreign studies in 1898 was, therefore, a decisive break with the canons of respectability held by his class and a sign of his strength as an individual. Furthermore, because the Nanking School taught barbarian languages and had a military flavor, it seemed to repudiate the gentry code at every point.[13] The decline of his family had forced him into unconventional paths, and not just for financial reasons. He wanted "to seek out other kinds of people." Haunted by memories of contemptuous looks and scornful insinuations, the young Lu Hsun had come to know and hate the narrowness of the gentry and the hypocrisy present below its idealistic surface. He had developed, in William Lyell's phrase, "a life-long sensitivity to sham."[14] In a few years, however, members of the gentry throughout the country were to trim their prejudices to fit the very apparent needs of greater institutional and military strength, and with these, the survival of a gentry-dominated China. Foreign studies became *à la mode,* and what had been unconventional for Lu Hsun became commonplace for other gentry families, falling and prospering alike. But he did not forget, and his later fictional portrait of traditional scholar-officials and the large gentry family was unsparingly critical.

For Ch'ü Ch'iu-pai (b. 1899), a childhood of poverty in a falling gentry family also embittered him against the institution of the large family or clan. His grandfather had been an official under the Manchu dynasty, but his fortune and the comfortable life that it secured did not last more than a few years of Ch'iu-pai's childhood. He was fated to experience a poverty that degenerated from the genteel sort into the abject. The blame seemed to rest at his father's feet; for he was a decadent and unemployable young man, whose hobbies were occult Taoism and opium. The family lived for several years by liquidating the family treasures—paintings, calligraphy, art objects, and fine furniture. Trips to the pawnshop were frequent, and the loss of family lands forced them to live for a time in the clan temple. After the father finally abandoned the family to take up a subsistence job as a schoolmaster in another province, the mother and six children were left to their own wits to survive. Ch'iu-pai's mother was educated, strong, proud, and domineering; but as T. A. Hsia commented, she shared "the fatal weakness of the gentry class: she did not know where to look for a source of income." They lived frugally, but mounting family debts forced Ch'iu-pai at age fifteen to leave middle school before graduating; his education cost precious resources, and as a teacher he was able to be self-supporting, thus leaving more for his four younger brothers and one younger sister. Yet his mother, made desperate by debts and by the accusations of relatives that she was an unfilial wife, mother, and daughter-in-law, thereafter committed suicide by drinking phosphorous matchheads mixed with tigerbone wine. The brothers were split up among relatives and the saga of one branch of the Ch'ü clan ended.[15]

Ch'iu-pai spent the next six years largely on his own in Wuchang and Peking, cities where the family clan had supportive relatives. He was a loner, absorbed in the world of poetry, classics, Buddhism, and Russian language study until the May Fourth movement of 1919 pulled him into the swirls of cultural and political turmoil. By the early 1920s, when he became the first Chinese reporter in the new Russia, Ch'ü Ch'iu-pai had come to relate his own family experience to the fate of the institution of the large family in China; and he was to describe it feelingly from the inside. He could not tell the story of his gentry family without now seeing it as a victim of the tides of history; he could not relate his own story without sensing the powerful shaping force of society and class. Individuals, like his father, mother, and himself, seemed small and insignificant compared to the twins giants of History and Society. Yet his imagination was alive to future alternatives. His time in history was transitional: social institutions were temporarily malformed; confusion and disorder would pass. And he himself, "molded and cast" in this setting, was not content to be a mere reflection of social and historical realities.

> "Human life is entirely the imprint of social phenomena. Social phenomena are all mirages reflected in human life." Society swallows everything, and everything flows and turns according to it. If I were to entertain the idea of an "unconventional life" and wanted to assault the fortress of "society," and wanted to carve and draw [for myself] the imprint of social phenomena, and wanted to . . . well, perhaps people would judge me to be oversensitive . . .
>
> Only in this most recent century has the pale light from a lighthouse overseas reached a drowsy China that has long been in the Land of Sleep. Steamship whistles woke her from foolish dreams. The engine of the automobile wounded her inner life. The old system of family production was being destroyed, and the old gentry class could not avoid bankruptcy. Because of the shaky economic foundation, these malformed social institutions were especially tottering, confused, and unbearably disordered.
>
> My birthplace was inside a family from the fallen gentry class . . . This

most crippled social existence, like being near death from a certain kind of disease, was absolutely contradictory to the inner needs of my soul. Thus anguish,
bitterness, grief, and misery all accompanied me into life. Because of the basic
unsteadiness of our social existence, my family got caught up in the tides of the
time and truly broke apart. Poverty was not accidental. Despite family ties and
mutual support among relatives, the family was a wrecked boat on a stormy sea.
Although the members seemed to help each other, at best they could only share
their sad feelings, wail, and tear each other's clothing, or more likely, just huddle
together and cry bitterly. Who could help whom? My mother was driven out of
this universe by Poverty; my father is nothing but jetsam cast off by the same
force. What will become of my disposition, molded and cast in the midst of this
lumpen-proletariat-style social existence, I am not able to know. The bitterness
of that dying family system, during those few fitful revivals before its death, shot
its reflections into my heart and influenced my life. It became an unerasable image
that pierced my mind and shook my innermost self, rolling up into a deep sound
wave inside this society of mirages. But after a short time, a flame of heart shot
through, piercing the heavy net of uncertainties.

My childhood setting was entirely under the shadow of the declining large
family system. This system, now quivering and shaking, will topple and gradually become lost from sight . . . The best one can say of the system is that under
it, everybody lives a dry static life. On the side of its evils, one can see that
because of the conflict of economic interests and the looseness of family ties,
especially between husband and wife, the members of such a family—fathers,
sons, brothers, sisters-in-law, uncles—while staring blankly at each other under
the mask of Confucianism, will stop at nothing to give vent to their jealousy and
hatred in secret, to grumble, to murmur, to curse, and to kill with their ven-
omous tongues.[16]

Poverty had exposed the ugly possibilities within the system. Like Lu
Hsun, Ch'ü Ch'iu-pai felt he had seen the "true face" of gentry life
during his childhood, both the surface mask and the underlying realities. But the memory of the world he left behind was not all hateful.
There was, at the very least, the treasure of his mother's love, the "flame
of heart" that pierced the heavy net of uncertainties. And there was the
artistic inspiration he had received in his early education, despite the
impoverished family circumstances: poetry at his mother's knee, painting from his father, the carving of seal stones from an uncle. His early
studies gave him a strong feeling for Chinese lyricism and Buddhist
philosophy which continued to punctuate the style and perspective of
his writing, even after he became a Marxist-Leninist convert and mem-

ber of the Chinese Communist Party. His two journalistic reports on his stay in Russia during 1920–1922—*A Journey to the Land of Hunger* and *History of the Heart in the Red Capital*—contain long, lyrical, mood passages, "sighs of personal grief" Hsia calls them, that seem incompatible with political reporting.[17] But the two were always fused, or confused, by him, in his person and in his work. Just prior to his execution by the Kuomintang in 1935, Ch'ü Ch'iu-pai confessed to his dual personality: first, a "half-baked" man of letters, shiftless, faint-hearted, sentimental; and second, an inept political fighter, who happened to become a leader of the Chinese Communist Party.[18] Despite his deep inner ambivalence about who he really was, and what his life had been worth, he had found a self-expressive, unconventional path, and through political action had assaulted the fortress of an old society. Although he knew that society was not as yielding as a lump of clay or as impressionable as a silk scroll, yet he persisted in thinking and acting for basic social reform.

PATRICIAN REBELS. The critique of the old family system by those who had enjoyed "dry static lives" within it necessarily lacked the razor edge of one with Ch'ü Ch'iu-pai's experience. But there were other ways to get a critical grip on the old system without direct negative experience within a falling gentry family. New ideals emphasizing the individual and the nation crowded in upon the family's claim to be the most significant matrix of social life. Armed with these ideals, young people attacked the family for victimizing the young and women, for constricting human potential, and for being hypocritical even on its own terms. The old family system was not only dying through changes forced upon it by the environment; it was also being assaulted by resistance fighters nurtured within it but now alienated from it by a revolution in consciousness, a revolution acquired largely through reading books and reinforced by peer contacts outside the family.

   The writer Pa Chin (b. 1904), who dissected the family as an evil system in his trilogy *Turbulent Stream* (especially the first volume, *Family*, published in 1931), epitomizes the well-born son without personal experience of poverty or great injustice who turned against the traditional system. Unlike Lu Hsun or Ch'ü Ch'iu-pai, who experienced the

decline of their families, Pa Chin had a secure, happy childhood, and
had to think and feel his way into the lives of victimized others.[19] Pa
Chin's family lived in Chengtu, Szechwan, as absentee landlords; and
with four generations living together, it approached the ideal of the
large family. Materially, the environment of Pa Chin's childhood was
rich with space, flowers, food, and servants. And the key people in it—
mother, old tutor, elder brother and sister—approximated the Chinese
ideal of loving kindness and mutuality in human relationships. The father was remote, but favorably remembered. The foreign missionaries
turned out to be sympathetic figures, and even the stepmother was kindly!

Only after the death of his parents in 1914 and 1917 placed Pa Chin
and his brothers and sisters under the direct hand of the grandfather,
did he become conscious of the "despotism" in the family. This education came largely through witnessing the suffering of others, especially
his vulnerable elder brother, and through reading avant-garde material
that heightened his consciousness of the negative aspects of large family
life. His grandfather did interfere with his plans to study in a modern
school, but even this "tyranny" was softened by the old man's warmth
towards Pa Chin before his death in 1919. Pa Chin's plans for a modern
education proved to have been blocked only temporarily, as the family
consented later to let him study in Nanking and Shanghai. Pa Chin's
experience in the family can be considered "negative" largely because of
his highly sensitive nature, which made the sufferings of others vicari-
ously his own. He did feel persecuted, but he did not have his life
warped by the direct misuse of power over him. His later fictional de-
piction of family life, as his biographer Olga Lang notes, presented "the
conflict of generation in a fashion not only more dramatic, but actually
more true to life [i.e., to the lives of many others of his class back-
ground] than his own story."[20]

Pa Chin's early mental world bore the marks of upper-class sensibili-
ties suddenly harnessed to the cause of social revolution: the daring idealism of anarchism, the tendency to view the family as the focus of
oppression, and the journey to politics through cultural criticism. In his
fiction, the bitter tragedies he describes are primarily those of upper-
class youth, whose plans in marriage or career or revolution are frustrated by the power of the older generation or by an education in filiality

that fatally impaired their capacity to resist. Precious and naive in many ways, this orientation was the reflection of "revolution" in the minds of "noble youth with warm hearts" from well-to-do educated families, who wanted to love and serve society and to liberate the masses below. Taking such diffuse enthusiasm and disciplining it to serious revolutionary work presented problems for professional revolutionaries. Mao Tse-tung criticized writers whose works were self-expressions of the class they came from, caught up in its perspectives and its dilemmas. They lacked a sense of proportion, missing essential tasks and prime needs; they added "more flowers to the brocade" rather than providing "fuel in wintery weather."[21]

TRADITION CARICATURED AND ABANDONED. The marks of a changing historical time are everywhere interwoven with the fate of these gentry families, whether in decline or under attack by the younger generation. Behind a seemingly natural process of decay long observed by Chinese thinkers may lie economic dislocations caused by foreign competition. Behind the dissipation and listlessness of some elders and young people may lie the loss of self-fulfillment and self-respect in social roles, occasioned by the collapse of traditional institutions. Behind the "lack of imagination" in meeting the times lay the crisis of a shifting, unpredictable economic and political order demanding greater inputs of initiative and talent if one were to make a successful changeover from old patterns of wealth and power to new ones.[22] There was nothing that was simply "traditional" anymore. There was much that was degenerating into a caricature of tradition, a distortion true enough to discredit, in the eyes of the young, the whole past as anachronistic and oppressive.

In the childhood of Hu Wei-han (b. 1924), one can see how small historical contingencies had thrown off the balanced workings of the traditional family model.[23] Hu's father was a highranking Kuomintang official in the 1910s, compelled by political events to be constantly on the move; this movement led to his marriage in a frontier region to a woman of undistinguished background. Hu's mother, as a result, was never fully accepted in his home district, and she was even looked down upon by the servants. The father was absent for years on end, making the family interplay almost exclusively one of females and children. Since

Hu, like his father, was the eldest son within a prominent, old family, he was nurtured as a Young Master, destined to lead the family into the next generation; but his presumptive and self-assertive behavior ran directly counter to the dominating position of his step-grandmother, the only surviving member from her generation.

An embittered woman, his step-grandmother lorded it over the household, skillfully and correctly using traditional prerogatives of authority while disregarding the spirit of compromise and moderation which had usually helped to achieve a semblance of social harmony. Young Master Hu felt he was a special target of her abuse and came to hate her. There could be no question of respect, let alone unforced love and trust; filial emotions in this context had to be more counterfeit than real. The mother, herself cowed and powerless before the step-grandmother, could offer little support, and in fact often had to turn her son's care over to others, because of her own sickliness and nervousness. This hostile interplay ended in the forced exodus of young Hu into his uncle's family at age ten, after a seemingly insignificant incident was skillfully parlayed by the step-grandmother into a major confrontation. This was the family beginning of an odyssey in which Hu experienced the great emotional extremes and personal insecurities inherent in an unstable age. Unlike the earlier generation of the 1890s, among whom relatively traditional childhoods were still common, Hu experienced irregularities right from early childhood: a perennially absent father, a mother in a weakened status position, an unchecked grandmother. These led to the ultimate irony, in a family-based society, of a Young Master's being expelled from the family he was supposedly being trained to head. To many like Hu who grew up the in the 1920s and 1930s, Pa Chin's dark portrayal of the "traditional" family life corresponded to the true face of things, without even the soft edges that Pa Chin gave to some of these relationships.

Within the traditional image of life in large families, the lack of freedom for the young had been stereotyped at least since the eighteenth-century novel *Dream of the Red Chamber*. Decisions on marriage and work were presumed to be family decisions, not personal ones; and the prerogatives of the elderly and the males could weigh heavily on youth, females, and misfits, who had little recourse short of the monastery or suicide. But the transitional republican situation, with its sense of a passing "old" arrangement and an emerging "new" one, greatly altered the perception of these relationships and the consequences of resistance. In the minds of educated youth, the "old" came to be correlated with the elder generation and tradition. And when authority over the young was badly abused, as in the case of Hu and his grandmother, the past also was felt to be "irrational."[24] Many elders for their part held on with increasing tenacity, relying on fundamentalist assertions of doctrine and authority, and trying to interpret the "rebellion" in terms of tested categories. The grandmother of Sheng Cheng (b.1899), for example, thought foreign barbarians were cannibals and devils, and hoped that Yuan Shih-k'ai would exterminate young Chinese "disciples of foreign devils" just as Tseng Kuo-fan in the nineteenth century had destroyed the Taiping rebels.[25] Queueless young men with army uniforms and heretical ideas—so appeared Sheng Cheng and his friends after the Revolution of 1911—could only evoke images of horror. He and his grandmother both viewed the family struggle as a mighty test between Tradition and Progress. She viewed "progress" as treason against the age-old civilization of China, and he thought "tradition" was degenerate and bankrupt but blindly determined to hold the young in its grip. Imprisoned within such conspiratorial viewpoints and deeply suspicious one of the other, they saw, or explored, no avenues of accommodation. Distrust escalated into deadlock, mutual incomprehension, loneliness, and silent anguish in each other's company.

The break away from the family came, as it had to, whether as a forced expulsion in Hu's case, or as a prudent move to preserve harmony in Sheng Cheng's case. But unlike those breaks in the *Dream of the Red Chamber* that led away from society, this generation was propelled by its progressive self-image to act in society and to find or create new organizations within which to live its ideals, thus bringing the inner self and the outer world once more into correspondence. The large families of the gentry class and the sanctuary cities of the foreign-tinged coastal strip were the incubators of this youthful counterculture, creating cultural heretics who were to become vipers to some, prophets to others.

RECORDS OF BITTER STRUGGLE: THE SONS OF COMMON FOLK

Children not born into families "fragrant with the scent of books" grew up with a radically different set of problems and expectations in becoming modern educated youth. First of all, they could not take education for granted. The old examination system in some ways had facilitated the upward mobility of sons from such families, while the new system introduced extensively after 1905 further constricted their opportunities. The books needed to prepare for the old exams were few (essentially *The Four Books*) and readily available. The fees paid to the tutors were elastic, though supervision might vary according to the amount paid; tutors seldom turned students away simply for lack of finances. Frequently clans or villages offered free instruction to identify promising students for further education. At the higher levels, there were prizes and stipends that enabled good students to continue, and even prosper.

The wider scope of learning for the new-style education, however, required more books. Other costs rose, too, for schools needed diversified teaching staffs, more physical equipment, and reference materials. There were also additional expenses for travel and boarding, as the new-style schools were concentrated in district towns and provincial cities, and the colleges proliferated in the coastal strip, especially Shanghai. Under the old system there had been traveling allowances, and examination and study centers were distributed throughout the empire. More important, after 1907 fees became common in government schools as well as in the private sector.[26] The fees alone made it virtually impossible for those from poor backgrounds to follow the path of the New Learning. To send two children to primary school in the 1930s was financially impossible for families with fewer than thirty *mou* of land, or in other words for about 90 percent of the rural population. Fifty-*mou* families could afford to send one child to an upper primary school, and 200-*mou* families (less than one per cent of the rural population) to secondary school.[27]

To be sure, commoners respected education, for they knew that scholars ranked first in the four traditional status groups, followed by peasant cultivators, craft workers, and merchants. But when they thought of education concretely for their sons (never for daughters), their respect for learning and dreams of family advancement had to be tempered by the simple truth that education was a luxury, paid for by whatever precious surplus they could manage to save by their labor. The justification for making such sacrifice differed with parental aspirations. For some it was simply a useful literacy training: to have sons capable of managing accounts, reading and writing letters. Others wanted their sons to know enough historical anecdotes and classical phrases to be regarded as distinct from other villagers, approximating local gentry. And a few aspired to a mastery of the Confucian canon and the arts of writing and composition that would allow a son to succeed in the examinations and enter the "forest of scholars" *(shih-lin),* bringing glory to the family, and perhaps even power and wealth. This latter kind of success, while not impossible, depended upon a seldom assembled combination of talent, parental ambition and determination, and good fortune.

PARTNERSHIPS OF LOVE AND AMBITION. The case of Shu Hsin-ch'eng (b. 1893) allows us to see these elements in motion and the ironies of fulfillment. For generations his family had been simple tenant farmers in a mountain-rimmed valley in western Hunan province. They owned only the land the house stood on, but got along by supplementing the rented fields with growing fruit and other crops on odd pieces of land. Once, his grandfather had been insulted and had determined to send his sons to school; thus his father, "in the midst of a hardship-filled life, studied for a few years and could keep accounts and write letters . . . [I]n terms of the family's past record, he was considered a literate person." [28] It was not the father, however, who became the driving force behind his education but his illiterate mother. A spirited, obstinate person, orphaned in her childhood and brought up in the house of her financé, she came to dominate the entire household. Her skillful management made their material life more secure, and they were able to buy several *mou* of poor land. Her son, the only child until a daughter was born five years later, received the same strict care as the family resources.

Since the men were away in the fields all day and there were no servants, Hsin-cheng's mother's influence bore on him with particular intensity. She did not want him to follow in his ancestors' footsteps, but prayed and struggled to make him into a scholar. He was not al-

lowed to tend the water buffalo or cut wood or climb trees or go swim-
ming or engage in any of the "coarse and wild" *(ts'u-yeh)* activities of
other village children. He had to wear different clothing and learn to
speak a language that did not reflect the vulgar phrases used by ordinary
people. As she hoped to enlist him among the ranks of the scholars,
"her every work and action were carefully calculated to nurture 'the style
of the Superior Man.' " Constantly she reiterated the family's poverty,
and the necessity to plan and to push forward. One of her frequent
sayings was "Eating and using things will not impoverish one, but not
being able to plan will doom one to poverty for a lifetime." [29]

His mother started him off in a nearby tutorial school with ceremonial pomp that demonstrated to him that "those who study are truly
different from ordinary men." Each day that he did well, the tutor would
paint a red circle on his forehead, a sign to his mother who had promised him an egg a day for steady improvement. [30] In actual fact, he liked
classes because they released him from his mother's tight control into a
circle of friends; and he was talented enough to do the work with relative ease. He became known in the village as a "prodigy" *(shen-t'ung),*
and various families began to court him as a possible son-in-law. On all
sides, he was being stamped as a scholar in the making. His studies
progressed rapidly, and he switched tutors often as his mother quested
for better qualified instructors. When he was ten, a crisis occurred that
jeopardized the entire effort. Hsin-ch'eng had helped as an accountant
for several months in a general store started by his father and a partner.
After the partnership collapsed, the father and both grandparents wanted
him to take over accounting duties in the shop permanently. The lad
himself was powerless to reject their combined will; but his mother
insisted that the others stop "fussing over small amounts of money," for
her son was not going to become a merchant, but "a high official with
a generous salary." No one dared challenge her authority. She proceeded
to seek out a distinguished teacher in a nearby district and offered up
her private effects to meet his higher fees. [31]

This determination and willingness to sacrifice are intelligible not
only because of that "generous salary" but also because of the desire to
bring some measure of glory and fame to the family. Fame was so intimately connected with success in the state examinations that it was hard

for poor rural families struggling upwards to conceive of other standards of achievement. Just as young Hsin-ch'eng's behavior was molded to conform to an age-old model of the superior man, so his studies followed the prescribed pattern of the past, oblivious to the new world forming on China's coast. On the very eve of the abolition of the old system in 1904, he was carefully learning the much scorned eight-legged essay. While Hsin-ch'eng himself was quickly pulled into the contemporary scene by his next tutor, who broached reform issues and put the publicist Liang Ch'i-ch'ao into his hands, there was no way for his parents to grow with him into this larger world. They were disappointed when he left the classical academy to enter a "foreign-style" school in 1908. He had to lie about his eagerness in order to make the shift acceptable to them, claiming that his teacher had honored him by selecting him to go.[32]

In 1909, he joined a competition to qualify as a primary school teacher, and the atmosphere of the event was heavily reminiscent of the old civil service examinations in all the participants' minds, examiners, candidates, and families alike. It was held on the old examination grounds of the prefectural capital, complete with fireworks, drums, and dramatic calling forth of the candidates. But somehow the old ferment was lacking, and the candidates barely filled a third of the seats in the vast hall.[33] Hsin-ch'eng knew it was not the same. His "graduation" from a modish academy of law and politics (*fa cheng hsueh-t'ang*) in Changsha after a five-month course in 1911 created a more distinct feeling of bizarre incongruity between family and self. The mutual sharing of honor and fame, such a powerful cement between them only two years before, was no longer strong enough to hold in the conflicting emotions on each side. Hsin-ch'eng knew that his diploma was a hollow achievement; and his jubilant mother, upon seeing that the returning scholar had cut off his queue, could not hold back her fury and almost drove him out of the house.[34]

Mother and son grew further apart after his formal marriage in 1911. The match had been arranged ten years before; and as the daughter-in-law was the mother's first choice, there should have been a harmonious family circle. But as soon as the chosen daughter-in-law arrived in the family, the strains appeared. Within three years, Hsin-ch'eng, out of

compassion, sent his wife home to her own family. This bitter period of
deteriorating relationships, with his mother treating her husband, her
son, and her daughter-in-law "beyond the bounds of normal human
sympathy," set off years of troubled introspection in the son. Why had
it happened in this most promising of circumstances? In his account of
his uncertain steps towards understanding, we have a rare chance to see
how poverty and the will to escape it through sacrifice and denial distorted the strong emotional bond between mother and only son. There
is none of the simplicity that sees Tradition confronting Progress, but a
rich awareness of limited human understanding.

> For the last twenty years not a day has passed without my seeking an answer,
> but for over ten years I never found a fully satisfying one. When this deterioration
> began, I only felt that my wife, in disposition and behavior, was an ideal daugh-
> ter-in-law. From a humanitarian point of view, I was dissatisfied with my moth-
> er's treatment of her; so on several occasions I would use all my strength to save
> her from the various traps of the old society. After each disturbance, I would
> analyze my mother's temperament and behavior from every angle, but the only
> conclusions ten years ago were a few words: "[She had] a peculiar obstinate tem-
> per, [she was] a moody, changeable person." In the last few years I have come to
> know that these words decidedly do not explain our difficulties . . . [T]he major
> cause lies in the heart, in the jealousy born of her love. I was the only son, and
> her love for me was the most pure and sincere. In our family, she and father did
> not get along well, and because of custom and habit, girls were not taken seri-
> ously . . . so I became the only refuge and consolation for her spirit . . . [I]n
> my childhood she considered me as a "small adult" and controlled me too strictly,
> until I became very afraid of her and did not love her very much, even though
> this close concern was the expression of her deepest love. Given my kind of family
> setting, she was willing to exchange the labor of her hands for my school fees, to
> make me study and become famous . . . As her love was so deep, her uncon-
> scious naturally drove her to try to possess my heart forever. But suddenly a wife
> rushed into my inner life, crowding her out, and she was obviously disturbed.
> The more harmonious we were, the more upset she was. Society being what it is
> also did not permit her unconscious to surface, and her only recourse was to find
> another outlet for her disquiet, and the daughter-in-law became the target of her
> transferred anger.

It had taken Shu Hsin-ch'eng years of daily moral self-examination, in
the spirit of Confucian introspection, to come to a broader understanding, one that extended sympathy not only to his wife but also to his

mother. This understanding went beyond a narrow accounting of right and wrong to probe their lives as social beings, each caught in a dimness of half-understanding. Still he felt guilty that his "present understanding" had only come about "in the midst of a many-sided depression after my mother's death in October, 1927."

> Today perhaps I could find ways of not hurting my mother while still extricating my wife, allowing both of them to be complete and happy . . . If my mother is conscious, may she smile from the underworld and forgive me.[35]

This kind of mother-son partnership, or as Robert J. Lifton has called it, "an alliance of love and ambition," was a major way for poor families to break out of the cycle of poverty and necessity.[36] But such intensive alliances and bitter sacrifices could create dependencies and expectations that warped the relationship between parent and child. And the shifting standards and goals in a transitional age made "success" less and less of a unifier, creating different, unshared and unshareable inner worlds between the partners. The mother measured achievements in terms of the old literati standards of the traditional community, while the son got drawn into the counterculture of educated youth, a world that had to be covered over with lies and could not be directly communicated because it was subversive to the mores of the village and his elders.

Educated upper-class families had better resources for adapting to new trends in that larger world, especially after 1900. The human environment of a son in such a family would include brothers or relatives or friends who had been to the cities, read new journals, or had some exposure to the New Learning in China or Japan. More exposed to this world, they were able to plan "modern futures" for their sons, and were doing so even before the imperial examination system ended. The young Hu Shih, for example, whose scholar-official father died in 1895 when he was three years and eight months old, grew up in partnership with his mother, who, like Shu Hsin-ch'eng's mother, concentrated upon his education with singular intensity.[37] She was careful to nurture the precocity of her only child and channel it into his studies, and not to spoil him in the process. But unlike Shu, Hu Shih had elder half-brothers who had studied in Shanghai, at an academy run by a friend of their father and at Nanyang Normal school for teachers. They became channels for books and opinions that led him in his tutorial work beyond the eight-legged essay and the questions and themes on the interpretation of the classics *(ts'e-lun ching-i)*. He also received various novels from opium-smoking relatives, and even acquired a translation of stories about Greek patriots from his second half-brother. In 1904, when he was just over twelve, his mother sent him along with his third half-brother to Shanghai.[38]

Hu Shih's tie with his mother also remained central to his emotional life. After she had hardened her heart to send him away for further study, he never forgave himself for returning home only three times between 1904 and 1918.[39] This relationship with his mother remained inviolable to the reform spirit he displayed in other areas of life. In 1917, upon his return from years of study in the United States, he accepted a marriage, arranged by his mother, to a simple, illiterate girl and despite great difficulties lived with her for the rest of his life. This was hardly typical of returned students, many of whom got divorced or refused to abide by family arrangements, and sought instead more compatible, independent, "modern" women as marriage partners. After his mother's death in 1918, he also thought through his views on immortality and broadened the traditional definition beyond the words, works, and virtues of the famous to include the least of men and women—such as his mother—who lived on in the lives of those they had touched. His essay "Immortality: My Religion," was first drafted at the end of 1918 during his mother's funeral. Though he remained impeccably filial in relation to his mother and her memory, Hu Shih did alter the funeral rites as well as his concept of immortality.[40]

MAKING IT ALONE. Alliances of love and ambition seem most likely to occur in small families, particularly between widows and only sons. Mencius and his mother provide a classic example. In larger families, parents and sons were caught up in a network of relationships that diffused financial resources and human energies among many rather than concentrating them on any one pair. The simple increase in mouths, in fact, depressed the general level of a family, making the moderately well-off very economy conscious and the poor almost desperate. For the poor and relatively poor, not only education but also other issues became

mountainous burdens in their inner landscapes. Food was basic: The
number of meals per day is often specified in autobiographical memoirs.
The kind of rice (dry-cooked rice or washed-rice congee), to say nothing
of the vegetables or meat that went with it, is remembered in exact
detail. Next, the major ceremonial expenses for engagement and marriage had to be faced. Beyond food and ceremony came education. The
schoolroom, that traditional pathway into office, prestige, and wealth,
was an expendable goal in the survival struggle of the poor. Within
large families, where numbers pressed upon limited means, a son determined upon educational advancement had to rely upon his own wits and
audacity to break the constraints imposed by an entangling web of debts
and obligations. Two cases, one set within a lower-gentry family with
six sons, another within a poor peasant-tradesman family of four children, illuminate this kind of struggle.

Shen Tsung-han, the fourth of six sons, was born in 1895 in a clan
village in Chekiang, not far from Ningpo, one of the original five foreign treaty ports on China's coast. His family combined farming and
studying, and was on the middle rungs of the economic structure in the
village, where some families owned as much as two hundred *mou* and
others as little as seven or eight *mou* of land. His great grandfather had
once owned four hundred *mou* and had started the studying tradition in
the village. By Shen's father's generation, there were several degree winners in the family, including his father and uncle, both *hsiu-ts'ai;* but
the lands had since slipped from their control. During Tsung-han's
childhood, the elder generation had already divided up the family assets;
their family income came from his father's salary as a tutor, from twelve
mou of rented land worked by a hired long-term laborer and a boy water-
buffalo tender, and every other year from the rent on twenty *mou* of land
set aside after the grandfather's death to maintain ancestral sacrifices.
His mother prepared the food, made the clothing, and without servants
managed a six-son, seven-mouth household. Each day they had three
meals; but the noon meal was washed-rice congee, in order to "save tea
water and rice" as she explained. They used vegetable oil instead of
kerosene, and a flint stone instead of foreign matches. She cultivated
silkworms in the spring and in the winter sold several hundred young
chicks to make "cake money" for her sons. Her thrift also permitted

them later to rent thirty-two *mou* of land on a long-term lease, especially satisfying since these lands had formerly belonged to the grandfather but had been sold to pay off his debts.[41]

In this family, the problem of basic education for the sons was solved rather easily, as the father had arranged to have one son at a time join his two tutees for common instruction; when they had reached a certain level, they graduated to their uncle. In this fashion, the eldest, second, fourth, and fifth sons acquired their basic classical education. The third son was brought up to work the family fields from the beginning, while the sixth son simply came too late for this arrangement.[42] Tsung-han spent the four years from age five to age nine with his father in a rich man's house, enjoying equal treatment with the sons in the family. Then he had two years with his uncle, who also was a resident tutor in a family. After finishing these family educational arrangements in 1906, he entered a private school founded by a wealthy merchant in the district town of Yu-yao. Through a push from the rich patron who had been his father's employer, he secured one of the two scholarships for needy students, freeing him from the usual fees. Because he was a needy student, and younger than the others as well, he suffered the ridicule of his rich and older classmates, and knew that he had to be outstanding in his studies to make up for these handicaps. In this context of ever present threats of ridicule from fellow students, high expectations from his rich patron, and his father's threats, the young boy quickly learned to discipline himself and to set himself up as a model of correctness and determination.[43] The strength of will forged in four years in this difficult setting made it possible for the young man to resist his father's wish that he then help the family by becoming a salaried school teacher and give up his plans for further study. His bitterest struggles centered on financing his further education in the midst of family resistance, including the ultimate accusation from his father that he was *pu-hsiao* or unfilial.

Tsung-han's father deeply believed the old teachings of propriety, and considered his major responsibility to be the proper instruction of his children and the management of their marriages. He engaged his sons when they were three or four years old, and expected them to marry at about age twenty. As each marriage was calculated to cost 300–400 silver dollars, or about twice the family's annual income, this was an enormous outlay of resources to plan and save for. The father loved orchids, and he began breeding them on the side, eventually selling them; in time he accumulated about 1,000 silver dollars which were set aside for the marriages of his second, third, and fourth sons.[44] It was assumed that the sons, for their part, would become part of the collective economic life of the family as soon as they were able. This included contributing part of their salary—in Tsung-han's case 30 out of 40 dollars that he earned as a young teacher—to current expenses, supporting younger brothers through school, and finally taking over the debts of the older generation and supporting the parents in their old age.[45] Tsung-han did not deny these obligations; but in the effort to fulfill them and yet make his own future, he was driven to despair and agony. A sense of struggle remained the dominant impression of his youth and early adulthood, as reflected in the title of his autobiography, *A Record of Overcoming Difficulties and Bitter Study*.

The story of Shen Tsung-han, whose persistence eventually won him a Ph.D. from Cornell in 1928, highlights the effort to secure a complete education along the sanctioned, orthodox path *(cheng-t'u)* in its altered twentieth-century form. A less respected path for advancement, the military, was becoming a major channel of mobility for the sons of the very poor, for whom the orthodox path of formal education was so distant as to vanish over the horizon.[46] The story of Ts'ai T'ing-k'ai illustrates this pattern.

Ts'ai T'ing-k'ai (b. 1892) came from a poor peasant family in Loting county in southwestern Kwangtung province. They owned a plot of land which produced two *tan* of grain, or about one-half *mou*.[47] They had inherited one *mou* from the grandfather; this field, however, had been mortgaged to pay for the father's marriage, an event that poverty had forced him to postpone until he was twenty-nine years old. They also farmed some rented fields. T'ing-k'ai's mother worked these fields by herself, managed the household, and brought up T'ing-k'ai, his older sister, and two younger brothers. His semi-literate father was a man of varied skills; he occasionally helped in the fields, but normally plied the trades of tailor and of herb doctor for both men and animals. He was well known in the village; and those whom he had helped would reciprocate at the Mid-Autumn Festival by bringing a chicken, duck, or moon cakes, things which the Ts'ai family otherwise would not have had because of their poverty and that of their relatives. The daily fare, though it consisted of three meals, was spare and monotonous: washed-rice congee or yams. Only for a few days right after harvest did they eat dry-cooked rice.[48] The boy learned the reasons for these habits by asking innocent questions that were bitterly and directly answered: Why couldn't they eat some dry rice after so many weeks of congee, or why didn't they go to the cemetery in sedan chairs or on horseback like others to pay respects to the ancestors?[49] Their life was a constant rhythm of planning, saving, borrowing, calculating investments in a water buffalo or tools or a year of education, and—if the debt load was not too great—purchasing small luxury items at New Year's, such as candles, meat, and special foods.

Because he was the eldest son, his father hoped to be able to send him to school to learn some characters; and one day, when T'ing-k'ai was six years old, his father promised, with a bitter, defeated expression on his face, to send him. This hope became a possibility two years later, after the thirteen-year-old debt for his father's marriage was finally repaid in full, the repayment costing five times the original amount.[50] The coming of two relatives, a paternal uncle and a young aunt, also increased their labor force for that growing season; and with a good harvest, they approached the new year in 1900 with lighter hearts. It was at this time that T'ing-k'ai's engagement was arranged, and a year of schooling planned. The school brought some ten village boys together under the instruction of a teacher who had studied for many years but never passed the first degree. The teacher lived from the school fees: one *tan* of grain, two bushels of rice, and two hundred coppers per pupil.[51] T'ing-k'ai took to memorizing easily and avoided a syndrome of punishment-truancy-punishment that often ended the schooling of children from poor families.[52] He was made to feel conscious of the privilege of learning; for at his engagement ceremony, which cost the family 30,000 coppers, his mother could not refrain from reiterating the extent of their sacrifice for him, "causing me to feel at once awesome respect and bitter sorrow." He did not "dare to be lazy" and studied diligently in the morning while tending the water buffalo in the afternoons.[53]

For three years the small surplus in family savings enabled T'ing-k'ai to study. Things were going forward as intended, that uncommon state of affairs so ardently wished for in the New Year's greeting: "May ten thousand events conform to your hopes!" But during the third year, when he was ten, the normal perversity of events undermined the family's economic base and wiped out the surplus. Drought sharply reduced the harvest that year, and his thirty-four-year-old mother died when an epidemic combed out the weak and overworked from the village. For the sake of the family, his father was advised to remarry; but in order to raise the necessary money, they had to mortgage, once again, the single *mou* of land inherited from the grandfather.[54] The stepmother soon protested strongly against T'ing-k'ai's "unproductive schooling." In retrospect Ts'ai blamed her for being both tyrannical and lethargic, but her protest was not unusual in the circumstances. The father supported his son's schooling until the month of June, that period of greatest crisis among the rural poor when the new grain was not yet ready and the old supply was running out (*ch'ing huang pu chieh*).

> At this time, poor families either pawn their possessions or borrow at high interest or come to the extremity of selling their sons and daughters in order to obtain money to buy rice. The situation was indeed miserable. Although my family did not reach the point of selling its sons and daughters, my studies were sold away by my stepmother . . . At that time I detested her greatly, but dared not express this hate openly. I only hoped Father would not consent. How could I know Father had no resoluteness whatsoever, and ended up being persuaded by Stepmother. He went to see the teacher and said that because the family was poor they wanted me to return home to work . . . [H]e had come to ask that I might be excused and give up my studies. After this, and for a long time to come, I did not reenter the gate of a schoolhouse.[55]

With his schooling ended, T'ing-k'ai was confronted with the question of his future. Sensing himself, in strength and responsibility, to be an adult already at age twelve, he determined that he would not allow himself any self-pity for his fate but rather would set his will in action and become a full man. As he had few opportunities, he started by learning his father's skills: farming, tailoring, treating sick animals. But even during this apprenticeship he yearned for something with a more promising future, for a way out of the insecurities of life in rural villages. This "other vision," this alternative, grew in his own mind out of some personal encounters in the district, until it crystallized in the form of a decision to join a new-style army that was recruiting in the area. As in the case of Shen Tsung-han, this personal future was bitterly opposed by his father, and for the same reasons: his labor was needed to support the family, to provide for his aging father and younger brothers. He had to proceed behind his father's back, with only the inner support of his own self-confidence and determination and vision of becoming a military officer. Even this vision was barely enough; for in the first ten years thereafter, he vacillated between the village and the army, venturing out but then returning home to open a shop or try peddling, before army life finally absorbed all his energy and attention.

Friedrich Nietzsche, in his 1874 essay *The Use and Abuse of History*, wrote of several ways in which the view of the past serves basic human needs.[56] In particular, two of these postulated ways—the monumental and the critical modes—speak to the experience of facing adversity. The monumental mode addresses the existential problem of finding the very courage to act; past models, whether heroic public figures or persevering parents or ancestors, support the courage to act by allowing persons not to feel alone, unsupported, unwatched. A symbolic buoying and nurturing across time helps set the will and fix determination. The critical mode addresses the hope for deliverance from suffering. The past is seen as dark, evil, oppressive, worthy of being condemned and cast away; the future is bright, hopeful, liberating, a vision of a more just and humane society. The language and imagery of these modes may help us understand how the inchoate early experiences of adversity can be translated into conscious ideas later held as adults.

The monumental mode is almost second nature within Chinese culture, with its longstanding emphasis upon teaching children and governing society by models and exemplars, both historical and contemporary. We have seen that models, by a kind of moral magnetism, were to pull the child along and support its will to do good. The mothers of Ch'ü Ch'iu-pai, Hu Shih, Shu Hsin-ch'eng, and Sheng Cheng, whether they were present, dead, or absent, were just such powerful presences urging their sons on to achievement, persistence, and hope. Adolescents and young adults seeking the "human path" *(tso jen)* also seemed to need past models to overcome the fear that, unaided, they might be unable to act morally, and might instead succumb to paralysis of will and intellect or be immoral through weakness and inertia. Psychological needs, real or imputed, lay behind the pervasiveness of modeling as a motivational support. The story of Shen Tsung-han is particularly illustrative of the widespread use of models to secure one's moral bearings; for he not only explicitly modeled himself on others as a youth, but he also became a model for another generation of adolescents through his memoirs.

As a young man, Shen Tsung-han found his moral examplars in an elder brother, whose influence led him to Christianity, and in contemporary and historical figures: Liang Ch'i-ch'ao, who fired his patriotic fervor; Wang Yang-ming, who taught him that knowledge without action was tantamount to ignorance; and Tseng Kuo-fan, who led him to cultivate the habits of diary-writing and daily self-examination. These models helped him to live a life of conscious, purposeful striving, after he had once made up his mind "to be good and to do good for my people and my country."[57] His memoir presents excerpts from the journals he kept as a youth, recording his struggles with drinking, smoking, masturbation, sex, and dishonesty. A confessional Christian side perhaps assisted him in making these struggles public, he said, but the primary thrust for a life of self-examination came from Chinese sources, particularly Tseng Kuo-fan. Learning later that Tseng had smoked and played chess, and even had a concubine, did not deter him.[58] Shen Tsung-han's memoir has been widely reprinted in Taiwan as a didactic autobiography directed at youths aged fifteen to twenty-five; it is a continuation of a tradition of promoting models of self-cultivation, past or living, to inspire young people to overcome difficult situations and be useful in the world. Shen himself tied the practice of self-cultivation to the promise of the *Great Learning (Ta hsueh),* a Confucian text that envisions the ordered inner self as the foundation for an ordered outer world (and which, as one of the Four Books, was memorized by all youngsters pursuing a Neo-Confucian education).[59]

In contrast to the monumental mode, Nietzsche's critical mode finds no support for future action in past experience; from past to future is a

passage from nightmare to utopia. This way of thinking, seemingly un-
characteristic for Chinese, became a dominant one for thousands of Re-
publican-era intellectuals. Lu Hsun's despair in the 1910s over China's
prospects was deep and almost overwhelming. He perceived society as
suffocating and oppressive towards its individual members; he could find
hope only in unsocialized young children and rebels. He sought to be
among the awakened men who would burden themselves with the weight
of tradition and shoulder up the gate of darkness, giving unimpeded
passage to the child-rebels "so that they may rush to the bright, wide-
open spaces and lead happy lives henceforth as rational human beings."[60]
Such melodramatic contrast was part of the language of battle during
the May Fourth era, when old and new, Tradition and Progress, elders
and educated youth, squared off against each other. In his militant advocacy and deep loathing, Lu Hsun was one of the architects of this
prose of conscious rebelliousness.[61] Ch'ü Ch'iu-pai went beyond prose to
implement a political program. His pathway beyond the gate of darkness became closely defined by a Marxist-Leninist view of history and
class liberation, yet underlying his ideological stance was the same diffuse imagery of history as an oppressive prologue to a brighter future.
Politics, like literature, has an expressive side in myths, metaphors, and
yearnings rooted in our lived experience. Those who overcome harsh
experiences are still fated to live with the memory of them.

A Young Master with his parents, ca. 1900. Courtesy, Essex Institute, Salem, Mass.

SIX

Privilege

Perhaps the most distinctive mark of the old scholar-official elite was the aura of a qualitative difference between themselves and the rest of Chinese society. The outer symbols—the long gown, the slow deliberate movements, the ceremonial largesse, poetic refinement of language, and leisurely pursuit of the arts—reflected an inner sense of difference. In theory, this social distinction was not based upon inheritance or ascription, but upon achievement in the form of mastery of the classical literature. As this literature enjoyed a kind of magical charisma in the culture, this charisma was transferred to those who had grasped the wisdom of these books and who were felt by all classes to be able to discern the will of heaven and to maintain the tranquility of the social order. Correspondingly, there was a basic two-layer structuring of society between those who were qualified for the highest human standing relative to a cultural definition of heaven, man and earth and those who stood in some more distant relationship to this norm.[1] It is inherent in this arrangement that those who "qualify" require a body of those who "do not qualify" for their sense of who they are. The superior man was set off against the common man he had surpassed; the man who lived by the *li,* regulating his conduct by a moral code, found his definition in those lesser men who had to be controlled by the outer compulsions of *fa* or law.

In an important sense, this status was inherited, for the children born behind the gates of gentry and official residences were assumed to be participants in a different world from that of ordinary children and accordingly were treated and addressed differently. This status was not something they had to achieve but something they derived from being identified by the surrounding community as their fathers' children. It was, moreover, something that led fathers to encourage sons to behave like gentry, for men saw their own status mirrored in their sons' manners and pastimes and in the deference accorded to those sons.[2] If the experience inside a falling gentry family tempered the consciousness of this gap in status, the experience inside a rising family or inside an established family that still enjoyed the difference, confirmed its existence. The name that catches this early training in superiority and command is *shao-yeh* or Young Master.

Young Master was not a casual nickname, but a status designation that accurately reflected the treatment of sons (especially eldest and only or otherwise favored sons) in prospering scholar-official families as "masters" in the making. The makers were not only kinsmen and servants, but also the surrounding neighborhood or area where public opinion was an ever present factor in drawing the life of myriad households into conforming cultural patterns. And the ideal result was the cluster of traits—language, deportment, style—associated with the superior man of Confucian morality, the sanctioned holder of wealth and power within society.

The previous chapter showed how Shu Hsin-cheng's mother, aspiring for her son to join that elite group, tried to form him according to her image of this cultural ideal.[3] In the case of some others, the name, the status role, and actual behavioral traits came to be subtle reinforcements bending the child in certain directions and not in others. One boy, seven years of age, from a nationally prominent family was called "Your Small Excellency" (*hsiao ta-jen*) by villagers because of his developed sense of manners.[4] The young Hu Shih, at age five or so, was given the name *hsien-sheng* or "Mister." Then it fit; later it became a constricting label.

> My body was weak when I was small, and I was not able to play together with rough kids. Also my mother did not allow me to run and jump about wildly. During my childhood I never developed the habit of vigorous play; no matter what context, I was always somewhat slow and gentle [*wen chou-chou-ti*]. So the elder generation in the village all said I was "like a Mister," and consequently

called me Mister *Mi*. After I had this nickname, everyone knew that Mister Three's son was now called Mister Mi. Since I had the name of Mister, I was unable not to pretend somewhat to the style of a Mister, and I certainly could not run wild with rambunctious boys. One day I was outside the gate of our house with a group of children playing the game "tossing coins." One of the elders walked past, saw me, and laughed: "Does Mister Mi throw coins, too?" I heard this and felt so ashamed that I blushed. I felt that I had lost much of the prestige of my Mister status. As the elders encouraged me to pretend to the style of a Mister, and as I was not accustomed to or capable of simply having fun, and as I honestly did enjoy reading books, one can say that in my whole life I never enjoyed the play life of a child.[5]

YOUNG MASTERS IN THE MAKING.

The autobiography of Li Tung-fang (b.1907) allows us to see how Young Master treatment was built into the early experiences of a son of the gentry, at home and at school. During the last years of the Ch'ing dynasty, his father, a *chü-jen* degree winner, was an official in the salt bureau in Yangchow, Kiangsu. He was the youngest child and the second son, and especially beloved by his mother because he had been born shortly after the death of her favorite nephew, and in a way replaced him.[6] His reception beyond the yamen walls was equally enthusiastic:

> The excitement of the common folk in the entire village, once they heard that a Young Master had been born to His Excellency Li Chen-tang, was no less than that of the Japanese people upon hearing that a "little emperor" had been born to the Emperor. Each household made a contribution to cast a three *liang* weight gold lock and chain to give to me. The top side had four characters: Long life, riches, and honor.[7]

Born into material security, with a special servant mother to care for and protect him until he was age nine, the lad had few demands made upon him before he went off to school. His memories, like those of many others with yamen childhoods, are full of journeys of discovery among the many interior rooms and courtyards, with little contact beyond the walls: "The household itself formed a world, with inexhaustible treasures to dig up and never-ending new continents to explore."[8] Objects were matters of curiosity and delight, from the intricate embroidered designs on his clothing to the varieties of flowers all about him.

At the age of five, he entered a private tutorial school nearby to acquire a basic classical education. His servant mother took him there; and, while ritualistically turning him over to the teacher's control for "scolding and beating as necessary," she noted that Young Second Master was a "very good child, not corrupted, just a bit melancholy." She implored the teacher's wife to intervene on his behalf if necessary, for the lad had never been disciplined with the rod before. His expressive nature was not easily brought under control. By his own estimate, he developed into an unmanageable adolescent who would not submit to anyone—mother or teacher—if it did not please him. "The monkey in *Journey to The West* did not submit to the Jade Emperor, but submitted to Kuan Yin. In my case, no one at all could control me, except for that strict yet merciful older maternal uncle."[9]

This conservative maternal uncle was able to discipline him, but only with an exquisite, almost sadistic, blend of sternness and mercy. Once he was called before this uncle for having satirized an old-fashioned tutor whom young Li (who had just spent two years in a new-style primary school) felt was beneath contempt; the old tutor, Tutor Ku, threatened to resign.

I entered Eldest Uncle's study. He put down a volume of Ch'ing dynasty commentaries on the classics which he had in his hand, and looked at me for a while. He picked up the commentary once again and read it for a few minutes. Then he said, "Sit down." I sat down, but he still did not say anything, only watched me steadily. Slowly he started to speak. "Have you read the *Book of Rites?*"

"No."

"You must read it. In the *Book of Rites,* it says, 'If a parrot could speak, it would nevertheless still be a flying bird. If an ape could speak, it would nevertheless still be a walking beast.' " I understood why he wanted to see me, and he continued. "If a man possesses knowledge of propriety, he will be at peace. Without such knowledge he will be in danger, and for this reason it is said that the rule of propriety must be studied. Have you forgotten the *Analects?* 'The philosopher Yü said, there are few who being filial and fraternal are fond of offending against their superiors. There have been none who, not liking to offend against their superiors, have been fond of stirring up confusion.' Haven't you read the *Classic of Filial Piety?* 'He who loves his parents does not dare to do evil towards others. He who respects his parents does not dare to be rude to others.' If your mother knew what you have done, ai, she would hang herself!" Only then did I realize the seriousness of this affair. How could I be so cruel as to drive my

mother to hang herself? Tears filled my eyes and Eldest Uncle said "All right, go
now." [10]

This distraught boy of twelve was rescued by an aunt who had been
listening outside the door. She gently led him to her room where she
had prepared a bowl of fried noodles. The eating calmed him, but the
threats worked: "Because I feared my mother hanging herself, and wanted
to avoid another instruction session before Eldest Uncle, I did not dare
to commit any more improper actions toward Tutor Ku." [11]

Growing up in a nurturing setting and spared that cruel taskmaster
of material necessity, young Li and many others of his generation had
become accustomed to freedom and security, and asked much of life as
they came of age. Authority had to have more justification than the
appeal to tradition; physical beatings and authoritarian tactics served
only to incense them. After spending two years, from ages ten to twelve,
in a new-style primary school (1918–1920), young Li might have learned
to curb his expression of contempt for Tutor Ku, but he could no longer
assent inwardly to old-fashioned ideas and methods of instruction. In
that new school he had picked up some of the progressive ideas of the
May Fourth movement which Tutor Ku could not comprehend, let alone
accept: The tutor equated "freedom" with the denial of superiors *(wu-
chün)* and "equality" with the denial of fathers *(wu-fu)* and regarded the
combination as "beastly doctrines." As late as 1920, Tutor Ku still believed that the old examination system had to be revived to save China.
He was suspicious of this pupil who had picked up "evil habits" in a
"foreign-style school." [12] But Tutor Ku was confronting more than a
progressive student across a generation gap; for this young man and
thousands like him were the favored sons of the rising generation, and
they had been told and come to believe that they were chosen young
men of genius and destiny.

THE MYSTIQUE OF EDUCATION. Both those who studied by birthright,
as it were, and those from uneducated families who enlisted in the ranks
of students knew or quickly learned the psychology of qualification. The
young Shu Hsin-ch'eng, from the latter background, was made aware at
three years, eight months, that "students truly differ from common folk."
Inasmuch as this sense of difference was based upon learning, many a

child was driven to excel in order to partake of the distinction promised to him by the culture. One was "chosen"—almost in a religious sense—by his educational qualification. A student, after all, was a potential sage as well as an apprentice official, and the sage participated in the mysteries of heaven and earth. [13]

The beginning student was ceremoniously initiated into the life of learning. On his first day of school, Hsin-ch'eng's mother led him through a family ceremony of three kneelings and nine prostrations before the ancestral tablets, followed by a single prostration before the entire elder generation in succession: grandfather, grandmother, uncle, aunts, hired hand, father, mother. [14] In the room of a small Buddhist temple where classes were held, his grandfather led him in kneeling and prostrating himself before a large, red, overhead tablet with strange black characters on it. He did the same before the teacher, and ended with bows toward the other students and their accompanying adult. Then the entire class was led by the teacher in kneeling and kowtowing towards Confucius' commemorative tablet. Such ceremonies were typical for beginning students, rounds of ritual in a room filled with the fragrance of burning incense being calculated to mark a break between the life of play now ending and the serious life of study now beginning. [15] Equally important, these ceremonial practices imparted a sacred aura to the transmitters of classical learning and to that learning itself. Visits to a Wench'ang temple dedicated to the patron god of literature, who presided over the civil service examinations, imparted the same aura. Many even believed that written or printed words had magical power against evil spirits, and that the destruction of written characters was desecration. [16]

In Imperial China, where so much was at stake in the examinations, the examination itself came to be a focal point for anxieties and mythmaking. Considerable lore held that success in the examination was preordained by fate and heaven, and was not simply a measure of intelligence and knowledge. Unsuccessful candidates and their families, as Ch'en Tu-hsiu wryly commented, "would always grumble that the *feng-shui* ['wind-water'] location of their ancestors' graves was not auspicious, and dig up the bones of the corpse for reburial elsewhere." [17] Successful candidates, especially those for higher degrees, were commonly viewed as incarnations of the gods, and thought to possess magical charisma. In this argument, a scholar, having perfected himself through mastery of the ancient wisdom, mirrored in himself the harmony, order, and beauty of the transcendent order, and participated in the power of protecting these values in society. It was believed that successful scholars were men in whom the *shen* or good spirits had triumphed over the *kuei* or demonic spirits. The examinations "proved" that a candidate possessed such qualities, and his subsequent deeds confirmed that charisma. High officials could in this way become objects of a cult while still alive.[18] The names of successful local and provincial candidates were enshrined in a Confucian temple and known and revered by those young students who sought by studying to gain entrance into that most exclusive company.

These conceptions persisted in some places into the early years of the Republic and beyond. In the cultured city of Yangchow in 1918, when Young Master Li entered a new-style lower primary school, the study of mathematics, English, the natural sciences, and Chinese proceeded within the traditional symbolic framework. The school was established in the old city, northwest of the Wen-ch'ang pavillion, in the huge area surrounding the Confucian temple that served as grounds for a prefectural academy serving eight districts. At the center of the academy was the Hall of Great Accomplishment (Ta ch'eng tien), approached by three ascending terraces, each edged with white stone railings in the manner of the Hall of Great Harmony in Peking. The tablet of Confucius was placed behind an immense alter with ancient, bronze incense burners. Around it was arranged a hierarchy of tablets: the four disciples, followed by the seventy-two sages and other notable Confucians, including two early-Ch'ing scholars added by a Peking ministry after the Revolution of 1911. Behind the Hall of Great Accomplishment was a smaller hall with overhead tablets in red with gold characters. The center tablet listed all the highest degree winners *(chuang-yuan)* from Yangchow during the preceding dynasty; other tablets commemorated lesser degree winners, and successive fathers and sons or grandfathers and grandsons who had achieved fame.[19] It was a setting ideally designed to encourage a *"chuang-yuan* mentality" in the young students who lived and learned there, to make them aspire to that mystique that linked them with the undying sages and brought them fame in the eyes of their contemporaries and fellow kinsmen.

The *"chuang-yuan* mentality" was an explicit target of one of my interviewees in Taiwan. An academic psychologist, he viewed it as a poisonous part of the Chinese heritage, arguing that the profferred rewards in status and success were dangled in front of young boys, who like white rats went scurrying after them, learning obedience and respect in the process. The examination was the maze they had to master, turning their minds into memorization devices, and eliminating critical thought in favor of correct interpretation. They learned that obedience paid off, that book knowledge paid off, that conformity paid off; and the currency was status and success. "Always agree, agree, agree; never any initiative!" he said, slamming the table. He personally fought the continued use of the term *chuang-yuan* in Taiwan to identify the top scholars in examinations; the term was finally dropped in the mid 1960s.[20]

THE IMMUNITIES AND CONCEITS OF TALENT. While the physical space of an old Confucian temple could inspire and provide a symbolic framework for learning, the human environment, even in an illiterate village, could grant immunities to a precocious lad that further enlarged the scope of his self-assertion. A child who did exceptionally well in his studies, as young Shu Hsin-ch'eng did, soon acquired the appellation "prodigy" or *shen-t'ung* (lit. "good-spirit child"). The underlying belief was that an unusual spiritual force resided in him, and a *shen-t'ung* could for this reason become an object of awe and respect in the village. At age fourteen, Hsin-ch'eng was emboldened to write and post a long essay condemning the "despicable behavior" of a local deity. Although his horrified parents believed the claims made by a poor literatus that this image possessed divine powers and the boy's attack stirred up the entire town like a storm, no one dared dispute him directly. It was common in society then, he explained, "to believe that a *shen-t'ung* was the incarnation of a god. That I had the gall to act in this way meant that I must have other spirit powers supporting me secretly. Thus my parents did not even reprimand me seriously."[21] The privilege and license that was given spontaneously by villagers to young men of genius had in the past been translated through the examination system into institutionalized privileges, especially the freedom from corvée labor and from corporal punishment enjoyed by higher degree winners.

When a Young Master or a *shen-t'ung* outgrew his boyish airs and became more serious, he could easily evolve into a *ts'ai-tzu* or "young man of talent," keenly attuned to the scholarly fashions of the day. After the closing of the imperial examination route in 1905, a *ts'ai-tzu* aspired to acquire the New Learning; to develop a mode of life that fit the image of a modern student; to travel and study in the foreign-tinged coastal strip, especially Shanghai and Peking; and eventually to study abroad. This new image and sequence of qualifying steps became a means for measuring oneself and being measured when few had more than superficial understanding of the New Learning. Reaching the large coastal cities became an achievement in itself:

> It did not matter whether your studies in Shanghai were good or bad or what school you entered; when you returned home to your local place during winter and summer vacation, it would always draw out the admiration and envy of others.[22]

Completion of the sequence of steps, especially the culminating study abroad, was becoming an end in itself; and those who did not go the full way had to answer before an invisible tribunal of fashionable opinion. The distinction between returned students and those who had never left China was one of the lines of division in Republican China's intellectual circles and even in her political life. It became a personal sore point for those who never had the "qualifying" experience. Among professors, for example, it was assumed that all had been abroad. A common opening question was "What year did you return to China?" In a similar way, the scholars under the old system had asked "What year did you pass the examination?" It often took years before some could answer straightly, "I have never been abroad" without feeling somehow inferior in making that admission.[23] These inner insecurities sometimes found expression in the great importance and display attached to later trips abroad for research or travel. These trips seemed to be functional equivalents for those who never had the earlier "qualifying" experience.[24]

In the more advanced stages of this fetishism, vulnerable egos lived by minute calculations of status and fed on appearances instead of reality. One man reported the apocryphal story of the five status levels for editorial staff at the Commercial Press in Shanghai, where desk size, salary, and type of chair and other items were correlated with one's formal educational background, ranging from Chinese college, Japanese college, Japanese imperial university, Western college, to Harvard, Yale, Oxford, and Cambridge.[25] The craze for *étrangerie,* especially among young modern "men of letters" *(wen-jen),* has been catalogued elsewhere.[26] Many observers of the urban scene could see through the superficiality or "gilding" of some returned students and recognized a "false foreign devil" when they met one. But like the eponymous Ah Q in Lu Hsun's famous novella, they would often rail at the imposter while themselves being guilty of the same hypocrisy. There were few who could resist the temptation to recount their literary triumphs, to establish their credentials, to parade foreign words and models, to record in solemn detail all the places they visited abroad and the distinguished personages they encountered. Sometimes this boasting is even preceded by assertions of unworthiness, insignificance, and utter "commonness."[27] At best, one can say that the conceits of "young men of talent" reflected a class of people who took education and distinction for granted; at worst, they reflect a toying with language and are a sign of social myopia. One looks in vain for such pretensions to individual prominence among the peasants in Jan Myrdal's *Report from a Chinese Village* or among the Communist revolutionaries whose life stories Nym Wales recorded in *Red Dust.*

Such mannerisms held over from the traditional gentry and transmitted from one student generation to the next affected the tone of the youth movement until the War of Resistance against Japan (1937–1945). That war radically altered the life situation of students in China, and hence their consciousness. One participant, and observer, commented:

> The pre-1911 revolutionary youth pursued revolution but couldn't always avoid the boastful, paternalistic [*ching*] airs inherited from the old gentry. The [discussion of] patriotism by May Fourth youth and those talking about the New Culture and New Thought was like their discussion of love, i.e. it often couldn't avoid the Young Master–Young Miss airs of middle-class families. The youth of the Nationalist Revolution often pursued revolution with the romantic airs inherited from the intellectuals of the May Fourth period. But the spirit of the youth in the War of Resistance, for the most part, threw off these mannerisms. Their lives were hard and bitter, more like those of the common people. And for this

reason their consciousness was also relatively more simple and straightforward [*p'u-shih*], less frivolous and vain.[28]

The genesis of such mannerisms (what Mao Tse-tung might have called a gentry tail) lay in early class socialization in a dual society, even in its fractured twentieth-century form. The cluster of attitudes surrounding work and "respectability" provides significant clues to this early class education.

A PSYCHOLOGY OF "RESPECTABLE WORK"

Families of sufficient means protected their children from manual labor, except for girl children, who still learned to weave and sew and cook. Manual labor was essentially "coarse" work, and like rough games, it did not fit the refined sensibility that a scholar-official ought to possess. Freedom from corvée labor was one of the gentry's longstanding prerogatives, and their long gowns and curving fingernails contrasted sharply with the peasants' dress and stubby field-worn hands. The sharpness of these distinctions blurred considerably, however, as one moved down the status scale into the lower gentry, rich peasants, and small merchant families. There necessity tempered pretensions, as some examples illustrate.

Shen Tsung-han (b. 1895), one of six sons in a lower-gentry family, did work in the fields as a young boy, tending water buffalo, raising water for irrigation, pulling weeds, spreading night soil, harvesting rice, sunning the grain, and growing silkworms and chickens. This living experience carried over into his later agricultural schooling; and the formula "using both hands and brain" was a guideline through his years as a student and agricultural researcher.[29] Those from farming-studying families had brothers and other kinsmen whose livelihood was farming; even if they themselves were channeled upwards via school education, they were at least used to the smell of a dung heap and had had daily contact with animals, hired workers, and tools for a period of years. Others from peasant backgrounds began farm work at the age of five or six and continued to work despite schooling. When young Mao Tse-tung began studying at a local primary school, he still worked on the

farm in the early morning and at night because his father hated idleness
and extravagance of any kind. The elder Mao also pressed his son to
acquire practical knowledge. First this meant learning the abacus and
bookkeeping for the family rice-transport business; later it meant studying the classics, which could be used in winning lawsuits by out-quot-
ing adversaries.[30]

Wang Yun-wu (b. 1888), the son of a Cantonese merchant living in
Shanghai, had less than five years of formal study before he began a
regimen of half work, half study at age thirteen. He was apprenticed to
a merchant during the day and attended English school at night. His
father was not anxious for him to pursue the path of scholarship, for an
elder son had died suddenly at age twenty after obtaining a *hsiu-ts'ai*
degree. Being a follower of geomancy, the father was wary of the warning of one "overturned cart," and did not want to send another son
down the same path. Young Yun-wu, therefore, had to coordinate his
studies with a business apprenticeship, and learning English was one
way to make the one seem to promote the other. His father, however,
was wont to exercise his claim on the boy and, when he was sixteen,
asked him to stop his studies entirely to handle the foreign correspondence of the firm.[31]

School-bound youngsters (lower or upper class) quickly picked up "the
ways of the student," which included the upper-class prejudice against
manual labor. It did not seem to matter whether they attended an old-
style classical tutorial or a modern-style school. In one gentry family, a
twelve-year-old, precocious lad who came to fancy himself as a "favorite
son of heaven" *(t'ien chih chiao-tzu)* turned against an old tutor because
he cooked his own rice. "At that time I did not understand this at all,
and had imperceptibly fallen under the influence of the social prejudice
that treated manual labor with contempt, and I did not much respect
the tutor or take his teaching seriously. I constantly looked for pranks
to make it difficult."[32] In traditional schools for older students *(shu-*
yuan), it was common for the students, in groups, to help around the
school and to prepare and cook their own rice and vegetables. Sometimes
a group would hire a servant to cook their rice and prepare the vegetables, but the actual cooking of the dishes was done by the students. The
young Shu Hsin-ch'eng, being the greenest student and late to join such

a group, was prodded into "supervising" the servant and cooking for the others.

> Before this I had always eaten food prepared by others, and naturally did not know how to handle oil, salt, firewood, and grain . . . [T]his practical problem really gave me a lot of trouble. But as it had come to this, I did not lack self-confidence. First I asked the servant to be my instructor; and then, through my own mental effort and the method of trial and error, I actually was able to season the food myself and received the acclaim of my fellow students.[33]

Cooking was an esteemed art among the educated; furthermore such work was shared within the privacy of the academy walls and did not extend beyond the gates. It still would have been unthinkable for a young apprentice official to carry his own baggage from home to school.

The modern schools that were set up, in some cases, seem to have intensified rather than arrested this expectation of being served. It is difficult, however, to have confidence in generalizing about the modern school system, for it included many different types of schools—private, governmental, and foreign (usually Christian missionary)—with a great variety of approaches and personalities. To the extent that the sons of the poor were squeezed out by the fee system, more obvious play was given to the vanity of children of means, who as mentioned earlier, had few internalized restraints against the display of their status and wealth. This also intensified the psychological burden on those poor boys who did become students. Young Shu Hsin-ch'eng, after leaving the old-style *shu-yuan* to enter a new upper primary school, was struck by the "Young Master scale of the living arrangements" *(shao-yeh ti pai-tou).*

> I knew that the sons in official families were called Young Masters, and Young Masters were such that anything requiring physical labor had to be done by some-one else. As the school gave us country kids Young Master treatment, too, the servants were especially plentiful. Besides the various workers in the porter's lodge, the registry office, and the kitchen, every two reading rooms and dormitory bed-rooms had a special attendant. In everything to do with drinking, eating, and daily needs, one did not have to move oneself—not even for an extra bowl of rice—because it was all done by them for us.[34]

There were moments when the "country kids" felt ill at ease in this company because of their coarse clothes, their provincial speech, their rough hands, their pasts, and their families. But as a minority, they could not contest the prevailing mores without being isolated, shamed, and perhaps even ridiculed. Not only in visible behavior but also in inner feelings, they were apologetic and accepted the standards of their "betters" who were somehow "cleaner" and more respectable and deserving. The eyes of contempt, real and imagined, drove them to conform, as is seen in this reflection by Mao Tse-tung:

> [A]t school I acquired the ways of a student. I then used to feel it undignified to do even a little manual labor, such as carrying my own luggage *in the presence of my fellow students,* who were incapable of carrying anything, either on their shoulders or in their hands. At that time I felt that intellectuals were the only clean people in the world, while in comparison workers and peasants were dirty. I did not mind wearing the clothes of other intellectuals, believing them clean, but I would not put on clothes belonging to a worker or peasant, believing them dirty . . . their hands were soiled and their feet smeared with cow-dung.[35]

Another boy named Third Son, fatherless, poor, and living at his well-to-do maternal grandmother's estate, anxiously contemplated a future that was not likely to include the ways of a student, but rather to make him into the peasant farmer or the businessman that he did not want to be. He respected the peasant laborer, but doubted his personal ability to go barefoot in winter and work without rest in summer. He doubted he could bear carrying out the night soil in March and April, with not only his clothes but also his face and nose smeared with filth. But his greatest fear was something else: When he was older and his elder brother and his cousins had gone off to the city to study, would he be able to bear his shame when he had to accompany their sedan chair to send them off at the station?[36] If it came down to it, he would prefer the life of a businessman, based on his comparison of the life of a neighboring herbalist with that of the hired laborers on his grandmother's estate. Though poor, the herbalist wore shoes and sat in his shop, smoked his water pipe, read some, conversed with friends, and was invited to all the social affairs in the village. Although this lacked the majesty of wearing glasses and foreign suits and carrying a walking stick as the apprentice officials did, the herbalist at least never had to roll up his pants.[37]

Third Son's tale is an autobiography told in the third person. This detached perspective, which avoids the problem of shame and appearing too confessional, allows for more detailed and honest commentary on his reaction to class prejudice, as in this passage: "[B]eing demeaned by others was the most painful thing for Third Son's soul. He was willing to bear hardships secretly, but did not want to suffer ridicule from others. The desire for glory and wealth is probably highly developed in rather unintelligent, poor children. Because of his poverty and sense of inferiority, he always wants to break out and reveal a bit of his own strength and worth."[38]

SCHOLARSHIP AND POLITICAL OFFICE: THE BROKEN LINK

If little or none of the energy of the upper-gentry sons had traditionally gone into physical labor, it had gone into book learning, but book learning of certain kinds and with certain motives. The basic learning was a long immersion in the history, philosophy, and literature of China, with *tso jen* and the goal of moral living—bringing the outer world into harmony with the discriminating moral mind—as the primary content. The teachings of the sages had charted the pressures and snares of the outer world, just as they had transmitted through the classics proper ways of acting that kept alive the hope of withstanding temptations and even transforming that outer world. What lay beyond this basic learning was a career in public service for those who passed the state examinations.

For the generation of the 1890s, the base remained more or less intact; the classical corpus, or at least its emphasis upon the moral life, was taught in private tutorials well beyond the changeover from the examination system to a school system. The passage into public office became complicated, however, when the link between classical scholarship and office was snapped by the abolition of the examination system in 1905. The scholar-official as a type of leader was gone; classical learning and politics separated. Scholarship developed freely beyond the classical corpus, taking in the natural and social sciences, foreign languages, and the comparative historical, literary, artistic, and cultural experiences of non-Chinese societies. Those of scholarly bent from this generation eventually split into two groups: a dominant one oriented toward work and research within the framework of modern professions, and a minority that felt itself to be living and transmitting the values of the Chinese cultural tradition. An important part of this minority of scholars gathered in Hong Kong after 1949, with New Asia College (now part of the Chinese University of Hong Kong) as their center. The college was started in the early 1950s by a group of expatriate scholars, including the historians and philosophers Ch'ien Mu (b. 1895), Mou Tsung-san (b. 1909), and T'ang Chün-i (b. 1909).

These "New Confucian" scholars, or humanists as they have also been called, have sought to establish the continuing validity of the Neo-Confucian vision of humans as moral beings, capable of perfecting themselves through self-cultivation and of transforming the outer world.[39] The twentieth century has been bruising to their faith. They themselves have had to depart from tradition, rejecting the institutional Confucianism of Imperial China in order to define an essential "spirit" serviceable for the future. Yet theirs is a critically developed body of thought, drawing on Western as well as Chinese sources, and finding room within its vision for the ideals of science and democracy. It is a reconstructed synthesis of the combined ideals of moral education and public commitment, grounded in a traditional Neo-Confucian understanding of the cosmos. Although professional academics themselves, they have asked for a wider consciousness and identity than that of "mere" scientists or professionals.[40] The very birth of this trend in Chinese conservatism in the 1920s was a reaction to the "scientism" of the May Fourth period; these tradition-minded scholars were not about to allow the deepest meanings of their personal lives and work to be diminished by positivist assumptions.[41] In creating a new synthesis, as Thomas Metzger comments, they may have succeeded in demonstrating that "the essential ideals of the Confucian tradition are as noble, as pertinent to the modern world, and as epistemologically defensible as those of any other tradition."[42] Perhaps in Taiwan they are helping reconnect the broken link between humanistic scholarship and politics.

Politics, following the collapse of the Ch'ing dynasty in 1911, involved an unstable interplay of forces that excluded any orderly selection of "qualified talent," in the old sense of scholar-officials who commanded a deferential respect from the various groups in society. Politics had become an arena for rising social groups competing through factions that were usually armed and sometimes imbued with new political ideas.

Those who had been thoroughly brought up on the old conceptions were generally unable to make the transition to the era of militarists, party cadre, and revolutionary soldiers. Some among the older generation of traditionalists had not even been able to make the transition into the Republic. Their concept of loyalty bound them to the preceding dynasty, and they conscientiously refused to serve as officials in the Republic.[43] One respected classical scholar and royalist, Wang Kuo-wei (1877–1927), retreated to Japan for five years after 1911. He continued to pay homage to the last Ch'ing emperor P'u-yi, and in 1923–1924, worked as a tutor on P'u-yi's staff in Peking until the royal family was expelled from the Imperial Palace and had to take refuge in the Japanese embassy compound. In June 1927, when the National Revolutionary Army under Chiang K'ai-shek was poised for a final advance into North China, Wang quietly drowned himself in Kunming lake on the grounds of the former imperial Summer Palace. The testimonial he left behind read in part: "Now at the age of fifty all I owe to myself is death. Having passed through so many political upheavals, as a matter of principle I see no reason why I should be humiliated once again."[44]

The proper Confucian "political" attitude was one of receptivity to a call to service, not a hankering after position and profit. One did not run or compete for office; one stood, and was proud if he never had to make a campaign speech. An old gentleman in Taiwan in 1969, though admitting he was close to the political leadership there, indicated he would never be willing to seek or accept a real official post beyond that of advisor or representative on some commission. Asked why, he said he was "not quite cut off from the old civilization." As a young man, he had been trained to take upon himself the disinterested responsibility of the state and now would feel ashamed to compete for office. The word *competition* itself had overtones of selfishness and superior airs.[45] Even some younger people who grew up amid hybrid cultural patterns developed strong reservations about the modern politics of parties. Despite the prestige attached to official service, contemporary politics was viewed with contempt as the art of the immoral, the corrupt, the cunning, and the expedient. Political parties, whether parliamentary or revolutionary, few or many, seemed to be only self-seeking factions. One academic administrator in Taiwan openly voiced his distrust of parliamentary democracy and the concept of the will of the majority. The majority, he felt, was largely foolish in its judgments and desires. Representation was an illusion; for, as he concluded from personal observation of the 1968 American elections, big money, gangsters, and power blocks decided things.[46]

Though the old trajectory into political office from a base in scholarship was no longer obligatory, its shadowy path lingered on well into the early Republican period. When one interviewee, as a lad in middle school, for example, was presented with a choice of a *wen* course of study or a *li** course—roughly the difference between liberal arts and sciences—his tradition-minded father urged the *wen* course, as it was the old channel into political office and all that this promised.[47] Sometimes a pattern of study that on the surface seems an unusual mixture to an outsider becomes intelligible in terms of the classical curriculum and the traditional path from classical learning into political service. For example, one woman in her student days in China took two baccalaureate degrees, one in Chinese literature, writing an extended paper on "The Thought of Pre-Ch'in China," another in the English department in preparation for going abroad. In the United States she studied English literature, writing a master's thesis on "The Beginning of Chinese Studies in the Western World," and then switched to take up political science. Asked how this sequence fit together, she reflected that Chinese *wen* (literary) studies combined literature, philosophy, and politics, and that the training of officials had long demanded broad reading in the liberal arts. In this tradition, her early interest in literature was never simply "literature for its own sake," but took in philosophy and history and the goal of purposeful service. She capped this "orthodox" education by becoming a legislator.[48]

The mushrooming of "academies of law and politics" (*fa-cheng hsueh-t'ang*) in the early Republican period embodied the need for a new link between learning and office-holding in a modern constitutional system, however imperfectly understood. There is some evidence, however, that the real importance of these schools was not in acquiring substantive knowledge but rather in bagging a qualifying diploma. Shu Hsin-ch'eng, who graduated from such a school, cited the superficiality of knowing a few legal terms.[49] Mao Tse-tung commented on the alluring pitch of a law school in Changsha: "It promised to teach students all about law in three years and guaranteed that at the end of this period they would instantly become mandarins . . . I wrote to my parents . . . I painted a bright picture for them of my future as a jurist and mandarin."[50] Was this an open prostitution of scholarship to politics, using shoddy learning for access to political office? Was "the phantom republic" creating its own counterfeit sanctions? Many sons of the literati in fact came to regard the split between scholarship and politics as irrevocable, and sought nonpolitical careers in which they could preserve some of the literati flavor, using their pens and their minds as editors, essayists, writers, and university teachers in the large cities.

The War of Resistance against Japan, however, just as it radically altered the life situation of students, altered the world of their elders, drawing many of those who had followed nonpolitical careers into the vortex of political events. A scion of an old scholar-official family from South China, for example, spent much of his youth and young adulthood abroad in America and England. Upon returning to China, he taught Western literature at several universities, until he was "called" in 1940 to work in the Ministry of Information for the Nationalist Government. For over fifteen years after the war, he remained active in government service in the Ministry of Foreign Affairs. In retrospect, with echoes of the ambivalence of Ch'ü Ch'iu-pai, who had never felt cut out to be a Communist revolutionary, this man thought the war had deflected his life. He had never particularly enjoyed government service and would have preferred to continue his original loves of teaching and writing.[51]

CLASS BLINDERS AND AWARENESS

All of us acquire a sensitivity to our surroundings that allows us to see and comprehend only parts of it. Certain experiences, people, and possibilities are present to mind and visible, others remote, invisible, unimaginable. That some members of this Chinese generation had class blinders was often painfully obvious: One with a view from "on top," for example, might apologize that for two hundred years there had been no *chin-shih* degree winners in the family; or have agonized over whether to become a lawyer, doctor, or professor; or have preferred fruit to rice for dinner as a child; or have found the experience of wartime inflation "rare and exciting" because money was measured by the wheelbarrow-ful.[52] It was possible for people to live on in enclosed worlds, hardly aware of the dramas being played out around them. Some did discover that they were wearing blinders, but often painfully and too late, when the only profit to them was insight and understanding.

Chou Yentung (Chou Yen-t'ung, b. 1886), born into a gentry family in Szechwan, slowly became aware of how his life had been skewed by class learning. Under the catalyst of criticism directed at intellectuals and scientists after the founding of the People's Republic of China, he wrote some autobiographical memoirs. Two were official reports of six to eight pages, required by the regime in the early 1950s as a kind of security measure; they were essentially catalogues of events in his life, checked and counter-checked by the government. He also composed an unofficial autobiography—"detailed, personal, and incomplete"—which was written for his own eyes and only accidentally unearthed and pieced together by his daughter, Han Suyin, after he died in 1958. This frag-mentary autobiography is a rare document of an old man's personal struggle to understand his past life, rare because written inside the People's Re-public of China and available by 1965 to others outside China.[53]

These autobiographical fragments are suffused with the tone of la-ment: lament for the narrowness of his social vision; lament for the limitations of the person that he became; lament for the blind spots in his understanding of politics, history, and ethics. Under the harsh judg-ment of personal failure, he relives his life and dwells on his flawed perceptions. He blames his self-enclosed childhood for the failure of his marriage to a Belgian woman.

> Because of childhood happiness I wronged my wife, for when I met her and told her of China, it was of this China, the China seen on Delft porcelain, a China of palaces and bridges, of satins and gardens, of mountains and rivers wildly beautiful, of obedient servants and benevolent kinsmen, which I described to her. I was only describing my prosperous, secure family. I thought it China . . . I forgot, or perhaps I never knew well until today, my country, the tumul-tuous, angry, and starving land, where millions died of famine, where blood

flowed so readily, where there had been revolt every year for nearly a hundred years, where Revolution was building its hurricanes, and where her people, my wife's people, the Whites, had come to fulfill their rapacity, their greed for possession of lands not theirs, their wealth built upon our disastrous misery.

I wronged her by not telling her any of this; my only excuse is that I did not know it myself, or rather I never thought of it. I was of my class, the gentry, and childhood betrayed me.[54]

In his last years he saw the people and things that he had not seen in earlier years; he knew the words that would have named other realities around him had he but learned them; and he lived with the alternative selves and lives that had been hidden by that first world of childhood. Language, early family learning, his class situation, the evolving bent of his personality were all there subtly interwoven to make him into the particular person he became. But he could not accept that person; ghostly memories of the past would not go away.

One unerasable memory centered on his boyhood friend, Liu Tachun (Liu T'a-ch'un), like Chou a son of the gentry, but unlike Chou a "patrician rebel" against his background. In the spring and summer of 1898, on the eve of the Reform Movement, Yentung, a lad of thirteen, and Tachun, fifteen, were "tasting the spring" as young scholars preparing for the district examination were wont to do. The bursting natural world they saw and felt around them was imprisoned in poetic images and well-turned phrases of the past, as if "at thirteen my song of life was written for me out of the massive accumulation of past sayings." Chou could see that his younger self had accepted the endless toil of the pale, stubby field workers as "part of the landscape, almost its due, at least due to us, as we lounged about, looking for a felicitous phrase." He remembered the skeletal, opium-addicted chair bearers who carried them into the hills and contrasts their wretched dependence on the drug for strength to the occasional enjoyment of it indulged in by the gentry. And he recalled a different air about his friend. "Tachun became at times moody, looking around him, but my eyes were not his, and I never knew whether he saw it then, as in my memory's eye I see it now."[55]

Chou was then a squeamish, studious, delicate young scholar, lacking the curiosity and courage that induced his friend Tachun to face up to the hidden, dreadful rumors of insurrection and revolution that filled the teahouses and the streets. Or so it looked in retrospect to an old man fifty-seven years later.

> As we walked among the flowers and heard the muttered phrases, I sometimes smelt blood and was seized with fear, for I dreaded bloodshed, and desired lofty visions in men, brought by natural virtue and wise concord, thinking them possible by moderation and virtue alone. I knew not then that men are both noble and vile, that nothing is begot but through pain and action . . . I saw the beauty of the plain, but not its heart-searing toil; joyed in the speckle and glint of water, and knew not each furrow turned in its life-giving mud fertilized not only with water and manure, but also with the blood of man . . . But not so my friend. As the spring deepened I saw a shadow over his piercing eyes, his smooth forehead darkened. He read much, many books of the New Learning, forbidden but which he somehow procured. He would speak of machines and inventions, and I begged him to be careful.[56]

Later that summer, after the conservative *putsch* ended the brief spring of reform, Tachun left Szechwan for Canton to join the Revive China Society of the arch-renegade Sun Yat-sen. He took part in armed uprisings in 1906 and 1907 and was captured. "Dressed as a peasant, he refused to recant, insulted the magistrate, and was beheaded." He was an only son, and a branch of a great family became extinct with him; yet in the remembered emotions of an old man, the presence and vision of this childhood friend in those short days of decision shone brightly against his own tarnished self-image. And the doubts could not be stilled: "Perhaps I should have gone with him . . . but I was not a revolutionist, I would never be a pioneer of any kind."[57]

A QUESTION OF PERSPECTIVE

A tone of self-recrimination haunts the reflections of many older men whose lives spanned this era of vast change in China. Chou Yentung wished he had been a revolutionary in 1898, criticizing those like him who "had so much but gave so little." But what did it mean "having much," when this very abundance entrapped one in certain living patterns and ways of thinking only to expose one later to self-recriminations for having failed to go in the right direction? The record of modern Chinese history, within the Communist movement as well as the Kuomintang and the "third force," is strewn with the wreckage of men and ideas, for the "right direction" was not apparent within the confining perspective of the present. Any retrospective effort to understand—whether by an actor or by an historian—contains within it, explicitly or implicitly, a certain evaluative stance. An actor's stance is likely to remain caught in the partisan perspectives of the period of history through which he lived, took sides, and apportioned blame to self and others for things done and not done. One aging expatriate, living comfortably but bitterly in Hong Kong after 1949, talked with me about his contemporaries. Integrity, radicalness, and dedication were the criteria he used to judge them. *Were they men of conscience?* Did they make money heartlessly; collaborate with the Japanese; think only of themselves and their families; compromise their liberal principles after the split between the Chinese Communist Party and the Kuomintang in 1927 by sticking with a corrupt, authoritarian regime? *Did the quality of their thought correspond to the nature of the times?* Did they understand Marxism, or were they mired in reactionary or traditional ideas? Was their response to China's desperate situation a "normal" one, namely a sense of injured pride, anger, and a concern for China's respect and parity with the other major nations of the world? *Were they activists dedicated to the pursuit of their professed ideals?* Did they drag their feet in following through on what they said they believed in? Were they "secret radicals," combining progressive ideas with conservative behavior?

In his mid sixties, when I visited him in Hong Kong in 1969, this man was going through a reevaluation of this span of modern Chinese history and his own place in it. And his self-evaluation was harsh, despite the obvious desire to interpret his own life favorably in the light of his construct of the ideal historical actor. Closest to his ideal were members of the Chinese Communist Party and a few others outside it who had been activist men of conscience with a political analysis that fit China's situation. "If I were back in the 1920s now, I would join the Communist Party." But he never did, then or later. He remained, in his own eyes, a "true liberal," working with some of the "third force" people after 1927 until a short imprisonment by a local "warlord for the

Kuomintang" completed his progression into inaction and finally silence. Had he done enough? No, he said he was a man of conscience,
but not an activist. Even now he was dragging his feet, unable to give
up his present way of life, although the whole thrust of his reevaluation
led him back to the People's Republic. In the early years of their rule,
the Communists had asked him to return; and there were radical acts in
his past of which he felt they must approve. But observing China in
1967 and 1968 in the midst of the Great Proletarian Cultural Revolution had made him terribly unsure and afraid. What did it mean? Where
was it leading? How could hardened Communists be overthrown and
repudiated? Would the Red Guards kill a person such as himself? Were
his chances of being accepted back getting worse and worse? With nar-
rowing eyes, he looked out the window of his high rise apartment in
Kowloon towards the range of hills that separate this alienated peninsula
from the rest of China. "I must wait a few years to let the dust settle." [58]
He died a few years later in Hong Kong.

   In a brief encounter between such unequals as a young foreign observer and a scarred veteran participant, there is much unsaid, much
unasked. Was he a prisoner of his past—the bookish influence of his
scholar father; the classical learning etched in his memory; his wealthy,
landowning-family background; the path from private schools in China
to study abroad; and finally work in that "modernized" but peripheral
group, the Chinese diplomatic corps? Could he detach himself from the
terrible dilemmas he had faced and still faced? Could he transcend self-
recrimination and scapegoating, and look with more forgiving, understanding eyes upon this awesome spectacle of modern revolution? Such
questions could be asked of him and of thousands of educated gentry
sons like him who suffered perplexity, confusion, and guilt; the world
they had known and the future they had expected had been altered beyond all expectation and recognition, invalidating the privileged roles
for which they had been prepared. The larger meaning of the questions,
however, lies in redefining our sense of the predicament they faced, which
was not simply personal but historical. A profound understanding of
history, as Herbert Butterfield has argued, cannot be based on events as
recollected by participants, for contemporary formulations of human
conflict have the structure of melodrama (unless, as Butterfield also notes,

they are written "after great prayer and fasting"). As we become less partisan, more able to comprehend the motives and reasoning of actors who were not like-minded with ourselves, the actual structure of the narrative and the formulation of the issues changes.

> Behind the great conflicts of mankind is a terrible human predicament which lies at the heart of the story . . . Contemporaries fail to see the predicament or refuse to recognize its genuineness, so that our knowledge of it comes from later analysis—it is only with the progress of historical science on a particular subject that men come really to recognize that there was a terrible knot almost beyond the ingenuity of men to untie.[59]

China coming into the twentieth century was caught in such a knot. Some who were young then knew at least that they faced unprecedented challenges and demands for ingenuity in seeking a Way Out of the national dilemma. And the past, if it offered no clear program for the future, did provide a legacy of supportive beliefs in a human nature that was essentially good and educable and a view that individual life was purposeful in the larger scheme of things. These beliefs made their twentieth-century search, in part at least, a moral exploration for a more inclusive community with more fulfilling lives than the dual-structured, beleaguered society of late Imperial times made possible.

PART FOUR
Seeking a Way Out

The Cornell Club, 1913. Hu Shih is seated on the floor at the right. Photograph from the Chinese Students' Monthly (1912–1913).

SEVEN

The Undertow

"The grip of custom has been too tenacious upon us," said K. T. May (Mei Kuang-ti), a twenty-five-year-old Harvard graduate student, writing in English for the *Chinese Students' Monthly* in 1916. "And to shake it off requires an explosion of volcanic force and brilliancy." [1] So the turmoil and excitement of the present age was unavoidable, even necessary. But May feared that moderation would be lost sight of: "We are liable to oscillate from the extreme of servile imitation of the past to the extreme of iconoclasm." He counseled against the "modern warrior" who indiscriminately tears down not only the institutions but also the museums and libraries of his foe:

> It was perfectly right to abrogate the Literary Examination System, but along with this we have nearly murdered our language itself; the high school boy who is able to use it well is indeed a prodigy . . . Official Confucianism and superstitious Buddhism must be left to while away the idle hours of the historical researcher, but is it sane to insist that the genuine Confucianism and Buddhism that constitute all that is good, true, and beautiful in our national life should go? Nor does the age of science and rationalism, which tolerates medieval humbugs such as astrology and witchcraft, need wage war upon those national myths and beliefs which have inspired some of our best art and literature and which long sustained our yearnings and imagination for the infinite and eternal.

The supreme task of this generation he proclaimed, was "to find a way out of this unprecedented national crisis . . . to readjust the existing and rising conditions in such a manner as to harvest the best fruits of both the old and the new through a process of harmonization." And he concluded that "neither the stand-patter nor the Jacobin is a safe person to be trusted with the destiny of our nation."[2]

The grip of custom, the energy required for release, the necessity of moving beyond tradition, the difficulty of determining which road to travel in an unprecedented historical situation, the intense commitment to the nation—all these themes were part of the predicament that young Chinese found themselves in as they pondered China's fate from abroad in the pages of the *Chinese Students' Monthly* over the years 1909 to 1921.[3] The writings in the *Monthly* mirror, and sometimes lag behind or anticipate, the changing configuration of attitudes and concerns within China itself. But as a collective voice of some thoughtful members of the now maturing 1890s generation, the *Monthly* also spoke with undertones, confirmed by individual voices elsewhere in memoirs. One can detect the ambivalence of liberation, the weariness of being forced marchers in new territory, the struggle to come up from under in a world that labeled races and countries as inferior and unfit. One overhears what it was like being caught up in the immensity of social and political turmoil, like a drop in the floodtide, or a rider on the waves, or one lapped by the tides from the West.[4] One listens to the collective voice tell of the search for a Way Out *(ch'u-lu)*, which meant then and still means having a sense of direction and hope for the future.[5] The way to become fully human *(tso jen)* had to be discovered in a world that had few familiar mooring points, and a strong, unfamiliar undertow.

The fastening of an alien, hybrid civilization onto the body of China and the ambivalent reactions among Chinese that this process engendered formed a large part of this concrete historical situation that those born in the 1890s came to face. The post-1895 opening towards the values and institutions of this new world, in the spirit of defensive nationalism, had certain consequences for the young people who were to become the educated youth of the early twentieth century. It meant above all that they would live through a disjointed sequence of settings: childhood in a relatively traditional family context, a middle school encounter with the New Learning in a provincial capital or in the modernizing coastal strip, and occasionally a direct experience abroad in Japan, Russia, or the West as a young adult. This was the last generation to memorize the Confucian classics in the traditional private tutorial schools *(ssu-shu)* and the first to be exposed as a group to the foreign-tinged New Learning, initially in hybrid institutions and then in the post-1905 school system. The major break occurred between childhood and the middle-school experience, when a sharp contrast between old and new, Chinese and foreign, tradition and progress, became an inescapable perception.[6]

A first casualty of this discontinuity was the end of a sense of life as repetitive, familiar, predictable within the rounds of the cycles of human life and the imperial dynasty. A thirteen-year-old boy growing up in the interior province of Szechwan in 1898 still knew the past as a dense inheritance of words and concepts. This inherited web of meanings was so pervasive that it seemed to anticipate his discoveries, describe his sensations, and almost rob him of a fresh, spontaneous encounter with the life around him.

> Four-square and moated city, gates older than Peking and a history of three thousand years, Chengtu basked and dawdled in the plain. In and around her the epic feats of the Three Kingdoms had been enacted, and we knew them all . . . All legend was history as history became legend about her. Along her river and about her plain and far beyond, her fortresses and tumuli, temples and shrines, her trees over a thousand years old, were witness of battles fought, phrases said, stratagems of war and politics; all was in place, known, written, and recorded.[7]

Present experience, in personal and public life, resonated with centuries-old themes. Between 1840 and 1880 the barbarian managers of the Ch'ing dynasty had themselves fit the Western intrusion into tested traditional categories. The assumption of superiority, the confidence in the art of statecraft, the belief in an ethical order of priorities all found corroboration in events within what seemed to later observers to have been an unprecedented historical circumstance.[8] Words from the past served to cover up unpalatable new truths with time-tested old ones. Given substance by inscriptions and historical illustrations, these words were also the first line of defense for elders frightened by the changes forcing their way into Chinese gentry life in the late nineteenth century.

> As long as we were mindful of the maxims inscribed in all their gold upon the large lacquer boards, we would be safe, safe from time and from change. Thus the elders asserted, and spoke largely of virtue and tradition.

> At times the real was the calligraphy, and not what really happened; the
> maxims on the wall were alive, not the revolts and the humiliations, the defeats
> and the hatred. There was always escape.[9]

By the turn of the century there was no more escape. The consciousness of cumulative threats to the life of an endangered nation came to
frame the era. "I was born in the fall of 1892," wrote one young man.
"That was two years before the Sino-Japanese War, seven years before
the Reform Movement of 1898, nine years before the Boxer Expedition-
ary Force entered Peking. It is unnecessary to say that my boyhood was
the darkest time for the old, great Chinese nation (*ta chung-hua lao ta
kuo-chia*)." [10]

The usable wisdom from the past had been called into question. The
insights into reality from elders and teachers, of course, never had been
monolithic, for lived experience and the cultural tradition had always
been filled with tensions and contradictions. But reality fragmented further when the break between family and new-style school occurred and
the genie of the New Learning was set free in young minds. In the peer-
group environment of the post-1905 schools—often now under the direction of nationalistic-minded teachers and administrators—young Chiense
became conscious of possibilities that before had been suppressed within
the small system of the family or hidden by the self-evident splendor
and reason of Old China. Far from being the world, China was now a
fragment of the world: the universal became the provincial, the natural
became the peculiar. Time-ordained values became obsolescent, even
harmful and obstructive; the possibilities for new self-discoveries and
larger identifications multiplied. A backward-looking China was vulnerable and transparent to a new generation of cultural critics.

THE AMBIVALENT LIBERATION

The encounter with Western ideas was a complicating, often crippling
experience. While it liberated one out of the confines, however broad,
of a single cultural standard, it initiated one into a state of confusion
and uncertainty. The encounter thus demanded a second liberation perhaps more decisive than the first, namely the release from confusion into
a higher integration or synthesis. The initial step beyond tradition had

become a condition of life, not contingent upon individual will and choice; it was partly this experience of broken connections, imposed on their inner lives, that sets this generation of educated Chinese apart from earlier ones. The second liberation was more decisive precisely because it could not be assumed, and indeed was even rare; for it depended upon a conscious personal integration of a fragmenting experience of the world. The cleavage between the past, with all its associations with childhood, tradition, parents, and village life, and a whirling revolutionary present was something that each had to attempt to bridge. Two ways of life, two styles of thought appeared to stand poised in contrast to each other, as separate as that non-China of the treaty-port fringe world seemed when viewed from the vast Chinese hinterland.

The initial images of the West encountered by this generation were often ambiguous, made up of jarring, contradictory evidence. Young Chou Yentung knew both the liberation of reading Huxley's *Evolution and Ethics* and the shock of seeing evolutionary theories condemned by a Christian fundamentalist. He felt excitement in discovering insights from outside his known world and horror at observing the behavior of Westerners in China. Chou wrote this about his first serious encounter with the New Learning in 1900 at age fifteen:

> I began mathematics, borrowed what I could find to read on world history, acquired two books on physics and on biology. I became enchanted with Western Science, the sublimity of its logic. I do not think it extravagant to call it enchantment . . . The discovery that the Universe was regimented by laws mathematically proven, that all phenomena, regarded as mysterious and transcendental, were predictable, within range of man's reason, exhilarated me. Here was, at last, what I was looking for. What tremendous power lay in Man! Verily Man could be Master of his earth, would he but recreate his earth in wisdom and nobility . . . I felt the discoverer of a new universe. As when a star explodes, comets swing into the sky and set it afire, innumerable questions now came to me, to be answered by the New Learning. I discovered a virtue which our classics had not emphasized, the spirit of curiosity, of independent inquiry. So that was what the West meant by freedom! For it was in Europe that the spirit of speculation had found itself most free. There man had boldly questioned all things, even his own body, and his own convictions, even at the risk of disrupting the universe and killing himself. No moral code, no ethics, stood in the way of this outrageous passion to know . . . In euphoric mood I read the first Chinese translation of Huxley's *Ethics and Evolution* . . . After reading that, I could not sleep for some

nights. It was the most wonderful book I had ever read, questioning Man himself.
I was overwhelmed.[11]

The intensity of this reaction expresses the Copernican nature of the
discovery. An older set of questions and answers, framed within the
bounds of one culture, is jolted by a new set of questions from outside
the culture. It was an experience at once liberating and disorienting,
particularly when accompanied with insight into the diversity and flux
of questions and answers within Europe itself and the impossibility of
reducing Western thought to a packet of "science" or "religion." Chou
confided to his brother as he prepared to leave for France in 1903, having recently journeyed from Chengtu to Shanghai:

> I feel more frightened than when I was crossing the rapids [on the Yangtze].
> Then, I knew my life was in danger; now, it is my mind which seems to hover
> above a dizzying precipice. I no longer know what to believe, and I even doubt
> the categories: hard and soft, liquid and solid, everything is topsy-turvy . . .
> where is the essence of the West, and how shall I ever understand it?[12]

The individual mind could eventually make sense out of these shock
experiences, especially if they were spaced out over time; but it was
difficult for young people to avoid a sense of growing incongruity between themselves and much of the surrounding society. New-style learning began to mean cleavages within schools and families, but the deepest
divisions and contradictions were inner. The ideal world they proposed
for themselves as progressive Chinese students was often a reverse image
of that past world embedded in them as well as in their elders. They
came as young people to question, even condemn and reject, parts of
their culture within themselves. The educational odyssey of young Chiang
Monlin (b. 1886) reveals this growing sense of incongruity within schools,
families, and self, and the means by which the mind sought to cope
with a fragmenting world.

Chiang Monlin's father, a small landowner with an entrepreneurial
spirit, was favorably disposed toward Western education; and after some
years in a traditional Confucian family school, young Chiang began to
attend a string of the hybrid institutions that were already appearing in
the 1890s. The first was a Sino-Western Academy in the nearby city of
Shaohsing, Chekiang, which taught elementary science, English, French,

and Japanese in addition to the required Chinese curriculum for the civil service examinations. Imported Western material goods like clocks, watches, kerosene, and soap were already taken for granted in his native Yu-yao, a district capital in Chekiang; but this was his first encounter with Western "mental imports." A succession of schools followed after 1898: a French Catholic school in Shanghai until the Boxer Uprising, a local school in his home town, and then an American missionary school in Hangchow. Despite two missionary schools, his mind was "closed tight as a clam against any spiritual foreign elements"; he remained an agnostic for life, conforming he felt with the basic teachings of Confucius. A student strike broke out at the Hangchow school, however, as the "new literati" composed of the student body and some faculty squared off against the "old literati" represented by the school authorities. The students left the academy en masse and organized a new short-lived School of Reforms and Progress in its place. Seen in retrospect from the 1940s, Chiang felt, these student strikes in Hangchow and Shanghai in 1902 marked the coming of age of the new intelligentsia.[13]

At sixteen, however, Chiang himself remained on a dual track. Although the school that he attended next, Chekiang College, was no longer called a *shu-yuan* or academy, it offered the old-style examination preparation alongside modern science and foreign languages. And even though he was reading Liang Ch'i-ch'ao's fiery anti-Manchu and reformist writings from Tokyo, he planned to take the civil service examination in 1904. Chiang claims in his memoirs that he stayed afloat in the crosscurrents, and never made the fatal mistake of being "swept away by the advancing tides." But being buffeted continuously by crosscurrents also meant increasing mental strain in maintaining his own independent and integrated stance. After he passed the examination, the family ceremony following his success dramatized for him the way the old system bound men to the past and attached their success to the ongoing life of the family. On returning to his new-style college, the contrast and strain finally overwhelmed him:

> It seemed a transformation overnight from immutable medievalism to the whirlpool of a new revolutionary world. I felt as if what had happened had been a dream . . . All the conflicting ideas, as between new and old, constitutional reforms and revolution buzzing around in this topsy-turvy world of mine, were

more than an immature mind could endure. I became restless and often had a
fantasy in which, by a sort of sommersault, I rocketed high into the air and then
whirled down rapidly to the ground, where I burst to bits and was gone forever.[14]

What Chiang describes here is the chaos of fragmentation, the madness
of feeling oneself literally broken into pieces that defy assemblying and
coherence. He surmised that this feeling manifested a streak of insanity
in the family; more likely it reflected the intense centrifugal pressures
he felt in trying to maintain a grip on his widely diverging experiences
and feelings.

Chiang's inner chaos seems to have taken on order when he went to
a more thoroughly Westernized school, Nanyang College in Shanghai.
The preparatory department was like a United States high school. Modern subjects were taught in English, and Westerners were highly visible.
The layout of the school was Western, complete with a clocktower; and
the guiding philosophy was derived from the English philosopher Herbert Spencer (1820–1903), with equal emphasis upon intellectual, moral,
and physical education. In this setting, young Chiang had the leisure to
order his impressions in a more systematic way, to compare, differentiate, and seek underlying unities and thus achieve the important second
liberation out of chaos. He did so by making reason into the "sole arbiter" of what was right or wrong. This decision freed him from inherited beliefs and practices that could not survive this test. "I felt as if I
had stripped off clothes that were altogether too tight and stepped forth
naked and free."[15]

Young Chiang's insight thus not only liberated him from the grip of
tradition, but more importantly it liberated him from the unbearable
centrifugal pressures that the discovery of Western ideas had imposed on
him and others of his generation. His empowering of reason, however,
answered only one question thrown up by this confrontation with the
West: How do we think clearly? How do we differentiate essentials from
nonessentials, the fundamental from the superficial? The problem of clear
thinking, addressing both the study of moral philosophy and comparative history, was his *idée fixe*. His resolution of this primary concern
largely determined his choice of a Way Out of China's historical predicament. In his Ph.D. thesis "A Study of Chinese Principles in Education," completed at Columbia University in 1917 and published in

Shanghai in 1918, he extolled education as the correct way to remedy China's plight. Education was at once "a method to spread culture, a scientific method, a means to individual development, a method to social progress, a means to the training of citizenship and leadership." Education, in other words, was an eminently "logical" and "demonstrable" solution to China's problems, as philosophical and historical studies illustrated. [16]

Other questions swirled in other young minds, and other insights both logical and demonstrable were to provide direction and some release from the pressures of chaos and uncertainty. The pages of the *Chinese Students' Monthly* allow us to assess the range of definable problems, which like the range of insights into them had burst beyond the recognition limits of tradition. Time and politics were to play the reaper—not the final arbiter—in cutting down the less significant questions, the less convincing answers. Some of the problems, if not the answers, were familiar: What did it mean to be a Chinese scholar in this new era? What was the leadership responsibility of the new intelligentsia? Other problems were rooted in the transitional situation—how to change long-standing social habits, how to redefine China's spiritual heritage, how to master science, how to overcome a divided consciousness, how to uplift the "ignorant mass" in China and in Chinatowns, how to deal with a pervasive labeling as an inferior people and culture.

THE ELUSIVE IDENTITY OF THE NEW SCHOLAR

Who indeed was the new Chinese scholar? There seemed to be agreement that whatever he was, he was in the process of becoming, and would not, could not be like the old scholar. "He will be a normal human being in society, not a solitary and centrifugal being out of it," asserted K. T. May in a 1916 *Monthly* article. This article, entitled "The New Chinese Scholar," catalogued bad traits of the traditional scholar: a supercilious attitude of disdain for ordinary men and affairs, an erratic and emotional romanticism, ostentatious moaning over the abuses and evils of society, ignorance and carelessness about money matters. These patterns of individual decadence, said May, were symptoms of a "decrepit and vitiated social order." The new age, with its popular education, democratic citizenship, and international travel would check the scholars' tendency towards self-aggrandizement, "nourished largely by their contemplation of the greatness and splendor of their past history." The new scholars must be "moral realists and see life as it actually is before their eyes, and not build up 'idealisms' in reverie." He noted that the irreconcilability supposed to exist between the actual and the real world was more often an excuse of moral weaklings for dread of responsibility than an absolute truth. May was optimistic that the very trends in contemporary society, including the beneficent influence of educated women, would humanize the new scholar, leading to a renaissance of "superior men" that had not been seen since the age of Confucius. In addition to the Chinese cultural heritage, the Western heritage could be appropriated to add greater variety and brilliance to this upcoming epoch of scholarship.[17]

This sweeping overview of the new scholar—perhaps itself an idealistic reverie—noticeably accepted the demise of the traditional scholar-official as a *fait accompli* in the real world; it was a role supposedly beyond reconstruction, let alone restoration. Yet the perception that the emergent new Chinese scholars in America in fact were more bookish "grinds" than world citizens was a painful recognition of an undesired continuity. They lived a "seclusive life" in the United States, with no time for anything beyond studying, charged one in 1911.[18] The "hermitic temperament" of Chinese was etched into relief by the preference for isolated purity, said another.[19] C. Y. Chin noted in 1912 that what was often missing from the lives of Chinese students in America was participation in voluntary activities and informal encounters with people; he blamed this not primarily on American exclusiveness but upon old Chinese habits and conceptions, seriousness of purpose, and inherent modesty. "These habits of meeting others, exchanging ideas, discussing problems, cultivating public spirit, learning to cooperate are what will be needed in the future"; and the Chinese Students' Alliance, which published the *Monthly*, was intended to fill this void.[20]

By mid decade in America, such warnings and recriminations about their restricted lives had become almost ritualistic. K. F. Mok summed it up in 1915: "Mere education does not make a man. We have so many exhortations to study that we have almost got accustomed to them. And do they get us anywhere except giving us some exalted feeling concerning work and duty in some deep recesses of our mind?" The grind had "his rudiments of a sense of appreciation [of nature and men] smothered in his perpetual pursuit of mere learning . . . All the learning of the world cannot compensate the loss of health or the inability to associate with others due to our isolation." Even the failure of cooperation among returned students in China was due to "our narrowness of mind and purpose, the provinciality of our field of thought, and the lack of sympathy in our intellectual make-up."[21]

Similar criticisms of the returned students were not only echoed but confirmed later in the decade from China, where considerable information on returned students had begun to be assembled. V. K. Wellington Koo, the Chinese Minister to the United States in 1917, had spent five years in China organizing the American-European Returned Students Association, and drew conclusions based on a sample of over two hundred queried returned students. The students went abroad, he told an Eastern Conference of the Alliance, with a definite purpose in mind, but this was "blighted upon return." Analysis of this blighted promise identified various inner disabilities: pride in demeanor and manner that led to non-communication with older, Chinese-educated co-workers; contempt for small opportunities that could be stepping stones to larger achievements; disregard for detail and a failure to be conscientious workers in modest roles; neglect for present work in favor of daydreams about the great occasion when they could play the roles of Napoleon, Lincoln, Cavour; lack of practical experience, leading to disputes and often quick resignations; lack of capacity for hard work on the part of "sedan chair engineers" and "agriculturists who rejected the plow." Yet the chief remedy could be inferred from the fundamental fault: the want of a steadfast purpose, of determination and will.

> Life, to be complete, to be worth living, must have a purpose and the will to carry it out. Life without a purpose is like a ship without a rudder; no one knows where it may drift, nor where it may stop. And life without the will to fulfill its purpose is like a ship without fuel; it can only remain idle in the haven of the unreal; the want of motive power deprives it of value to the real world.

Self-vigilance is needed, Koo said, a selfless dedication to China, "a spirit of consecration by her loyal sons and daughters." "China," Minister Koo told them, "must march in double time."[22]

EXPERIENCING A FORCED MARCH

Marching in double time is a forced march; and that was indeed as much China's problem as any alleged or actual shortcomings of her people, including the returned students from America. The belief that will power and a sense of purpose were all-conquering helped disguise the nature of the problems and difficulties that they were being asked to conquer. The demands of the real world, the objective circumstances, would thin and even ravage the ranks of the forced marchers. How heavy was the burden of new tools and skills that they were asked to take along in their backpacks? How much of a drag on their feet was the fatigue of minds divided between old and new, the past they could not discard and the future that was not yet theirs?

The burden of new tools and skills was indeed heavy. Acquiring facility in foreign languages was a major undertaking, and a precondition for successful study abroad. Language deficiency lay behind the shyness that Chiang Monlin felt in his early years in America; more than shyness, it was a sense of inferiority, "like an intelligent dog listening to its master, understanding the meaning but unable to talk."[23] Beyond language mastery lay other often difficult tasks: navigating an unfamiliar world of choices; arranging for one's room and board; negotiating with immigration and visa authorities; and constant sparring with the ill-informed and stereotyped images of Chinese that were commonplace in the America of the 1910s. In their American education itself, which was most often in technical fields, they had to plumb the meaning of "expertise." The modern state required experts in many spheres, declared Loy Chang in 1916, but China had none, except foreign ones, owing to the "amateurish spirit of the nation." And Chinese B.A. graduates from America were hardly sufficiently qualified: "[T]hey will be only as effective as amateurs in the line of work for which they have had only the beginnings of the preparation . . . He has still before him a hard road for training and discipline, before he can be of any great usefulness."[24]

Yet, others argued that too much time spent training in America was often a sign of an unproductive "degree fever," and could even lead to an excessive Americanization that "has cost many a student the vitality of our own national character."[25] Many were the snares on the road to becoming a "liberally educated expert," a subtly different cultural type from the superior man of Confucian morality. Language and thought, sound and symbolic meaning, grow together over a lifetime of experience, pointed out Yuen R. Chao (Y. R. Chao): "By no symbolic contrivance can you get a liberal education quick by trying to go around hard and solid experience and life [by just learning the ideas]. This common psychological fallacy comes from the fact that we Chinese students have had the relatively abnormal condition of having to learn a new language after having acquired a rich stock of ideas."[26]

One persistent temptation in this situation, also reinforced by traditional learning approaches, was to settle for an imitative style of learning: memorizing and copying. But this, the students were told by Westerners and by each other, would never do, if there were to be true advancement in China. C. C. Woo, exploring the link between scientific research and industrial manufacturing, spoke of the futility of simply copying the processes of others. Chinese conditions may lead to the necessity of modifying the existing processes to a great extent and hence preliminary research in China was essential. "What is available to us [in America] in the literature contains only the principles and hints which should be advantageously utilized." Chinese technical students in the United States needed to undertake "independent exhaustive work" in laboratories and libraries, and more observation of industries and self-study. More degrees were only a handicap, for they built up expectations of status that inevitably made it harder to adapt foreign learning to Chinese conditions. The very speed of the industrial transformation in the United States and his awareness of the difficulties of translating it into China dazzled and depressed him. "Are we going to be left behind forever and forever?" he wondered.[27]

Scientific research, direct observation, and inductive reasoning were themselves no panaceas. In two reflective comments in 1914, Zuntsoon Zee explored the double-edged sword of scientific training. Letters from home and his own educational experience convinced him that scientific determination of facts and direct observation of living things were "a much needed corrective for our traditional aptitude for verbosity and empty formulas, and for the contemporary craze for glittering generalities of politics and literature." Yet, some months later, he added this cautionary advice:

> Scientific training has . . . to be guarded against chilling scepticism, whence it is only too apt to lead. Where definitions and postulates differ widely, the utility of stiff reasoning and close argument is, likewise, mighty little, as all can tell who have traveled far enough that way. Perhaps one who, thanks to the enlightening effects of a liberal culture, is permitted to thrust out feelers hither and thither and to peep in here and there will fare better. He may, if he perseveres, at last return to a radical revision of his fundamental ideas and reconcile himself anew to authority, life, and history. But then an average lifetime is pretty short, whereas the path of Truth is long.

Foreshadowing the stance that science had little to offer in understanding the larger questions of life—except a chilling skepticism—Zee argues for a more meandering, less syllogistic approach to learning, so that the broader context is not lost. Many of his generation had rejected traditional authority, yet were despondent about finding a Way Out of the present historical predicament. What new authorities could take the place of tradition? Were science and reason potential dead ends as new sources of authority? Had the earlier youthful rejection of the Neo-Confucian Chinese world view been ill-founded and premature? Could the way forward in his own thinking be found by looking backward once again, to reconsider those earlier choices? Zee wonders whether an unlearning of the supposed wider utility of science might not be necessary for him to progress in his own evolving world view. "There is much in the saying that we forget in order to remember. Few are those who always learn right that they never have to unlearn." Sitting in modern, scientific America and remembering his own intellectual journey seems to evoke the perennial concerns of his early Confucian education: how to live a purposeful life in society. The "fundamental ideas" that he started with are still intact in his memory, however much revised by his interim experiences. As on a great circular route, he may once again pass over familiar terrain and come to a new reconciliation with authority, life, and history, perhaps by combining a liberal democratic tradition with the Neo-Confucian tradition of his ancestors. The iconoclasm of his early youth seems behind him, a stance once taken, now also discredited.[28]

Like answers to the larger, ultimate questions about life, the new social skills that Chinese students were asked to acquire were not readily secured through formal education, in China or abroad. As we have seen, the Alliance, in fact, was set up to be a training ground for certain habits that were felt to be weak among Chinese students; these included the practice of individual skills, such as meeting people, exchanging ideas, and discussing problems, as well as the cultivation of collective virtues, such as public spirit and cooperation. Promoting these values under the umbrella of the Alliance allowed the activities to be "especially fitted to Chinese habits and manners."[29] But the success of this training function is difficult to assess. Other concerns, such as maintaining a national focus, recruiting membership, and financing its programs and publications, were more pressing. Keeping the welfare of the whole group in view was a constant struggle. The national Alliance itself had been created in 1911 out of three separate regional bodies. And not all Chinese students belonged to the Alliance; membership was stable at 600–850 members for the decade of the 1910s, which represented about half of the Chinese students studying at that time in the United States.[30] This membership clustered in different ways. Although over half were males hailing from Kwangtung and Kiangsu provinces and half had scholarships from Tsinghua College, the students came to be scattered across dozens of campuses throughout America, and organized themselves into many local, professional, alumni, and interests clubs in addition to the Alliance.[31] Factionalism and sectionalism did rear their heads many times inside the Alliance, most dramatically in 1915–1916, when a confrontation occurred between the Alliance leadership and the major alumni group. The Alliance President H. K. Kwang had intoned in December 1915 that the Alliance "is a junior republic of China in which there is no distinction as to age and knowledge. All those who belong to it have an equal voice in the conduct of its affairs. I am glad to say that the opinions we have expressed and the works we have carried out have been marked by that moderation and practicality which becomes true democracy." In March 1916 the *Monthly* editorialized that the Tsinghua Alumni Association was threatening to break the Alliance into two warring factions. "Sectionalism and provincialism have been the bane of our organizations, whether as a nation or as smaller societies."[32]

But the Alliance survived, not least because it was a training ground in federalism, democracy, and constitution-making for these young self-consciously Chinese adults who wanted to demonstrate their self-governing capability to the world. The accounts were audited regularly to forestall fraud and to maintain a high managerial standard.[33] The *Chinese Students' Monthly* had from early on prided itself as a forum for freedom of expression; a frank exchange was desired and articles, most solicited through open competitions, were not emended. The *Monthly,* like the Alliance itself, was a sober-minded vehicle for expressing diversity within a common organizational format. It showed that many young Chinese, within the context of a liberal culture, were quite able to manage a business efficiently, run an organization democratically, grow together in fellowship, and disagree with each other without personal and partisan attacks. At least, that is the story that emerges from the pages of the Alliance's official publication. But, however full and frank that story appears, it is assuredly not the complete story of what happened in the editorial and business offices of the *Monthly,* in the planning sessions for the summer conferences and national meetings of the Alliance, and in the feelings and minds of some individual young Chinese. That intimate human detail is lost to us, but we should not assume that that hidden story is more important than the visible signs of achievement which are reflected on the public stage. That stage, as many Chinese have long recognized, is where the important encounters that sustain social, cultural and political life occur; hidden realities are consequential only if they disrupt the action on the stage.

Even if the Alliance were the "junior republic of China" that Kwang called it, it was, as a training ground and democratic stage in America, still miles and miles, in physical distance and cultural terms, from China itself during the 1910s. The Alliance President in 1914, smarting from sectional disputes within the organization, could well argue that the spirit of cooperation was essential to making an organization work; but he left the realm of the possible when he argued that such training in cooperation was a preparation for the future when "several hundred of us, acting together, will form an army, invincible for China's advancement."[34] That unity of thought never appeared, in America or China, for there were too many different Chinas, too many different perceptions of advancement. The forced marchers were forever breaking ranks, with groups of them going off in their own direction. Although Chinese nationalism was a near universal sentiment that colored all points of view, there were troublesome issues that prevented unanimity, even in the most dramatic crises. Were Chinese Christians "traitors to their country" as some accused them? Although this view was branded illiberal and dangerous in an article by Y. C. Ma (Ma Yin-chu), the many Chinese Christian students within the Alliance had to wonder how to draw the boundaries between their Christian beliefs and their Chinese citizenship.[35] Patriots also had to defend their creed against "the philosophers of mankind," who saw nationalism as a necessary but lamentable stage towards developing broader international organizations and beliefs.[36] Cosmopolitan student clubs were attractive to Chinese students, some of whom, like Hu Shih, took active roles in them as well as within the Alliance.[37] But when a Pan-Asiatic League was formed in December 1915, the *Monthly* did not see much benefit from it for China. Asian societies were highly divergent, an editorial argued, and China could not identify closely with her aggressive neighbor, Japan. It was necessary "to see the interests of the country above benevolent and sentimental exuberations."[38] Chinese students also had to justify their patriotism to outsiders, who seemed to perceive in China nothing but two extremes: either no sense of public virtue or only a xenophobic one![39]

The quest for "true patriotism" was only one in a long litany of similar quests for true reform, true loyalty, true Confucianism, the true teaching. All were symptomatic of a loss of a sense of givenness in the realm of values following the collapse of the imperial Confucian civilization. What was to take the place of Confucianism? Could Confucianism itself be reformed, revived, restored? Would the new *chiao* or "doctrine" have to come from the West? Was it better to replace old gods with new ones or with one God or with no God? All these questions were asked and debated in young minds. It was tempting with these questions to look to ready-made answers from authority figures. Yet some pushed for a deeper analysis. "Will it not be far more fruitful and

far more proper for us to do some study and some thinking on our own
. . . than to resort to Dr. Legge and Dr. Beach and the learned writer
in the *China Review* for arguments pro and con Confucianism?" wrote
twenty-two-year-old Hu Shih. He did not endorse the "new morality"
of liberty, equality, democracy, patriotism, and freedom that had arisen
in Chinese thought between 1898 and 1913—in fact, he called this
revolution in thought a set of "new superstitions." His critical, questioning mind was always challenging what his contemporaries were willing to accept as fact, as a new givenness, which made him seem odd to
many, even cold-blooded and unpatriotic.[40] But in this commitment to
the critical life of the mind, Hu Shih had perhaps only deeply internalized a peculiar Western mode of individualism. It was not a Way Out
of the Chinese predicament that his Chinese contemporaries could follow. They did not want one hundred schools of thought to contend;
they wanted a common faith, a Way Out for all China. James Pusey has
captured this longing well:

> The search for a new faith . . . became a grim search for a new unifying faith
> . . . [Chinese] looked West for an "ism" to replace their *chiao*. That is why Hu
> Shih's famous plea, in 1919, "Raise more problems and talk less of 'isms' " fell
> on deaf ears. For Chinese wanted an "ism." They were not comfortable each on
> his own. They wanted to *ch'ün* [to group]. They wanted a Way. They wanted a
> Sage. They wanted to book to replace the *Analects*. They wanted a compass, a
> polestar, a helmsman.[41]

If the collapse of the common faith was the root of the historical
predicament, then the divided consciousness was the branch, the psychological fact that shadowed their feelings and thoughts. "We are being
re-created," said Runtien J. Li in April 1910.[42] Not just institutions,
but people were taking on new forms and meanings. For women perhaps
even more than for men, this involved changes in self-definition. Compared with the set stages and roles in a woman's life before, there was
now being developed what one young woman writer, Pingsa Hu, called
a completely new ideal: self-realization and independence.[43] Many modern Chinese men found this change in their counterparts desirable; but
approval had its costs, for many of them had to endure guilt at deserting
"old-fashioned wives," often arranged for them by their parents before

they came to America.[44] Nor did the old forms and meanings conveniently disappear for either sex; they dogged the feet and minds of the forced marchers. In her article on "The Women of China," Hu expressed this directly when she said of herself, "I am at once the girl of yesterday and the girl of tomorrow. That is, I was brought up according to the old standard of life before I was ten years of age, and since then I have lived under the new influence and have been educated even in America." She contrasted what observers saw in the behavior of modern young Chinese women like herself with the more ambivalent inner experience: "You think she is a regular suffragette but remember that she is also the daughter or granddaughter of the woman of yesterday. She cannot help but inheriting the spirit of self-sacrifice."[45]

Three selves are interacting in Pingsa Hu's mind: a social self that others see, a hidden self embodying the past, an idealized self imagining a modern future. The inner tension among these different selves could result in perpetual conflict, a negotiated coexistence, or even a resourceful resolution. Or it could result in simple, numbing denial of part of oneself (especially the hidden self embodying the past), with the individual will as field marshal instructing the mind what to do: Look *forward* into the future, *up* in hopefulness, and *out* into the world, not backward, down, and in, admonished the *Monthly* in 1910.[46] Of course, *backward* meant facing the Chinese past, including their own traditional families and childhoods; *down* meant plumbing the despair over the brokenness in China and in themselves; and *in* meant looking inside oneself and the Chinese past for the resources to repair the brokenness.

From the very familiar traditional ground of moral training to the smallest acts of daily life, the new American world crowded in on their minds. An ethic that called on individuals to adjust to a given environment had worked well in late Imperial China, argued Mabel Lee in 1916, but now a more dynamic set of individual skills was needed. "Our new ideal must be to develop the individual so that he will be able not only to adjust himself to one form but to changing norms of society. He will thus be the master instead of the bondsman of the situation." The present was a "period of maladjustment," in which "rival guides of progress, good in their intention, yet having been trained only to adapt themselves to a static society, found themselves at sea under the new conditions."[47] Yuen R. Chao urged the reform of letter writing the same year, to encourage spontaneity and genuineness.

> Our letters should be free from their "polite" nonsenses to give room for sincerity. Relatives and friends should write as they would talk. I am not speaking from the point of view of efficiency alone. An extra page or two of formalities not only wastes time, energy and money, but it wastes attention and interest, and, as we say . . . puts a film between you and me.[48]

At every turn China and its people seemed to lack something. Like the quest for the "True Version" of whatever, the cataloguing of Chinese shortcomings consumed many pages in the *Monthly*. Indeed, the question seemed to be were the Chinese fit enough to make it in the twentieth century? In the resounding "yes" of young Chinese, we see the one area where givenness endured and cultural confidence remained adamantine.

INNER IMPERIALISM: COMING UP FROM UNDER

The encounter with the West meant more than the enlarged vistas of intercultural learning, more than cognitive and emotional dissonance associated with being forced marchers into a new world. It meant a response to the agents of that force: the intrusive and proliferating Western presence, which through missionaries, ministers and consuls, advisors, merchants, adventurers, and journalists had fastened a grip on coastal and riverine China and many scattered points in the interior.[49] And beyond individual Westerners, it meant a response to the larger concept of Western imperialism. This force, for better or worse, had initiated world history by bringing hitherto largely self-sufficient and separate empires in Asia and Africa into a common framework, in which the terms of encounter, initially at least, were set by the stronger imperialist powers. In an era dominated by cultural myopia in general and assumed Western and white superiority in particular, the interaction among these diverse peoples was very unequal. For China, a large agrarian empire with tenacious traditions, this unequal interaction meant a massive failure of reciprocity between Chinese and foreigners, with the "weaker"

Chinese increasingly on the short end, labeled not merely "different" but inferior, backward, unfit. The inner experience of imperialist domination, or what I would call "inner imperialism," and the constellation of emotions attached to it—fear, humiliation, resentment, shame, envy, dependence, hatred—drew heavily on the psychological resources of this generation. For some it further complicated that second liberation out of chaos, doubt, and dissonance. For most, it seems to have helped provide the one fixed point in a whirling world: their Chinese identity, their long-term faith in their endangered country.

To many boys who grew up away from the treaty ports in the late nineteenth century, foreigners were simply "predatory savages with magical powers and with potent medicines, and their main purpose of life was to take advantage of others and make profit for themselves."[50] This was a safe and reassuring view, for the foreigner could be assigned to the known world of eccentric beings—spirits, demons, fools—that peopled rural China. For young Chiang Monlin, who first saw Shanghai at around fifteen years of age, foreigners split into a dual image:

> The foreigner appeared . . . half divine and half devilish, double-faced and many-handed like Vishnu, holding a electric light, a steam boat, and a pretty doll in one set of hands, and a policeman's club, revolver, and handful of opium in the other. When one looked at his bright side, he was an angel; on the dark side he was a demon.[51]

As one drew nearer to the centers of foreign power in China, the image could become even more disturbing and personally threatening. *He has ordained where I shall walk and live. He lives in a world apart and looks down on Chinese. He has strongmen to enforce his will and I am a shrunken being in his presence. He hears no argument. He does not want to hear.*

Chang Fu-liang (b. 1889), recalling his childhood in Shanghai, conveyed a sense of having been segregated, demeaned, belittled.

> At the turn of the century, boys of my age who lived in treaty ports like Shanghai grew up with a strong inferiority complex. The best buildings in Shanghai were occupied by Westerners and most carriages were owned and used by foreigners. Racial segregation was unashamedly the order of the day. Public parks had signs at the entrances that dogs and Chinese were not admitted inside, and a tall Sikh police man, whom the Chinese called "the Redheaded Devil," enforced

the order with a big stick. As a boy, I was afraid even to look at foreigners, for they all seemed nine feet tall.[52]

One learned to be inwardly wary: "[I]n Shanghai to approach a European was to court trouble: one never knew whether he would hit or merely curse, and there could be no redress."[53] Foreigners seemed a great perplexity; their behavior was incomprehensible, unpredictable, assertive, and self-confident. Once Chou Yentung was called before his French teacher, who was about to criticize the "sacrilegious idea" of evolution in one of his essays.

> He sat behind the desk. Suddenly his beard quivered, and he started shouting. I was so frightened that I could not understand him at first. Then his mouth opened wider, and he came nearer, shouting in my face, so that I saw his teeth and palate . . . He paced, shouted, beard wagging in profile. At any moment his flaying arms (for he moved them about as he paced) would hit me, and what would I do? I would lose dignity. I could not submit to being struck by anyone, and therefore would possibly have to kill him, or to kill myself, that my spirit might exact revenge upon him after death. He towered above me by a head and must have weighed twice what I did. I wanted to run away, but pride kept me nailed, standing in front of him. I sweated with fear . . . I walked out, my essay in hand, torn across. It took years before I began to comprehend.[54]

But comprehension did not mean that young Chou ever mastered this fear of foreigners. After years in Europe, he still was "uneasy and restless in the houses of Europeans, never natural, anxious not to draw the so ready violence, verbal or physical, so that he became almost obsequious with them . . ."[55]

Behind these individual experiences lay an unstable, even volatile, combination of Chinese historic pride and Western intrusive arrogance. Historic pride ran deep in China. It was particularly intense among the educated, who were accustomed to viewing outsiders with disdain, or at best complacency. The equation of *foreign* and *inferior,* as we have seen, seemed a natural one, for there was much evidence to shore up the Chinese sense of achievement: a record of continuous civilization stretching across the centuries and an acknowledged cultural superiority over other peoples around the rim of territorial China. These achievements gave substance to a myth of superiority, a theory of world order that claimed to be at once impartial and inclusive and that placed China at the center of the civilized world.[56] Lucian Pye has argued that this Chinese historic pride became rooted in a highly self-conscious biological identification with past greatness, an identification that took on near mystical proportions. To be Chinese was to feel "the significance of their own beings as part of immortal history," manifested in ancestor worship and in pride in an unbroken genealogical continuity.[57] From this perspective of perceived greatness, the modern period was experienced as a time of great frustration and impotence, especially in two areas of past Chinese superiority: governmental management and material plane of living. Nineteenth-century treaty-port administration contrasted with confusion elsewhere in China; and standards of Western living seemed as far above the Chinese level as the Chinese had once been above the "barbarians."[58] For Pye the crucial problem has not been Chinese identity as a people, which was secure, but "the fact that they have been weaker and poorer on the world scene than they have felt it right and proper for them to be." This perception led to a persisting dissatisfaction with their leaders and "deep cravings for the decisive power of truly effective authority." The Chinese have thus experienced modernization as "the agonies of a great civilization in turmoil and not just a traditional culture adapting to modern ways." Their modernization has been marked by a distinctive crisis of authority, a prolonged state of disarray, and a politics of hatred, none of which, according to Pye, would have occurred in this manner without the psychological millstone of the Chinese identification with historic greatness.[59]

Pye's perspective is extreme because it looks for cues to understanding behavior almost exclusively within the inherited culture and not within the historical situation confronting China.[60] Western imperialism becomes an almost beneficent vehicle for the demands of modernization. Western intrusive arrogance, however, was not just a fantasy of nationalistic Chinese; it is the theme of a story that is easy to document. The story began with the "unequal treaties" negotiated with the Ch'ing dynasty in the nineteenth century, reached a climactic reversal with the founding of the People's Republic of China in 1949–1950, and continues to unfold in significant ways into the 1980s in post–Cultural Revolution China.

Westerners were not only efficient administrators of cities or produc-

ers of vast material wealth; many were white racists, religious dogma-
tists, and bullies. The creation of the treaty-port world involved clear
restrictions on the sovereignty of Chinese authorities to oversee the activities of foreigners, to set their own tariff duties, or to patrol their
own inland waterways. Consequently, concessions to the foreigners in
the nineteenth century were made only reluctantly, even though they
were rationalized to the emperor as traditional techniques for barbarian
management. Within the treaty-port world, the actual interaction of
Chinese and foreigners was similar to that in colonial enclaves, with
assumptions of white superiority, discrimination in residence and em-
ployment, and segregated patterns of social intercourse.[61] Beyond the
treaty ports, the two principal foreign exports—opium and Christianity—were felt by many educated Chinese to have been introduced and
sustained through trickery, threat, and force; both were sources of constant friction and deep resentment. Given the nature of contacts between
the races, the Chinese image of foreigners could pass easily from barbarian to bandit, and the corresponding attitude from condescension to
resentment and rage.[62]

Throughout the twentieth century, there was a concerted effort by
various Chinese groups to recover the rights lost in the nineteenth century through the "unequal treaties." These Chinese felt themselves to be
acting to redress a wrong, to unbind the ties fastened upon China's free
development and self-determination by the system of Western imperialism. This historical movement entered its final stages in 1949–1951,
when the Western presence in China was systematically liquidated.
Extraterritoriality, nominally ended by the United States and Britain in
1943, had continued under a Sino-American wartime agreement; it finally became a closed issue in a People's Republic that would no longer
tolerate it. The foreign concessions, settlements, and leased territories
were reincorporated into the Chinese communities that had long surrounded but not dominated them. The last foreign gunboat on the Yangtze
was fired on by Chinese Communist troops in April 1949, and forced to
retreat towards the open sea. In the early 1950s the Christian churches
in China were pressured to become autonomous, national bodies, sever-
ing their connections with foreign personnel, money, and institutions.

The cumulative effect, described by one Westerner who lived through those years, was a final accounting for a century of abuse and violation.

> Everywhere the Westerner has been made to feel the weight of Chinese authority and has been forced to realize that he is at most a guest who is temporarily tolerated, but possesses no rights in China . . . There were probably very few Chinese who were entirely free from a feeling of satisfaction, however slight or perhaps even unconscious it may have been, at the way the Westerners had been put in their place.[63]

Over thirty years later, in the 1980s, the West and China seemed to have entered an era of coexistence and greater mutuality. The United States' recognition of the Peoples Republic in 1979 ended a long period of treating the PRC as an international pariah. And China's post-1978 "opening to the outside" led to ever-widening circles of negotiated economic and cultural contacts with other countries, on bilateral and multilateral terms. In the spring of 1978, a French destroyer entered Chinese waters at the official invitation of the Chinese government, the first Western warship since 1949 and a forerunner of limited military cooperation with the West. Even though personal contact with foreigners remained suspect for some, because of inconsistencies in governmental policy, there seemed to be greater ease in relations with foreigners. It was in fact a Westerner in 1980 who counseled "Watch out for the Foreign Guests!" while the Chinese, with both modernization ambitions and enhanced cultural confidence, sent thousands of students abroad again in the 1980s and, within limits, experimented with new economic and ideological emphases at home.[64]

The story of the psychological impact of imperialism in China has been little studied. If there is a consensus on the emotions that have set the tone to the relations between Chinese and Western foreigners in modern Chinese history, there is as yet little consensus on the ultimate explanation of these emotions or their deeper meaning. The arguments, so far, have clustered around two standpoints: that the emotions express something distinctively Chinese, rooted in inherited self-image and world view, or that they are comprehensible as a natural counter-pressure to foreign insults and intrusion.[65] In one sense, these differing explanations matter little: whether a Chinese in the twentieth century was an historical actor confronting an unjust situation or a cultural actor expressing a sense of injured historic pride, or both, in international contexts he had to struggle to come up from under. He could not assume a place in the world hierarchy, then being determined in Europe, America and Japan, as an equal, let alone as a superior. His personal worth in the interaction with Westerners was inseparably linked with China's international status as the "Sick Man of East Asia" (*Tung ya ping-fu*). No more than a Westerner in China could a Chinese in the treaty ports or abroad shed his physical features or his national origin and be treated simply as a person. This sense of being labeled, graded, and rated, and the felt counter-need to establish one's personal and national worth in the eyes of others, especially Westerners, was an important understanding of their situation by educated youth in the early years of the twentieth century.

The following "entreating voice in China" appealed to the Chinese students in America through the pages of the *Monthly* in the fall of 1915, several months after the Japanese humiliation of the Twenty-One Demands.

> They say I am old. They call me a sick man, a very sick man. I was wounded in 1894. I was almost hopeless then, but your birth at that moment gave me a new hope. I was robbed in 1898. I looked to you in that year but you were only five years old. I was about to be divided among the nations in 1900, but you were only seven years old. I was dumb as a sheep before her shearers in the Russo-Japanese War, but you were still too young to help me. I was again most helplessly robbed last May. You remember those days very well. My limbs have been cut away from me one by one, only the breath still remains. You are now about ready to help me. Will you not determine to keep my life so that I may recover gradually? I must have a strong government, a united people; will you be my Bismarck? I have to free myself from my enemies; will you be my Cavour? I need an intelligent people to be at the back of my Bismarck and my Cavour; will you educate them? I need wealth, prosperity and strength; will you be my engineers? . . . Oh, my sons and my daughters, you are my hope, my greatest hope. Remember my past shames and see my present sufferings. Will you not respond to my call?[66]

The imploring parent, crippled by the immoral actions of robbers and thieves, was an almost irresistible image in the land of filial piety and lofty moralism. But the precise formulation is no less interesting than the appeal. That China is sick and decrepit is not acknowledged; "they" only say so. China has been mutilated and beaten, its affliction coming from outside, not from within. From within comes the salvation of the younger generation, born in the time of greatest affliction, and maturing with precisely those strengths of courage, intelligence, skill, and unity that will permit a gradual recovery of strength to China. This is not a land whose people lack long-term confidence in their survival and vigor and place in the world.

This faith in China's capacity for long-term survival, however dire the present situation, was an anchoring buoy that gave young Chinese some stability in the midst of the storms raging between China and the West. Two ways to navigate in these uncertain international waters were reflected in the *Monthly:* an ideal one emphasizing reason, cooperation, moral suasion, peaceful means; and a darker, threatening one, in which China would have to compel respect, entirely on her own if need be. The pivotal year seems to have been 1919, when the balance swung from the former approach to the latter. The ideal approach was to be expected in the years surrounding the Revolution of 1911, because the American Republic was viewed as a model and a potential ally of the young Chinese Republic. Yet even in the early years, a darker undercurrent was present in the Chinese experience of contempt in America and in the perception of American hypocrisy.

The very word *Chinaman* was offensive to the Chinese students. One commented that it is a violation, philologically and otherwise; "a measure of contempt is implied consciously or unconsciously in this word."[67] Instances of alleged discrimination were frequently aired in the *Monthly*. American immigration policies that excluded "Orientals" from the country were a running sore. The health tests for hookworm as part of the immigration procedure in San Francisco were degrading, but no less so than the hissing at an American student seen walking with a Chinese student.[68] Such incidents served to remind Chinese students of a bigoted, ignorant, and fearful side of Americans that contrasted with their frankness, generosity, and congeniality. Which was reality? After being verbally accosted on a bus as "Japs!" and being told by a drunken passenger that the next President of the United States would throw them out of the country, one student surmised that the lies of civilized discourse were preferable to the "disconcerting truths" blurted out when drunk.[69]

The students generally attributed bigotry to ignorance, or at least sought vigorously to promote a more enlightened view through the *Monthly* to the two-thirds of its readership who were not members of the Alliance. Presenting the "other side" on numerous China questions had been one of the major goals of the publication since the editorial policy was first defined in the November 1907 issue. Throughout the decade, popular books were reviewed, often critically; and perceived misconceptions, misjudgments, and misrepresentations of China and her people were challenged. Were the Chinese cowardly? No, was the answer; instances of past valor and bravery were cited, as well as China's anti-militaristic ethics, derived partly from Buddhism.[70] Are Chinese students too serious? "Well, the Observer does not feel tormented by such remarks. He feels that at present the Chinese people cannot be gay long with impunity."[71] Seriousness is a distinguishing characteristic of the Chinese race, added another. "We look serious, we talk seriously, and we act seriously."[72] Were the Chinese inert, docile, and procrastinating, as charged in an article by E. F. Baldwin in *Outlook* magazine in 1910? No, China is not inert but moving now, like Japan, said C. T. Wang (Wang Chengting) in response. But Chinese, he claimed, are docile and proud of it, and also slow-moving in their conservatism. As to "backwardess," Wang replied: "We candidly confess that our people as a people are about a century behind time, whether in government, industry, education or community life . . . But we dislike criticism that is loaded with self-conceit."[73]

The pervasive thinking in terms of racial hierarchies did not seem to be attacked by the young Chinese early in the decade, only the specific ranking that they were assigned within this structure. The better class of Chinese students was pulled down, unjustly they felt, by the lower class of Chinatown. "As plain and indelible as the Italian and the African laborers are photographed in the minds of us Chinese students, and as easy and natural as we recall their detestable pictures and repulsive peculiarities, even when we see their brethren in higher statuses of life, so is the case with the Americans in regard to us Chinese."[74] Americans associated Chinatown Chinese with sacred queues, grotesque houses, opium, rats, gambling, and tong wars. "Very often, as travellers and visitors, we are put in a very annoying, embarrassing, humiliating, and painful situation by the questions of our inquisitive American friends, whose conversation always turns on these topics."[75] The Chinese underclass in America needed to be lifted up, and the *Monthly* urged local clubs to form General Welfare Committees to deal with this "unattractive and unpleasant work."[76] A similar concern was expressed by a student who had accompanied a group of American professors to China to survey conditions. While there was much upon which to build a basis for hope, he was dismayed when he came to discuss "the qualifications of our people." Two observations stuck out: the Chinese people's attitudes towards beggars and unfortunates and "hereditary squalid practices." "In numberless places . . . I was completely dejected by the constant and numerous appearances of beggars, men and women, old and young . . . absolutely homeless and foodless." There seemed to be no corresponding sense of civic responsibility, as the presence of such people produced no effect in people's minds. "I was equally uneasy and was abased . . . by the frequent squalid practices by the people of every class, from the highest to the lowest" which he left undescribed "for lack of courage." These things, Y. Tsenshan Wang said, disgrace the nation. There needed to be public programs for indigent people and public and private sanitary reform, "to remove foreign prejudice against us."[77]

This agonizing over what foreigners thought and said and saw was, of course, aggravated by the students' being in America, competing in American schools, and wanting to qualify by American standards. Foreigners were all around them, much more pervasive than they were in the treaty ports in China, let alone anywhere in the vast Chinese interior. What is important to note, however, is how little evidence there is of obsequious behavior, despite Han Suyin's earlier comment on her father's reaction to foreigners in Europe. China had shortcomings and a long way to go, just as the students had limitations as "modern students." But so did the United States have shortcomings and blemishes that prevented the Chinese students from being entrapped as if inside some sort of "modern utopia." It is doubtful, even in a more perfect America, that they would have seen this country as anything more than one source of ideas for China's future, not a model for China to follow. They were in America to acquire new skills and tools needed by China;

and however Sisyphean that task sometimes proved to be, or however seductive aspects of American life appeared, few of them seemed to have lost their basic identity as representatives of an endangered land and people. To this end the racial stereotyping of the day perhaps gave an unwitting assist.

Certainly opportunities to identify with and adopt the foreigner's perspective abounded. In countless lectures at summer conferences and club meetings, they heard the viewpoints of Americans; many of these were reprinted in the *Monthly*. They were proselytized, counseled about the dangers of study in America, told what to keep in their own culture, and warned not to push the slogan "China for the Chinese" too far. A state governor, thinking wrongly that the Alliance was an organization of Christian students, found no need to change his topic when he learned that they were not all Christians; the students were, he said, "forerunners of a band of people that will sometime . . . put China where she ought to be, and where it is in her interest to be, i.e. among the Christian nations of the earth."[78] The solicitous concern by Westerners about the students' losing their own culture seemed to focus on manners, that they not become coarse, pert, commonplace but keep the "serenity and fine consideration and graciousness of the literati and gentlemen . . . Cling to these things, use them as a fine polish on any substance you may be able to attain among us."[79] Compare this with the aside of one Chinese student that the literati's mind was "like an antiquarian armory full of curious old weapons—as compared with a well stocked arsenal containing all the most approved warlike implements fit for service."[80] But the advice against overzealous patriotism probably fell on the least receptive ears. While they might add a dance at a summer conference to show Americans that they could mix and were "up-to-date," or seek to run the Alliance well to demonstrate to Americans their capacity for self-government, it was another matter to allow outsiders to define the limits or nature of Chinese sovereignty.[81]

Stubborn national self-reliance increasingly pushed to the fore as a slogan during the decade of the 1910s. From being in 1910 "the best friend our country has" among the Powers (except for its exclusionary immigration policies), the United States had become by 1919 a suspect friend—one who at best had stood aloof from ratifying the disastrous peace-making process that followed World War I. Individual Americans were championed—Henry Cabot Lodge, for example, who had refused to ratify the Treaty of Versailles or support the League of Nations—but America was, after all, a part of the West; and the West, after five years of suicidal warfare, had shown itself near moral bankruptcy. What had been learned about war and the perilous paths leading to it? asked an editorial commentator in the *Monthly*. In its refusals to learn from experience, its self-indulgence, its fixation with material progress, the West had shown itself no less bankrupt than a drifting and superficial China.[82]

Many Chinese students had slowly become less enchanted with the American republic. Had it not delayed overlong in recognizing the birth of the Chinese republic in 1911? Was its political system really the best for China?[83] Was not the Lansing-Ishii Agreement of 1917, in which the United States acknowledged that Japan had special interests in contiguous areas in China, "a warning to the Chinese people that too much trust cannot be put in friends"?[84] Were not China's hopes for a redressing of her grievances against Japan and the West, in part stimulated by President Woodrow Wilson's idealism, now dashed by the rebuff accorded her by erstwhile allies?[85] The Honorable Quo Tai-chi, a former student in America and a technical advisor to the Chinese Peace Delegation in Paris, told the students at the annual Alliance Conference in the summer of 1919 that "the Shantung settlement by the Peace Conference in Japan's favor amounts to a moral and legal sanction by the civilized world of Japan's policy of aggression and despoliation in China as expressed in her notorious Twenty-One Demands [of 1915]. That is why China so bitterly resents and strenuously opposes that decision."[86]

After the news from Versailles, the *Monthly* editorialized that China was "painfully disappointed and her faith in the dawn of a new era rudely shaken." Was the Peace Conference merely "an assemblage for the division of spoils," for the stronger allies to prevail over the weaker ones? "The world had been taught to believe that the war was a great moral struggle, that the Central Powers were faithless brutes, devoid of any sense of justice; but when in a company of friends one member should be permitted to cut another's throat, I can hardly conceive anything much worse."[87] The League of Nations itself offered no prospect of hope, for it was not designed to overcome national jealousies and racial inequality. "The present form of the League is really a means of exploitation of the weak by the strong." The conclusion seemed obvious: "It is up to the weak to work out their own salvation from the peaceful conquest and domination by the so-called Great Powers."[88] The lesson of these years, discovered from the actual politial situation and not from democratic political theory, was that "to resist Japan, to escape the fate of Korea and Egypt, we must rise up like a man, disdaining any protection from whatever source, the United States or the League, and we must rely absolutely upon ourselves."[89] This disillusionment and cutting of the ties with the Western allies coincided with the May Fourth outbursts in China itself, which gave fresh hope that the Chinese people—not just the returned students but youth, merchants, workers—would create an independent Way Out. China's destiny lay in its own hands, as the students in America had increasingly predicted it would.[90]

The darker, more threatening approach to changing China's position in the world had come into full view. Already in 1917 there had been statements in the *Monthly* calling for all-out patriotic discipline as the answer to China's disunity and weakness. Y. C. Yang (Yang Yung-ch'ing) argued that the present crisis "demands an absolute, unconditional and unreserved subordination of the self to the community, of private interest to national welfare, of the individual will to the organized will." With this attitude, he maintained, "North and South shall be united in one sentiment and the old and the new forces shall be guided by one vision, then the progressives and the conservatives shall live in harmonious co-operation and the militarist and constitutionalist shall work in perfect unison." There would be no internal dissension, no threat of civil war, no chronic disturbance to retard the progress of the nation.[91] This totalistic approach marked an extreme response to the disunity and the brokenness within themselves, within China, within the world as a community. But there were, in fact, only a few tactical approaches available to those who were determined to come up from under, who insisted upon being treated with equality and respect in the face of discrimination, contempt, or simple nonrecognition. Over this decade, the Chinese students in America reacted in several ways: with sober analyses and refutations, based on fact and argument; and with satire and parody, aimed at hypocrisy but also at their own pretensions.

They were willing to see China tested and challenged as an underdog in the international game of fitness and success. But China would be recognized, if it took sending her youth into the streets of Shanghai in dare-to-die squads in the fall of 1919.[92] Sovereignty and self-determination had been non-negotiable, long before this generation of Mother China's educated youth. Y. C. Yang anchored his patriotic call in China's historic pride: "Four thousand years of unbroken and independent development. Is this not a prestige worthy of your ambition?"[93]

A crowd of onlookers, Shanghai, 1908. Courtesy, Essex Institute, Salem, Mass.

EIGHT

Breaking the Hold of the Group

Twelve years before C. Y. Yang, a student in America, called for iron-handed group discipline and total sacrifice of the self for the cause of national unity and progress, another Chinese student in Japan saw a news slide on the Russo-Japanese war of 1905 and drew a different conclusion: Instead of more group discipline and self-sacrifice, his compatriots needed to become more self-critical. The news slide showed a group of Chinese, strong in body but apathetic in expression, waiting for the Japanese military to execute a bound Chinese accused of being a spy for the Russians. The shame he felt in this scene, not only for the Chinese spy who was used and executed by other nationals but also for the pathetic Chinese onlookers who had come to enjoy the spectacle, forced him to reconsider his medical study in Japan and his analysis of the locus of China's problems. "The people of a weak and backward country, however strong and healthy they might be, could only serve to be made examples of or as witnesses of such futile spectacles; and it is not necessarily deplorable if many of them died of illness. The most important thing, therefore, was to change their spirit."[1] This young man, the future writer Lu Hsun, was to see literature as the way to change the inner spirit of the Chinese people, to awaken them to a sense of their national failings, and to point out how they might become "real human beings" freed from the tyranny of the group and tradition.

The spectacle of the conformist, mindless crowd that so struck Lu Hsun's attention in this incident in Japan recurs again and again in his short stories of the late 1910s and early 1920s. In "Medicine," during an execution scene the people "craning their necks as far as they would go . . . looked like so many ducks, held and lifted by some invisible hand." In the story "K'ung Yi-chi," the fierce-looking employer and the morose lot of the customers are as important thematically as the pathetic figure of the old scholar-failure. In the "Diary of a Madman," the protagonist is tormented by the strange, fierce expressions in people's eyes, even in those of children, and by their ghastly pale, long-toothed faces that come alive with derisive laughter. Ordinary villagers who have themselves endured shame and wrong are still unable to identify with the protagonist: "Some of them have been pilloried by the magistrate, some slapped in the face by the local gentry, some have had their wives taken away by bailiffs, some have had their parents driven to suicide by creditors." Yet these experiences only make them more frightened and fierce, more ready to persecute than empathize.[2]

In his short stories, Lu Hsun presented individuals caught in this callous, self-righteous group setting. The environment of the traditional group bound them with a thousand threads. Sociologically, whole classes of people, particularly women and youth, were held in a state of servile dependence; psychologically, all participated in binding themselves as they grew up and internalized the cultural style. Change was predicated on breaking the hold of tradition within oneself as well as others. The pathos of the reformer or rebel lay in the almost futile effort to free oneself from four thousand years of history. As the protagonist in "The Diary of a Madman" finally realized, it was not just the others around him in a "man-eating" environment who were implicated in sustaining the status quo, but himself; for he, too, had ingested the tradition, unknowingly, as a child. Only the not yet socialized children of the future could be saved, could offer a Way Out of the predicament.

Becoming an agent of change within such an all-encompassing group meant, first, a conscious reorienting of the self, that is, a deliberate desocialization through awareness, an unlearning of the socially accepted habits and attitudes that had come to characterize one's own inner life and behavior. It meant, second, the even larger task of attempting to unmake the inner world of ordinary Chinese. Change could not happen as long as this great majority preferred to destroy an innovator as a "crazy man" rather than to open themselves to doubt about traditional wisdom and to the possibility of new ideas and forms in politics, ethics, and social life. This failing of ordinary Chinese was addressed by Lu Hsun most fully in his satirical piece, "The True Story of Ah Q." The nameless Ah Q was held up as a mirror in which all could see their reflections; by implication all Chinese shared his faults.[3] In the story, Ah Q is timid, even cowardly, full of resentments that he releases only when confident of getting away with it. He has a repertoire of ways to achieve subjective victory and wipe out objective defeats and losses. He has keen eyes to his own advantage in any situation, whether avoiding pain or securing fame and profit, despite the idealistic labels he may attach to his own behavior. And he readily inflates his own self-image and thinks himself above others, although he can also be very self-effacing if necessary: "I am an insect—now will you let me go?" Ah Q is a spineless creature, finely attuned to living within the prejudices of his group, yet trying desperately to enhance his self-image at every opportunity. He is open to manipulation and abuse by his social and political "betters" because of his ignorant imprisonment in the group's ways.

For someone like the character Ah Q, however, spinelessness was also a strength, for the capacity for subjective victory lent a psychological resiliency in the face of defeat and humiliation. Flexibility in different situations permitted a variety of behaviors, all in good conscience; this undoubtedly enhanced survival as it meant avoidance of clashes over principle with stronger parties as well as the absence of debilitating self-doubts and recriminations. The long-range costs of these "strengths," however, were continuing to live in a world of dangerous illusion and facing an eventual crisis of moral integrity and self-respect. Among the characters in "The True Story of Ah Q," individual identity and responsibility are reduced to role-playing, as condemned criminal, imitation foreigner, would-be revolutionary, disgraced mate, competent thief. Furthermore, for both the characters in the story and the real people they limned, such roles were played within a drama whose script was now outdated and inappropriate for twentieth-century Chinese society. China needed, in Lu Hsun's vision, strong individuals with empathy and honesty who could redefine roles and create a new drama.[4]

The interplay between self and group is richly posed in Lu Hsun's works, and I have built upon various of his insights in developing parts of this book, especially in Chapter Four on spiders without webs and marionettes on strings. But his vision is not the last word. It has a melodramatic quality, perhaps necessary in promoting change, that tells us as much about Lu Hsun's own struggles with adversity and shame as it does about a traditional-minded society in change. How powerful were society and tradition? The "group" is after all only a designation for special aggregations of individuals, organized as families, clans, villages, schools, neighborhoods, peoples, or nations, and each of these defined by certain physical spaces, social structures, rules, and sanctions. While some groups were clearly capable of "devouring" some individuals, society as a whole in China was neither omnipotent nor self-perpetuating; it was a debtor, borrowing its power from the support or acquiescence of individual members. And the individual, in hundreds of unconscious appropriations, habitual acts, and conscious decisions, negotiated and then renegotiated again and again how much power would be lent to others or reserved to self. Tradition in practice was no more monolithic than society. Indeed parts of tradition, such as the ideal of the superior man, could assist in the development of strong individuals with some of the traits that Lu Hsun admired. The old family system itself generated tens of thousands of imperfectly socialized children, with many more appearing through new openings in families and schools in the early twentieth century. Some of these young people were redefining roles, using traditional psychology to new ends; and through social dramas newly scripted by small groups, they were opening up pathways to a different future.

But while not absolute, the power of authorities wielding traditional levers of control within groups would appear awesome to a growing child. We have seen the pressures for conformity at work within the first world of childhood. Two unequal parties—powerful, towering adults and dependent, small infants and children—enter into a pact that is highly resistant to change because the parents' allies in this learning process are the fears, insecurities, and powerlessness of the child. The pact said to children, Learn and accept the importance of biological continuity within the family, the rightness of graded obligations to past and present family members, and the need to achieve a standard of worthy adulthood within the human group *(tso jen)*. Do this and you shall be accepted by us as a worthy family member, by your neighbors and society as a "good and decent man." The child's sense of his own worth and of the coherence of the world came to depend on these early internalized meanings; any attack on them, even on those meanings that victimized or tyrannized him, threatened his own sense of security in a coherent world. The child became his own taskmaster, his own ego the protector of a social world. In the wider society, the language of *lien* or "face" reinforced these norms by providing guidelines for respect before others as well as warning signs of social ostracism. The formal institutions and cultural ethos of the empire, from the orthodox moral teaching of the Confucian classics to the legal and coercive sanctions that could be brought to bear against cultural and political dissidents, provided an outer ring reinforcing social orthodoxy.

Of all these circles that encompassed Chinese lives, the family mattered most. The male kinship group was an "everlasting corporation," stretching back to past ancestors and forward to generations unborn. The actual family *(chia)* that lived together was the first and last station in life for an individual. Life was contained within this kinship circle probably because basic perceived social needs were met there better than through alternatives, real or imagined. In the formulation of anthropologist Francis L. K. Hsu, the satisfying of human needs for status, security, and sociability within the family and clan weakened any outward drive into private escapes or extra-kinship groups.[5] A child quickly learned that it had a status relative to others, and what degree of emotional involvement and obligation was necessary to maneuver successfully through the family network. This interaction within the group was well defined in customs, rules, and regulations. *Pao* or "reciprocity" built a hope of mutuality into these rules, stipulating that "every act of receiving means an obligation to return," even if equivalence was measured out over long periods of time. The restricted lives of young people and the suffering of women could be compensated for by the prospect of real authority and privileges as mature adults or honored elders. There was a cost of diminished individual freedom in this arrangement, but also a gain in individual security. Identity for most was automatic within the all-inclusive membership of the family: "I am my father's son" was a simple, well understood credo. Indeed, active participation in Chinese family life made a person part of a meaningful drama, which through ancestor worship transcended the here and now. It schooled one in exacting social interaction that required a finely adjusted set of calculations about the other actors, sensitivity to interpersonal signals and cues, and considerable emotional self-control. A skillful performance demanded great attentiveness and knowledge, and had its intangible reward in contributing to the harmony of the whole living group as well as its practical advantages in mutual support and help.

This system, Hsu has argued, did not produce many visible dissidents, nor many with new ways to offer who were willing to fight hard for their realization.[6] The logical recruits to movements for change—the misfits and the ambitious—were effectively neutralized within the system. Was one living up to the ancestral name? Did one have sons to continue the family line? Was one's "face" exposed through breaking with customary practices? Those vulnerable to social ostracism typically reacted by making greater efforts to conform in every way possible. Exceptional individuals who were more ambitious and talented tended to compete along traditional lines in order to become illustrious sons of the kinship group. Their competitive efforts led to bigger funerals, temples, and graveyards; ostentatious weddings; feats of filial piety; extensive genealogical records; and larger families under one roof—changes in scale but not in kind.[7] While this blocking of dissent and channeling of ambition seems demonstrable in studies of West Town, Yunnan, and other villages, it is also true that too little investigation has been directed at the limitations of the hold of the traditional group upon individuals; thus our generalizations about conformity are overstated. Three areas in particular warrant a closer look: the mechanism of the inner/outer split as it defines the limits of conformity; the operation of secondary customs that modified cultural demands in the light of certain psychological needs; the traditional ideal of the superior man as leverage against the power of shame.

THE INNER/OUTER SPLIT

The emergence of one child's special awareness of an inner self distinct from the person implied by her outer, public behavior was outlined in

Chapter Four above.[8] What the author of "My Secret Self" describes is a common defense mechanism that must have been a part of the psychological makeup of many other Chinese children. The rich detail on her early childhood world sets this autobiographical piece apart from most memoirs and allows us to enter realms that existed in other lives but remained unexpressed. The author spent the first fifteen years of her life in a port city of China during the Nationalist era of the 1930s, where her father had some prominence as a public official. Subsequently, she lived briefly in an overseas Chinese community before coming to the United States, attending college, marrying an American-born Chinese, and studying as a graduate student at Columbia, where she wrote "My Secret Self" as part of a research project. Her exposure to more than one culture and her extensive, bilingual schooling may have contributed to her articulateness and her ability to objectify her experience. Certainly they made her somewhat atypical. Nevertheless, her childhood and youth were spent in a traditional extended family of parents, paternal grandparents, siblings, and other relatives; and it was dominated by a father whom she portrays as conservative. The pressures for conformity that she experienced were those felt by others, and the limits of their hold on at least this one child can be explored directly through her account.

Conformity to group expectations had to be learned, and most Chinese children, like children elsewhere, were imperfect learners. What they did learn was to give up the illusion of omnipotence experienced in infancy, when the world seemed to exist for them and their needs, and to take on a larger world in which their needs had to be negotiated with others who were powerful, and not always moral or praiseworthy.[9] For the young girl whose life is recalled in "My Secret Self," this larger world meant a disillusioning experience with her grandmother, the teasing and judgmental attitude of her parents, the sparring and outright fighting with her elder sister ("I doubt my parents ever knew half that went on behind our closed doors"), the experience of being manipulated and used by others as well as the thrill and guilt of participating in "wanton" mischief with her peer group. Each generation of children had to learn out of hard and varied experience what was expected from them; "the group" and "tradition" were embodied in people and viewpoints, sometimes minority viewpoints, that emerged through real life encounters. Life proceeded in all its untidy fullness and contradictions, no mat-

ter what the moral blueprint and its interpreters (who were also its en-
forcers) said. The language of *lien,* we should recall, assumed falls from
grace; the stages of slippage, of loss of face, were noted and recorded.

Although many different kinds of messages came through to children
struggling to navigate or thrive in that larger world beyond the dependency of infancy, one message appears to have been particularly clear:
Compensate for group restrictions imposed on your outer behavior by
building up an active, private, inner life. This inner resistance, as we
called it in Chapter Four, was a response to the minutely prescriptive
rules based on generation, age, and gender that governed every social
act within the family; such prescriptiveness made it very difficult for the
young to have their own spontaneous feelings, hopes, wishes, or decisions recognized as legitimate by those with authority over them. So the
"real self" inside split off from the "social self" that others saw. Although the awareness of an inner/outer tension is a universal phenomenon, in the Chinese case this natural awareness intensified into a deliberately cultivated, conscious split because of the authoritarian style of
kinship and of other institutions modeled on kinship (e.g., secret societies and the state). The cultural distinctiveness of this inner/outer split
is further corroborated by the informant's observation that she lost her
"inner life" after coming to the United States; now she could speak and
act out directly what was on her mind.[10]

The informant's sharpened sense of her inner self was created through
certain experiences of revelation, two of which are given in her account.
The first, at age three-and-a-half, took place during a vaccination in a
doctor's office, when her mother tried to distract her attention with an
alarm clock. Thinking her mother's efforts foolish, she nonetheless played
along, consciously, as in a game, while keeping one eye on the doctor.
The event revealed to her that the actions of adults could be contrived
and inappropriate. By seeing through her mother's acting and playing a
part herself, she had discovered her own inner self. This situation is
similar to the child's discovery that one can lie to others and get away
with it; parents are not omniscient, it says, for they cannot see through
my pretense. The inner self becomes the hidden, secret self that others
cannot see and see through, the self behind the self that is acting consciously and visibly out in front of others.

The second experience, at eight years of age, did not reflect such a universal dimension of human social interaction but posed for the growing child the specific predicament of the Chinese organization of family life. After the girl had remarked to her grandmother that she saw rings before her eyes, she found out later, to her bewilderment, that she had somehow appeared to be insubordinate. As we have seen, Chinese rules governing the appropriate behavior of children were very strict; and although younger children might be excused or dealt with more leniently, children after the age of six were made to understand that they were not legitimate partners to a negotiation process. The decisions of traditional authority figures were supposed to end arguments.

> "Children should not open their mouths indiscreetly," my father said to me sternly. "How could you have eye trouble at your age!" I felt terrible inside. I wanted to say, "Why not?" Yet I could not find the words to express my feeling, so stirred was I by what seemed to me a frame-up. I stammered, "But it was the truth," only to bring sterner remarks from Father. I bolted from the room.[11]

An innocent remark on an actual experience had become a heated issue because the grandmother apparently chose to present the remark in a critical fashion to her son and he, taking the criticism upon himself, displaced his anger onto his indiscreet daughter. She in turn felt anger, and calmed herself by "a discourse I had with myself." Through such experiences she became "a quiet child . . . full of observations, feelings, and thoughts, but lacking in speech and action. Externally I was passive, internally I was seldom inactive."

The difference between these two experiences of revelation is instructive. The discovery of pretense or pretentiousness in others, like the discovery of one's own power to convey illusions by lying and pretending, is an enlarging experience. Seeing through her mother's pretense gave the daughter insight into the forms and possibilities of social interaction. But in having her words manipulated by her grandmother and her negotiating power snatched away by her father, she learned to put restrictive boundaries around her interaction with adults and to cultivate her own internal resources. It was the unpredictable and unanswerable nature of parental prerogatives that caused this sharp inner/outer split. What had she done wrong? Disobedience was monitored so closely that virtually anything, if it struck an authority figure wrong, could become "indiscreet." Raising the question was itself counterproductive, indeed fresh evidence of the very "crime" at issue. In her presentation and resentment of this compound injustice, we can hear strong echoes of the attitudes described in the testimony of Yan Phou Lee, who, recalling his boyhood in the 1860s, remembered ruing his own imprudence in contradicting his elders and observed that a subordinate in China fared better by keeping silent than by protesting innocence.

Alternative courses of action did exist, although she chose not to exercise them fully. First, she could have displaced her anger upon other persons, creatures, or objects within her control. An "unpardonable incident" with a bachelor relative is illuminating in precisely this context. As children of the head of the household, she and her sister and "little auntie" were protected in their mischief-making by the father's authoritative status; to criticize them was to criticize the father who had responsibility for them, and this the lower-status bachelor relative, unlike the grandmother, hesitated to do. "With a forced smile on his flushed face," he had to beg the brats to stop putting beauty marks on his calendar pictures of seminudes. A second alternative would have been to seek solace and support from others. Instead she chose the hard and lonely path of self-cultivation, a highly valued course within the traditional culture because it was revered as the moral way of the sages. She sought to control her reactions, to exhibit patience and tolerance and understanding, to examine her own feelings and motives, and eventually to overcome the inner/outer split by bringing her inner sentiments into harmony with proper external behavior. It provided some solace for her that sages sometimes looked like fools.

Although she had reservations about the truthfulness of her behavior, she did come to act outwardly in ways that encouraged family stability. Despite considerable rivalry with her older sister, the ideal—and a good bit of the substance in their schoolwork—was mutual help. She was willing to compensate for her sister's feeling less attractive and intelligent by deliberately praising her sister's character. She was prepared to let her parents' judgmental attitude towards her own character go unchallenged for many years out of the same regard for her sister's feeling of inferiority. After the disillusioning experience with her grandmother, she let adults have their way by not being open with them and not putting herself in situations where her self-disclosure might be hypocritically betrayed again. To this extent, she acted consistently with a success-in-creating-harmony orientation rather than a truth-in-honesty orientation. "Truth" had to be applied empirically to situations, and thus could involve dissembling, outright lies, and tolerance of illusions in the surface interactions as the partial and legitimate means of creating and keeping the peace.[12]

Within this orientation, there was much stimulation for the development of individual ego awareness. After the experience with her grandmother, her introspection became intense and she had frequent "debates with my inner self." This process heightened her knowledge of who she was as a particular person, as she differentiated her needs and perspectives from others; what she actually did or said came to be one part of a repertoire of possible responses to situations, which included her own inner thoughts and feelings as well as the conscious assessment from which words and acts selectively followed. For example, her post-tantrum approach to the sibling rivalry with her sister involved consideration of many dimensions: the overt deeds and words of her parents and sister, the underlying motives and needs that their words and deeds seemed to convey, the ideal action that group harmony enjoined upon her, her own need for self-respect, her obligations as younger sister and filial daughter, the decisions on how much to disclose of herself overtly and how much to withhold and deal with internally. As argued in Chapter Three, learning to act responsibly within the group was much more than taking orders; it meant an ongoing dialogue between self and various others, a continuing exploration of boundaries for self-expression in feelings, thoughts, speech, and deeds.

The inner/outer split, seen from the perspective of the individual growing child, has implications for the nature and hold of tradition. In theoretical discussions by philosophers and historians, tradition as a body of norms, values, and knowledge is easily reified into a monolithic structure; but in the lives of individuals, tradition accrues bit by bit, as features of it are encountered and appropriated. Tradition in China was a world of possibilities, embodied first of all in people and only secondarily in books and artifacts. The psychological mechanism that transferred these diverse possibilities from adult to child was identification, a process that was selective, incomplete, and even contradictory, as in the case of sons of the educated who often came to inhabit one world with their nurses, another with their mothers, and a third with their fathers. Tradition meant diverse interpretations of the world, drawing on plain-speaking bits of peasant folklore and popular religious beliefs as well as conflicting schools of classical learning and social criticism. Was going to school a way to fulfill one's human capacities, a way to attain prestige as an official, or a way to be held in harness? Was footbinding a way to perfect one's female nature or a device perpetuated by men in order to restrain women? Was praying to spirits and propitiating demons a praiseworthy, prudent act, or a superstitious practice? Individual identity was never a mere replica of social beliefs, but reflected the diverse ideas within society that had been concretely encountered and appropriated.

Appropriation itself was complicated, for children might act out a behavior as part of a social drama but retain reservations about the sense or fairness of what was required. The inner/outer split thus introduces a huge question mark into our theorizing about Chinese behavior; the relationships among deeds, speech, thoughts, and feelings might well be discontinuous at each step, progressing from inner feelings and thoughts to outer speech and deeds. We have, for example, hypothesized that some filial sons were filial sons by default. They did not necessarily want to be what the social drama required them to be; and they kept alive, inside, a hidden, alternative viewpoint. They were held in the filial role not so much by internalized values as by the overwhelmingness of concrete situations that offered them only disastrous alternatives. When situations changed, prescribed meanings and roles could quickly lose their hold for this group of young people; alternative meanings and roles were retrievable in the shadows of the mind. The persistent effort by Chinese moral philosophers and political rulers, both traditional and contemporary, to probe behind deeds to the thoughts that give rise to them, perhaps reflected a clear recognition that compliant behavior did not mean internalized values, that much publicly manifested action was a mask, and that an explosive potential existed below the surface of an authoritarian society committed to harmony. The inner sphere of the individual could be touched, bruised, seduced, overloaded, and indoctrinated by others; but it was, and is, finally a private and uncontrollable reality.

Certain secondary customs, or backhanded ways of satisfying psychological needs, also acknowledged the limits of the hold of the group; in so doing these customs created institutionalized ways to give expression to the unconventional or "deviant" underside of individual and social reality. The expression was often deceptive: A visible public stance, such as a large, extended family's facing the community as one family under one roof, concealed compromises and patterns of tolerated deviance, such as the division of the household into separate living units with their own kitchens. Outwardly, the face of conventional morality could be preserved, while the needs of persons, families, and even whole communities to be different, to have some respite from hierarchical control and moralistic gossip, could be given some degree of protection, even if not legally guaranteed. These secondary customs thus reveal a complex field of negotiation between cultural demands and psychological needs.

One of the more unusual formulations of such a custom is Leon Stover's argument that the entire underside of the society—the myriad folk cultures of village China—was in part preserved in its differentness by the widely accepted myth of elite moral leadership over a unified Confucian society. He claims that the Confucian elite did not really speak for the entire society, because peasant communities largely regulated themselves and were neither Confucian nor oriented toward the imperial center. Nevertheless the pretense of moral leadership of a unified society was useful to the elite because it allowed them to claim that they offered peasants something in return for the taxes they extracted and resources they controlled. And on their side of the bargain, so long as they paid those taxes and did not threaten the peace, peasant communities were left alone in their local cultures and targeted only with the moral indoctrination of the *Sacred Edict* (a bi-monthly lecture on Confucian orthodoxy delivered in paraphrased form in rural areas after 1659, but mostly a meaningless exercise after 1850). In Stover's controversial argument, the thin veneer of upper-class Confucian culture did serve to solidify the elite, which was spread geographically throughout the empire; but it left the varied folk cultures undisturbed beneath this veneer. This arrangement permitted an outward acceptance by all of the authority and moral leadership of the cultural center while acknowledging in practice the reality of two separate subcultures.[13] Stover finds a similar fictive gloss in the elite's use of such terms as *friendship* among peers and *contentment* among peasants; in each case the terms tell only an idealized part of the story and conceal underlying realities that he argues are more accurately defined as "formalized informality" for friendship and "sanctimonious husbandry" for contentment.[14] The outer, more idealized impression is held out for public viewing.

At the level of villages, some types of unconventional behavior were tolerated, and even expected. As recorded by Margery Wolf in *The House of Lim,* the dominant clan in one Taiwanese village had a tradition of pride in being apart, in innovating, in leading. Eccentricities were simply felt to be inherited in these strong individuals, and it was taken for granted by villagers that their behavior would be somewhat unpredictable. Yet there were limits: The clan elder could spend hours idly with foreigners as long as this appeared to be an alternative outlet for the release of inner strains and desires, much the same as spending time with prostitutes or gambling, but not if this contact began to draw him away from the village and its established ways.

> In the closed life of a Taiwanese village, the usual quirks of a man's personality are accepted in the same way as a crippled leg: that's just the way he is. But even the slightest suspicion of a more basic peculiarity—a man who questions the premises his neighbors call fact—leads to doubt and distrust. Because of the long hours he wasted talking with us, some of Lim Chieng-cua's neighbors wondered at his patience, others grew suspicious of his motives and ours, and the more acute were uneasy at his obvious enjoyment of profitless discussion . . . I hope his neighbors concluded after our departure that the hours Lim Chieng-cua wasted with us were only a modern variation of the hours he wasted in the company of his mistresses.[15]

Village morality chiefly emphasized the inhabitants' duties as parents, neighbors, friends, and providers. Knowledge of the bonds of human relations was the core of traditional teaching; as revealed in the language of *lien* (face), it was believed to distinguish human beings from the rest of nature. "Humans have *lien,* trees have bark. Without *lien,* a hundred evils can be done," as one proverb related. Anyone disregarding these bonds was not only thought to subvert tradition, but to be an inhuman monster as well. On the other hand, if in their public performance individuals met, or appeared to meet, conventional moral expectations, they could be forgiven much in their private lives. For example, in the particular Taiwanese village cited above, it was interpreted as a filial act for a poor daughter to sell her youthful body as a prostitute and thus help support her parents; prostitution had little respectability as a vocation, but a prostitute might gain community respect as a filial daughter.[16] Circumstances, such as poverty, which could limit choices and create strong conflicts among values, were considered in village morality.

Not all situational constraints counted equally, however. Maxine Hong Kingston recounts the fate of an aunt—"No Name Woman"—in a Kwangtung village in the 1920s where there was no apparent margin of understanding and forgiveness. Hers had been one of seventeen hurry-up weddings in the village, just before the men, including her husband, sailed for America. When she became pregnant several years later, it was a transgression beyond redemption, beyond argument. Her family "expected her alone to keep the traditional ways, which her brother, now among the barbarians, could fumble without detection. The heavy, deep-rooted women were to maintain the past against the flood, safe for returning. But the rare urge west had fixed upon our family, and so my aunt crossed boundaries not delineated in space." Her act was a violation of kinship obligations that could not be tolerated. The villagers, counting the days of her pregnancy, swooped down on the household one evening, tearing it apart as a way of re-establishing the social (and cosmic) equilibrium destroyed by her actions. That night her aunt gave birth, and the next morning both mother and baby were found plugging up the family well. "Misallying couples snapped off the future, which was to be embodied in true offspring. The villagers punished her for acting as if she could have a private life, secret and apart from them."[17] Of course, what Kingston neglects to add, some did have different lives at night, hidden from their neighbors' eyes, until the consequences caught up with them. And here, as in many other instances, women and youth were severely disadvantaged. Parents and in-laws, with the backing of elderly community leaders, could initiate the punishment of unchaste women, unfaithful wives, and even grossly disobedient children, all of whom could be condemned to death by force ("drowned in a pig's cage") by an unforgiving community.[18]

The unconventional behavior permitted by tradition to scholar-officials in their private lives was acceptable as long as it was part of a rhythm between dedication and release, work and leisure, and did not threaten to undermine their primary roles and public performance. In a contemporary version of this phenomenon, a "modern" social reformer could become more palatable to traditionalists on Taiwan if he were conventional in his interpersonal relations, that is, filial to his parents and faithful to friends. When Hu Shih, for example, is cited by traditionalists as being in some ways very Confucian, this is usually what they mean. He is widely respected for enduring his unhappy marriage and being devoted to his mother.[19]

In varied ways, some straying of individuals beyond the normal boundaries of conventional behavior was known to happen and was not automatically condemned. Francis L. K. Hsu has postulated that these secondary customs or "safety valves" were built into Chinese social life at precisely those points where unqualified insistence upon primary cultural demands and regulations would have produced unmanageable psychological and external conflicts. He cites in particular the architectural arrangement of division under one roof, which allowed mature sons within an extended family some scope for economic decision-making, self-expression, and conjugal intimacy. The importance attached to form, particularly to grandiose funerals for deceased parents, also worked to appease the guilty consciences of sons for less than devoted filial behavior.[20] The conspicuous value placed on dutiful public performance in certain key roles also took pressure off individual performance in less primary roles. In minor relationships, such as those between mother and son, brother and sister, and grandparent and grandchild, affection and intimacy were permitted, as well as in major relationships at certain times and places, such as between father and son during the infancy-toddler period and between husband and wife in the privacy of the inner room. Even the sharp division between men as "outside persons" and women as "inside persons" gave women a special sphere where men were not expected to intrude; if village women were barred from speaking about what went on outside the house, village men were also kept in the dark about what the women said among themselves in the women's community. Thus not only a physical boundary but also some psychological protection was built into the distinction between inside and outside persons.[21]

The secondary custom of seeing supernatural force in precocious youngsters was important in the socialization of talented young male children; this earned them not only praise and indulgence, but immunity from normal expectations and an enlarged scope for self-assertion. We have seen in Chapter Six how young Shu Hsin-ch'eng acquired the appellation "prodigy" (*shen-t'ung,* lit. "good-spirit child") for his exceptional study achievements, which seemed to indicate to his awestruck neighbors that an unusual spiritual force resided in him. They dared not dispute his public posting of a long essay condemning the "despicable behavior" of a local deity. With or without imputed supernatural assistance, many children in the late Ch'ing period, as they had in earlier periods, developed into stereotypical *t'ao-ch'i* or "mischievous" children. As we have seen in Chapter Three, *t'ao ch'i* children could emerge and even thrive within the filial system, not because they were deliberately encouraged (quite the contrary), but because of the tardy impact of paternal disciplining, the delegation of authority to teachers, the interventionist style of the father, and the supporting network of mothers, nurses, grandparents, sisters, and kindly males. In combination, these openings guaranteed a steady stream of "poorly" socialized children who could not easily be bent to the will of the group. And many parents themselves had ambivalent feelings about bending them. Unconventional activities, especially immoral behavior, could not be openly encouraged; but uncommon vigor and intelligence in children could win secret approval from parents.

THE TRADITIONAL IDEAL AS A CRITIQUE OF CONVENTIONAL MORALITY

Besides taking advantage of secondary customs, the individual psyche could break the stifling hold of tradition by setting the highest ideals of that very tradition against the conventional decency described in the language of *lien*. Choosing the nonconformist stance of the superior man gave one a counterweight to the shaming power of gossip. These swipes and cuts of hostile opinion—so noticeable in Lu Hsun's fictional recreations of the early Republican era—were a major prop of conventional morality, which, except in the treaty ports and some progressive circles, was still very much intact in China during the early twentieth century. Cultural and political reformers often had to convince themselves as well as others that they were not heretics, rebels, or fools. They had to have unusual strength and self-confidence, and the ability to confront gossip, disdain, and even ostracism. Otherwise, like many returned students from America, they would find themselves scattered and isolated in different parts of the country, disheartened and discouraged. They would "too easily lose themselves in the immensity of things" and be unable "to wrestle successfully against the forces of conservatism and opposition."[22]

The plight of one such man in a rural village in Hupei is recounted in Hu Ch'iu-yuan's autobiography, *Collected Fragments of Early Writings (Shao-tso shou-yi)*. He describes the situation of his father, who had taken over responsibility for two innovative local ventures, a school and a railway, but then had been imprisoned for default when higher authorities claimed them without assuming local debts. In the summer of 1930 when Hu Ch'iu-yuan returned to the village of Huang-p'i, Hupei, his father was facing another crisis and another possible prison sentence. Relatives and friends argued the indignity and uselessness of his going to prison and urged him to leave Huang-p'i and retire in the face of the public clamor over the case. But his father, using traditional concepts, kept turning the arguments back upon them, and in the process redefining "shame" and "respectability." The following words, as recollected, were part of his self-defense to his nineteen-year-old son, explaining why he refused to give in and leave the village. His self-defense is worth quoting at length; for not only does it juxtapose portraits of the inferior man of conventional morality and the superior man of Confucian wisdom, but it also discloses how the pressures generated by fear, insult, and shame were brought to bear on a nonconformist by his friends and relatives in addition to his enemies.

If as soon as I hear that someone doesn't like me I must move to Wuchang, and then someone else doesn't like me and so I go to Nanking, and then someone else doesn't like me, how can I avoid going abroad? Although the world is large, if it goes on like this, there will eventually be no place to rest my body. I have already retreated [to this village], and there is no other place I can retreat to. I will go out to stroll when I please, and I will not be intimidated into fleeing. They are not emperors, and they cannot force me. If we have broken the law or done some shameful thing, then we should be afraid even before a three-year-old child. But if we have committed no crime nor disgraced ourselves, then we need not fear heaven, earth, or spirits, let alone emperors. This matter really should not be considered very important, and there is nothing to fear. These friends and relatives only know that even falling leaves may break open one's head. They do not know that if one does not consider strange things as unusual, their strangeness disappears. We must know [the limits of] our virtue and our strength, and not provoke disputes. [But] we shouldn't fear people without reason or be excessively afraid of doing things.

I do not consider it dignified to sit in prison and to present oneself in court; but if one has committed no crime, then there is no shame connected with it . . . Some friends and relatives say, If you have to sit in prison, go sit in the large prison in Nanking. You should not be seized and handled here like a chicken. That's no different from saying that the beggars in Nanking are a bit more dignified than the beggars in Hankow. This expression reveals an impure heart, and a hankering after fame and profit . . . We should know that for a man to act in this world he can only look for the resources in himself. He can really only ask about the rightness of things, and inquire into his own conscience. I do not concern myself with profit and loss, glory and shame. One must also take a long range view, counting on the judgment of posterity . . . No matter whether one is an emperor or bandit, acts done without regard for the right way are shameful. In the Ming dynasty, many eminent persons had their buttocks beaten by the eunuchs, and who will say that beating people is dignified but being beaten was disgraceful? One must consider the "why" in all matters . . .

I have already said these things to the relatives and some friends, but they never understand. When they speak out, they all say that I am provocative. Because I'm not thinking of leaving, they say there's trouble. What kinds of words are these? These friends and relatives naturally are decent people, but they are also "yes men." Some of them even listen to the propaganda of those people [his enemies] on the streets, who say that they only want me to leave Huang-p'i and can help me find work elsewhere. These words are not only nonsense but insulting. I eat only my own rice. Each grain is earned by bitter toil and tastes good and sweet. I also have some small talents, and each time after the family resources were exhausted I was able to restore them. Because they [his enemies] don't have this small talent, or wouldn't value this kind of talent, they can only pick up a signboard, look for some position of influence, and live off other people. And what great talents do they have?

Actually these relatives and friends do not understand the principles of things and do not understand insulting words when they hear them . . . They take in the insulting words of others, and even want to convey them to my ears. This is to fall into their trap, to do their bidding, and use my friends and relatives to surround me, intimidate me, insult me. I can be shamed but I cannot be made to shame myself . . . [T]his kind of yes man is none other than those Confucius called local hypocrites [*hsiang-yuan*]. I would call them "pig's intestines." They cannot stand up, and they cannot comprehend principles. Since they cannot distinguish truth and falsehood, they also cannot understand profit and loss. They only fear this and that. You can go tell them that I only believe in Heaven and fate . . . If fate decrees that I should die, fleeing will not keep me alive, and if fate decrees that I shall not die, no one will be able to kill me! Only because decent men are useless do bad men acquire power. From the conditions in this little village, one can see a microcosm of all of China. If the macrocosm is like this, there isn't much individuals can do. But spirit can both expand and contract. If the principles of the superior man [*chün-tzu*] spread, then those of the inferior man contract. If those of the inferior man expand, those of the superior man contract. In whatever time or place, we can only stand on our principles and let correct principles slowly spread and pernicious ones slowly contract. At the very least one must not permit one word or act to spread the inferior man's principles. Doing this is what we call "changing customs" or "turning back the trend." To do these things we must measure our strength. This is then the meaning of "grasping the opportunity and exhausting one's effort" [*sui-yuan chin-li*]— the only path that you will be able to follow.[23]

The elder Hu portrays the inferior man as above all a weak individual who drifts with the prevailing tides of opinion and rumor. He is attuned to conventional definitions of crime and shame which he assents to out of fear or self-effacement before authority ("emperors, demons, and gods"). He is motivated by the desire for profit, fame, status, the fear of loss and shame; he has no ability to go beyond these to the discrimination of truth and falsehood *(shih-fei)* and the discernment of correct moral behavior. He is anxious to preserve appearances and to avoid undignified situations. He is likely to nod his head towards the Will of Heaven as a ready explanation both for difficulties and successes. He cannot stand up to the world and penetrate the conventional face of things in his environment because he has failed to anchor his ego firmly in something other than the small world he knows. He has no independent stance, economically or intellectually, with which to face the world and so is doomed to exist as a reflection of conventions, authorities, fashions. He is the "decent man" who lives within the inherited or prescribed definition of the personal and non-personal world.

In contrast, the social type of the superior man is revealed as an unconventional person, distinguished above all by the personal stamp he places on the world about him. He defines shame and crime and sin not solely by convention and appearance, but by the context of the acts and the truthfulness of the charges. If truly wrong, he feels under judgment before a weak child as much as before a strong official or powerful deity. He has a long-range view of reputation and shame and trusts in the considered judgment of posterity, not in the instant judgment of community approval or condemnation. He is not intimidated by the powerful or by the threat of ostracism and isolation nor is he afraid that "even falling leaves may break open one's head"; he even anticipates the unfamiliar and strange. He accepts neither himself nor conventions at face value, and recognizes the need to reexamine the integrity of his own views as well as to penetrate the falsehoods, injustices, and delusions of life around him.

Handling the shame that others might thrust upon them was a major inner struggle for those attempting to break free from conventional morality and group face. How could the individual become invulnerable to the barbs and stares and gossip? How could one conquer the resentments that seemed bound to arise, especially if self-reflection confirmed the correctness of one's stand? There were two approaches and elder Hu's self-defense employs them both. One was to inflate his own self-image and denigrate the opposition as mere "wolves, a pathetic lot." Hu tried to establish his superiority by satirizing the abilities of his tormenters, calling them poor calligraphers or mere clerks, and assuring himself that he could do better. "My not doing so is a matter of intent, not ability." By such defenses, he could keep his equilibrium and endure the shame that "inferior men" inflicted on him. This is similar to the story in *Mencius* about the traditional superior man, who worn down by the perversity and unreasonableness of lesser men, would say, "This is a man utterly lost indeed! Since he conducts himself so, what is there to choose between him and a brute? Why should I go to contend with a brute?"[24]

The second approach—reversing the perspective on who or what was shameful—was a more profound response, for it went beyond the conventional calculation of ability and righteousness that still characterized the first approach. It embodied the recognition that "shameful" acts contain a double revelation: they expose the alleged social failings of the individual, but also reveal the limited nature of social mores to the individual. Were those who perpetrated the act shameful or those who suffered from it? "Who will say that beating [the buttocks of] people is dignified, but being beaten is disgraceful?" In the experience of shame— of being out of step with society—lay the possibility of being stretched to think beyond the common morality of the particular social group and its prescribed rules. It permitted the discovery of other standards by which to measure oneself and one's society, and could liberate a person into a larger historical and human perspective. That larger awareness itself, while it may have left those who held it more isolated and unprotected in the particular social milieu, also gave them a certain sturdiness through being able to "discern and ally themselves with men and values over wide ranges of time and space." The sense of kinship with past sages and the sense of knowing and living ancient truths may have more than compensated for the loss of the comforts of a narrower but well-adjusted life.[25]

From the perspective of social reform, persisting through the experiences of shame and incongruity without being pulled back into the group's sway was a touchstone capacity, a final testing of character in the actual historical situation of early twentieth-century China. For social reform in China did not happen abroad, within the liberal training ground of America, nor in a human vacuum in China. It had to be achieved in groups, old ones, new ones, and mixed ones. This required courage and persistence by individuals in the face of active opposition as well as vigilance against passive backsliding into old habits and conventional ways of thinking and acting. And to maintain that courage and persistence and vigilance, young persons and adults had to draw upon a range of supports gathered over a lifetime, some of them deep and invisible, others quite conscious and explicit. For young men there was the positive early experience of maternal bonding that gave them an underlying faith and hope in a responsive and good world. There was the deep

memory of that earliest sense of autonomy and initiative, when as toddlers (and some of them as mischievous boys) they first tested their own
powers against the world. There was the experience of disciplined effort
as older boys, when they had learned to cooperate with other people and
master tasks in school, family, and field. There was that active inner
world of the "real self," where resentment at the unfeeling strictness of
rules, the harshness of paternal discipline, and the experience of shaming
and humiliation could be harbored and transmuted into alternative ways
and desires. There was the undergirding support of others, a mother, a
brother, friends and neighbors, schoolmates, groups of like-minded people. There were the examples and models of success—a Tseng Kuo-fan
who showed them what self-cultivation could do, an image of the traditional sage or superior man who was not intimidated by the crowd, a
Liang Ch'i-ch'ao or Ch'en Tu-hsiu who fearlessly spoke out and wrote
down what was on his mind. Girls born in this generation had fewer
opportunities than boys to exploit openings within traditional socialization, or to join the emergent counterculture of educated youth that provided a way station to unconventional lives. Still some succeeded. I do
not know what gave these girls and young women the strength to sur-
mount the additional obstacles that Chinese society put in their paths:
the secondary value placed on their arrival in the family as infants; the
unequal treatment they received compared to their brothers, including
the greater tolerance of mischievousness in boys; the restrictions imposed
on them as "inside persons" barred after puberty from access to the
world beyond the household; the prejudice within the male kinship family that valued them, and feared them, only for their reproductive power;
the lack of encouragement in society for them to aspire beyond the roles
of wife and mother; the widespread belief that education, and hence
higher levels of moral being, was unnecessary for them to be complete
persons.[26] In the end, both young men and young women, if they were
to make a difference in society, needed the courage and ability to translate their own feelings and thoughts into words and actions, or into
visible silences and non-actions, for only in the public arena would the
group's hold be challenged.

The Way Out for China and themselves could not, at first, be a group
way, but had to be achieved in individual minds breaking free from old

norms, or in the case of the traditional ideal of the superior man, in
individual minds giving a fresh moral meaning and institutional form
to the all-important virtue of *jen* or "human-heartedness." This new way
had to take shape in personal ideals: new or modified values about what
was good for people and society, visions of what might come into being
in history. These were ideals that could, with leadership and time, become embodied in new ways of life and thought for the Chinese people.
The ability to frame such ideals in turn reflected overall ego strength,
that sense of hopefulness, autonomy, initiative, competence, and identity that undergirds the courage to think and to act in new ways in the
world. For many, such ego strength and such action were precluded as
much by certain biases toward group dependency in traditional socialization as by the undertow engendered by the altered historical situation.
The great changes and contradictions they were experiencing were
understood simply as a victimizing process whose significance was best
captured by the age-old categories of timing *(shih)*, fate *(ming)* and luck
(yun). For a few, this wrenching process revealed discernible patterns,
prescriptions for action, ways to tame change; they were able to sustain
the fragile connection between inner thought and affect and outer action, in part because of other biases in their socialization experiences,
some of them very traditional, that encouraged ego strength, intellectual
synthesis, and conscientious action.

LU HSUN AND KUO MO-JO: LEADING THE GROUP BEYOND THE TRADITION

Lu Hsun (b. 1881) and Kuo Mo-jo (b. 1892) were two men among
these few who were able to transform the fragmenting experience of their
portion of history into new visions, forms, and directions for their fellow
countrymen. They had the courage and ability to be leaders, to challenge the group's hold in the public arena. In a typology of personalities
developed by Helen Lynd, both were "restless" persons who form their
identities in terms of evolving ideals of their own making; they were
not "normal" persons who find continuity in their lives by acting upon
what superiors have taught them they should do and should not do.
Restless persons discover their own lines of direction, but at greater

emotional cost than normal people; experiences of shame lead them to revelations of the innermost self as well as to the central dynamics of society.[27] Both these men knew shame firsthand, and had learned how to deflect, and even turn to their own use, this most powerful weapon in the arsenal of the traditional group.

LU HSUN. Lu Hsun we have met in these pages as a boy dwarfed by the high counter of a pawnshop, as a young man who chose to break with his family's gentry tradition by going to a new-style school in Nanking, and as an unrelenting critic of traditional China and its upper class through his short stories. He became the leading Chinese intellectual of the twentieth century and a mentor to some of the 1890s generation of educated youth. As a leader, he was a fearless critic of hypocrisy and weakness in himself as well as his fellow Chinese (with some indulgence toward youth and the poor) until his death in 1936. He was a man who expressed his leadership through his vision of reality and the power of his written words; out of intellectual integrity, he declined to commit himself fully to the morality, ideology, or historical mission of any political party.

Lu Hsun exemplified, in his life and through his works, one of Helen Lynd's "restless persons" measuring himself by his own internally evolving standards. In the autobiographical preface to *Outcry (Na-han)*, Lu Hsun recounts several experiences through which he came to shed earlier views as outmoded, provincial, unworthy, or uninformed. He sought to identify broader, more universal standards of human behavior and thinking, standards which in turn stood in judgment over aspects of his own behavior and that of his fellow Chinese. He was keenly aware of the double-edged power of shame either to hold the individual within the conformist crowd or to sharpen individual insight into society's claim and how that claim might be, or should be, contested. The "inferior men" of the village wine shop, the Ah Q's of China and the world, knew shame as a prod to conformity. Lu Hsun's early pessimism about social reform in China was grounded in his assessment that the villagers could not be shaken out of their familiar self-righteous worlds. The teahouse scene from his short story "Medicine" is clear on this point. Mr. Kang is the village bigot whose ego feeds upon being center stage and cajoling bystanders into agreement. The bystanders, because of disability (the hunchback), youth (the man in his twenties), or experience (the greybeard), might be presumed to be empathetic towards the young man who had just been executed for his unorthodox political beliefs; but they are all unwilling, or unable, to express any support. The young rebel, in their eyes, had been a rascal, a scoundrel, a rogue, a wretch, a criminal, a crazy fool. His expression of pity for the jailer was incomprehensible to them; this pity reflected a world view that perceived the jailer as a victim of society and not an enemy, a point of view that Lu Hsun wanted at least his young readers to comprehend.

> [T]he greybeard walked up to the man in brown and lowered his voice to ask:
>
> "Mr. Kang, I heard the criminal executed today came from the Hsia family. Who was it? And why was he executed?"
>
> "Who? Son of Widow Hsia, of course! Young rascal!"
>
> Seeing how they were all hanging on his words, Mr. Kang's spirits rose even higher. His jowls quivered, and he made his voice as loud as he could.
>
> "The rogue didn't want to live, simply didn't want to! There was nothing in it for me this time. Even the clothes stripped from him were taken by Red-eye the jailer . . . That young rogue was a real scoundrel! He even tried to incite the jailer to revolt!"
>
> "No! The idea of it!" A man in his twenties, sitting in the back row, expressed indignation.
>
> "You know, Red-eye went to sound him out, but he started chatting with him. He said the great Manchu empire belongs to us. Just think: is that kind of talk rational? Red-eye knew he had only an old mother at home, but had never imagined he was so poor. He couldn't squeeze anything out of him; he was already good and angry, and then the young fool would 'scratch the tiger's head' so he gave him a couple of slaps."
>
> "Red-eye is a good boxer. Those slaps must have hurt." The hunchback in the corner by the wall exulted.
>
> "The rotter was not afraid of being beaten. He even said how sorry he was."
>
> "Nothing to be sorry about in beating a wretch like that," said Greybeard.
>
> Kang looked at him superciliously and said disdainfully: "You misunderstood. The way he said it, he was sorry for Red-eye."
>
> His listeners' eyes took on a glazed look, and no one spoke . . .
>
> "Sorry for Red-eye—crazy! He must have been crazy!" said Greybeard, as if suddenly he saw light.
>
> "He must have been crazy!" echoed the man in his twenties . . .
>
> "Crazy!" agreed the hunchback, nodding his head.[28]

In a first person reminiscence, "A Small Incident," written in July 1920, Lu Hsun revealed how he, too, could identify with being caught up in the web of conventional, protective reactions. One evening in Peking, a rickshaw in which the narrator was riding accidently knocked over an old woman. It was disgusting, he thought, that the old woman should pretend to be hurt; the rickshaw puller deserved the mess he was getting into for helping her to the nearby police station. His own impulse was to "go on" and avoid trouble.

> Suddenly I had the strange sensation that [the rickshaw puller's] dusty retreating figure had in that instant grown larger. Indeed, the farther he walked the larger he loomed, until I had to look up to him. At the same time he seemed gradually to be exerting a pressure on me that threatened to overpower the small self hidden under my fur-lined gown.
>
> Almost paralyzed at that juncture, I sat there motionless, my mind a blank, until a policeman came out. Then I got down from the rickshaw.
>
> The policeman came up to me and said, "Get another rickshaw. He can't take you any further."
>
> On the spur of the moment I pulled a handful of coppers from my coat pocket and handed them to the policeman. "Please give him this," I said.
>
> The wind had dropped completely, but the road was still quiet. As I walked along thinking, I hardly dared to think about myself. Quite apart from what had happened earlier, what had I meant by that handful of coppers? Was it a reward? Who was I to judge the rickshaw man? I could give myself no answer.
>
> Even now, this incident keeps coming back to me. It keeps distressing me and makes me try to think about myself. The politics and fighting of those years have slipped my mind as completely as the classics I read as a child. Yet this small incident keeps coming back to me, often more vivid than in actual life, teaching me shame, spurring me on to reform, and imbuing me with fresh courage and fresh hope.[29]

Lu Hsun's unconventional reaction was to confront his shame, to forego the easy labels "ridiculous, pointless, troublesome," and to turn inward after the moment of the glassy stare. The secure, even smug, relationship between the self and others dissolves in such moments; the self-image is shaken and the world may never look quite the same again.[30] What turns the unconventional reaction into a promise for social change is using the insight gained through such experiences to break outward, from feelings to thoughts, from thoughts to words, from words to actions. Breaking free meant seeing through the opacity of habit and convention.

Through such apparently minor incidents as this encounter in Peking, or the news slideshow in Japan during the Russo-Japanese war, Lu Hsun was driven to plumb his inner depths and to reassess the integrity of his actions in society. His life was a restless dialectic of growth in understanding and ego-assertion that knew no boundaries. In a prose poem written after the incident on 18 March 1926, in which several of his students at the Women's Normal School in Peking were killed and wounded, Lu Hsun presumed to have insight into the meaning of creation itself. The creator was playing a game with mankind, using time and forgetfulness and a daily fare of "sweetened bitter wine" to make humans wish to live on, ignorant of the truth. But this would change.

> A rebellious fighter has arisen from mankind, who, standing erect, *sees through* all the deserted ruins and lonely tombs of the past and the present. He remembers all the intense and unending agony; he faces squarely the whole welter of clotted blood; he understands all that is dead and all that is living, as well as all that is being born and all that is yet unborn. *He sees through the creator's game.* And he will arise to resuscitate or else destroy mankind, these loyal subjects of the creator.
>
> The creator, the weakling, hides himself in shame. Then *heaven and earth change color in the eyes of the fighter.*[31]

He who has made the world look different has already changed it.

KUO MO-JO. Kuo Mo-jo left behind a troubling legacy as an intellectual leader. As a major representative of what Leo Ou-fan Lee has called "the romantic generation of modern Chinese writers," Kuo had a restless ego that was unabashedly in the forefront, yet prey, over the course of his lifetime, to the extremes of romantic individualism and individual self-sacrifice. From 1918 to 1924, during his first phase of intense literary creativity, Kuo assumed the role of the poet as hero, as creator of new paths for consciousness. Not content with praising others as heroes, from the Chinese poet Ch'ü Yuan to Beethoven and the English romantic poets, he reserved the most extravagant eulogies for himself. In one pantheistic rapture, Kuo imagined himself as a "hound in heaven" swallowing the stars and the universe: "My ego is about to burst," he proclaimed.[32] His conversion to Marxism-Leninism in 1924 transformed the focus of his romanticism away from the emotional experiences of the unfettered individual to the future happiness of the masses in a communist utopia. The hero now became the self-sacrificing revolutionary who would bring about this future society where all people, not just a privileged and sensitive few, could be permitted the free and complete development of their individuality. The poet gave way to the political cadre, flights of fantasy to party propaganda.

Kuo entered the political scene in the 1920s on the side of the leftist Kuomintang and the Chinese Communist Party, and can legitimately be viewed as having played a role, then and during World War II, as a midwife to the new China. The founding of the People's Republic of China brought him new honors as an established intellectual in literary and scholarly circles; it also brought new heights, or depths, to his hero worship as he contributed his share of poetic panegyrics to the cult of Mao, now portrayed as the grandest of the romantics. During the Cultural Revolution, Kuo was the only major writer to survive relatively unscathed, in part by declaring, in a preemptory self-criticism, the worthlessness of all his previous writings.[33] Since his death in 1978, the adulation and attention directed at his legacy as a versatile communist intellectual have eclipsed the memory of his earlier pre-Marxist phases of heroic individual rebellion. They have also obscured a major question about his life: What is the meaning of his failure, as an intellectual leader, to find a steady, reasonable balance between the rights of individuals and the claims of society? Was Kuo a reflection of a transitional era, a time in which some dislocated and alienated individuals felt compelled to fall back on themselves, to oppose the value of their own egos to the rest of society? Can this explain the self-intoxication and hero worship, the cultural iconoclasm and demands for total cultural rebirth that characterized the thought of some of China's intellectuals?[34] This perspective of a disinherited generation is certainly part of an answer. But there is another way, more specific to China, of viewing the historical predicament at this time: Those who tried to bring something new into being were almost driven to extremism by the grip of tradition, the power of shame, and the immensity of the task of changing mentalities, their own and those of ordinary people in society. This was no sober revolution on the American model, where the pre-existing rights and practices of a citizenry could be reaffirmed within a new political structure; the Chinese revolution touched deep-seated cultural instincts and images, where the bedrock had to shift before lasting, new structures could be built upon it.

It is instructive to return to Kuo Mo-jo's boyhood, where in one phase of one life we can see that cultural bedrock shifting in small but significant ways. Before his later reputation marked him as the archetypal rebel-hero, Kuo was just a bright, young boy in competition with some teachers, older students, and elders to define what it meant to be a proper, educated, young Chinese in the early twentieth century. The autobiography of his early years focuses on his struggle to establish and maintain self-esteem, that fragile compound of positive self-image and social respect that everyone needs to sustain a life in society. He portrays his vacillating self, his inner doubts and bouts with shame. These years do not explain why Kuo became a romantic poet or a Communist cadre, but they do tell us about the inner costs of confronting the traditional shaming power of authorities paid by those who would be cultural innovators in an ancient land.

At thirty-six years of age, writing an autobiography in Japan in 1928, Kuo Mo-jo reflected back over his earliest childhood schooling in the small market town of Sha-wan in remote Szechwan province. A number of perspectives—some strictly Chinese, some inspired from abroad—mingled in his memory. There were familiar country proverbs about beginning school as being similar to "piercing the ox's nose," and other maxims about methods and results, such as "Beating is the discipline for instruction" and "Without beating, one won't become a man; with beating, one could become an official." He remembered the strictness of Teacher Shen Huan-chang, who conducted the tutorial school in a back courtyard of the Kuo family compound, and the obscurity of the philosophical problems in the first primers they had to memorize. He recalled his truancy and his father's using force to carry him back into the classroom, while others laughed at him, calling him "Truant dog! Truant dog!" In considerable detail he related Teacher Shen's punishing technique:

His punishing instrument was a strip of bamboo, one-eighth to one-quarter inch thick and about three and one-half feet long. His informal way of beating was to beat wildly right through the clothes and hat. His formal way was to beat the palm or the buttocks.

The punishment of beating the buttocks was the most barbarous of all. The little criminal had to carry a bench to the front of the memorial tablet for Most Accomplished and Revered Sage Confucius, and very respectfully pull out his shirt, take down his pants, stick out his buttocks, and allow the incarnation of Most Accomplished and Revered Sage Confucius to take up the bamboo stick and beat him wildly. How the flesh on the boy's body trembled with fear beneath that instrument. How a boy's sense of shame and self-respect were trampled by others until not a single trace of them existed.[35]

This passage is significant because it reflects a new theme in the Chinese narration of childhood. Childhood was now viewed as a time for the unfolding of a distinct personality in children, a time when children had needs of their own and a vitality *(hsing-ling)* to develop, a time when adults through their actions and non-actions could facilitate or block healthy growth of body and spirit in children. This mode of thinking had been absent in traditional Chinese conceptions of socialization, which focused overwhelmingly on education and the formation of moral character as defined by adults and tradition.[36]

Kuo described his early schooling in the bantering way of one who has outgrown not only the first world of early childhood but also the confines of a cultural world. That each person's self-respect and personal identity have a history in childhood that can be viewed from the child's perspective was indeed a novel idea. And Kuo was ready to narrate his story from that perspective. As a creative poet in his late twenties, he had nurtured the life force and dynamism he felt inside himself; he knew it could be damaged or even destroyed, and projected that fear back into his description of traditional Chinese education. He regretted "the chronic tendency of education in the past to wipe out the child's vitality. I fear that this is much more harmful than using a hemp rope to break open the nose of a young ox." "Dumping obscure philosophy on a child's head," he wrote, had the effect of pushing aside the child's own mind. "You teach it to him, but how can he understand it? How can he be interested in it?" He recalled his resentment and temporary powerlessness in being forced by his father and ridiculed by his class-mates.[37] In retrospect, Kuo hated the traditional teaching methods that he had been subjected to from age four-and-a-half to twelve, but he recognized that Teacher Shen was not a sadist. In a letter Kuo had written home from Japan, dated 9 November 1919, he asked solici-tously about the condition of his old tutor.[38] He recognized some posi-tive contributions from those tutorial years for his future work as a scholar and writer. In fact, as David Tod Roy has emphasized, Kuo's early clas-sical education took place within a curriculum and format already being altered by the late Ch'ing educational reforms; he even practiced calis-thenics, to incomprehensible Japanese commands, at a neighboring ele-mentary school promoted by his older brother.[39]

Writing about experiences is one way to make the self as fully con-scious of them as possible, to possess them in a personal and orderly way. But long before he wrote these words in the 1920s the young Kuo Mo-jo had become, as we shall see, highly self-aware through intense social encounters that at times nearly overwhelmed him. He, like so many young people caught in this transitional age, was living on shift-ing socio-cultural boundaries; experiences of both social isolation and restless self-assertion tested and shaped his evolving personality. Perhaps that is why he wrote so much in an autobiographical vein: He realized that his anxious self was a fiction of his own making that required con-tinual exploration, definition, and public affirmation. At least up to his conversion to Marxism in 1924, when he found an ideological home for his restless mind, he could not live easily within inherited or prescribed identities and roles. At certain times during his early years he had ex-hibited the literati mannerisms of a "young man of talent"; at other times his behavior appeared indistinguishable from that of shameless gentry sons whose self-indulgent lives mocked the conventional morality of *lien*. But he never succumbed permanently to these pressures and temptations; instead he had the inner strength to assert and reassert himself, to think and act in innovative ways, and even to emerge as a leader. In his description of his experiences in his first year away from home and family in 1906–1907, we can see the dynamics of shame and self-respect at work and witness the emergence of a new-style student rebel.

In September 1905, young Kuo Mo-jo, not yet thirteen years of age, made a river trip along with his father to Chia-ting (today Lo-shan), the nearby prefectural capital in Szechwan, to take the competitive entrance examination for the upper primary school. Over one thousand candidates, many in their thirties and forties, crowded together in the old examination stalls to compete for places in this new school; for with the abolition of the civil service examination, graduation from upper primary school was now considered the legal and social equivalent of the lowest degree in the old system. Young Kuo was one of the youngest successful candidates, but still very much a country boy who took his local habits and reflexes along with him to the city. Although he knew that the practice of first-time visitors bowing three times towards the prodigious city gate was something of a put-on, he could not suppress a feeling that one must bow to this symbol of splendor and power. During his early months at the primary school, which opened in a converted Buddhist temple in the spring of 1906, he also retained his family habit of tying his queue with a red string.[40] His face was round and red-cheeked, and he had the boyish chubby appearance of one who was healthy and well-nourished. These features and habits set him apart from his fellow students, many of whom came from the city of Chia-ting itself and most of whom were much older than he was, half in fact in their thirties.

This young boy, third smallest in his class of ninety, brought to Chia-ting a sharp mind and restless disposition, along with a "baptism in science," which he had already received in his tutorial education at home. Except for some accusations that he had a "peculiar relationship" with a young classmate, he got on well enough during the first semester, spending most of this time playing and exploring. An iconoclastic incident, in which young Kuo broke into a fenced-off structure behind the school, knocked down and then urinated upon a set of "superstitious" images, indicated that he had quickly outgrown his awe of symbolic powers. The academic work itself was not taxing for him; when engaged, he did very well, when not, poorly.[41] His sociopolitical difficulties and education really began following the first semester examination. His top placement was a blow to the self-respect of the older students, who started a movement for redress.

They chose representatives to go and surround Teacher Shuai. They wanted to examine the papers. While the representatives were discussing inside at the dean's office, a large crowd gathered outside the window, all shouting wildly, "Unfair! Unfair!"

"What a pity our faces are ugly . . . Let's go buy a red string to tie up our queues! Buy a little face powder to rub on! Smear on a little rouge."

At first I did not know what the commotion was about. I went over to see what was happening.

An older student named Hsu, at that time he was already 31 years old, suddenly grabbed hold of my right wrist. He held on and wouldn't let go, shouting "How do you do, how do you do!" In about ten minutes my fingers began to get numb. When he finally let go of my hand, circles of blood marks showed through on top of my wrist, as though I had worn several bracelets.

The examination list was pulled down and the papers examined, but they still couldn't find any evidence of unfairness. From the dean's office to the principal's office, from the principal's office to the reception room, no matter what [they heard], they wanted Teacher Shuai to change the list of examination grades. Teacher Shuai was pushed into a corner, and the only thing to do was to reduce my grade by several points: I was marked down to the eighth name on the list before most of the older students regained their composure.

The small humiliated student returned home for summer vacation. With bitter anguish and care, he planned how he would scrub away his shame upon returning to school in the fall.

He knew that these older students were very timid, taking advantage of the weak but afraid of the strong. The strategy he decided upon, therefore, was to concentrate on opposing the teachers that these students trembled before . . . Almost none of the old or new teachers in the school had ever been opposed.[42]

Since the demotion crisis, Kuo Mo-jo had lived behind the bars of shame and humiliation; for he felt that Teacher Shuai, in giving in, had accepted the older students' charge that he was sexually perverse. This was an unspeakable insult. "Could I endure it or not?" he asked himself that summer when he decided upon his plan for revenge. The strategy that the young Kuo adopted was a modern variation of an old proverb: "To shoot down a mounted rider with bow and arrow, first shoot down the horse; to capture thieves, one must capture their chieftain."[43] The target, however, was not a peripheral group, such as the mounted barbarian horsemen of old or a group of bandits, but rather a respected authority group within the traditional structure: teachers and school administrators. Such cultural heresy had become possible because, with the abolition of the civil service examination, there was little experience and no consensus on how new-style schools should be governed. Individual schools and small groups within schools began scripting new arrangements for learning, teaching, and administering. Already in Hangchow and Shanghai in 1902, student strikes had broken out and led to such experimentation in educational policy.

Young Kuo's hatred for Teacher Shuai came to be directed at the school principal Yi Shu-hui, nicknamed "the tiger," who taught local history and inspired the greatest awe and terror among the students. "His expression was just like the powdered wicked official from the stage . . . [his voice] when he started yelling had a commanding force like the sound of wind and waves."[44] In this confrontation between young Kuo and Principal Yi Shu-hui, their individual histories cast long shadows against a new historical backdrop: Progressive youth, entering into an enlightened age, were preparing not only to supplant their elders but to "overturn the Master's image of Heaven." Theirs was a confrontation over the politics of culture, over how members of society negotiate standards for shame, humiliation, respect, and face among themselves.

The first confrontation was a conversation on a Saturday evening in the Self-Cultivation Hall, a place feared by most students because behind it was a hillside of graves and "wailing ghosts." Kuo Mo-jo was there with a friend when Principal Yi, slightly intoxicated, suddenly came upon them.

"Ah, you two small students really have a lot of courage, not being afraid of ghosts."

[The friend said]: "We are not afraid, Teacher Yi. Are you afraid?"

"Me, afraid?" he replied. "Ha, ha, ha, ha. On the contrary, ghosts are afraid of me! Evil forces are no match for righteous forces. People like me are 'Clear and bright in body, determined and energetic like [good] spirits.' How would an evil spirit dare to enter me? Ha, ha, ha, ha, ha."

I said, "Teacher Yi, your views are not very profound [lit. "you have not ascended to the hall and entered the inner chamber"].

"Heh?" he rolled the whites of his eyes.

"Those of us who have studied physics know that this kind of thing, whether ghosts or spirits, doesn't exist at all."

"Ha, ha, ha, ha, ha. Today's students want to overturn the Master's image of Heaven."

He patted the back of their heads a few times and went away seemingly unangered.[45]

The second confrontation centered initially on an issue raised by the older student named Hsu who had squeezed Kuo Mo-jo's wrist in the earlier demotion crisis. He complained that the younger students at his eating table were deliberately depriving him of food. They were in fact trying to demonstrate to him, by taking small portions and controlling the passing of the food among themselves, that he always ate more than his share at the table. They had not expected that he would complain to higher authority. Principal Yi called the seven small students together to face student Hsu. Outside the window milled a crowd of other students who sensed excitement.

> "Why didn't you give him any rice to eat?" Tiger Yi questioned us fiercely.
>
> "Who didn't give him rice to eat? The rice pot was in the middle of the table," a fellow student replied.
>
> Older student Hsu said, "You kept the rice ladle and didn't give it to me." [It was] a pitiable kind of cry. Outside the windows laughter broke out.
>
> "You know-nothings! What are you laughing at?" Tiger Yi began putting on a stern face towards the students outside the window. The spectators scattered for a minute, but as he glanced away they began assembling once more.
>
> "Why didn't you give him the rice ladle?"
>
> "We don't have enough rice ladles. Eight people only have one. But he's really stupid. If the rice ladle doesn't come to him, he could use his bowl [as a ladle]," another fellow student answered.
>
> "You little devils. You think you're the smart ones. You don't fear a short life. You think I don't know you're just stirring up trouble!"
>
> Outside the window laughter again broke out.
>
> The tiger once more turned a stern face towards the window, that the people out there should break up. But soon they gathered together into another group.
>
> "We certainly can't outgrab him. He's usually very assertive. Today he didn't succeed in outgrabbing us, but came to tell on us instead." A small student in the B class said this, and those of us standing in front of Tiger Yi all laughed.
>
> Tiger Yi seemed to want to restrain himself, but could never let down [on an issue of] face [*lien*]. He probably wanted to act decisively in order to preserve his dignity. Suddenly he boxed the ear of the small student. The small student began to cry.
>
> I couldn't restrain myself: "Teacher Yi, this is nothing but barbarous behavior!"
>
> "Right, barbarous! Barbarous!" The crowd outside the window began shouting with one voice.

"Barbarous principal! Barbarous principal! How can anyone want to hit students in this enlightened age? Too inhumane, insulting to our dignity as students."

The crowd outside the window milled around shouting wildly. Tiger Yi wanted to get up and say something, but he saw that his stern face had been completely undermined. He suddenly stood up and walked into his study.[46]

After the encounter, Principal Yi asked to retire from office and the entire school was thrown into great chaos. Classes stopped for the day. Teachers and older students went to persuade him to stay on, which he finally agreed to do. For Kuo Mo-jo, this encounter marked his ascendancy into school politics. "After I had opposed Tiger Yi, my authority began to be firmly established among the students, and I became a little leader in the school." A small minority of older students would have nothing to do with him; but he felt this meant little, for they were only concerned with grades and pleasing teachers. "Besides lifelessly biting into textbooks, they didn't concern themselves with any of the administrative issues [about governance] among the students."[47]

But this was not the last of it. In the spring term of 1907, students and school authorities got embroiled in a confrontation over the cancellation of the Saturday half-holiday. Elected student delegates asked that it be restored and Kuo Mo-jo, as representative of his class, proposed that the student body should threaten to strike if their demands were not met. Teacher Yi and a new teacher, Tu Shao-shang, managed artfully to conciliate the student's demand yet isolate their leadership. In school assembly, Teacher Yi said that the students could keep the holiday, but that threatening to strike classes was evil and wrong. He said he knew that only a few "failures" in the students' midst urged this action, and he wanted the group to repudiate them, for otherwise when they went home, how could they face their fathers? Since these tactics seemed likely to fail, Teacher Tu suggested that an anonymous vote be taken to determine who was the strike leader. The vote was taken, and while some students submitted blank ballots, more than 110 singled out Kuo Mo-jo. The result was his summary expulsion from the school.[48]

Kuo Mo-jo spent a lonely night in an inn in the town. He felt disappointment with the students instead of feeling personal regret for what he had done. Still the strategy of Teacher Yi remained to be tested. Would the boy's elders be a more effective force in bringing him into harness than his teachers? Would he be able to live with the hurt and anger that the humiliation of his expulsion had caused them, especially his father? Initially Kuo Mo-jo's father played his expected part in the drama with great energy. On the same day the son was expelled, a letter written by Teacher Tu was sent by messenger to the father in Sha-wan eight miles away. He came immediately and on the afternoon of the second day intercepted his surprised son in the inn.

> [F]ather walked into the room with a grieved look on his face holding in angry and unhappy feelings. The more I looked, the more frightening and severe he appeared. I did not know that Father might come, and I was wearing a long queue as usual. As soon as Father saw me, he grabbed the queue from my head and used it as a whip to beat me several times. "You worthless thing!" he cursed.[49]

School officials came by to pay their respects to the father, explaining that the school authorities only wanted to help his son. If he were remorseful, he would be allowed to return, and they expected he would have a great future. As one of them put it, "[The younger Kuo] has great intelligence, but lacks refinement. He only needs to be softened up a bit, and his future will be promising beyond measure." His father accepted this rationale and decided to "exhibit" *(shih-chung)* Kuo Mo-jo among the nearby elders in the family clan, in order to let the meaning and gravity of the offense come home to him.[50] First he was taken to the village where his eldest paternal uncle and many other relatives lived. The private primary school there prided itself on being more free than the official county school, and had in fact a number of progressive teachers. His father led him into the school yard for his first public humiliation, but the anticipated effect was not forthcoming.

> My literary fame in primary school had already spread a great distance, and now the notoriety of my expulsion was added to this. As soon as I arrived in Wen Ch'ang Hall, a great commotion arose among the students . . . As I was led around by my brother to see the various parts of the school, all the students crowded around expressing the greatest respect. I was like a general in a triumphal march in their midst. I was received as a guest. Whether eating or conversing, I was treated on a par with the teachers.[51]

Not only was the student reaction decisively in his favor, but the teachers at the school, when informed in detail about the dismissal, opposed the method used and decided to write a letter to Teacher Yi. In the letter, they appended a caution against ruining a child's spirit through unnecessary humiliation, and inquired when young Kuo would be readmitted. They were prepared to accept him as a "special research student" at their school, so that he would not fall behind in his studies. They urged the father not to continue his humiliation tour and instead to await the reply from Teacher Yi. The letter came and, while it was unyielding in principle, said that he could return to school immediately. The young Kuo laughed secretly at this precipitous, unexpected about-face, and his father also relented in his anger. His case, he thought, was "iron proof" of the bankruptcy of Teacher Yi's educational principles. Furthermore, through the administrators' behavior, he felt he had learned to detect falseness and vanity: "As soon as the expulsion notice disappeared, another one—'after repentence and self-reform, permitted to return to school'—appeared to take its place. It was all vanity, the vanity of administrators preserving face *(mien-tzu).* This was one of the great lessons they gave to me." Back at school a few days later a handsome, talented new student grasped his hand on the path to the ball field and addressed him as "Mr. Kuo." This small gesture of recognition and respect made him feel as though "all the humiliation he had received had been tossed away into the East China Sea."[52]

But Kuo Mo-jo did not escape unscathed. He noticed that as his actions were denigrated and his "face" *(lien)* broken by others, he had become inclined towards "shameless behavior." "Since my face was already broken, what difference did it make?" He had worked listlessly and taken to smoking, visiting brothels, drinking, gambling, and carousing; these behaviors also marked his later middle school years in Chia-ting and Chengtu until he left for Japan in 1914 at age twenty-one. For Kuo Mo-jo this pull towards a shameless way of life was a temporary phase, a rebound fascination with the devalued underside of conventional society as well as a playing at being an adult and enjoying adult pleasures.[53] However, for some others, as we have seen in Chapter Four, this "shameless" life of dissipation, arrogance, and defiance grew out of deeper and more fundamental personal curses; it had little to do with the process of personal growth and much more to do with patterned social incompetence.

HISTORY THROWN ON THE BALANCE. The young Kuo Mo-jo's vacillating behavior did point to that indefinite but recognized limit beyond which humiliation could cease to have its desired effects, and indeed might even destroy the desire to compete and push forward. The "progressive teachers" stressed this limit in their argument against the shaming strategy of Teachers Yi and Tu. How far could one break the face of a child before these counterproductive effects began to appear? Within traditional circles there was undoubtedly disagreement, just as there were differing theories of education and learning. But in the world of the modern schools, especially among progressive students and teachers, the balance of opinion was clearly shifting against heavy-handed authoritarian methods. The movement of history develops situational answers that may make contemporary debates seem academic and insubstantial, as though suspended above the sociological and historical trends that condition the success or failure of ideas.

By 1911 the larger structures that had helped contain the "misdirected" energies of the young and the unconventional had collapsed, particularly the imperial Confucian state and the civil service examination system. And within the traditional filial system itself the mischievous child was finding supports undreamed of before. Not only scattered individuals, such as elder brothers, relatives, or teachers, but also organized reform groups beyond the family called for new values, new ways, new institutions, new leadership. These historical realities promoted the cause of the cultural and political dissident; they lay behind the argument over the "merits" of changing practices in childhood education. *In such an enlightened age,* went the argument, *it is barbarous to hit students, to trample on their self-respect, and to exploit their sense of shame. Ethics aside, the practical result of such traditionally sanctioned practices is to depress talent and stop up the well springs of the spirit. This is an intolerable prospect in an age demanding the utmost exertion and intelligence from the future Napoleons, Washingtons, and Bismarcks of China.* And the dissidents, by the tens of thousands, from adolescent student rebels to middle-aged cultural critics, seized the moment opened up to them by historical timing.

Epilogue

Inside the Kuo Family Residence Museum, Sha-wan, Szechwan, 1986.
Courtesy of Christine Saari.

The Few and the Many

In the spring of 1986 I walked the streets and byways around the Buddhist temple-*cum*-school in the city of Lo-shan, Szechwan, that had served as stage for Kuo Mo-jo's emergence as a student rebel almost eighty years before. I could not repress an eerie feeling imagining the crowd outside the window of Principal Yi Shu-hui's office in 1907 shouting, with one voice, "Barbarous! Barbarous Principal!" Were their cries another symptom of the grip of tradition? Was a new type of leader being anointed by the same conformist crowd, mired now in boisterous but deferential behavior to a new set of slogans? The question echoes across the decades to the Red Guards of the late 1960s, marshaled into action to attack the capitalist-roaders and revisionists inside the government and ruling party of the New China. How much was actually being changed in the early twentieth century? Perhaps in the long run, the creation of a more inclusive stage for youthful learning within the human life cycle—the time of *ch'ing-nien* or youth (ages fifteen to thirty)—will look important to us as a permanent change in Chinese culture. For all but a handful of Chinese boys in late Imperial China, the lack of an adolescent peer experience apart from family certainly reinforced the continuity of values across generations and held the individual close within the embrace of the group. In theory, the advent of more universal schooling away from home, for girls as well as boys, enhances the possibility of separate peer cultures; the resultant comparison between family and peers can allow individuals to develop stronger self-identities and, in particular, lead to belief systems based on a reexamination of the cultural and family learning inculcated in childhood.[1]

The generation of educated Chinese born in the 1890s went through such a reexamination with a vengeance. They had little choice in the matter, for they fell between worlds. Born into still traditional families in the late Ch'ing, they matured in the foreign-tinged setting of new-style schools and coastal cities. They questioned much of what they had been taught, or were forced to modify and reintegrate traditional ways and meanings into their new or refurbished selves. And they were always on the march, a forced march as I have called it. It was a never ending struggle to keep up, for a continuous flow of new perspectives outflanked old ones with startling rapidity. The barrage of ideas and demands often left them feeling harried, alone, cut off. "We were hermits on the desert wandering into a radiation field, being bombarded with rays of various sorts with various intensities," reflected one.[2] There was sharpened controversy on many substantive issues and decreased toleration and forebearance. Yet on one issue their minds were made up and seldom wavered: their identity as Chinese. In the 1910s a deepening sense of urgency and despair for China as a nation served to make individual pursuits seem decadent, selfish, and unsocial. The fascination with individual liberation and self-fulfillment had flared for a long moment and then been absorbed into what many Chinese felt were more important tasks: national salvation and class struggle. By the late 1920s collective thinking had become a habit among intellectuals, and politics narrowed down to the struggle of two armed, Leninist-style political parties; the dominance of this political struggle and of thinking within the categories of nation-state and class virtually precluded the emergence of any new orientation.

It is not difficult to disparage the limited achievements of many men caught in this historical situation. Unable to feel a harmonious interweaving of inner being and outer environment, some held rigidly to ossified traditions or fixated for years on one or another "foreign meaning" that had ceased to hold sway in the West or that was no longer pertinent to China's evolving situation. Unable to possess the whole, they made a fetish of parts. Unable to be in reality the independent, progressive-minded "modern men" that had become their inner ideal, many accepted outer appearances and correct forms as substitutes. One participant, looking back from the 1960s, saw the "storming of the [Confucian] prison" as merely leading Chinese intellectual life from the bondage of the Ancients to uncritical compradoring from the West, choking off any truly independent, creative, and scientific thought.[3] Mao Tse-tung, although excluding "scientific Marxism" from the list of compradored goods, would have agreed: "[Returned students from abroad] become gramophones and forget their duty to understand and create new things."[4] Younger scholars of Chinese descent have sometimes criticized this elder generation for the superficiality of its "scientism," the rashness of its "iconoclasm," the shallowness of its romantic yearnings, and, above all, the failure to develop a "creative reformist" approach to China's crisis.[5]

Such judgments seem unnecessarily critical. How, after all, did the ancient ideal of *tso jen* translate into twentieth-century realities? There was no literal translation, only nuanced variation in well-lived lives, because those seeking to find the right translation grew up, thought, felt, acted, and dreamed in ways that differed one from another. The perspectives of past actors cannot be reduced to data in a theory, in this case not even to a theory that a creative, reformist approach to China's problems would have been possible and preferable. Yet the seekers had much in common, enough to make examining them together illuminating; and from the perspective of time and distance it is possible to conclude that to judge them as shallow failures is to oversimplify their task and to underestimate their personal strengths and accomplishments. In weaving together a rich human story of modern Chinese intellectuals, Jonathan Spence was struck by "how flexible, how courageous, and how subtle the Chinese response to crisis in our own time has been." Many made commitments in the face of danger, hoped when hope appeared futile, and threw themselves with energy and daring into "the task of surviving in a disintegrating or murderous world." Spence concluded that these life stories spanning eighty-five years challenge any simple clichés about Chinese apathy and the narrow range of Chinese vision.[6]

But this generation of educated Chinese did more than survive as human beings in an unfavorable time. In the pattern of their separate interests in the 1920s, they also etched in the outline of a new synthesis for China. This new synthesis would first of all incorporate the New Learning in one version or another; for, with China now a particular fragment within the larger world, a thoroughgoing reassessment of the completeness and universality of its own intellectual tradition was necessary. Second, it would require an activist orientation toward the immediate problems of imperialist encroachment and the increasingly visible social problems in village and urban China, for this historical situation demanded corrective action. And third, it would be informed by a traditional concern for the morality of action, since "bad philosophy" was the ultimate root of social and political disaster. Each of these starting points defined a grouping of like-minded men (and some women)—the New Knowledge Enthusiasts, the Action Intellectuals, the Neo-Traditionalists. Each had its characteristic criteria—respectively, truthful complexity/false simplicity, effectiveness/ineffectiveness, morality/immorality—that it is used against the others and in promoting its cause.

Together, they were the paradigm-makers, the ones who opened up new and fruitful pathways for their ancient culture in scholarship and literature, social organization and politics, philosophy and morality.[7] They were "the few" among the educated who were able to secure an overview, an integration, a partial synthesis out of the disorienting world they faced. They discovered patterns in the interplay between a tradition-bound China and an irrepressible new world already organized in her coastal cities. They differed in describing what "tradition" actually was, and what the interplay between China and the world beyond really meant in terms of both politics and ideas. And they differed greatly in temperaments, in philosophies, and in the prescriptions for action that they thought would take China beyond an unacceptable present. But they merged in the desire to tame change, to make it comprehensible, and in their ability to grasp opportunities amid disorder and turn them to advantage. The revolutionary program of the Chinese Communists, who were mostly Action Intellectuals, addressed the immediate historical situation and combined the perspective of "scientific Marxism" with the sense of initiating a new moral order. Through their programs they integrated these three concerns in ways that the other two groups of thinkers did not. This is a matter of historical record; but, as is also a matter of record, the Chinese Communists did not then, or now, have a monopoly on truth, workable solutions, or morality.

With the founding of the People's Republic of China in 1949, a new synthesis prevailed, at least for the 95 percent declared to belong to "the people." The society was once more relatively unified in peace, this time behind a program of national development and social reform. Individuals could find meaning within a supportive context of self-transcending social ideals, a renewed sense of community, critical perspective on tradition, and a secure place in the unfolding of history, temporarily at least spared from the modern limbo of the "homeless mind."[8] Even amid the disorder of the 1910s and 1920s, when young people struggled to find and create a Way Out, something of this supportive background was present, whether in the belief in a beneficent cosmos and human nature or in the confidence that China would ultimately survive this era of troubles as she had others in the past. Ch'ü Ch'iu-pai caught this element of faith in his reflections on the eve of his trip to Russia in 1920: "The relations between man and man have troubled me as a great puzzle. The meaning of life is absolutely obscure to me. Though I believe I have within me a harmonious chord, no harmonious music can I play."[9] Ch'ü Ch'iu-pai's puzzle was still troubling in the 1980s, and perhaps always will be. Widespread disillusionment in the wake of the Cultural Revolution, coupled with the often confusing reorientation of reforms, led to a "crisis of faith" in the People's Republic. Many young Chinese openly admitted feeling cast adrift, no longer securely moored within socialist morality and Marxist ideology. The pro-democracy movement of 1989, despite the terrible crushing of its supporters, may over the long term nourish a new commitment and faith in a more free and democratic China, one that will finally make utopian hopes, political repression, and intellectual despair unnecessary.

Appendixes
Notes
Bibliography
Glossary

APPENDIX A
Notes on Interviewing Elderly Chinese in Taiwan and Hong Kong

Interviewing can be approached in two basic ways: with a detailed questionnaire or standardized test in hand, or with some general but uncodified ideas in mind. The first approach is open-ended only after the question has been asked; the second is open-ended about the nature of the problem itself, allowing its possibilities to be brought out in an informal, conversational way, largely from the perspective of the person interviewed. A researcher working in a foreign country is in danger of formulating an argument too soon and codifying it into a questionnaire. Initial hypotheses are usually based on knowledge from books and often prove too abstract to be appropriate in posing questions to real people, who, after all, are the final bearers of culture and the agents of history. Understanding people, the way their minds appropriate knowledge, and the various contexts that give "facts" their form and relevance is the goal of studying another culture. To be useful, therefore, research must be open to surprises, and arguments must be subject to continuous revision as answers cast doubt on the very questions asked. To me as a young interviewer in a foreign culture, curiosity, a sympathetic interest, and the willingness to let questions emerge seemed the most productive approach for talking to Chinese of the generation I wanted to learn about.

In 1969, I talked with about forty persons over sixty years old in Taiwan and Hong Kong (mostly Taiwan) and filled some twenty notebooks with the results. Most individuals I interviewed at some length;

that is, I spent at least six hours with them as I discussed their early life histories and present attitudes towards the past. Some of the interviews were quite brief, allowing me to acquire only a sense of the person and to get a personal introduction to his or her written works. My questionnaire was short and general, and I used it only where it seemed to be necessary to get talk started. I preferred to make these encounters into free-flowing conversations, gently held on course by occasional questions. The "real" inner world in different persons remained hidden, like the proverbial underside of the iceberg. It would have taken the relationship of an analyst and patient to bring that dimension out in most cases, and I did not consider myself an analyst nor did they consider themselves patients. Only with a few people—an academic psychologist, a Christian convert, and one man fond of rigorous, open self-examination—could this inner world be explored directly. Although few of these interviews were ultimately incorporated into this book, they were crucial in the early stages in helping me form impressions about significant childhood patterns and define the right questions.

Contact with potential interviewees was made in a variety of ways. I brought along several letters from friends in the United States introducing me to people there. I also developed some institutional contacts shortly after arrival; I discussed my project with them and told them the kind of people I hoped to see: educated Chinese born roughly between 1890 and 1905 who were articulate and thoughtful; who had perhaps written about themselves; and who were likely to be willing to see a young American scholar to talk about their early life histories. This kind of institutional contact was rather easily made in Taiwan, either through groups sponsored by the United States or groups with strong American ties, such as the American University Club, various alumni groups, or the Joint Commission on Rural Reconstruction.

Although these institutions in Taiwan were fine for a start, they were clearly biased towards Chinese who were most like ourselves. To approach people who were either more traditional or more maverick in outlook, one had to look elsewhere. One way was to locate several "pivotal persons" who had a wide range of personal friends. I was introduced to one such man by one of my original contacts. This man had extraordinary empathy for people of all types and persuasions. Having worked as an educational administrator in China, he had former students and colleagues from all parts of the country. Besides the pivotal person with many kinds of friends, there was the pivotal person whose power and influence extended into many corners of Taiwanese life. Through a Chinese student friend of mine in the States, I made contact with a cabinet minister in Taiwan who was also on the governing board of the conservative College of Chinese Culture. Through him I was introduced to the vice-president who was helpful in getting me in touch with five of his faculty members. His secretary, who did the legwork, also turned out to be a former student of this same minister, which all the more redounded to my advantage. Drawing upon these reservoirs of friendship and influence seemed to be a quick way of securing access to a number of potential interviewees. Access, however, was only the beginning.

The key problem in the "conversational interview" is how to establish a good rapport. This is often half-achieved before you even see the person if he or she is well disposed towards your contact person and attracted to the project as explained in your introductory letter. I had several carefully worked-out versions of one basic letter that I sent to most potential interviewees. The basic letter included an escape clause, saying that I sought only one brief meeting to talk more about my project and that after this meeting recipients could decide whether they had the inclination and time to participate. If not, I hoped they would be frank about it; and some were. In some cases the general letter was unusable, for I assumed that I would be able to meet some prominent people only once, if that. In writing to such people, the approach was specific, personal, and direct, revealing advance preparation.

Some people did decline to participate in the project. The most common reason was probably a fear of embarrassing or painful subjects or a distaste for open-ended conversations with a young foreigner, perhaps particularly with a young American on account of smoldering resentments left over from the Chinese civil war of the 1940s. The reasons given overtly were more circumspect: "My experiences are not worth studying," or "Mine is an uninteresting life." Some people never answered my initial letter; others I had to pursue by telephone and a second letter. Some of these hard-to-reach people were not hiding, but simply absentminded; others were more openly reluctant, as the one who wrote in reply to my second letter, "Since you insist, I guess I must not grudge you an interview." This happened only once in such a frank fashion, and even this gentleman ended up giving me all of his relevant written works and a further reference to a friend in Hong Kong. Overall, the reluctant were a decided minority, and reluctance itself was not a fixed state of mind.

In my interviewing, I did not use a tape recorder or administer any tests. I felt that to do either would interfere with rapport. I relied upon only a notebook and a pen, and often these were invisible during the interview. About two-thirds of the interviews were conducted in English and one-third in Chinese. In only two of the interviews in Chinese was an interpreter present, one chosen by the interviewee himself. Except in these two cases and two others—an interview of a brother and sister and one of a husband and wife—the interview took place as two people talking directly to each other. Beforehand I had emphasized the need for a quiet place where we might not be interrupted, and often I was invited into their homes. I took no gifts, unless invited for a meal, and gave no compensation, except to perform such friendly favors as writing up an outline of our talk for one man's future reference and writing letters to a publisher in the United States to find out what had happened to a manuscript. The talks themselves often turned up out-of-the-way autobiographical materials, ranging from theses done abroad years ago to articles written or collected by the interviewees to a family chronology (*nien p'u*).

Several reasons seem to account for the responsiveness of this older generation in 1969 to a young foreign scholar exploring their early lives. One was the lively interest in Taiwan in biographical and autobiographical literature, an interest generated by this older group. The appearance and growth of the periodical *Chuan-chi wen-hsueh* (Biographical literature), begun in 1962, testified to this interest and need. Another reason was that my subject seemed innocent enough; the sensitive topic of politics, especially Kuomintang history or the current situation, was not a direct point of inquiry. A third reason was that, prior to American recognition of the People's Republic of China in 1979, many of this generation in Taiwan felt that this phase of international politics demanded strong cooperation between Taiwan and the United States. Some people I interviewed in 1969 might have been less cooperative without this line of reasoning to give our meeting some larger rationale. Many also had sons and daughters in the United States, and this reinforced the sense of mutual ties and mutual destiny. Their strong belief in the need for basic Taiwan–United States cooperation overrode lesser issues that could have kept us apart, such as the general belief that American academic circles were badly deluded by liberal perspectives on world affairs.

A final consideration, especially in the case of Chinese in Taiwan, was personal: I had traveled all the way to Taiwan and taken pains to meet and listen to them. I suspect that meeting elderly Chinese in their own cultural setting lent a certain self-confidence and generosity to their dealing with foreigners that might well have been lacking in colonial Hong Kong and would have been even less sure in an alien setting like the United States, for there was still something of a carryover among intellectuals from the time not long ago when the foreigner clapped and the comprador or coolie came running. Moreover, the fact that I welcomed follow-up meetings and had time to befriend those who participated in the project helped overcome the unhappy memories a few of them had of interviewers who came full of questions and enthusiasm but disappeared after one meeting.

APPENDIX B
Persons Interviewed in
Taiwan and Hong Kong, 1969

TABLE 1 Persons Interviewed in Taiwan between February and
August 1969

Name	Year of Birth	Native Province or Birthplace
1 Cha Liang-chao	1896	Chekiang
2 Chao Pao-ch'uan	1907	Kiangsu
3 Chang Ch'i-yun	1901	Chekiang
4 T. K. Chang	1900	Kwangtung
5 Ch'en Ch'i-t'ien	1893	Hopei
6 Anonymous	1899	Fukien
7 Ch'en Ta-tsi	1887	Chekiang
8 Ch'eng Fa-jen	1894	Hupei
9 Chiang Fu-tsung	1898	Chekiang
10 Ch'ien Mu	1895	Kiangsu
11 Ch'ien Shih-liang	1908	Chekiang
12 Gunson Hoh	1899	Kiangsu
13 Hu Ch'iu-yuan	1910	Hupei
14 Y. C. Koo	1901	Kiangsu
15 Li Chi	1896	Hupei
16 Liang Shih-ch'iu	1902	Chekiang
17 Liang Tsai-p'ing	1911	Hupei
18 Lin Yutang	1895	Fukien

Table 1 Continued

Name	Year of Birth	Native Province or Birthplace
19 Anonymous	1906	Peking
20 C. H. Liu	1911	Jehol
21 Liu Chung-p'ing	1897	Fukien
22 Ma Hsin-yeh	1909	Chekiang
23 Sah Meng-wu	1897	Fukien
24 Shen Kang-po	1897	Hupei
25 Shen Tsung-han	1895	Chekiang
26 Stephen Tsai	1896	Hunan
27 Tseng Pao-hsun	1894	Hunan
28 Tseng Yueh-nung	1894	Hunan
29 T. C. Van	ca. 1900	Chekiang
30 Wang Chia-hung	1900	Hupei (?)
31 Elizabeth Wang Te-chen	1912	Kiangsu
32 Wei Ju-lin	1908	Hopei
33 John C. H. Wu	1899	Chekiang
34 Yeh Kung-ch'ao	1904	Kwangtung
35 Yü Ta-wei	1898	Chekiang

Table 2 Persons Interviewed in Hong Kong between September and December 1969

Name	Year of Birth	Native Province or Birthplace
1 Chang P'i-k'ai	1904	Shantung
2 P. H. Chang	1905	Kwangtung
3 Chang Yi-tsuen (Daniel Y. Chang)	1906	Kiangsu
4 Hsu Fu-kuan	1903	Hupei
5 Kuo Jen-yuan (Zing Yang Kuo)	1898	Kwangtung
6 T'ang Chün-i	1909	Szechwan

Notes

PREFACE

1. A dictionary is, as R. H. Mathews pointed out in 1931, a graveyard of a language; for words are ever evolving beyond current usage. In more recent dictionaries, *tso jen* has acquired different connotations from those it had at the turn of the century. In Lin Yutang's *Chinese-English Dictionary on Modern Usage* (Hong Kong, 1972), entry 1274, *tso jen* is simply a matter of conducting oneself in society, or knowing how to get along with people. In Chao Yuen Ren and Lien Sheng Yang's *Concise Dictionary of Spoken Chinese* (Cambridge, Harvard University Press, 1947), it is "to be a human being," which seems to include anything that a human being might do, namely acting justly, shrewdly, or foolishly. In *Mathews' Chinese-English Dictionary* (rev. American edition; Cambridge, Harvard University Press, 1943), originally compiled in 1931, more of the original meaning of the term is conveyed. *Tso jen* means "to exert an influence upon others; to stimulate others to goodness; to act as becomes a man." The concept of a moral model for human behavior is central to the usage that I am adopting in my translation. Similarly, the term *ch'eng jen* means both an end result and a process; in Mathews' formulation, it is "to become a man; to act as a full grown man; to succeed in life; an adult." To become an adult person is to become a good or decent person; proper behavior and attitudes are essential, not years of age.

2. Chang Po-hsing, *Hsiao-hsueh chi-chieh* (Taipei reproduction, 1962), first preface (dated 1713), p. 1.

3. Thomas A. Metzger, *Escape from Predicament: Neo-Confucianism and China's Evolving Political Culture* (New York, 1977), chs. 1–3.

4. Ibid., p. 19.

5. For the most wide-ranging critique, see Frederick W. Mote, "China's Past in the

Study of China Today—Some Comments on the Recent Work of Richard Solomon," *Journal of Asian Studies* 32.1:107–120. See also Thomas A. Metzger, "On Chinese Political Culture," *Journal of Asian Studies* 32.1:101–105.

6. Richard H. Solomon, *Mao's Revolution and the Chinese Political Culture* (Berkeley, 1971), p. xi.

7. For a perceptive discussion of the usefulness and shortcomings of social science theory applied to China-centered historiography, see Paul A. Cohen, *Discovering History in China: American Historical Writing on the Recent Chinese Past* (New York, 1984), pp. 180–186.

8. For an elucidating comparison of Confucian self-assertion with Western notions of individualism, see Metzger, *Escape*, pp. 42–45. T'ang Chün-i's standpoint, via Metzger, is that the idea (not to speak of the ideal) of a clearly bounded ego directly pursuing its own gratification is a distortion—or a perversion—of human experience, for it blocks the natural flow of empathy among humans. Metzger comments (p. 45) that some anthropologists of Chinese background or descent "feel a need for theories of human behavior avoiding that bias towards Western individualism which they detect in Western theories of personality." For a brilliant critical essay on individualism as a recent Western cultural and historical phenomenon, see Yi-fu Tuan, *Segmented Worlds and Self: Group Life and Individual Consciousness* (Minneapolis, 1982). For a critique illuminating the negative aspects of American individualism by an anthropologist of Chinese descent, see Francis L. K. Hsu, *Rugged Individualism Reconsidered: Essays in Psychological Anthropology* (Knoxville, 1983).

9. The best introduction to Erikson's theory of the life cycle is in Erik H. Erikson, *Identity: Youth and Crisis* (New York, 1968), pp. 91–141. The evolution of Erikson's viewpoint, along with cautions against its mechanical application, is addressed in Robert Coles, *Erik H. Erikson: The Growth of His Work* (Boston, 1970), chs. 5 and 6. For an emphasis on Erikson's thoughts on the life cycle as a set of theories not facts, as a vehicle for ethical idealism as well as clinical description, see Paul Roazen, *Erik Erikson: The Power and Limits of a Vision* (New York, 1976), pp. 119–120. On the complex matrix of human development, see Kenneth Keniston, "Psychological Development and Historical Change," in Robert Jay Lifton with Eric Olson, eds., *Explorations in Psychohistory: The Wellfleet Papers* (New York, 1974), pp. 149–164.

10. Ida Pruitt, *A China Childhood* (San Francisco, 1978), pp. 1–5.

11. Agnes Hankiss, "Ontologies of the Self: On the Mythological Rearranging of One's Life History," in Daniel Bertaux, ed., *Biography and Society: The Life History Approach in the Social Sciences* (Beverly Hills, California, 1981), pp. 203–209.

12. Erik H. Erikson, "On the Nature of Psycho-Historical Evidence: In Search of Gandhi," *Daedalus* 97.3:695–730; Jon L. Saari, "The Human Factor: Some Inherent Ambiguities and Limitations in Scholarly Choices," in Amy Auerbacher Wilson, Sidney Leonard Greenblatt, and Richard W. Wilson, eds., *Methodological Issues in Chinese Studies* (New York, 1983), pp. 89–91.

13. From the concluding paragraph of Lu Hsun's 1921 short story, "My Old Home," in Lu Hsun [Lu Xun], *Selected Works*, vol. 1 (Peking, 1980), p. 101.
14. Taiwan Interview No. 13.

1. Arthur Kleinman, *Social Origins of Distress and Disease: Depression, Neurasthenia, and Pain in Modern China* (New Haven, 1986), p. 199.
2. Paul Riesman, "On the irrelevance of child rearing practices for the formation of personality," *Culture, Medicine and Psychiatry* 7.2:103–129.

1. *CHILDHOOD AS CRISIS: A CULTURAL PERSPECTIVE*

1. Silvan S. Tomkins, "Affect and the Psychology of Knowledge," in Silvan Tomkins, ed., *Affect, Cognition and Personality: Empirical Studies* (New York, 1965), pp. 72–97.
2. R. H. Tawney, *Land and Labor in China* (London, 1932), ch. 2, pp. 47–48.
3. Marianne Bastid-Bruguière, "Currents of Social Change," in John K. Fairbank and Kwang-ching Liu, eds., *The Cambridge History of China*, vol. 11, part 2 (Cambridge, 1980), pp. 582–589.
4. D. K. Lieu and Chiang Min-chu, "Statistics in Farm Land in China," *Chinese Economical Journal* 2.212–213, cited in Tawney, p. 71.
5. Fei Hsiao-t'ung and Chih-i Chang in *Earthbound China: A Study of Rural Economy in Yunnan* (Chicago, 1945) discuss family budgets and standard of living in several rural communities in Yunnan during the 1940s. They describe these communities as "old China in miniature" (p. vii), which justifies the use of them to understand late Ch'ing rural psychology. The pressures and patterns described in these paragraphs are drawn from the discussion on standards of living on pp. 81–108, 157–165, and 245–265.
6. On the phenomenon of "contentment" in Chinese rural society, see Fei and Chang, pp. 82–84. For a general and more controversial interpretation of this phenomenon, not restricted to China, see George M. Foster, "Peasant Society and the Image of Limited Good," *American Anthropologist* 67:293–315. Foster has been criticized for, among other things, assuming the internal homogeneity of peasant communities and for characterizing them as closed systems. In the case of China, homogeneity and closedness are clearly inapplicable, although the nature of the connectedness to the ideological traditions of the towns and cities is a topic of continuing dispute. See John G. Kennedy, "Peasant Society and the Image of Limited Good: A Critique," *American Anthropologist* 68:1212–1225. On the concept of rural "contentment" as in reality an idealistic gloss for "sanctimonious husbandry," the acting out

of a cult of poverty so as to minimize envy and suspicion, see Leon E. Stover, *The Cultural Ecology of Chinese Civilization: Peasants and Elites in the Last of the Agrarian States* (New York, 1974), pp. 133–140, and Leon E. Stover and Takeko Kawai Stover, *China: An Anthropological Perspective* (Pacific Palisades, Cal., 1976), pp. 207–212.

7. Liu Ta-chieh (b. 1905) recalled a boyhood friend who disliked school and was planning to be a peasant cultivator, and who had exactly this "buried treasure psychology." He felt schooling was unimportant, for money was what mattered after all. Money was to come to him in the way it had come to the neighboring Chao family: by his uncovering gold bricks while plowing. It all depended upon luck *(yun-ch'i)*. His mother had already told his fortune *(suan-ming,* "calculated his fate"), and this indicated that he could become rich after he was 19 years old. He was simply going to wait it out. See *San-erh k'u-hsueh chi* (Shanghai, 1935), pp. 112–114. See also Stover and Stover, pp. 209–212; and Fei and Chang, pp. 277–290.

8. A remark by John K. Fairbank in *The United States and China* (Cambridge, 1983) is of interest in this context: "Nothing can so vividly convey a feeling of man's impotence in the face of nature as to watch the swirling coffee-colored flood of the Yellow River flowing majestically within its dikes across, and twenty feet above, the crowded plain 200 miles from the sea; and to realize that this vast yellow torrent is steadily depositing its silt and building its bed higher above the surrounding countryside until the time when human negligence or act of God will allow it again to burst from the dikes and inundate the plain" (p. 11).

9. See Francis L. K. Hsu, *Religion, Science and Human Crisis* (London, 1952). This study is based on the response to a cholera epidemic by a Chinese rural community in Yunnan Province; the problem posed is the validity of the distinctions between magic and religion, and particularly religion and science. Hsu uses the term *real knowledge* for science or "rational knowledge." He argues that an outside observer can distinguish between magical-supernatural beliefs and "real knowledge," but that most cultural participants, whether in preindustrial societies or the United States, do not do so. The two types of knowledge are mixed, but the dominant interpretative pattern is set by the overall culture, whether scientific or magical-supernatural.

10. The phenomenon of spirit sadism is discussed in Fei Hsiao-t'ung, *Peasant Life in China: A Field Study of Country Life in the Yangtze Valley* (London, 1939), pp. 35–36 and 85–87. Fei's study is based on a village in East China, but the practice of giving children derogatory names to protect them from evil spirits was geographically widespread: For Yunnan province, see Cornelius Osgood, *Village Life in Old China: A Community Study of Kao Yao, Yunnan* (New York, 1963), pp. 264–265. For North China, see Mrs. [Mary Isabella] Bryson, *Child Life in Chinese Homes* (London, 1885), pp. 14–15; and Harriet Monroe, "The Training of Chinese Children," *The Century Magazine* 83:644. For Foochow, see Rev. Justus Doolittle, *Social Life of the Chinese* (New York, 1885), p. 132. For Kiangsu and Anhui, see Henry Doré,

Researches into Chinese Superstitions, vol. 1 (Shanghai, 1914), pp. 11, 15–16, 20, and 23. For Hong Kong, see E. J. Hardy, *John Chinaman at Home: Sketches of Men, Manners and Things in China* (London, 1906), pp. 182, 274, and 277.

11. On the *t'ou-sheng kuei,* and the thirty childhood barriers, see Doré, vol. 1, pp. 9–10, 13–14, 22, and 26–27.

12. Francis L. K. Hsu has pointed out that the Chinese peasant attitude toward gods and spirits tended to be "negative," that is, an attitude that conceived of them primarily in terms of specific requests and needs, rather than "positive" in the Indian sense, in which the effort was made to establish a unilateral dependence upon an all-embracing, all-giving Reality as a framework for life. The first line of dependence, he argues, was upon one's fellow men, especially one's kin; the gods served to strengthen these bonds and to assure prosperity in the community. See Francis L. K. Hsu, *Clan, Caste, and Club* (Princeton, 1963), p. 274ff. Indeed, the gods did function in part as a supplementary source of strength for this-worldly ends. The heavenly realm reproduced the human realm, complete with a bureaucracy; and gods could be influenced by human feelings and appeals, and even disciplined. Far from being omnipotent, some gods were actually beaten or burned or both in public by earthly magistrates and priests for committing wrongs. Yet in his functional study of 1,786 major temples distributed over five major sections of China, C. K. Yang discovered that 55 percent of the major temples were directed towards other-worldly ends of personal holiness or salvation. Of these, almost half were oriented towards the moral order of heavenly and underworld deities as a system in itself, involving sin, judgment, salvation, heaven, and hell; over half were monasteries and nunneries, primarily Buddhist. Thirty-four percent may be interpreted as embodying appeals to the gods to buttress the solidarity and strength of social organizations (families, local communities, and state), while 9 percent were instrumentally directed towards specific economic and health functions. See C. K. Yang, *Religion in Chinese Society: A Study of Contemporary Social Functions of Religion and Some of Their Historical Factors* (Berkeley, 1961), pp. 7–16.

13. Passage from the novel *Long River* quoted in Jeffrey C. Kinkley, "Shen Ts'ung-wen: Short Story Writer of Ch'u" (unpublished workshop paper, August 15, 1974), p. 37. See also Jeffrey C. Kinkley, *The Odyssey of Shen Congwen* (Stanford, 1987), pp. 176–179. A personal document that reveals the interplay between effort and supernatural dependence is Ida Pruitt, *A Daughter of Han: The Autobiography of a Chinese Working Woman* (New Haven, 1945). Ning Lao T'ai-t'ai, the woman whose self-understanding is revealed in this autobiographical account, believed firmly in fate, but largely as a final appeal after energetic efforts had failed to achieve her goals; her general orientation towards life was not passive and resigned.

14. Zing Yang Kuo and Lam Yut-hand, "Chinese Religious Behavior and the Deification of Mao Tse-tung," in *The Psychological Record* 18:455–468, published at Denison University, Granville, Ohio. So-called "feudal superstitions" continue to be reported in China in the 1980s. The causes are familiar ones: not just the "trickery"

of wizards, shaman, and healers, but also unfulfilled hopes among the masses for healing and health care, for delivery from natural and man-made disasters, for securing male offspring. See Elizabeth Perry, "Rural Violence in Socialist China," *The China Quarterly* 103:434–435.

15. Rudolf P. Hommel, *China at Work: An Illustrated Record of the Primitive Industries of China's Masses, Whose Life is Toil, and Thus an Account of Chinese Civilization* (New York, 1937).

16. The *li* represented the forms of correct social behavior. Articulated by China's great philosophers, they were felt to be the natural and self-evident ordering of society, assuming scarcity, a hierarchical order of merit, a need for the division of labor, and a favorable view of the potentialities of human nature. The case for the *li* played down any resort to coercive governing tactics and instead emphasized individual self-cultivation in the style of the ancient sages. The Legalists had been less sanguine than the Confucianists about man's potentialities and more impressed with the imperative of state control and the need for specific institutional devices to maintain such control. The actual system that emerged during the Han dynasty was based upon the "Confucianization of law." It was a compromise between the two points of view. Legal norms were not applied universally as the Legalists might have desired. Instead the domain of civil law remained the domain of custom and popular usages as these were interpreted and enforced by clans, guilds, and villages. State law was overwhelmingly penal in nature and used primarily as a backstop behind the less punitive local control groups. But the domain of penal law extended beyond acts of criminal violence to include acts of moral or ritual impropriety as defined by the *li*.

On balance this system of law interwoven with *li* "tended to terrify the public into good behavior rather than redress disharmony." The law was one link in the state system of control that relied first upon other agents to secure its ends. When these resources were not enough to encourage conformity, then the law in its harshness could serve as a final inducement. As the alien Ch'ing dynasty wore on, in fact, there are suggestions that it tended to rely more and more on the law as an instrument of pacification. There were tight controls on any display of insubordination against constituted authority, on any religious cults that might have a prophetic message, on any writings that might be subversive, and on any weapon larger than the kitchen knife. The Confucian and Legalist arguments are concisely given in Derk Bodde and Clarence Morris, *Law in Imperial China, Exemplified by 190 Ch'ing Cases* (Cambridge, Mass., 1967), pp. 20–21, 23–24, 184–192, and 542.

17. Joseph Needham, *History of Scientific Thought* (Cambridge, 1956), pp. 472–485.

18. Chu Hsi, however, invites misinterpretation on this point, as he conceives of *li** as logically prior and existent before *ch'i*. He has even been called head of a "school of Platonic Ideas" by one student; see Feng Yu-lan, *A Short History of Chinese Philosophy*, Derk Bodde, tr. (New York, 1948), ch. 25. The conclusion of Wing-tsit Chan seems warranted: that Chu Hsi was both a monist and a dualist, as he thought of

li* as both immanent and transcendent, but that these terms and usual Western polarities are simply not helpful when applied to Chinese philosophy; Wing-tsit Chan, *A Sourcebook in Chinese Philosophy* (Princeton, 1963), pp. 634–635, and 640–641. See also Metzger, *Escape,* pp. 82–83, 110, 210 and 261. For a balanced discussion of Confucian rationalism and the subsystem of religious ideas within it (Heaven, predetermination, divination, the theory of yin-yang, and the Five Elements), see C. K. Yang, pp. 244–257 and 272–274.

19. Metzger, *Escape,* ch. 3, esp. pp. 61–68, 108–113, 127–135, 153–154, and 160–165.

20. Ibid., pp. 68–70, 125–126, 153–154, and 172–177. Metzger's work is pathbreaking here in bringing both psychological and philosophical evidence to bear in a sophisticated analysis of Neo-Confucian thought and thinkers. The interface for him is the diffuse dependency anxieties traced to childhood socialization by Richard Solomon and the need for Heaven as an "unmatchable counterweight" that both enjoins and facilitates moral action in the world. He rightly argues that the Neo-Confucian writings must have formulated the problems of life in a way that made sense to those who turned to them as a compelling vision of reality. I have, however, included fixity as another aspect of such psychological-philosophical interface. Metzger treats the desire for fixity as a goal related to the need for control or mastery but does not see fixity in relation to the problem of reification itself. Heaven was only one such reified concept. Why was reification itself so attractive? I see the practice of reification and the attraction to fixity as counterweights to the perceived fragility and vulnerability of the mind, which seemed to need such supports to initiate and sustain moral action.

21. Ibid., p. 153.

22. For a particularly illuminating discussion of a cultural parallel, Puritan New England, see Perry Miller, *The New England Mind: From Colony to Province* (Cambridge, Mass., 1953), pp. 19–146, esp. pp. 27–39 on the jeremiad.

23. Phenomenalism was the belief that natural calamities depended upon the ethical errors of human leaders. See Needham, pp. 346–395, for a discussion of the "pseudo-sciences and the sceptical tradition." The distinction that Needham makes between pseudo-scientific theories and proto-scientific theories, however, is unclear; for both kinds of hypotheses were early efforts at comprehension and control of the environment. Skepticism needed to be directed at both kinds of hypotheses.

24. Needham, pp. 66–67. The Taoist theory, as Needham has summarized it, is that he who can plunge into nature, determined not to flinch from anything as too trivial, too painful, too disgusting, or too horrible to be named and investigated, will conquer fear, becoming invulnerable, and "ride upon the clouds."

25. *Hun-po* represented the two souls of human beings: the spiritual soul *(hun)* ascended upon death, the animal soul *(po)* descended. The Neo-Confucians rationalized these terms by defining *hun* as a rising, light variety of *ch'i* and *po* as a heavier, sinking variety. Similarly, *shen* and *kuei,* the ancient terms for god and demon, came to

express the abstract concepts of expansion and contraction for the Neo-Confucians. See Needham, pp. 490–491.

26. Wang Ch'ung quoted in Needham, p. 376. Metzger has commented that Chu Hsi ascribed to the peasant masses the feeling of subjection to "unmalleable cosmic forces," which Metzger contrasts with the elitist feeling of scholars that they could shape a malleable cosmos (*Escape*, pp. 132–133). Metzger's comment that the masses indeed seem to have felt that way, "as suggested by the well-known peasant saying *k'ao-t'ien ch'ih-fan* (depend on heaven for one's livelihood)" (p. 133), overlooks or underestimates the activist effort by peasants to shape the outcome of events, by natural efforts or supernatural means. The morality of common people was shaped by a focus on family, neighbors, and supernatural beings; but I do not share Metzger's conclusion that the common people, because of more limited goals and lesser expectations, had no feeling for an ultimate, existential predicament within their "intractable" world. I would contend that the supernatural world was a problematic, existential reality for peasants, not just a form of self-help or insurance. See Metzger, pp. 252–253, n. 15.

27. Lu Hsun [Lu Xun], *Selected Works*, vol. 1 (Peking, 1980), pp. 1–2, 396–403. For a description of the actual remedies and the rationale for using them, see Leo Ou-fan Lee, "Genesis of a Writer: Notes on Lu Xun's Educational Experience, 1881–1909" in Merle Goldman, ed., *Modern Chinese Literature in the May Fourth Era* (Cambridge, Mass., 1977), pp. 166–167.

28. Hu Shih, *Ssu-shih tsu-shu*, Overseas Chinese ed. (Hong Kong, 1954), pp. 41 and 44.

29. Francis L. K. Hsu, *Under the Ancestors' Shadow: Kinship, Personality, and Social Mobility in Village China*, rev. ed. (Garden City, N.Y., 1967), p. 177. See also C. K. Yang, pp. 275–277. For an autobiographical description of the role of spirits within a Chinese and American context, see Maxine Hong Kingston, *The Woman Warrior: Memoirs of a Girlhood Among Ghosts* (New York, 1977).

30. These thinkers found Neo-Confucianism too metaphysical; they reasserted the naturalistic immanent reality of *li** and the primacy of *ch'i*. Needham, pp. 506–515; Fang Chao-ying's entry on Tai Chen in Arthur W. Hummel, *Eminent Chinese of the Ch'ing Period* (Washington, D.C., 1943), pp. 695–700; Wing-tsit Chan, pp. 693, 700–701, and 703–705; Metzger, *Escape*, pp. 162–163 and 173–174.

31. Wing-tsit Chan, p. 700.

32. Ibid., p. 701. S. Y. Teng, "Wang Fu-chih's Views on History and Historical Writing," *Journal of Asian Studies* 28.1:111–123.

33. Wing-tsit Chan, p. 698. As one of my graduate students in China wryly noted in 1986 upon reading this passage, this is an argument for "seeking truth from facts," a major slogan in post–Cultural Revolution China.

34. John Meskill, *Academies in Ming China: A Historical Essay* (Tucson, 1982), pp. xvi and 69–159, esp. 69–79, 99–100, 138, 146–150 and 156–159.

35. T'ang Chün-i, "The Reconstruction of Confucianism and the Modernization of Asian

Countries," in *Report: International Conference on the Problems of Modernization in Asia* (Seoul, 1965), pp. 101–113. On the rejection of Confucian fundamentalism and institutional Confucianism, see Metzger, *Escape,* pp. 7 and 193.

36. Edwin D. Harvey, *The Mind of China* (New Haven, 1933). This study, a detailed portrayal and commentary on Chinese popular religion or "the world of the spirits," is filled with examples of the overlay of meanings in daily life. "It is a simple truth to say that every kernel of rice sown, every silk cocoon reared, every ton of coal mined or tree hewn, every pupil beginning his school career, every birth, and every death, is surrounded with high religious or cult sanction or authority. It will be instructive to follow the interpretations of these religious notions in the real business of living; to discern how a highly accomplished people have had their social, political, and economic interests modified by these all-pervading ghostly sanctions" (p. 4). This "inveterate animism," as Harvey calls it, reflected for him an overelaboration of religion in the life of the ordinary Chinese, who in the 1920s still lived apart from the symbolic worlds of the traditional upper class or the modern intelligentsia. "The great masses of the Chinese people have but the flimsiest notions of the lofty ethico-political systems of Confucius or of Dr. Sun Yat Sen" (p. 5).

37. Kuei Wen-ts'an, ed., *Hsiao ching chi-chieh* (Taiwan ed., 1968), p. 25. A comprehensive study of this text is Harry Hsin-i Hsiao, "A Study of the *Hsiao-ching:* with an emphasis on its intellectual background and its problems" (Harvard Ph.D. diss., 1973). Hsiao traces the development of the concept of filial piety from antiquity to the Han, when the text crystallized in its present form; he also compares its themes and emphases with other literature of filial piety, particularly the *Twenty-four Examples of Filial Piety,* the *Li Chi,* tales and biographies of exemplary filial children in the standard dynastic histories, and themes of filial devotion in fiction, drama, and opera. A clear class difference stands out in the appeal and content of this literature. The *Hsiao ching,* with its "moderate-rational" appeal and general norms, influenced the upper class, whereas the more popular tales were "emotional-inhumane" in appeal and filled with examples of exceptional filial devotion, often stressing its supernatural magical powers. Both types of literature had a wide appeal until the early twentieth century; but there were also countercurrents to the emphasis upon filial piety, countercurrents that went back to contending philosophers in the classical era as well as some thinkers within Confucianism itself.

38. Chu Hsi, "Treatise on *Jen,*" in Wing-tsit Chan, pp. 594–597.

39. *Mencius,* Book II, Part I, chapter 6. Translation from Wing-tsit Chan, pp. 65–66.

40. Ibid., p. 66.

41. Translation from Wing-tsit Chan, p. 98.

42. Chang Tsai (1020–1077), translated in Wing-tsit Chan, p. 511.

43. Chang Po-hsing, ed., *Hsiao hsueh chi-chieh,* first preface, p. 1. The *Hsiao hsueh* is an elementary text usually attributed to Chu Hsi. Chang Po-hsing (1652–1725) was a Ch'ing scholar-official and educator who founded two academies and was very devoted to the Sung Confucianists, especially Chu Hsi. A set of works collected and

edited by Chang, including his own works as well as works of earlier philosophers, was first published between 1707 and 1713, and subsequently republished several times in the late nineteenth century. See entry by Dean R. Wickes in Hummel, *Eminent Chinese of the Ch'ing Period,* pp. 51–52. See also Appendix A in Meskill, pp. 160–164, for "Ch'eng Tuan-li's Daily Schedule of Study in the Ch'eng Family's School According to the Age of the Student." The age breakdown in this schedule is as follows: before age eight *sui,* eight to fifteen, fifteen to twenty-two, and twenty-two to twenty-five. During the eight-to-fifteen or *hsiao hsueh* period, only plain texts without commentary were to be used; the first text was the *Hsiao hsueh,* which Meskill describes as "Six *chuan* of sayings and exemplary deeds of sages and worthies, recommended by Chu Hsi for the fundamentals of self-cultivation. Although commonly attributed to Chu Hsi, it was in fact compiled by a disciple under Chu Hsi's direction." The *hsiao hsueh* as a developmental phase was followed by the *ta hsueh* or "learning for adults." Generally Chinese *sui* or "years of age" are one year more than the equivalent Western age, as it was Chinese practice to begin counting from the time of conception. The period of *hsiao hsueh* was thus age seven to fourteen.

44. Carson Chang, *The Development of Neo-Confucian Thought,* vol. 1 (New York, 1957), pp. 267–268.
45. Wing-tsit Chan, pp. 547–548.
46. Chu Hsi on "The Mind, the Nature, and the Feelings," in Wing-tsit Chan, pp. 630–632.
47. Ch'eng I, in Wing-tsit Chan, p. 548.
48. Wing-tsit Chan, p. 608.
49. Charles P. Ridley, "Educational Theory and Practice in Late Imperial China: The Teaching of Writing as a Specific Case" (Stanford Ph.D. diss., 1973), pp. 294–295. Ridley, in an illuminating section on theories of internal growth held by some late-Ch'ing educators, cites the period of the *ta hsueh* (age fourteen years on) as the point at which the understanding arises as a tool of intellectual and moral growth, precisely because the onset of "contamination by material desires" cannot be handled by memory learning alone. This view differs from the Neo-Confucian one in placing the onset of "contamination" so late. Some forms of "contamination" undoubtedly intensified with the coming of puberty, but the legacy of uncontrolled feelings was believed to be an inherent feature of the *hsiao hsueh* period as well. This "contamination," as Ridley rightly emphasizes, was thought to be environmentally induced by deleterious influences and not a result of any innate perversity (pp. 279–280).
50. *Hsun-tzu,* ch. 23, "The Nature of Man is Evil," translated in Ch'u Chai and Winberg Chai, eds., *The Humanist Way in Ancient China: Essential Works of Confucianism* (Taiwan, 1965), pp. 232–233.
51. See T'ung-tsu Ch'ü, "Chinese Class Structure and its Ideology," in John K. Fairbank, ed., *Chinese Thought and Institutions* (Chicago, 1957), pp. 236–237. Donald J. Munro emphasizes the environmental interpretation of evil in both Mencius and

Hsun-tzu, and doubts the centrality of the chapter in Hsun-tzu that seems to define human nature as evil. He argues that the differences between Mencius and Hsun-tzu lie chiefly in Hsun-tzu's "adopting an approach based more on actual human and social conditions and less on their ideal forms." See Donald J. Munro, *The Concept of Man in Early China* (Stanford, 1969), pp. 71–78 and 88–90.

52. Neo-Confucians had two names for the mind, according to which "track" it was on. "The mind of Tao" was mind oriented to correct principles of Heaven and nature; it was a subtle mind, searching for the right. "The mind of man" was mind motivated by the desires of the physical world. It was full of danger, and likely to "go wild and become wanton." "The mind of Tao" is mind as Master; "the mind of man" is mind as slave. See Carson Chang, vol. 1, pp. 270–272.

53. Ch'eng I, in Wing-tsit Chan, pp. 567–568.

54. Chu Hsi, "A Treatise on Ch'eng Ming-tao's Discourse on the Nature," in Wing-tsit Chan, p. 599; and "How to Study," in Wing-tsit Chan, p. 605. On the general Neo-Confucian sense of the pervasiveness of evil and the elusiveness of the *tao*, see Metzger, pp. 108–113, 158–161, and 197–200.

55. Chu Hsi, in Wing-tsit Chan, p. 599.

56. Confucius, *Analects*, Arthur Waley, tr. (New York, 1960), Book 16, 9. "Master K'ung [Confucius] said, Highest are those who are born wise. Next are those who become wise in learning. After them come those who have to toil painfully in order to acquire learning. Finally, to the lowest class of the common people belong those who toil painfully without ever managing to learn."

57. One of my interviewees described his mother as a *shan jen*. She had little education, but was strict with herself, generous to others, and a devout Buddhist. In filial concern for her sick mother, she cut a piece of flesh off her arm to prepare a special soup, a technique of treatment viewed as especially efficacious and praiseworthy among the common people. Taiwan Interview No. 12. It is precisely this kind of act that is labeled by Harry Hsin-i Hsiao as "cruel, inhumane, foolish behavior." Such "unreasonable self-sacrifice" was praised in the popular tales and biographies, even though it was foreign to and even contrary to the principles in an upper-class text such as the *Hsiao ching* (Classic of filial piety). The *Hsiao ching*, for example, stressed the noninjuring of one's own physical body, which "filial" fleshcutting clearly contradicted. Harry Hsin-i Hsiao, pp. 233 and 258–266.

In a male-dominated society, women could be virtuous as chaste widows and dutiful mothers, but they could not progress far along the path of learning and sagehood. For a discussion of these historical limitations upon women, as well as the need for a contemporary Confucian philosophy to transcend them, see Tu Wei-ming, *Confucian Thought: Selfhood as Creative Transformation* (Albany, 1985), pp. 143–145.

58. Tcheng Ki-Tong, *The Chinese Painted by Themselves*, James Millington, tr. (London, 1884), p. 20.

59. Yang Lien-sheng, "The Concept of 'Pao' as a Basis for Social Relations in China,"

in John K. Fairbank, ed., *Chinese Thought and Institutions* (Chicago, 1957), pp. 304–305.

60. On family and clan rules, see Hui-chen Wang Liu, *The Traditional Chinese Clan Rules* (Locust Valley, N.Y., 1959), esp. ch. 3. On the use of the *Sacred Edict* within the examination system, see Ichisada Miyazaki, *China's Examination Hell: The Civil Service Examinations of Imperial China* (New Haven, 1981), pp. 23–25, 29, 35, and 38. A section on the *Sacred Edict* was dropped for the provincial and higher examinations. As Miyazaki noted, "Since this law was composed for the instruction of beginners and commoners, the emperor himself held that there was no need to include it in higher examinations" (p. 38).

61. These principles and regulations are translated and discussed in Meskill, pp. 50–58. For a comparison of a control-oriented set of regulations, emanating from official supervisors, with the more flexible learning-oriented pedagogy of Wang Yang-ming, see p. 96–101 and 164–166.

62. Chung-li Chang, *The Chinese Gentry: Studies on Their Role in Nineteenth-Century Chinese Society* (Seattle, 1955), pp. 97–98; Miyazaki, pp. 18–19. Younger students were probably more likely to be admitted to private academies.

63. On this and other pitfalls in social psychology, see Reinhard Bendix, "Compliant Behavior and Individual Personality," in Neil J. Smelser and William T. Smelser, eds., *Personality and Social Systems* (New York, 1963), pp. 55–67.

64. This specific formulation is from one of the worthies cited and recommended by Chu Hsi. See Chang Po-hsiang, ed., *Hsiao hsueh chi-chieh* (1962), pp. 93–94.

65. Cited in Ridley, p. 306.

66. Ibid., p. 287–288.

67. Ibid., p. 304.

68. Ibid., p. 305.

69. Ibid., pp. 308–315.

2. THE LOCUS OF INNOVATION, 1840–1920

1. Lu Hsun, "Random Thoughts (25)" and "What is Required of Us as Fathers To-day," in *Selected Works,* vol. 2, (Peking, 1980), pp. 26–28, 56–71. On the critique of *hsiao* as fostering anachronistic political submissiveness and cultural passivity, see Wu Yü, *Wu Yü wen-lu,* vol. 1, (Shanghai, 1927), pp. 14–23; and Chow Tse-tung, *The May Fourth Movement: Intellectual Revolution in Modern China* (Cambridge, Mass., 1960), ch. 12, esp. pp. 303–308. On the tendency to over-identify all Confucian attitudes with the norms of *hsiao,* and falsely to find all sources of moral autonomy in Western thought, see Metzger, p. 195.

2. See Ivan Chen, *The Book of Filial Duty* (London, 1908). Although quotations are from this edition, all references hereafter are to the more familiar rendering of the title, *Twenty-four Examples* and example number only. Chen excluded two tales on the grounds of propriety: one is of a man who tasted his father's excrement to see

whether the old gentleman would recover from a serious illness; the second is of a woman who nursed her toothless grandmother.

3. *Twenty-four Examples,* no. 6. The four cases involving married men are nos. 11, 12, 13, and 22; the five involving older men are nos. 2, 6, 21, 23, and 24. The value of this book as evidence has been questioned on the grounds that it is a bizarre and unrepresentative cultural curiosity; see Mote, pp. 110–111, 115, and 119. It was, however, widely read as a supplementary children's text to provide concrete examples of the principles contained in more substantive texts, such as the *Hsiao ching* and Chu Hsi's *Hsiao hsueh;* see Harry Hsin-i Hsiao, pp. 258–265.

4. *Twenty-four Examples,* no. 1.

5. *Mencius,* Book V, Part I, Chapters 1–5.

6. *Analects,* Book 4, 18. Arthur Waley translation, with slight change in punctuation.

7. Sybille van der Sprenkel, *Legal Institutions in Manchu China: A Sociological Analysis* (London, 1962), pp. 80–89, 125, and 128.

8. *Twenty-four Examples* no. 17. This argument of indebtedness is also stressed in the first maxim of the *Sacred Edict,* a set of ethical exhortations developed initially by the K'ang hsi Emperor to reach ordinary villagers. *The Sacred Edict . . . Together with a Paraphrase on the Whole by a Mandarin,* William Milne, tr. (London, 1817), pp. 36–38.

9. *San Tzu Ching,* ll. 37–38, in *San Tzu Ching: Elementary Chinese,* Herbert A. Giles, tr. (1910; New York, 1963); *Twenty-four Examples,* no. 16; Aisin-Gioro Pu Yi [P'u Yi], *From Emperor to Citizen: The Autobiography of Aisin-Gioro Pu Yi,* W. J. Jenner, tr., vol. 1 (Peking, 1964), p. 66.

10. Hu Shih, *Hu Shih wen-tsun,* vol. 1 (Taipei, 1968), pp. 690–692.

11. Ernest Becker, *Angel in Armor: A Post-Freudian Perspective on the Nature of Man* (New York, 1969), p. 55.

12. Charles P. Ridley in "Educational Theory and Practice in Late Imperial China," discusses internal debates in educational circles in China as well as offering his own commentary as a scholar and educational theorist. It is this latter perspective that I am presenting here.

13. Ibid., pp. 326–327.

14. Ibid., pp. 100–108.

15. Cited and translated by Ridley, pp. 310–311. For a brief biography of Ch'en Hung-mou, see Hummel, pp. 86–87.

16. Paul Cohen, *Between Tradition and Modernity: Wang T'ao and Reform in Late Ch'ing China* (Cambridge, Mass. 1974), p. 5.

17. The partial commercialization of the southeastern coast of China in the period 1500–1850 was the beginning of this process. The first European and American seafarers joined an already emerging world of international trade, creating a new "fringe civilization" which was a "deviation from the continental heartland on both sides of the world." See Frederic Wakeman, Jr., "The Opening of China," in Joseph R. Levenson, ed., *Modern China: An Interpretive Anthology* (London, 1971), p. 51.

18. Hosea Ballou Morse, *The Trade and Administration of China* (London, 1908), pp. 203–269, offers a survey, province by province, of the treaty ports. See also John K. Fairbank, *Trade and Diplomacy on the China Coast: The Opening of the Treaty Ports, 1842–1854* (Stanford, 1969), pp. 155–157; Rhoads Murphey, *The Treaty Ports and Chinese Modernization: What Went Wrong?* (Ann Arbor, 1970), p. 4; and George Cyril Allen and Audrey G. Donnithorne, *Western Enterprise in Far Eastern Economic Development: China and Japan* (New York, 1954), pp. 129–130.

19. Within a twenty- or thirty-mile radius of each treaty port there were signs of spill-over, such as the extensive commercial sale of agricultural goods, higher tenancy rates, and some industrial development in the hinterlands of Shanghai and Tientsin: Murphey, *Treaty Ports,* pp. 57–58. There were obviously some changes introduced by the presence of the treaty ports, above all "the beginnings of a more efficient and particularly concentrated commercial structure," changes in transport, long-distance marketing, and production for export (Ibid., pp. 49–52). Once this is said, however, the question remains: Is this much or little? Reacting against the picture often drawn of China progressively modernizing on the treaty-port model, Murphey is impressed by the limitations of this process, which finally aborted with the collapse of Kuomintang China. Other reasons for the limited economic impact of the treaty ports are given in John K. Fairbank, Alexander Eckstein, and L. S. Yang, "Economic Change in Early Modern China: An Analytic Framework," *Economic Development and Cultural Change* 9.1:1.

20. Milton Theobald Stauffer, ed., *The Christian Occupation of China; A General Survey of the Numerical Strength and Geographical Distribution of the Christian Forces in China Made by The Special Committee on Survey and Occupation; China Continuation Committee, 1918–1921* (Shanghai, 1922). By 1919, 1,598 out of 1,704 counties in China proper and Manchuria reported Protestant evangelical activities. See also Albert Feuerwerker, *The Foreign Establishment in China in the Early Twentieth Century* (Ann Arbor, 1976), ch. 3.

21. Irwin T. Hyatt, Jr., "Protestant Missions in China, 1877–1890: The Institutionalization of Good Works," *Papers on China* 17:67–100. For the continuation and expansion of these efforts in the 1900–1920 period, see Feuerwerker, pp. 41, 43, 48–49, 51–52, and 54–56.

22. There were in 1926 between 2,500,000 and 3,000,000 Chinese converts to Christianity, four-fifths of whom were Roman Catholics. The population in China then was well over four hundred million. See Kenneth Scott Latourette, *A History of Christian Missions in China* (New York, 1929), p. 831.

23. Murphey, *Treaty Ports,* pp. 66–67.

24. Cohen, *Between Tradition and Modernity,* pp. 68–69.

25. Fairbank, *Trade and Diplomacy,* pp. 176–177.

26. The ambivalence of foreign policy views during the 1860–1895 period is highlighted in Yen-p'ing Hao and Erh-min Wang, "Changing Chinese Views of Western Relations, 1840–95," in Fairbank and Liu, eds., *Cambridge History of China,*

vol. 11, part 2, pp. 142–201, esp. 172ff. The views of reformers and "enlightened types," such as Kuo Sung-tao are presented as "the rational, constructive and pleasant ones"; they are contrasted with "the belligerent, emotionally charged and occasionally xenophobic ones" triggered by Western imperialism and rooted in Sinocentric pride. These latter attitudes among scholar-officials produced "insurmountable institutional and political obstacles" to reform and, prior to the 1880s, doomed the new awakening in cultural consciousness to be "superficial and haphazard."

27. Fred W. Drake, *China Charts the World: Hsu Chi-yü and His Geography of 1848* (Cambridge, Mass., 1975), pp. 80–92, 115–117.

28. Teng Ssu-yü and John K. Fairbank, eds., *China's Response to the West: A Documentary Survey 1839–1923* (Cambridge, Mass., 1961), pp. 97 and 99–102. On the fate of Kuo Sung-tao, see Paul Cohen, "Ch'ing China: Confrontation with the West, 1850–1900," in James B. Crowley, ed., *Modern East Asia: Essays in Interpretation* (New York, 1970), pp. 50–51. On Hsu Chi-yü's struggle with conservatism, see Drake, pp. 44–51.

29. Cohen, *Between Tradition and Modernity,* pp. 69, 176ff.

30. Ibid., p. 75.

31. Y. C. Wang, *Chinese Intellectuals and the West: 1872–1949* (Chapel Hill, 1966), pp. 42–45 and 96–98.

32. Warner M. van Norden, ed., *Who's Who of the Chinese in New York* (New York, 1918), pp. 65–66. Lee's childhood memoirs are found in Yan Phou Lee, *When I was a Boy in China* (Boston, 1887).

33. Cohen, *Between Tradition and Modernity,* p. 62ff. On the breakdown of the association of foreigners with barbarism and beastlike nonhuman behavior, see Hao and Wang, pp. 181–186 and 188–190.

34. The general structural features of this historic confrontation are outlined in Peter Berger, Brigitte Berger, and Hansfried Kellner, *The Homeless Mind: Modernization and Consciousness* (New York, 1973), esp. ch. 6. The authors avoid making any assumptions about the inevitability or desirability of this process and, in fact, sympathetically portray various forms of tradition-inspired resistance to disruptive, alien cultural and intellectual forces.

35. Jung-pang Lo, ed., *K'ang Yu-wei: A Biography and Symposium* (Tucson, 1967), pp. 36 and 38.

36. Ibid., pp. 27 and 31. On K'ang's exalted self-assurance, its strengths and drawbacks, see Kung-ch'uan Hsiao, *A Modern China and a New World: K'ang Yu-wei, Reformer and Utopian, 1858–1927* (Seattle, 1975), pp. 18–21.

37. Richard Howard, "The Early Life and Thought of K'ang Yu-wei, 1858–1895" (Columbia Ph.D. diss., 1972), pp. 34–35, 46–54, and 111–115; Kung-ch'uan Hsiao, pp. 15 and 418–435.

38. Kung-ch'uan Hsiao, p. 434.

39. Quoted in Howard, p. 96.

40. Ibid., pp. 604–606; Kung-ch'uan Hsiao, pp. 331–335.

41. Howard, pp. 622–625.
42. Ibid., p. 626.
43. Metzger (pp. 216–220 and 275n) argues that Western means, particularly technology and political institutions, injected into Chinese thought a new sense of optimism about being able to transform the "outer" world and thus to find a way out of an apparently insoluble predicament in Confucian thought and practice. Although the cultural and linguistic "grammar" through which historical actors interpret their situation is obviously important in explaining their acts, I am more inclined than Metzger to lay weight upon the perception of the West in the 1890s and 1900s as a threat and stimulus for radical action than as a means and opportunity to regain utopia.
44. H. G. Barnett, *Innovation: The Basis of Cultural Change* (New York, 1953). Barnett cites three kinds of variables as particularly important in understanding the acceptance or rejection of novelty by individuals: 1) the intrinsic nature of the new thing or idea, 2) the persuasive power of those advocating for or against its adoption, 3) biographical determinants or the life situation of the individual person reacting. On the advocacy variable, see pp. 291–328.
45. Cohen, *Between Tradition and Modernity,* part 4, esp. p. 252. For an overview of the entire reform process up to 1900, see Kwang-ching Liu, "Nineteenth Century China: The Disintegration of the Old Order and the Impact of the West," in Ping-ti Ho and Tang Tsou, eds., *China in Crisis* (Chicago, 1968), vol. 1, book 1, pp. 93–178. This study stresses the extent of intellectual ferment and reform plans during the period 1860–1895. The publications, schools, and individual reformers are tallied up. From this longer perspective, however, 1894–1895 still marks a break: "[W]ith the appearance of reform periodicals, 'study associations,' and new schools, it may be said that nationalism (which implies the sharing of nationalistic sentiments by a larger sector of the community) had come into existence among China's upper classes" (ibid., p. 173). See also the conclusion by Yen-p'ing Hao and Erh-min Wang that nationalism as a state of mind emerged in the 1860s, but as a movement only in the 1890s; "Changing Chinese Views of Western Relations, 1840–95," in Fairbank and Liu, eds. *History of China*, vol. 11, part 2, p. 188.
46. Mary Clabaugh Wright, "Introduction: The Rising Tide of Change," in Mary Clabaugh Wright, ed., *China in Revolution: The First Phase, 1900–1913* (New Haven, 1968), pp. 1–3.
47. There were earlier versions of this phenomenon. The "Taotai-merchant," with an official title acquired through purchase or achievement, goes back at least to the court-authorized hong merchants of the eighteenth century. Most major compradors after 1860 found it convenient, even necessary, in their work to establish an official status through degree purchase. It was not only the degree but their performance of traditional gentry functions of social leadership in their home communities and treaty ports that earned merchants gentry status. Yen-p'ing Hao, *The Comprador in Nineteenth Century China: Bridge between East and West* (Cambridge, Mass., 1970),

pp. 7, 184, and 190. For the forms of alliance and amalgamation between a "nascent bourgeoisie" composed of compradors, merchants, bankers, industrialists, overseas Chinese, and the traditional landowning, degree-holding gentry, see Marie-Claire Bergere, "The Role of the Bourgeoisie," in Wright, ed., *China in Revolution*, pp. 237–242.

48. Han Suyin, *The Crippled Tree: China—Biography, History, Autobiography* (London, 1965), pp. 114–115. Soldiering had been traditionally devalued in popular lore as well as in Confucian teachings as an occupation unbefitting the "best talent." On the changing terms applied to foreign learning, see Hao and Wang, pp. 167–169 and 200.

49. On the comprador's preference for Western education for his sons over the traditional civil service route, see Hao, p. 7.

50. Two such innovative centers in the 1890s were Hunan province and western Taiwan where progressive governors-general had undertaken reform programs on their own initiative. See K. C. Liu, pp. 136 and 151–159; and Charlton M. Lewis, *Prologue to the Chinese Revolution: Transformation of Ideas and Institutions in Hunan Province, 1891–1907* (Cambridge, Mass., 1976).

51. Hao Chang, "Intellectual Change and the Reform Movement, 1890–8" in Fairbank and Liu, eds. *Cambridge History of China*, vol. 11, part 2, pp. 330–336.

52. The extent, vigor, and inventiveness of the resistance to imperialist territorial encroachments during the first decade of the twentieth century is stressed by Mary Wright; see Wright, "Introduction," pp. 3–19.

53. Ernest P. Young, "Nationalism, Reform, and Republican Revolution: China in the Early Twentieth Century," in Crowley, ed., pp. 151–179.

54. Chūzō Ichiko, "Political and Institutional Reform, 1901–11," in Fairbank and Liu, eds. *Cambridge History of China*, vol. 11, part 2, pp. 411–415.

55. Barnett, pp. 385–386.

56. Meskill, pp. 46, and 102–103. The relative weakness or even absence of the adolescent peer group experience, in which family and traditional values may be contested and even rejected, may have had important theoretical implications for the ability of many young Chinese to be independent-minded vis-à-vis the group and tradition. See my discussion of the work of Alfred Bloom and Kenneth Keniston in this regard in Jon L. Saari, "Breaking the Hold of Tradition: The Self-Group Interface in Transitional China," in Sidney L. Greenblatt, Richard W. Wilson, and Amy Auerbacher Wilson eds., *Social Interaction in Chinese Society* (New York, 1982), pp. 38–40.

57. On the changing definition of *ch'ing-nien*, see Marion J. Levy, Jr., *The Family Revolution in Modern China* (Cambridge, Mass., 1949), pp. 84–93 and 294–300. The question of the validity of *ch'ing-nien* as an age-group classification during the "traditional" era is raised by Levy, as peasants and women were generally excluded and the normal reference was to *ch'ing-nien-jen* or "green years men." During the period of the late Ch'ing dynasty and early Republic, the term came to include all major

groupings in Chinese society, peasantry as well as gentry, male as well as female. The frivolous aura of the traditional use of the term was gone.

58. On the limited spread of foreign learning in one provincial setting, coastal Chekiang before 1905, see Mary Backus Rankin, "The Revolutionary Movement in Chekiang: A Study in the Tenacity of Tradition," in Wright, ed., *China in Revolution*, pp. 328–329. See also Rankin's *Early Chinese Revolutionaries: Radical Intellectuals in Shanghai and Chekiang, 1902–1911* (Cambridge, Mass., 1971), p. 3. On the outreach of the new system, see Wright, "Introduction," pp. 24–26.

59. H. S. Brunnert and V. V. Hagelstrom, *Present Day Political Organization of China,* A. Beltchenko and E. E. Moran, tr. (Shanghai, 1912), preface, pp. 213–265 and 312–323. This was, of course, a bureaucratic organizational chart, not necessarily a description of existing schools.

60. For an example of such retrospective contempt, see David Tod Roy, *Kuo Mo-jo: The Early Years* (Cambridge, Mass., 1971), pp. 15–16 and 19–20.

61. Ku Chieh-kang, *The Autobiography of a Chinese Historian: Being the Preface to a Symposium on Ancient Chinese History (Ku Shih Pien),* Arthur W. Hummel, tr. (Leiden, 1931), pp. 18–19. The young Ku was unimpressed with some teachers, however, for they appeared "incapable of freeing themselves from slavish adherence to textbooks . . . The paltriness and vulgarity of such teaching comes home to me every time I think of it" (ibid., pp. 19–20). See also the reminiscence about a rural elementary school near Shanghai by Yu Tzu-i, "Erh-shih nien ch'ien hsiang-ts'un hsueh-hsiao sheng-huo-li ti wo," in *Chiao-yü tsa-chih* 19:30533–30545, partially translated by Jane Chen in Patricia Buckley Ebrey, ed., *Chinese Civilization and Society: A Sourcebook* (New York, 1981), pp. 254–258.

62. Young, p. 158.

63. Leo Ou-fan Lee, *The Romantic Generation of Modern Chinese Writers* (Cambridge, Mass., 1973), pp. 30–40, 62–65, and 258–262. Lee sets this development off against the traditional preference for the controlled expression of sentiment, the belief that the inner feelings should reflect and reciprocate the outer forms of the *li* or propriety. In Confucianism this inner-outer polarity dominates; in Buddhism and Taoism there is a counter-interpretation that denies the relevance of such a distinction. The flow of sentiments and instincts is the outer self, an end in itself, irrespective of conventional morality. Su Man-shu established an untraditional precedent "that a man's emotional nature not only needs no moral justification, but also when externalized in a unique life style, should be the only earmark of his personality" (Lee, *Romantic Generation,* p. 261).

64. Chow Tse-tsung, Table 1, pp. 379–380.

65. Kuo Jen-yuan, "The Confessions of a Chinese Scientist" (unpublished manuscript), pp. 57–58. For testimony on Liang's influence on this generation of youthful readers, see Philip C. Huang, *Liang Ch'i-ch'ao and Modern Chinese Liberalism* (Seattle, 1972), pp. 3–8.

66. Joseph R. Levenson, *Liang Ch'i-ch'ao and the Mind of Modern China* (Cambridge, Mass., 1953), pp. 92–101.

67. Philip Huang, pp. 56–67, 77–83 and 99–103. For a detailed account of Liang's crucial Canadian and American journey in 1903, see Jerome B. Grieder, *Intellectuals and the State in Modern China: A Narrative History* (New York, 1981), pp. 161–170.

68. Translation from Chow Tse-tung, pp. 45–46. On the pervasiveness of Social Darwinism during the May Fourth era and on Ch'en's contradictory use of the facts of evolutionary change both as an ideology for change and as a cause for hopelessness and pessimism, see Lin Yü-sheng, *The Crisis of Chinese Consciousness: Radical Antitraditionalism in the May Fourth Era* (Madison, 1979) pp. 56–59. On the earlier transmission and dissemination of Darwin's ideas in China, see Benjamin Schwartz, *In Search of Wealth and Power: Yen Fu and the West* (Cambridge, Mass., 1964), pp. 98–112; Grieder, *Intellectuals,* pp. 147–152 and 245–248; and James Reeve Pusey, *China and Charles Darwin* (Cambridge, Mass., 1985).

69. Translation in Teng and Fairbank, pp. 240–241.

70. Ibid., pp. 241–245. These traditional tendencies listed above became the core of the negative self-image in many young people, that is, the part of their culture which they felt to be within themselves but which they rejected.

71. For a study stressing the undemocratic and opportunistic nature of post–May Fourth student movements, see John Israel, *Student Nationalism in China: 1927–1937* (Stanford, 1966), pp. 1–9 and 184–198. For an argument that student movements were, at least initially, expressions of public opinion in China, see Wen-han Kiang, *The Chinese Student Movement* (Morningside Heights, N.Y., 1948). A close analysis of one student movement of the mid 1930s, John Israel and Donald W. Klein, *Rebels and Bureaucrats: China's December 9ers* (Berkeley, 1976), pp. 277–279, argues that party and students were "mutually vehicles for each other, with differing goals or understandings of national liberation."

72. Frederic Wakeman, Jr., "The Price of Autonomy: Intellectuals in Ming and Ch'ing Politics" *Daedalus* 101.2:67.

73. David M. Raddock, *Political Behavior of Adolescents in China: The Cultural Revolution in Kwangchow* (Tucson, 1977), pp. 41–44.

74. John Meskill has used this formulation in summarizing the significance of the Ming academies as perhaps attesting to "the growth of a civilization against the boundaries of the political order it had produced." In this Ming dynasty case, however, the growth was ended by the imperial despotism of an entire governmental system "which seemed disposed to be suspicious of an innovation in the society supporting it" (Meskill, p. 159). The comparison between this case and the post-1895 reform movement is illuminating, as both embodied critiques of the existing system of education and government, and created "cells of reform" within the larger society and polity. The differences, however, were substantial, lending support to the claim that the post-1895 movement was indeed an unprecedented development. See

Wakeman, "Price of Autonomy," for a comparison of the Tung-lin academicians of the seventeenth century and the scholarly reformers of the 1890s.

75. Wakeman, "Price of Autonomy," pp. 55–56.

76. Bastid-Bruguière, pp. 560–561; and Wakeman, "Price of Autonomy," p. 37.

3. *MISCHIEVOUS SONS: PERFECTLY HUMAN, IMPERFECTLY CHINESE*

1. An overall description of this process of humanization is given in Ernest Becker, *The Birth and Death of Meaning: A Perspective in Psychiatry and Anthropology*, 2nd ed. (New York, 1971), pp. 15–21, 41–44, and 55–56.

2. This reversal of perspective is an important emphasis within recent studies of the history of childhood. See Lloyd deMause, "The Evolution of Childhood," in Lloyd deMause, ed., *The History of Childhood* (New York, 1974), p. 54.

3. For some perceptive observations about what happened to various individuals who were all stripped of their past lives and "leveled" to an equal, vulnerable status within the extreme situation of a concentration camp, see Victor Frankel, *The Search for Meaning* (New York, 1963). Frankel has erected an approach to psychology and therapy based upon insights into this context; he emphasizes the margin for conscious choice that can give meaning and dignity to existence, despite the narrowness of choice that may seem to exist in a given situation.

4. Han Suyin, *The Crippled Tree*, pp. 18–19.

5. Lloyd deMause, in his claims for the new historical paradigm of psychogenic theory, goes significantly beyond the hypothesis that I am stating here. He claims "that because psychic structure must always be passed from generation to generation through the narrow funnel of childhood, a society's child-rearing practices are not just one item in a list of cultural traits. They are the very condition for the transmission and development of all other cultural elements, and place definite limits on what can be achieved in all other spheres of history. Specific childhood experiences must occur to sustain specific cultural traits, and once these experiences no longer occur the trait disappears" (deMause, "Evolution," p. 3). This argument seems to exaggerate the importance of child-rearing practices for the maintenance of different cultural expressions. Child-rearing practices themselves are dependent variables, influenced by a variety of conditions in the larger society. In Chapter One, we derived parental attitudes not from the details of child-rearing practices, but from the existential struggle on the land. Both are viable lines of argument, particularly in times of relative stability when outer circumstances and human logic reinforce themselves in many interlocking ways. The isolation of childhood experience as a critical factor seems more important in understanding change, whether the slow personality-induced change called "cultural drift" or the more accelerated change associated with historical dislocation, such as was occurring in China after 1895.

6. Robert A. LeVine, *Culture, Behavior, and Personality* (Chicago, 1973), pp. 157–158.

7. For the traditional age group classifications and an overview of the *ying-erh* and *yu-nien* periods, see Marion J. Levy, Jr., pp. 66–133.

8. Erikson, *Identity*, pp. 107–114.

9. Sheng Cheng, *A Son of China*, M. M. Lowes, tr. (New York, 1930), p. 131. The book was written in 1927 when he was 28 years old. Compare his remembered emotion with the maxim that Erikson says was the residue of the sense of autonomy from this early period: "I am what I can will freely" (*Identity*, p. 114).

10. Carolyn Lee Baum and Richard Baum, "Creating the New Communist Child: Continuity and Change in Chinese Styles of Early Childhood Socialization," in Richard W. Wilson, *et al.*, eds., *Value Change in Chinese Society* (New York, 1979), pp. 98–106. Cross-cultural research in Africa and Israel has shown that infants can bond with several caretakers, with frequency of physical contact the prime consideration. This bonding has also been linked to toddlers' subsequent independent exploration of the environment. See Charles M. Super, "Cross-Cultural Research on Infancy," in Harry C. Triandis and Alastair Heron, eds., *Handbook of Cross-Cultural Psychology*, vol. 4, *Developmental Psychology* (Boston, 1981), pp. 39 and 37.

11. On the responsiveness to the child during infancy see Osgood, p. 263; Bernard Gallin, *Hsin Hsing, Taiwan: A Chinese Village in Change* (Berkeley, 1966), p. 188; Marion J. Levy, Jr., pp. 68–71; and Solomon, pp. 41–46.

12. Hsu, *Under the Ancestors' Shadow*, pp. 206–207.

13. Hsu, *Under the Ancestor's Shadow*, p. 204; Marion J. Levy, Jr., pp. 70–71; Gallin, pp. 193–194. Contrasting evidence of limited care among poor families comes in a study of several generations of Hakka women in rural Hong Kong. Elizabeth Johnson observed that babies were left alone, unsupervised, "perhaps tied to a table leg," while overworked mothers, young and old, went about their tasks. "Previously," she was told, even less was done. "Children were not so precious—they just fed them and put them to sleep, and let them crawl on the floor so that they were very dirty, because the women had to work and didn't have time": Elizabeth Johnson, "Women and Childbearing in Kwan Mun Han Village: A Study of Social Change," in Margery Wolf and Roxanne Witke, eds., *Women in Chinese Society* (Stanford, 1975), pp. 215–241, esp. p. 218.

14. Arthur H. Smith, *Village Life in China: A Study in Sociology* (London, 1899), p. 238. Despite this determination, crying in the night was so common that it was described in one memoir as an incurable disease of childhood. See Yan Phou Lee, pp. 12–13.

15. Marion J. Levy, Jr., pp. 72–74.

16. On enforced sitting in a bamboo chair, see Bryson, pp. 17–18. On carrying children past the age of walking, see Smith, p. 241, and Bryson, p. 74. On dangerous play, see Smith, pp. 243–245. Smith unraveled the mystery of undisturbed crows' nests outside Chinese cities, where every twig was precious as fuel: "Extensive inquiries have satisfied us that the true explanation is simply the natural one, that the Chinese boy is *afraid* to climb so high as a crow's nest. 'What if he should fall?'

says everyone when applied to for information on the point, and it is this unanswered and unanswerable question which seems to protect young Chinese crows from age to age" (p. 244). Direct personal observation on Taiwan in 1969 of our two-and-one-half-year-old son in interaction with a Chinese *amah* (maid) and Chinese neighbors confirmed continuation of protective restraint in relation to "dangerous play," such as climbing rocks behind the house or running unattended in the yard, and in relation to unknown beetles and plants. On bedding practices, see Lee, p. 12.

17. There seems to be general consensus that weaning and bowel training were noncrisis issues in Chinese child-rearing practices. See Hsu, *Under the Ancestors' Shadow*, pp. 217–218; Marion J. Levy, Jr., pp. 71–74; and Gallin, pp. 193–194. On the basis of bowel training in particular, Caroline and Richard Baum have postulated that a sharp split developed during the toddler period, ages one to three, between the child's own gradual control over bodily functions and the parent's imposition of strict external discipline on outward behavior, the former promoting a healthy sense of autonomous self-control, the latter promoting doubt, shame, anxiety: Baum and Baum, pp. 107–108 and 111–112. Their portrait of "extreme freedom in bodily and motoric functions" seems to be overdrawn, particularly in the light of widespread protective restraint. The external discipline towards outward behavior was also more discriminating than the Baums suggest at this age, for it was primarily directed towards disruptive social behavior, such as fighting and quarreling among neighboring children; the child had not yet reached "the age of reason" which allowed discipline to be directed at a broader range of issues.

The practice of protective restraint can be identified as what Lloyd deMause calls "projective care." The adult was projecting its own needs and fears into the child, and the care was thus "either inappropriate or insufficient to the child's actual needs" (deMause, "Evolution," pp. 15–16). In protecting the child, parents were not only expressing their own experience that human life was fragile and vulnerable, but also nurturing the child as they themselves desired to be nurtured by the child in their later years. I would disagree with deMause, however, that such "projective care" could seldom amount to "good care" and provide a solid feeling of security through the first few years of life. The main problem lay in its prolongation into later years when the child was ready to explore and test its developing powers.

18. Wolfgang Franke, ed., *China Handbuch: Gesellschaft, Politik, Staat, Wirtschaft* (Hamburg, 1977), p. 56. In eighteen reports about infant mortality available from different parts of China over the period 1909 to 1934, the figures show wide divergencies, from 122.6 per 1,000 live births in Nanking to 555 in Canton in 1925. Ta Chen estimated the national infant mortality rate in 1934 as 275, which at that time was one of the highest in the world. Ta Ch'en, *Population in Modern China* (Chicago, 1946), pp. 34–36 and 103–104. In her village study in Hong Kong, Elizabeth Johnson determined that in the late 1960s women over sixty had lost 50 percent of their children, whereas those under fifty had lost almost none (p. 221).

In the rural North China community of Ting Hsien in 1931, the infant mortality was 199 per 1,000 live births, while the maternal death rate was 13 per 1,000 live births. Sidney Gamble, *Ting Hsien: A North China Rural Community* (Stanford, 1954), p. 46.

19. Martin C. Yang, *A Chinese Village* (New York, 1945), p. 11. In the general practice of deceiving harmful spirits about the identity of one's son by namegiving and deceptive dress, some little boys wore the dress of Buddhist priests until age eight or nine, when "the period of danger [was] past" (Bryson, pp. 14–15).

20. For example, see Shen Tsung-han, *K'o-nan k'u-hsueh chi* (Taipei, 1954), p. 13; Hu Shih, *Ssu-shih tzu-shu* (Hong Kong, 1954), pp. 18, 28, and 34–35; and Martin Yang, pp. 203–204.

21. Erikson postulates a continuum of negative states of mind that can emerge from malnutrition and understimulation: Oral pessimism, based on infantile fears of "being left empty" and being "starved of stimulation," can in extreme cases become oral sadism, that is, a "cruel need to get and take in ways harmful to others and oneself" (*Identity*, p. 102).

22. Fei Hsiao-t'ung, *Peasant Life in China*, p. 64.

23. Even when gratification was not limited in material terms, this same lesson could be conveyed. William Hung's early childhood alternated between a cramped house rented by his father and the spacious domicile of his wealthy maternal grandparents. When little William was about two years old, his mother was already teaching him his proper place. Insisting that a coin he had found on the street was his, William demanded that his mother, who had discovered the coin during his evening bath, not take it away.

> "Well," his mother said, "If you insist on dividing up what is yours and what is mine, I will give the coin back to you and you can leave the house."
>
> She placed the coin in Hung's tiny hand, folded up all his clothes . . . and bid the stark naked two-year-old child goodbye. William started to cry inconsolably and between sobs, told his mother he did not want the copper coin anymore. It was his first lesson on the nature of property ownership in a Chinese household.

See Susan Chan Egan, *A Latterday Confucian: Reminiscences of William Hung (1893–1980)* (Cambridge, Mass., 1987), p. 7–8.

24. In Taiwan during the 1960s, festivals still seemed to erupt against a background of sobriety and restraint. One observer noted the Apollonian-Dionysian rhythm in the contemporary celebration of Confucius' Memorial day, which began with an orderly, slow-moving, dignified procession inside the temple grounds and ended with a rush by ordinary people in the street to pluck hairs from the sacrificial cow: Discussion with filmmaker Tom Davenport.

25. Erikson, *Identity*, p. 113.

26. Tuan, p. 139.

27. Ibid., pp. 151–153.

28. Saari, "Breaking the Hold of Tradition," p. 42. An extended analysis of the extent

and nature of self-awareness engendered in a Chinese upbringing, as revealed in the document "My Secret Self," is contained in this article, pp. 40–46 and 55–59.

29. Ibid., pp. 42–43.

30. Solomon, chs. 3 and 4, esp. pp. 73–81.

31. This language reflects Thomas Metzger's preferred way of expressing what Solomon calls "the dependency social orientation." Balancing the obligations of authority figures alongside their prerogatives creates an image of interdependence, at least in the eyes of some social scientists. Metzger, *Escape,* pp. 21–27.

32. Isaac Headland, *The Chinese Boy and Girl* (New York, 1901), pp. 35–36. Headland noticed this trait partly because of his disapproval of the low moral tone of much of their conversation and activity. Understandably he especially disliked jokes directed at religious men, notably Buddhist priests (p. 23).

33. Lu Hsun, "Thoughts on a Child's Photographs," *Selected Works,* vol. 4, p. 83.

34. Considerate parenthood is defined in relation to adult responsiveness to the child's urges and needs. See Everett E. Hagen, *On the Theory of Social Change: How Economic Growth Begins* (Homewood, Ill., 1962), pp. 133–140. Hagen draws upon Erikson's insights into the healthy development of the child, and in particular stresses the early childhood experiences that facilitate an innovative or open stance towards the exploration of the world. His standard of considerate parenthood is thus lodged in Western child developmental theory of recent vintage. Chinese parents of earlier times and even today might consider the "normal" American child as hyperactive, and hyperactive children as subject to a psychopathological condition (such as the hyperkinetic disorder, which by definition is hyperactivity beyond the normal limits of tolerance). The sociocultural context is thus very important in what people perceive as normal and abnormal behavior. David Yau-Fai Ho, "Childhood Psychopathology: A Dialogue with special reference to Chinese and American Cultures," in Arthur Kleinman and Tsung-Yi Lin, eds. *Normal and Abnormal Behavior in Chinese Culture* (Dordrecht, The Netherlands, 1981), pp. 148–149.

35. The argument that I find most credible begins with certain observations about the structural framework of the traditional gentry family, including cultural norms as part of that structure, and then derives from this external configuration a set of individual attitudes that make this structure viable over time. One could, of course, argue the reverse, deriving institutional structures and norms from individual psychological patterns. It is plausible that parents were sensitive to the deviation of *t'ao-chi'i* children because these children were an indictment of the parents' earlier and continuing self-betrayal of their own needs for autonomy. They could not tolerate this expressiveness in their children without undermining the small share of autonomy they did possess within the system, namely, the power to control and guide their own children into prescribed roles. The structural arrangements thus become a formal expression of these psychological needs and reactions. Although these psychological patterns probably existed, it is also true that they occurred within a given structural constellation that encouraged, if not compelled, the same

behavior. Faced with such explanatory choices, my preference is to attempt first to explain behavior through examination of the external structural configuration in the environment of the actor, and secondly, when this external configuration is insufficiently illuminating, to explore the configuration inside the actor's mind. This progression of investigation from external to internal places a premium on explanations that see human beings as conscious actors responding to the situations they find themselves in. This guideline seems appropriate in acknowledging the dominant role that external environmental factors play in the shaping of consciousness and behavior, and it specifies the scope of intrapsychic explanations.

36. See Hsu, *Under the Ancestors' Shadow*, pp. 113–122 and 249–250; and Marion J. Levy, Jr., chs. 4 and 7.

37. Marion J. Levy, Jr., p. 173.

38. On the bewildered reactions of Chinese wives who were asked in public settings if they loved their husbands, see J. MacGowan, *Men and Manners of Modern China* (London, 1912), pp. 237–238.

39. Ch'en Ch'i-t'ien, *Chi-yuan hui-i lu* (Taipei, 1965), pp. 6 and 13.

40. Teng Ssu-yü, *Family Instructions for the Yen Clan, An Annotated Translation with Introduction* (Leiden, 1968). Particularly pertinent are the sections on "Teaching Children," "Brothers," and "Family Management," and within them, pp. 4–5, 10, and 17. This book was one of three famous works on family education. See Martin C. Yang, *A Chinese Village: Taitou, Shantung Province* (New York, 1945), p. 139; and James Hayes, "Specialists and Written Materials in the Village World," in David Johnson, Andrew J. Nathan, and Evelyn Rawski, eds., *Popular Culture in Late Imperial China* (Berkeley, 1985), pp. 79–80.

41. The time of *hsiao hsueh* or elementary learning (ages seven to fourteen) was, in fact, sometimes called *ching hsueh* or the time for "the study of respect."

42. Van Norden, pp. 65–66.

43. Yan Phou Lee, pp. 17–21. Young Lee's observations reveal the transforming effect of comparison upon a young curious person. This exposure, however, occurred *outside* China and without reference to a peer group *inside* China. As we saw in Chapter Two, at the turn of the century, and especially after the transition from the imperial examination system to a new-style school system in 1905, making comparisons became common *in* China within a peer group. From this point on, the personal experience began to have greater social and historical consequence.

44. Reinhard Bendix discusses this problem in "Compliant Behavior," pp. 55–67. In the 1970s studies began to be more attentive to individual variation. See Gustav Jahoda, "Theoretical and Systematic Approaches in Cross-Cultural Psychology," in Harry C. Triandis and William Wilson Lambert, eds., *Handbook of Cross-Cultural Psychology*, vol. 1: *Perspectives* (Boston, 1980), pp. 69–141, esp. 76–85.

45. These four "cracks" were chosen because they highlight situations in which parental discipline and control could assume different forms and intensities. Parental practice was not uniform across families, nor within families over the childhood years, nor

between family and school. The list is not exhaustive (sibling order, for example, might also be considered a permanent crack within the filial system, for elder and younger sons were socialized differently within the family). The important recognition here is that childhood socialization was replete with inconsistencies; parental treatment varied, and hence opportunities for development varied, too. Socialization was and is an imperfect process because "society" itself is a diversity of concrete individuals and structural constellations.

46. Marion J. Levy, Jr., dates the transition from the beginning of the *yu-nien* years, a change symbolized by the son being switched from the mother's to the father's side of bed, or by the male *yu-nien* being "sent to live in his father's section of the house" (pp. 72–76). These were not strict practices, however, and in some cases sons slept in the mother's bed into their teens. A more significant transition in gentry families seems to have been around age eight or nine, when nurses were sent away and the father came to have a more active role in the son's life.

47. Hsu, *Under the Ancestors' Shadow,* p. 225.

48. Martin Yang, pp. 128–129.

49. Li Tung-fang, *P'ing-fan ti wo,* vol. 1 (Taipei, 1969), p. 20.

50. Teng Ssu-yü, p. 3. Yen Chih-t'ui's recommendation to prevent this outcome was to start disciplining the child as soon as possible: "As soon as the baby can recognize facial expressions and understand approval and disapproval, training should be begun in doing what he is told and stopping when so ordered." His constant fear was that parents would be too lax and loving with their children, not that they would be too strict and despotic. A passage of this nature poses a serious problem of semantics. An "arrogant child" might be one who was simply asserting a sense of autonomy and independence, which to the parents appeared to be insubordination. A "greedy child" might desire a few extra toys or another bowl of rice. A "scoundrel" might be one who refused to surrender his self to larger family interests. We must always examine the meaning of such "crimes" in light of parental values and expectations.

51. *Mencius,* Book IV, Part I, Chapter 18. Translation from Wing-tsit Chan, p. 75.

52. Shu Hsin-ch'eng, *Wo ho chiao-yü* (Shanghai, 1945) p. 12.

53. Egan, p. 9

54. Lasting damage could and did result from these techniques. Ku Chieh-kang recalled his recitation experience in *The Autobiography of a Chinese Historian* (Leiden, 1931), p. 9:

> My tutor was naturally severe with his pupils . . . The more I feared to pronounce the words before me, the more he commanded me to do so. Whenever I showed inability to get the words out, he would clap his foot-measure violently on the table beside me; and when I was unable to recite from memory, he would bring it down recklessly on my head. Perpetually quaking with fear under this regime of sternness and compulsion, I became a confirmed stammerer so that ever since that time I have never been able freely to express my thoughts by word of mouth.

Another man described his youthful shyness as "something like stage fright, due to my family education." He overcame this difficulty as a graduate student in the United States, while preparing and delivering a twenty-minute report, followed by questions and answers. He "did a good job, *was congratulated, gained confidence,* and was no longer afraid." Taiwan Interview No. 11, emphasis mine.

Charles Ridley noted that some Ch'ing educators questioned the effectiveness of severe discipline and physical punishment. Wang Yün (1784–1854) argued that teachers should stimulate students' talent instead. "[W]hen you observe pupils and find that they are happy and enthusiastic and that they talk extravagantly about learning, you know they have a superior teacher. If, however, the pupils knit their brows in anxiety, drag along as if they were dead men, and you consider them to be stupid oxen, is their teacher not the same?" See Ridley, p. 477.

55. Martin Yang, p. 204. Although told in the third person, this account has the authentic ring of autobiography in its rich personal detail. The village Yang describes is his native village; the story of Tien-sze is "the story of a villager's boyhood" (ibid., p. xi). Probably the most extended and undisguised account of a truant in modern Chinese letters is in the autobiography of Shen Ts'ung-wen, which has been partially translated in Shen Congwen [Shen Ts'ung-wen], *Recollections of West Hunan,* Gladys Yang, tr. (Peking, 1982).

56. Martin Yang, p. 205.

57. On man as *homo poeta,* see Ernest Becker, *The Structure of Evil: An Essay on the Unification of the Science of Man* (New York, 1968), p. 172ff.

58. Sheng Cheng, pp. 142–149. For another description, with illustrations, of such unsanctioned military games by children, this time in the city of Taiping in Anhui Province in 1894–1895, see M. von Brandt, *Der Chinese in der Offentlichkeit und der Familie wie er sich selbst sieht und schildert* (Berlin, n.d.), pp. 102–103. The inspiration for such war games probably drew as much from traditional novels as from current events.

59. Hsieh Ping-ying, *Autobiography of a Chinese Girl: A Genuine Autobiography,* Tsui Chi, tr. (London, 1943), pp. 48–49.

60. Li Tung-fang, vol. 1, pp. 67–69.

61. Ibid., p. 29.

62. Shen Kang-poh, "Wo yu-shih suo shou ti chiao-yü," in *Chuan-chi wen-hsueh* 1.1:12. Shen was brought up by his grandfather under rather unusual circumstances. It was an intimate companion relationship; they ate, walked, and studied together. Grandfather prevailed in any guidance problems. His mother was in the background, caring for his physical needs. His father was remote, "indifferent." Taiwan Interview No. 24.

63. Yen Chih-t'ui, preface, in Teng Ssu-yü, *Family Instructions for the Yen Clan.*

64. Mao ran away from school and home at age ten; he wandered for three days in circles before being found by his family. Conditions improved somewhat: "My father was slightly more considerate and the teacher was more inclined to modera-

tion." At age thirteen, after being cursed by his father before guests, he threatened to jump in a pond. They argued. "I agreed to give a one-knee *k'ou-t'ou* [sign of submission] if he would promise not to beat me. Thus the war ended, and from it I learned that when I defended my rights by open rebellion my father relented, but when I remained meek and submissive he only cursed and beat me the more." See Edgar Snow, *Red Star Over China* (New York, 1968), pp. 124–126.

On the common use of threats by parents to secure leverage, see Gallin, p. 195.

65. Hsieh Ping-ying, pp. 52–55.

66. Chou Yentung [Chou Yen-t'ung], quoted in Han Suyin, *The Crippled Tree*, pp. 75–76.

67. Taiwan Interview No. 34. Before the Revolution of 1911, a false queue was a sign of anti-Manchu revolutionary convictions.

68. There are some instances of intimacy during the *yu-nien* years between a son and an adult male, as we have seen with Shen Kang-poh and his grandfather and his tutor. But it is more common for intimacy to develop later in life, when the son on his own can begin to minister and care for the father. For one story of reconciliation, see Martin Yang, p. 215.

69. Ibid., p. 76. The context was a family gathering to make *chiao-tzu* (meat dumplings) in preparation for New Year's Day: "With the New Year just ahead, the sisters and brothers tease each other more freely than at any other time. The mother says nothing except occasionally to scold them laughingly which only makes the youngsters more mischievous. This is one reason why it is best for the father not to participate in this work, for his presence would kill all the laughter and jokes."

70. Sheng, pp. 93–94; Li Tung-fang, vol. 1, p. 12. Li's nurse was also with him until age ten.

71. Martin Yang, p. 218.

72. Snow, p. 125.

73. Kuo Jen-yuan [Zing Yang Kuo], "Confession of a Chinese Scientist," ch. 1, esp. p. 10.

74. All such correlations based on historical data are bound to be impressionistic. But the early years of such reformers and revolutionaries as Ch'en Tu-hsiu, Hu Shih, Kuo Jen-yuan, Ch'ü Ch'iu-pai, and Sheng Cheng would seem to lend some initial plausibility to this pattern. In an article on the Russian intelligentsia in the eighteenth and nineteenth centuries, Patrick Dunn argues a similar hypothesis: untypical childhoods characterized by warm interaction between parents and child that allowed children to delineate some autonomy during these early years lie behind the movement for cultural change and revolution among a large segment of the Russian intelligentsia. See Patrick Dunn, " 'That Enemy is the Baby': Childhood in Imperial Russia," in Lloyd deMause, ed., *The History of Childhood* (New York, 1974), pp. 383–405, esp. p. 402. The main problem with Dunn's overall analysis is that he does not indicate what else, besides warm parent-child interaction, needs to happen in family life, individual biography, and history to make a cultural critic or

revolutionary. If a strong self-identity is requisite, for example, this results (in Eriksonian epigenesis) from a cumulative process that is lifelong and goes through many stages. The autonomy crisis centers on early childhood, and is not the first nor the last within the parameters of childhood, let alone the adult life cycle. The childhood experience can bias but not determine the character of the future adult; it certainly cannot predict who is going to become a revolutionary.

Another pertinent study analyzes the background family dynamics of adolescents in China during the early Cultural Revolution (1966–1969); it shows that male political activists could come out of both vertical "authoritarian" father-son relationships or horizontal "open" ones. Mothers are left out, but the horizontal father-son tie is suggestive of the pattern where both paternal and maternal modes are united and authority has a single face. Horizontal father-son ties, however, fostered a higher percentage of active political participants among sons than vertical ties: Raddock, pp. 90–137. According to Raddock, competition with father-surrogates was a major factor motivating and shaping the political participation of sons from both kinds of family contexts. But the difficulty in a vertical relationship is that "evolution of a political or social type tends to be more tenuous and susceptible to being aborted by the guilt engendered in defying father and by a greater need on the part of the young individual to have his behavior reinforced and supported by the outer social environment" (ibid., p. 135).

75. Paul Valéry, "Introduction" to Sheng Cheng, *A Son of China,* p. 21. The doctrine of universal love *(jen)* was indeed traditionally believed to have its roots in human nature, and its first visible expression in the parent-child relationship, as we have seen in Chapter One.

76. Sheng, pp. 124–128.

4. CULTURE TRIUMPHANT: THE MAKING OF SOCIAL SELVES

1. Lu Hsun, *Selected Works,* vol. 3, pp. 334–335.

2. Ibid., vol. 2, p. 27; and vol. 4, pp. 84–87.

3. Clifford Geertz, "The Impact of the Concept of Culture on the Concept of Man," in John R. Platt, ed., *New Views on the Nature of Man* (Chicago, 1965), pp. 93–118. The following quotation indicates the connection.

> Man is so in need of such symbolic sources of illumination to find his bearings in the world because the non-symbolic sort that are constitutionally ingrained in his body cast so diffuse a light. The behavior patterns of lower animals are, at least to a much greater extent, given to them with their physical structure; genetic sources of information order their actions within much narrower ranges of variation . . . For man, what are innately given are extremely general response capacities, which, although they make possible far greater plasticity, complexity, and on the scattered occasions when everything works as it should, effectiveness of behavior, leave it much less precisely regulated . . . Undirected by culture patterns—organized systems of significant symbols—man's behavior would be virtually ungovernable, a mere chaos of pointless

acts and exploding emotions, his experience virtually shapeless. Culture, the accumulated totality of such patterns, is not just an ornament of human existence but the
principal basis of its specificity—an essential condition for it. (Ibid., p. 108.)

4. Becker, *The Birth and Death of Meaning,* pp. 21–26 and 38–58.

5. Lloyd deMause, for one, might disagree with the inevitability of this process. In
   formulating an historical succession of "modes of parent-child relations," he has
   identified an emergent Helping Mode (beginning in mid-twentieth century) which
   is based on the proposition "that the child knows better than the parent what it
   needs at each stage of its life." The parents try to empathize with and fulfill the
   child's expanding and particular needs, without disciplining it or forming habits.
   Presumably, such parents would try not to make demands upon the child and hence
   initiate the blockage and outside-in construction of the self; the child would remain
   its own master. The child that supposedly results from this kind of upbringing,
   and hence deMause's standard for healthy existence, is "gentle, sincere, never depressed, never imitative or group-orientated, strong-willed, and unintimidated by
   authority." See deMause, "Evolution," pp. 51–54. This is an intriguing thought.
   Such a child would still be taking in a cultural world in becoming a social being,
   but would be doing it in an easier, more natural way, without having to exchange
   the original "organismic identity" that is formed in the free use of the body and
   the will for a social identity. I see deMause's view, however, as a variation, not a
   rejection, of the sketch of humanization made in the text. Certainly almost all
   Chinese, past and present, would view deMause's ideas with incredulity, for to them
   the need to train the child, "guiding it into proper paths, teaching it to conform,
   socializing it" has appeared axiomatic. In this they would be joined by the vast
   majority of nineteenth- and twentieth-century Western child-development theorists
   as well as educated parents. I find myself also theorizing within what deMause calls
   the Socialization Mode, not so much arguing that children ought to be trained,
   guided, and taught to conform to external standards, as noting that they do indeed
   pick up such standards in the process of growing up, as they internalize in different
   forms and to different degrees the normative culture or cultures in their surrounding
   environment. I view this process as descriptive rather than prescriptive.

6. Hu Shih, *Ssu-shih tzu-shu* (Taipei, 1954), pp. 28–29. Hu Shih's mother was perhaps
   uncommon in the deliberateness and exactness of her disciplining, although teaching children to endure pain in silence was not unusual. The early death of his father
   when Hu was three years, eight months old, and the isolation of Hu and his mother
   within the larger family lent an added intensity to this relationship, which is undoubtedly why he was able to remember and communicate it so clearly.

7. Talcott Parsons, "Social Structure and the Development of Personality; Freud's Contribution to the Integration of Psychology and Sociology," *Psychiatry* 21.4:321–340.
   Reprinted in Talcott Parsons, *Social Structure and Personality* (New York, 1964), pp.
   78–111. In this important article, Parsons clarifies the processes of identification
   and internalization during early childhood learning. I am assuming that these pro-

cesses operate cross-culturally, and that the analysis would apply to a more complicated extended family as well as a nuclear one.

8. All major theories of socialization seem to agree that an absorptive process of social
and cultural learning takes place during childhood, even if theorists have different
ways of formulating the process and different understandings of specific mechanisms
by which humans become social beings. Cultural anthropologists see the process as
the incorporation of culture through exposure (instruction, observation, and imitation) and parental use of rewards and punishments. Personality psychologists see
the process as the acquisition of impulse control, whether this is the taming by
adults of disruptive drives in children and subsequent channeling of these drives
into socially useful forms or the development of adaptive capacities by the child's
ego that can serve the child as well as the social order. Sociologists are inclined to
see the process as role training to insure an appropriate functioning of individuals
in society; this is an unproblematic training, or at worst an adaptive accomplishment between individual personalities and social structures. See LeVine, pp. 61–
68.

9. Peter Berger and Thomas Luckmann, *The Social Construction of Reality: A Treatise in
the Sociology of Knowledge* (Garden City, N.Y. 1966), pp. 134–135.

10. Richard W. Wilson, *Learning to be Chinese: The Political Socialization of Children in
Taiwan* (Cambridge, Mass., 1970), pp. 29–30 and 30n28. In using the present
tense in this section I am implying the continuing validity of *lien*-thinking beyond
the late Ch'ing period in China. In fact, a cogent argument has been made by David
F. Y. Ho that 'face' is a concept of universal applicability, distinctively human and
not just Chinese. Since the standards for judging the extent, loss, and gains of face
are rooted in value orientations, they will vary cross-culturally as well as over time
within a single culture; but the concern for face and for avoiding social bankruptcy
are held to be universal. See David Yau-fai Ho, "On the Concept of Face," *American
Journal of Sociology* 81.4:867–884, esp. pp. 874–875 and 882. Ho, an academic
psychologist in Hong Kong, may be expected to put the concept of face into a
framework different from that embraced by the academic establishment in China,
where face until 1980 had been viewed as a relic of Confucianism and feudalism. See
L. B. Brown, *Psychology in Contemporary China* (Oxford, 1981), p. 228.

11. Hu Hsien Chin, "The Chinese Concepts of Face," *American Anthropologist* 46.1:45–
64.

12. Ibid., pp. 54–55.

13. Wilson, ch. 1. One must be cautious in interpreting these observations as typical
for late Ch'ing China. Before the Western impact there was little sense of a separate
Chinese "nation"; people lived their Chineseness, but did not know themselves as
Chinese citizens. And there was no widespread peer group experience in schools
before the twentieth century. The group focus then was the multi-functional family,
clan, village neighborhood, or region.

A more recent study based on elementary and middle school textbooks in Taiwan has emphasized that traditional concepts of morality are still the core of moral education, with some modifications. Pupils are encouraged to think of moral learning as an outward extension of self into society, not as a denial of self. The very terms used for "individual" and "society", namely, the *small-I (hsiao-wo)* and the *big-I (ta-wo),* encourage children to identify with the larger group. See Jeffrey E. Meyer, "Teaching Morality in Taiwan Schools: The Message of the Textbooks" *The China Quarterly* 114:274–276 and 283.

14. Lucian W. Pye, *The Spirit of Chinese Politics: A Psychocultural Study of the Authority Crisis in Political Development* (Cambridge Mass., 1968), pp. 95–96.

15. Wolfram Eberhard, *Guilt and Sin in Traditional China* (Berkeley, 1967). Eberhard's intent is to correct the notion of China as a "shame-based" culture. He argues instead that, while the literati especially felt shame and the common people guilt, China was more accurately described as a "stratified society with one guilt-based value system." Eberhard defines guilt as "wrongdoing, an actual and tangible violation of sanctions, often coupled with a feeling of remorse or regret." His conclusion seems unwarranted. Even granting that shame with its code of propriety and guilt with its concept of sin are both internalized moralities that operate "in essence . . . in the same way," it need not follow that the whole system is based on guilt instead of shame. The controversy over shame and guilt cultures has largely ended in the West, as it has become clear that the distinction between shame and guilt is not universal but one of our peculiar folk theories. To concentrate on these terms and their supposed equivalents in China—"propriety" *(li)* and the sense of shame, or "sin" *(tsui)* and the sense of guilt—is not as useful as the effort to reconstruct the primary emotional states that prevailed in the culture. In this case *lien* seems to have escaped Eberhard's conceptual net entirely. On the shame-guilt debate see Hildred Geertz, "The Vocabulary of Emotion: The Study of Javanese Socialization Processes," *Psychiatry* 22.3:236. On the likely audience of the *shan-shu,* see David Johnson, "Communication, Class, and Consciousness in Late Imperial China," in David Johnson, Andrew J. Nathan, and Evelyn S. Rawski, eds., *Popular Culture in Late Imperial China* (Berkeley, 1985), pp. 64–65.

16. In *Shame and the Search for Identity* (New York, 1958), Helen Merrill Lynd succinctly catches this difference in starting points and the unusual nature of a cultural conception in which the individual and the group are commonly viewed as polar opposites (pp. 158–159):

> [I]t is a special version of life which regards society as external to the individual, mother love as something "given" to the child, emotional "needs" as something that must be felt and "met," the social group as a series of links rather than a continuum. There may be wide differences in the range of what is conceived as possible according to whether one starts with the assumption of separate individuals and then considers how they may be linked together or starts with the assumption of related persons and then considers how they may develop individuality within the group.

17. One integrated, perceptive account of the self and its behavioral environment is in Irving Hallowell, *Culture and Experience* (New York, 1967), pp. 75–110.

18. Sao-ke Alfred Sze, *Sao-ke Alfred Sze: Reminiscences of his Early Years as Told to Anming Fu,* Amy C. Wu, tr. (Washington, D.C., 1962), p. 1. Eighty-one generations is of course an exceptionally long memory.

19. Hu Shih "My Credo and its Evolution," in Clifton Fadiman, ed., *Living Philosophies: A Series of Intimate Credos* (New York, 1931), p. 235. Hu Shih was also the only Chinese contributor.

20. Hu Shih's father, for example, wrote a will to his wife and each of his sons just two months before he died. In the will to his wife, he stressed three-year-old Hu Shih's intelligence and the need for him to pursue studies. He said the same in the will to Hu Shih himself. Hu Shih felt that these wills exerted considerable influence on his later life, especially when these pieces of paper led his older half-brothers to accede to their father's wish and help him progress in his studies (*Ssu-shih tzu-shu,* p. 17). Another example of this genre is the *Family Instructions of the Yen Clan* discussed in Chapter Three, a means for one family patriarch to influence the continuing life of the family for generations after his passing.

21. Robert Payne, *Chiang Kai-shek* (New York, 1969), pp. 47–49. See also Pinchon P. Y. Loh, *The Early Chiang Kai-shek: A Study of His Personality and Politics 1887–1924* (New York, 1971), p. 4; Cheou-kang Sie, *President Chiang Kai-shek: His Childhood and Youth* (Taipei, 1954), pp. 3–5 and 37. The meaning of the past and the dead is, of course, fashioned by the living members of the group, whether in written or spoken form. The accumulated written memory of the culture, however, played only a small part in early childhood learning. Verbal transmission, from grandparents and parents to children, was more important. This living memory reached back in detail only three, at most four, generations, but the family altar kept alive the memory of nine generations, beyond which the ancestor became a name in a long series of names stretching back into a legendary past.

22. Hannah Arendt in *Between Past and Future* (New York, 1963), has captured the inequality of the situation in which a child confronts the group:

> [T]he authority of a group, even a child group, is always considerably stronger and more tyrannical than the severest authority an individual person can ever be. If one looks at it from the standpoint of the individual child, his chances to rebel or do anything on his own hook are practically nil . . . he is in the position, hopeless by definition, of a minority of one confronted by the absolute majority of all the others. There are very few grown people who can endure such a situation, even when it is not supported by external means of compulsion; children are simply and utterly incapable of it. [Cited in Wilson, *Learning to be Chinese,* p. 32.]

23. Sheng Cheng, p. 125.

24. Erikson, *Identity,* p. 124.

25. Ibid., p. 127.

26. Lynd, pp. 162–164. See also Ernest Schachtel, "The Development of Focal Attention and the Emergence of Reality," *Psychiatry* 7.4:309–324.

27. Erikson, *Identity*, pp. 126–127.

28. "My Secret Self," in Margaret Mead and Rhoda Metraux, eds., *The Study of Culture at a Distance* (Chicago, 1953), pp. 157–162. Document RCC-C11689, Informant 45F. This document has been reprinted and analyzed in my article "Breaking the Hold of Tradition," pp. 40–45 and 55–59.

29. Solomon's *Mao's Revolution and the Chinese Political Culture* contains the most penetrating discussion of the issue of dependency and its ramifications in Chinese social and political life. There is little positive valuation of dependency in our own cultural tradition, and Solomon's portrayal of the pervasiveness of this quality in China is likely to strike many Western readers as pathological. He would have us believe that it was "normal" in China for individuals never to become independent centers of decision and action but rather to await the dictates of specific authority figures in order to act. To me, he has taken an extreme form of dependency and made it into the central fact in the socialization of Chinese children. This degree of passivity and self-denial diminishes the documented variety of childhood experiences and falsely assumes that when people do something in a certain way, it necessarily reflects a personality trait. More attention to the continuum of possibilities would make the Chinese practice distinctive but not abnormal or pathological, even within a Western theoretical framework.

30. Lu Hsun, "Shanghai Children," *Selected Works*, vol. 3, pp. 334–335.

31. Becker, *Birth and Death of Meaning*, pp. 62–63.

32. See, for example, this commentary for readers on "Brighter Horizons for Children" in *China Reconstructs* 37.6:5: "The widespread acceptance of the one-child family policy is producing more and more spoiled single children. Adored by parents and grandparents, some become 'little kings' and 'little queens' in their families. Overweight from too much rich food, waited on hand and foot, and with an exaggerated sense of their own importance, they become a problem for their families, schools, and society."

33. On his bouts with these other powers, see Aisin-Gioro Pu Yi [P'u Yi], *From Emperor to Citizen: The Autobiography of Aisin-Gioro Pu Yi*, W. J. F. Jenner tr., vol. 1 (Peking, 1964–1965), pp. 51–53, 71–72, and 66–67.

34. Ibid., pp. 54–56.

35. P'u Yi was not brought up free of the "natural" assumptions that the fragile, precious child could not be trusted to act or eat on its own. There were protective restraints on his physical movement, his play, and his eating. He described these restraints in talking about his younger brother, P'u Chieh, whose environment and upbringing were the same as his own:

> Between the ages of four and seventeen he was dressed every morning by his old nurse. He could do nothing for himself, not even wash his feet or trim his nails. If he picked up a pair of scissors, the nurse would shout and scream, terrified that he might

cut himself. She would take him everywhere, and did not let him run, climb, or go out of the front gate. He was not allowed to eat fish for fear he might choke [Ibid., pp. 128–129]

In P'u Yi's case, the attention lavished on his eating habits took the form of deprivations, for the Empress Dowager Lung Yu believed that a diet of browned rice porridge was the only thing to cure stomach ailments; thus he knew some periods of real hunger in his childhood (Ibid., p. 48).

36. Ibid., p. 70.
37. Ibid., p. 71.
38. Ibid., p. 72. On the importance of wet nurses *(nai-ma)* vis-à-vis other authority figures, see the passage from *Family Instructions of the Yen Clan,* cited in Chapter Three. They indeed had a status different and higher than other house servants. They were selected not only for physical health but also moral character and reputation.
39. Ibid., pp. 70–72. At the age of seven P'u Yi had discovered that he could have the Administrative Bureau flog the eunuchs for minor offenses, if he chose. He disregarded the remonstances of his tutors and others.
40. Hsu, *Under the Ancestors' Shadow,* pp. 278–281, 222–233, and the chart on 289, emphasis mine. For the implications of this observation on the rise and fall of families and social mobility patterns, see Hsu's postscript, esp. pp. 302–306.
41. Chow Yung-teh, "Life Histories," in Fei Hsiao-t'ung, *China's Gentry: Essays in Rural-Urban Relations,* rev. and ed. by M. P. Redfield (Chicago, 1968), pp. 145–287. On the military commander, pp. 182–185; the bureaucrat, pp. 210–212; the gangster, pp. 248–250; and the reformer, pp. 276–278.
42. Ibid., pp. 205–206, 270–272, and 274–275.
43. Pye, pp. 140–141. There are some fine insights in the chapter "Willpower and Morality."
44. "The Master said, At fifteen I set my heart upon learning. At thirty, I had planted my feet firm upon the ground. At forty, I no longer suffered from perplexities. At fifty, I knew what were the biddings of Heaven. At sixty, I heard them with docile ear. At seventy, I could follow the dictates of my own heart; for what I desired no longer overstepped the boundaries of right." Confucius, *Analects,* Arthur Waley, tr., Book 2, 4.
45. Cited and translated in Ridley, pp. 320–321, with slight alterations. I am using Liu Tsung-chou in this context as an example of how those within the Neo-Confucian tradition practiced self-examination, in the spirit of the phrase from *The Doctrine of the Mean* that "the superior man is watchful over himself when he is alone." Liu was also popular during the Ch'ing as a moral philosopher, primarily on account of his famous pupil Huang Tsung-hsi. His collected works were printed in 1822, the same year his tablet was placed within a Confucian temple. For a biographical sketch of Liu Tsung-chou, see Hummel, pp. 532–533.
46. Wang Ming-tao, *Wu-shih nien lai* (Hong Kong, 1967), pp. 9–10. Wang was the

fifth of five children, three of whom died while very young. There had been two sons born before him, both of whom died (ibid., p. 2).

47. Ibid., p. 6.

48. Ibid., p. 6

49. Ibid., pp. 7 and 10.

50. Ibid., p. 12. Wang's stubbornness was a lifelong trait. As reported by Amnesty International in 1978, Wang was arrested in 1955 for his uncompromising stand on the independence of the Christian Church in China. He did sign a confession of wrongdoing, but then was reported to have informed the authorities that his confession had been made under duress and did not represent his true opinions. He was rearrested in 1957 and was still in detention in 1974; his fate and whereabouts were unknown in 1978. Amnesty International, *Political Imprisonment in the People's Republic of China* (London, 1978), pp. 153–154. He is not mentioned in Amnesty International reports for 1984 and 1987.

51. Ibid., p. 11.

52. Ibid., pp. 14–15.

53. Ibid., p. 15.

54. Ibid., p. 16.

55. Ibid., p. 17.

56. Lien Shih-sheng, *Hui-shou ssu-shih nien* (Singapore, 1952), p. 193ff.

57. Discussion with Parker P. H. Huang. Hamden, Connecticut (June 1973).

5. ADVERSITY

1. Hsieh Ping-ying, p. 31. The eldest sister of one interviewee was known in the family as a "poetic genius." She joined the father and his sons in playing games of wit based on the classics. She died at age seventeen, but a memorial volume of her poetry was later assembled. Taiwan Interview No. 14.

2. One version is in the *Three Character Classic* or *San Tzu Ching;* see *San Tzu Ching: Elementary Chinese,* Herbert A. Giles, tr., 2nd ed. (1910; rpt. New York, 1963), pp. 8–9. The version in Y. C. Wang, p. 8., suggests that the mother's act was a "warning to her son of the danger of approaching starvation."

3. *San Tzu Ching: Elementary Chinese,* pp. 144–148.

4. Hong Kong Interview No. 3. These family genealogies, in their omissions and emphases, provide a guide to community ideals and values. See Hsu, *Under the Ancestors' Shadow,* pp. 232–237.

5. There were some exceptions to this, such as purchased degrees and the practice whereby the sons of officials could enter the bureaucracy without passing through the examination system, but they represented minor channels to influence. The purchased degrees were mostly lower level degrees, equivalent to the *sheng-yuan;* and they did not qualify one for appointment to office. By the late nineteenth century, however, the hard-pressed dynasty sold more such degrees, and the "irreg-

ular" purchased degrees made up the qualification for a third of the 1,450,000-member gentry. John K. Fairbank, Edwin O. Reischauer, and Albert M. Craig, *East Asia: The Modern Transformation* (Boston, 1965) pp. 329–330. On the examination process itself, see Ichisada Miyazaki, *China's Examination Hell.*

6. Hsu, *Under the Ancestors' Shadow,* pp. 276–281. I agree with Hsu's argument that this style of behavior among the wealthy was a product of cultural expectations shared by the community at large, not simply the style of an exploiting few. See also Chow Yung-teh, *Social Mobility in China: Status Careers Among the Gentry in a Chinese Community* (New York, 1966), pp. 246–250.

7. Tseng Ch'i-fen, "Tzu-ting nien-p'u," in *Ch'ung-te lao-jen chi-nien ts'e* (Private publication, 1931), p. 27.

8. Taiwan Interview No. 6.

9. Chow Yung-teh, *Social Mobility,* p. 251.

10. Lu Hsun, *Na-han,* pp. 1–2.

11. William A. Lyell, Jr., *Lu Hsun's Vision of Reality* (Berkeley, 1976), pp. 15–17.

12. Ts'ao Chü-jen, *Lu Hsun p'ing-chuan* (Hong Kong, 1957), pp. 18–19.

13. Ibid., p. 24. Foreign mathematics and sciences were more respectable, for there were Chinese precedents for these subjects; there was no precedent for studying barbarian languages. Similarly the gentry had long disdained the military life and viewed soldiers as men unfit for anything else.

14. Lyell, p. 26. For Lu Hsun's fictional treatment of the traditional scholar, see pp. 141–161.

15. T. A. Hsia, "Ch'ü Ch'iu-pai's Autobiographical Writings: The Making and Destruction of a 'Tender-hearted' Communist," *The China Quarterly* 25:181–184.

16. Ch'ü Ch'iu-pai, *O-hsiang chi-ch'eng* in vol. 1 of his *Ch'ü Ch'iu-pai wen-chi* (Peking, 1953), pp. 12–13. This passage is partially translated in T. A. Hsia, "Ch'ü Ch'iu-pai's Autobiographical Writings," p. 184.

17. Hsia, "Ch'ü Ch'iu-pai's Autobiographical Writings," pp. 184–185 and 196–197.

18. Ibid., pp. 205–212. Despite the controversy over his last work in prison, *Superfluous Words,* I find T. A. Hsia's argument about its consistency with Ch'ü's earlier writings and ambivalence convincing. Ch'ü's description of himself was plausible. See also, Jonathan D. Spence, *The Gate of Heavenly Peace: The Chinese and Their Revolution, 1895–1980* (New York, 1981), pp. 252–255.

19. Olga Lang, *Pa Chin and his Writings: Chinese Youth Between the Two Revolutions* (Cambridge, Mass., 1967), pp. 7–57. There is ample evidence in Lang's book for the interpretation I am presenting, although she does not stress the vicarious nature of his suffering.

20. Ibid., p. 74.

21. Mao Tse-tung, *Selected Works of Mao Tse-tung* (Peking, 1975), vol. 3, pp. 82 and 77–78; and vol. 4, p. 243. These criticisms are general ones, and are not meant to apply specifically to Pa Chin's writings.

22. Some literati families clearly did make the transition from the top of the old order

into the vital sectors of the emerging Republican order. After all, they had better resources than the poor for doing so, if they could overcome psychological obstacles. After 1900, as we have noted earlier in Chapter Two, there was a rapid reversal of attitudes towards the foreign, outside world among gentry families. For an example of this successful transition, see Hu Kuang-piao, *Po-chu liu-shih nien* (Hong Kong, 1964), which describes the evolution of the author (b. 1897) from a scion of a scholar-official family into an engineer-industrialist, via Tsinghua and M.I.T. But it is difficult to know how common this kind of transformation was. The modern sectors of the Chinese economy after 1911 appear to have been dominated by people from rising social groups, based in the coastal provinces, adept at the new-style political maneuvering and moneymaking, and often enjoying some foreign contacts and experience. See, for example, the account of the Soong family and its rise from obscurity to prominence in Howard L. Boorman and Richard G. Howard, eds., *Biographical Dictionary of Republican China,* vol. 3 (New York, 1970), pp. 137–153.

23. Robert Jay Lifton, *Thought Reform and the Psychology of Totalism: A Study of "Brain-washing" in China* (New York, 1963), ch. 15, esp. pp. 275–279 and 288–289.

24. Ibid., p. 289.

25. Sheng Cheng, ch. 20. Sheng Cheng's case of a fatherless family dominated by a grandmother is very similar to Hu Han-wei's with the great exception that his mother and his nurse were sources of strength and comfort; they were able to protect this precocious *enfant terrible* from his grandmother. The mother was caught between "two fires": "She tried to follow the grandmother in Tradition, and at the same time leave us children free to move forward on the path of the future." Sheng Cheng finally left the family for Nanking at about age ten, so that there could be peace in the family; unlike Hu, he took his mother's love and trust with him into the larger world. See chs. 11 and 17, esp. p. 166.

26. There was public support in some government schools, such as the Kiangnan Arsenal Academy that Lu Hsun had attended in Nanking; and the government sponsored language schools, such as the one Ch'ü Ch'iu-pai attended in Peking. And there were provincial and national scholarships for studying abroad. The system of public supports, however, was top-heavy at the upper levels: higher education and study abroad. There was marked inattention to the needs of lower education. Y. C. Wang, pp. 150ff and 360–370.

27. Ibid., pp. 152–153.

28. Shu Hsin-ch'eng, p. 4.

29. Ibid., p. 7.

30. Ibid., pp. 15–16.

31. Ibid., pp. 35–36.

32. Ibid., p. 50.

33. Ibid., p. 63.

34. Ibid., pp. 75–76.

35. Ibid., pp. 78–80.

36. Lifton, *Thought Reform*, pp. 302–303 and 309. Such alliances were also promoted by the traditional emphasis upon mothers who inspired their sons to greatness. We noted the case of Mencius earlier. This theme, supported by many historical and even contemporary examples, such as Chiang K'ai-shek and Hu Shih, is a staple in the moral education of school children on Taiwan today. See Meyer, p. 278. Fathers could also instill ambition in sons to help break the cycle of poverty, but seldom did that father-son relationship have the power of love. The mother-son dyad within the larger family was so special that Margery Wolf has called it the "uterine family." It was particularly intense because in traditional China the loyalty and success of her sons were the only guarantee of security a married woman could have, inasmuch as she was essentially an outsider among in-laws. On the "uterine family," see Margery Wolf, *Revolution Postponed: Women in Contemporary China* (Stanford, 1985), pp. 9–11.

37. The relationship between an only son and widowed mother seems especially intense and focused when there is the memory of a scholar-official father in the background. Hu Shih's mother's life centered on raising him in the image and ways of his dead father, which meant concentration of limited means on his education above all else. *Ssu-shih tzu-shu*, pp. 17 and 23.

38. Ibid., pp. 24–26.

39. Ibid., p. 43; and *Hu Shih wen-ts'un*, vol. 1 (Taipei, 1953), pp. 788–791.

40. Hu Shih, *Hu Shih wen-ts'un*, vol. 1, pp. 696 and 701–702.

41. Shen Tsung-han, *K'o-nan k'u-hsueh chi*, pp. 7 and 9.

42. Ibid., p. 8.

43. Ibid., pp. 19–20.

44. Ibid., pp. 8–9.

45. For a discussion of these cultural expectations as a force oppressing the young, see pp. 7–8 of Hu Shih's preface to Shen's *K'o-nan k'u-hsueh chi*.

46. In some families and regions, the military was more than a "channel of mobility for the poor." After 1900, gentry sons were being sent to military academies to be trained "to defend our land" (Han Suyin, *The Crippled Tree*, p. 115). In some regions, especially border areas and garrison towns, military service had great prestige and was in fact the main vocational possibility. See Shen Ts'ung-wen, *Tsung-wen tzu-chuan* (Hong Kong, 1960), pp. 4–5 and 47. There were also old military families in which becoming an officer was traditional. In general, however, a military career was less valued than the path of scholarship; and often the son who took up the military was "not much of a scholar," and a truant from school. Taiwan Interview No. 32. See also Chow Yung-teh, *Social Mobility*, pp. 157–172.

47. A *tan* was what one man could carry on a shoulder pole, about 110 lbs. Roughly, one could produce four *tan* of rice per *mou* of land, and an adult would consume the equivalent of seven *tan* of rice per year. The plot of land they owned was, therefore, about a half *mou*, and its produce hardly filled their needs. See Snow, p. 123.

48. Ts'ai T'ing-k'ai, *Ts'ai T'ing-k'ai tzu-chuan*, vol. 1 (Hong Kong, 1946), pp. 10–12.

49. Ibid., pp. 6–7 and 12.

50. Ibid., pp. 18 and 23.

51. Ibid., pp. 26–27.

52. This syndrome was noted by Hu Shih, who observed that the truants in his own tutorial school were often beaten for slight reading mistakes and preferred to go hungry in the fields rather than face the exacting tutor. The poorer children also received less personal attention because they paid less in fees; and not knowing some characters through home instruction before they started classes, they were unable to understand the meaning of anything they read. Lacking interest and afraid of being beaten, they played truant until this was no longer viable (*Ssu-shih tzu-shu*, p. 22).

53. Ts'ai T'ing-k'ai, vol. 1, p. 30.

54. Ibid., p. 34.

55. Ibid., p. 34.

56. Friedrich Nietzsche, *The Use and Abuse of History*, Adrian Collins, tr. (Indianapolis, 1957), pp. 12–17 and 20–22.

57. Shen Tsung-han, short biographical sketch (untitled manuscript, dated 12/26/67), p. 2. In the author's possession.

58. Taiwan Interview No. 25.

59. Ibid.

60. Lu Hsun, "What is Required of us as Fathers Today," *Selected Works*, vol. 2, p. 57.

61. Tsi-an Hsia, "Aspects of the Power of Darkness in Lu Hsun," in Tsi-an Hsia, *The Gate of Darkness: Studies on the Leftist Literary Movement in China* (Seattle, 1968), pp. 146–147. Hsia comments that Lu Hsun "loathed the old and hailed the new with too much vehemence to allow his argument to be contained within an entirely rational framework" (p. 147).

6. PRIVILEGE

1. Talcott Parsons, *Societies: Evolutionary and Comparative Perspectives* (Englewood Cliffs, N.J., 1966), pp. 70–71.

2. Hsu, *Under the Ancestors' Shadow*, pp. 277–279.

3. See also Shu Hsin-ch'eng, p. 7.

4. Li Tsung-t'ung, "Yu Kuangchou ch'ung hui Peiching," *Chuan-chi wen-hsueh* 4.1:26.

5. Hu Shih, *Ssu-shih tzu-shu*, p. 27. The word *hsien-sheng* in various contexts can mean "mister," "teacher," or "sir," and carries connotations of respect and status. *Mi* has the connotations of "passive," "refined," and "gentle." In Hu Shih's case, connotations of status were, in fact, present from the beginning, for his scholar-official father was called Mister Three out of deference and respect for his place in the village.

6. Li Tung-fang, vol. 1, pp. 6–7.

7. Ibid., p. 12. Li probably overstates the enthusiasm of the villagers. Such contributions were customary. One *liang* is approximately 1.3 ounces.

8. Ibid., p. 17. For the importance of these exploratory experiences with physical objects in the development of autonomous will and initiative, see Chapter Three above.

9. Li Tung-fang, p. 88. The Monkey was a rebellious, Promethean figure who claimed he was the Sage Equal to Heaven, and who treated all authorities with disdain.

10. Ibid., pp. 68–69.

11. Ibid., p. 69.

12. Ibid., p. 67.

13. For mystical praise of the sage, see *The Doctrine of the Mean,* one of the basic Four Books memorized by every serious student. James Legge, *The Chinese Classics,* vol. 1 (Taipei, 1966), pp. 415–416 and 422–423.

14. Shu Hsin-ch'eng, pp. 12–13. The hired hand was considered a member of the household in this region, a touch unlikely to exist in the experience of a Young Master by birthright.

15. Ibid., p. 12.

16. C. K. Yang, pp. 270–271.

17. Ch'en Tu-hsiu, *Shih-an tzu-chuan,* p. 32.

18. Max Weber, *The Religion of China: Confucianism and Taoism,* Hans H. Gerth, tr. (New York, 1964), pp. 28–29, 131–132, and 135. See also C. K. Yang, pp. 265–268.

19. Li Tung-fang, vol. 1, pp. 44–45.

20. Taiwan Interview No. 29.

21. Shu Hsin-ch'eng, pp. 45–47.

22. Li Tung-fang, vol. 1, p. 73.

23. T'ao Hsi-sheng, *Ch'ao-liu yü tien-ti* (Taipei, 1964), p. 76.

24. Ch'en Ch'i-t'ien, ch. 6; and Chang Ch'i-yun, *Chung-hua wu-ch'ien nien shih* (Taipei, 1960), pp. 5–6.

25. T'ao Hsi-sheng, pp. 74–75

26. Leo Ou-fan Lee, *The Romantic Generation,* pp. 30–40.

27. Li Tung-fang's autobiography, entitled *P'ing-fan ti wo* or *My Commonplace Self,* raises this issue most directly. He discusses it in his preface: "Friends always consider my calling myself 'commonplace' as excessively modest. Actually to be ordinary is not easy. I deeply regret that in using these two characters [*p'ing-fan*], I raised the issue of boasting; but once I had written it, changing it was inconvenient" (n.p.). Boasting became an issue because excessive modesty, like too little modesty, is an exaggerated presentation of the self; and the self, in Li's account, is visibly in the forefront. His account, however, is straightforward and frank; and unlike some others, he is self-consciously aware of some of the Young Master mannerisms of his generation.

28. T'ang Chün-i, *Ch'ing-nien yü hsueh-wen* (Taipei, 1973), pp. 115–116. The word *ching* has the meanings of "pity," "boasting," and "dignity," catching within it the

different faces of the upper class, with its mixture of paternalism, pretensions, and respectability.

29. Shen Tsung-han, pp. 9–11.
30. Snow, pp. 124–125 and 127.
31. Wang Yun-wu, *Wo ti sheng-huo p'ien-tuan* (Hong Kong, 1952), pp. 1–2, 10, and 20–21.
32. Lo Tun-wei, *Wu-shih nien hui-i lu* (Taipei, 1952), pp. 5–6.
33. Shu Hsin-ch'eng, pp. 37–39 and 43.
34. Ibid., p. 51.
35. Mao Tse-tung, *Selected Works of Mao Tse-tung*, vol. 3 (Peking, 1975), p. 73, emphasis mine.
36. Liu Ta-chieh, p. 109.
37. Ibid. p. 110. These three possible vocations (peasant, businessman, official) are discussed on pp. 105–115.
38. Ibid., p. 111. Liu's remark about "unintelligent" children would also be problematic told in the first person, because of the appearance of false modesty.
39. Metzger, *Escape,* pp. 6–10. Metzger uses the broader "humanist" label for this group of thinkers, and even includes within it foreign Sinologists like Donald J. Munro and presumably himself. For a narrower focus on those in Hong Kong and Taiwan, see Hao Chang, "New Confucianism and the Intellectual Crisis of Contemporary China," in Charlotte Furth, ed., *The Limits of Change: Essays on Conservative Alternatives in Republican China* (Cambridge, Mass., 1976), pp. 276–302.
40. In establishing a school of thought outside mainland China, these thinkers have placed an unusually heavy burden upon themselves: to meet the standards of international scholarship as well as to carry on the moral and inspirational roles of the vanished scholar-official. Success can be difficult and elusive. T'ang Chün-i criticized himself as a "mere" academic compared with more "complete men" like his colleague Hsu Fu-kuan, whose life included a period as a political activist and military leader. Similarly, of his teachers he saw the philosopher Hsiung Shih-li as less complete than Liang Shu-ming, who in his rural reconstruction projects combined social and political action with ethics. Hong Kong Interviews No. 6 and No. 4. For an aside on the subtle ways in which a modern professional orientation can filter out a commitment to traditional language and ideals, see Metzger, *Escape,* pp. 6–7.
41. Hao Chang, "New Confucianism," pp. 276–288. Hao Chang, following D. W. Y. Kwok, defines scientism as "an inflated conception of science as an all-inclusive system of nature which not only informs us of objective reality concerning the physical universe but prescribes an outlook on human life and society as well . . . a conviction that science represented a mode of thinking, a methodology which promised to be the only valid way of understanding life and the world" (ibid., p. 283).

42. Metzger, *Escape,* pp. 9–10. While critical of some shortcomings in their work, Metzger is an unabashed supporter of the humanists' overall perspective. The entire second chapter of his book is an exposition of T'ang Chün-i's concept of Confucian self-fulfillment. He argues that Western historians, in focusing too much on the reaction against tradition, have failed to see and appreciate those thinkers who sought instead a transformation of the traditional commitment to the Confucian heritage (ibid., p. 6).

43. In *P'ing-fan ti wo,* Li-Tung-fang reported that one of his maternal uncles would have preferred death to cutting his queue and was unwilling to serve as an official under the Republic. These political attitudes were in keeping with his overall moral strictness: "Although he had no sons, he never kept a concubine . . . He read the whole day and liked to study; he didn't play cards or drink wine or barter in the marketplace" (pp. 87–88).

44. Translated in Boorman, vol. 3, p. 390. The former Ch'ing official Liang Chi, father of Liang Shu-ming, had committed suicide nine years earlier in 1918 as a warning against the moral deterioration among leaders of the Republic; he felt they failed to put their ideals into practice, and were guilty of a lack of sincerity, a Confucian touchstone for virtue. Loyalty to Confucian principles rather than to the former imperial regime seems to have motivated him. See Lin Yü-sheng, "The Suicide of Liang Chi: An Ambiguous Case of Moral Conservatism," in Charlotte Furth, ed., *The Limits of Change: Essays on Conservative Alternatives in Republican China* (Cambridge, Mass., 1970), pp. 151–168.

45. Taiwan Interview No. 28.

46. Taiwan Interview No. 24.

47. Hong Kong Interview No. 3.

48. Taiwan Interview No. 31.

49. Shu Hsin-ch'eng, p. 76.

50. Snow, pp. 139–140.

51. Taiwan Interview No. 34.

52. Taiwan Interview No. 23.

53. Han Suyin, *The Crippled Tree,* pp. 54–57.

54. Ibid., pp. 67–68.

55. Ibid., pp. 91–92.

56. Ibid., pp. 95–96.

57. Ibid., p. 108.

58. Hong Kong Interview No. 2.

59. Herbert Butterfield, *History and Human Relations* (London, 1951), pp. 16–17.

7. THE UNDERTOW

1. K. T. May, "The Task of our Generation," *Chinese Students' Monthly* 12:152. Mei Kuang-ti (1890–1945) was a leading figure in the conservative periodical *Critical*

Review in the mid and late 1920s; see Laurence A. Schneider, "National Essence and the New Intelligentsia," in Furth, ed. *Limits of Change,* pp. 57–89, esp. 73ff; and Howard L. Boorman and Richard G. Howard, eds., *Biographical Dictionary of Republican China,* vol. 3 (New York, 1970), pp. 24–26. The romanization of Chinese names in the *Chinese Students' Monthly (CSM)* varies considerably, reflecting several factors: the use of initials for the given name to aid English-speaking readers in distinguishing it from the family name, the use of adopted Christian or Western first names, and dialectical differences in Chinese pronunciation combined with an early lack of standardization in English romanization systems. In this chapter I use names as they were written in *CSM,* with a Wade-Giles romanization in brackets if one is recorded elsewhere.

2. *CSM* 12:152–154.

3. *CSM* was the official publication, first of the Chinese Students' Alliance of Eastern States (1905–1911), and then of the enlarged student organization, The Chinese Students' Alliance in the United States of America (1911–1931). It grew from a mimeographed circular concerned just with the student world to a general-interest periodical that discussed all the important educational, social, industrial, and political issues in China. In 1912–1913 its circulation doubled from 590 to 1,200; by 1914 almost two-thirds of its subscribers were non-members of the Alliance, mostly Americans and Europeans. It was published eight times each academic year, from November to June. From its earliest years it supported itself from subscriptions and advertisements, and by 1915 it was considered a settled institution of Chinese students. In 1919 it had a twenty-three member editorial board and a thirty-two member managerial board, and was exchanging publications with at least eighteen different organizations. Thus the years 1909–1921 were the maturing period for the magazine, the time when it, as a voice of the Chinese students in the United States, grew up. In listening to that voice over these years—at times troubled, self-conscious, thoughtful, angry, and shamed—we have a source into the collective emotions and thoughts of those members of the 1890s generation who were privileged to be educated abroad. See *CSM* 8:503; *CSM* 13:475; *CSM* 14: title page; see also P. K. Yu, ed., *Research Materials on Twentieth-Century China: An Annotated List of CCRM Publications* (Washington, D.C., 1975), pp. 21–22.

4. These images respectively are from the titles of memoirs by T'ao Hsi-sheng, Hu Kuang-piao, and Chiang Monlin.

5. This term, as well as the sea image, have been used by Fox Butterfield in *China: Alive in the Bitter Sea* (New York, 1982). See Ch. 8 "No Road Out—Youth," describing the attitude of many young people in China in the wake of the Cultural Revolution.

6. The significance of the demarcation between those who studied the New Learning in China and those who went abroad is controversial. I argue that the experience of studying abroad was a matter of going "further West," as Chiang Monlin characterized it in *Tides from the West: A Chinese Autobiography* (New Haven, 1947), ch. 9.

Although the student who studied abroad and returned to China often bore the stamp of the host country he had come to know, this experience by itself did not produce a group identity as basic and as fateful as the consciousness of being a progressive young Chinese. And although foreign study undeniably earned cachet and standing within the progressive group, this group identity was hardly limited to those who had been abroad.

In *Chinese Intellectuals and the West: 1872–1949*, Y. C. Wang portrays the returned students collectively as sharing an urban orientation, privileged social origins, decadent habits, exalted self-image, iconoclastic attitude towards tradition, and specialized professional interests. Yet it is difficult to establish that all these traits apply primarily to the returned-student part of the educated group, or that the experience abroad generated a distinctive kind of consciousness. The urban orientation was found in the entire group, though less in middle-school graduates; those educated in the cities rarely returned to the hinterland, if they could help it. Returned students did tend to come from the wealthier coastal provinces of Kiangsu, Chekiang and Kwangtung, and from business, official, and professional families; their origins set them apart as a group. But this only indicates relative privilege, for few children of peasant or worker families could afford a middle school or college education in China, let alone a foreign education. If Republican era China, as Wang believes, could be described as an "ethical vacuum" in which restraints against letting go weakened as the old morality was discredited, then the entire educated group, and not just returned students, must have been affected. The exalted self-image and the savior-of-China complex that characterized many returned students may be interpreted as expressions of the elite's long-standing consciousness of special privileges and responsibilities, a consciousness inherited by the new intellectuals. If the returned students acted as though they were "gilded with gold"—as they were described by detractors in China, who felt that their Western learning was only a thin, pretentious veneer—the middle school or college graduate also affected a long gown or Western suit; certainly all had shaken the mud off their shoes. If it is true that "a deep inferiority complex characterized most Chinese intellectuals in the first three decades of the twentieth century," it is also true that the subsequent desire to identify with foreign ideas and institutions and to discredit traditional ones was a general phenomenon; at most the returned students experienced this problem more directly and intimately. See Y. C. Wang, pp. 369, 375–377, 150–169, 92–93, 503. These examples could be multiplied, but the major point is that only a few of these "shared traits"—orientation toward professional specialties and prominence in education and national politics—seem to set the returned students apart from the whole group of Chinese intellectuals. I have followed Wang's China-specific usage of the term "intellectuals" *(chih-shih fen-tzu),* which is broader than the Western usage and includes all those with at least a middle-school education under the new school system. See also Chow Tse-tung, p. 9 fn.

7. Chou Yentung's autobiography cited in Han Suyin, *The Crippled Tree,* pp. 76 and

89–91. This passage illustrates a way of viewing experience in which present experiences seem "comparable" and "repetitive" in relation to past experiences.

8. John K. Fairbank, "The Early Treaty System in the Chinese World Order," in John K. Fairbank, ed., *The Chinese World Order: Traditional China's Foreign Relations* (Cambridge, Mass., 1968), pp. 257–275.

9. Han Suyin, *The Crippled Tree*, pp. 74–76.

10. Kuo Mo-jo, *Wo ti t'ung-nien* (1956; rpt. Hong Kong, 1968), p. 12.

11. Chou Yentung, in Han Suyin, *The Crippled Tree*, pp. 160–162.

12. Ibid., p. 164. In emphasizing the "Copernican nature" of this encounter, I am underlining not only the unprecedented historical predicament faced but also the protean intellectual response it generated. It was not just a question of new answers to old problems or new means to resolve old predicaments; the problems themselves—such as Chou Yentung's questions "What is Man after all?" and "What are the limits of human inquiry?"—have changed through an altering of perspective. The initial and ongoing fascination of Chinese intellectuals with eighteenth-century European Enlightenment thinkers, themselves taking on the world of Christianity with the scalpel of critical reason, is a sign of how deeply and broadly many of these intellectuals have perceived their own encounter with Chinese tradition, whether labeled Confucian or "feudal." On this latter point, see Vera Schwarcz, *The Chinese Enlightenment: Intellectuals and the Legacy of the May Fourth Movement of 1919* (Berkeley, 1986).

13. Chiang Monlin, *Tides from the West*, chs. 3–6, esp. pp. 40 and 47–49.

14. Ibid., pp. 53 and 58–59.

15. Ibid., p. 62; see also ch. 8 in its entirety.

16. Ibid., p. 59. See also Chiang Monlin, *A Study in Chinese Principles of Education* (Shanghai, 1918), ch. 15.

17. K. T. May, "The New Chinese Scholar," *CSM* 12:342–351. Other articles in *CSM* accord with this point of view. I found no articles expressly promoting the type of the traditional scholar, evidence that there was a general agreement that a new type of scholar had to emerge.

18. *CSM* 7:399.

19. *CSM* 7:641.

20. C. Y. Chin, "The Proper Meaning of the Chinese Students' Alliance," *CSM* 8:527–531.

21. K. F. Mok, "Culture," *CSM* 11:276–279.

22. V. K. Wellington Koo, "Address made at the Platform Meeting of the Chinese Students' Conference at Brown University, September 6, 1917," *CSM* 13:20–28. See also the article by T. L. Li, "What Chinese Students Should Do When They Return," *CSM* 13:163–167. Some returned students had hopelessly succumbed upon returning to China, he claimed, because "after mingling with the people for a while, they soon become merged with the general mass, just like drops of rain . . . having fallen into a polluted stream . . . ." Ibid., p. 163.

23. Chiang Monlin, *Tides from the West,* p. 74.
24. Loy Chang, "The Need of Experts," *CSM* 11:467–471.
25. *CSM* 11:55–59 and 124.
26. Yuen R. Chao [Y. R. Chao], "Proposed Reforms," *CSM* 11:589.
27. C. C. Woo, "The Value of Industrial Scientific Research to the Advancement of Manufacturing Methods," *CSM* 16:80–81; and "Some Suggestions on the Preparation of the Chinese Technical Students in the United States," *CSM* 16:168–172. Racial prejudice, Woo suggested, was also a reason why Chinese technical students had little direct access to American manufacturing plants.
28. Zuntsoon Zee, "Scientific Training for Efficiency," *CSM* 9:186–187; and "Learning and Unlearning," *CSM* 9:525. I use the term *foreshadowing* here because the full-scale debate between science and metaphysics did not burst out until after World War I, and particularly in the 1920s. See Charlotte Furth, *Ting Wen-chiang: Science and China's New Culture* (Cambridge, Mass., 1970), pp. 94–135. Zee's short piece is tantalizing; its full meaning must be drawn out by the reader; and even that, of course, is the reader's interpretation of its meaning, not necessarily what Zee himself meant.
29. C. Y. Chin, *CSM* 8:527–531.
30. The following estimates are taken from membership reports in *CSM* for these years: 385 members out of 650 Chinese students in the United States (1910–1911); 600 members out of 1,000 Chinese students (1914–1915); 830 members out of 1,200–1,400 Chinese students (1915–1916); 600 out of 1,300 Chinese students (1918–1919); 800 members out of 1,500 Chinese students (1919–1920). Dues-paying membership was often quite a bit lower than announced membership, ranging from 78 percent in 1915–1916 to 37 percent in 1918–1919. For the early history of the Alliance, see V. K. Wellington Koo, "An Account of the History of the Chinese Students' Alliance in the United States," *CSM* 7:420–431.
31. For the provincial origin statistics, see Y. C. Wang, p. 158; for Tsinghua College as a feeder of students to America from 1911 on, see Y. C. Wang, pp. 111–114.
32. *CSM* 11:125–127, 299–301.
33. For the creation of the constitution of the Eastern section of the Alliance, complete with provisions for initiatives, recalls, and direct popular votes, see *CSM* 7:260–267; on demonstrating their capability, see *CSM* 15.3:54 (volumes of *CSM* were paginated continuously, except for vol. 15). I disagree strongly with Y. C. Wang's generalization, based on several actual instances of embezzlement and forgery among Chinese students in the United States during these years, that Chinese students abroad had "a severe personality maladjustment" and "tendency to drift into dissipation and decadence" (p. 166).
34. *CSM* 10:172–173.
35. Y. C. Ma [Ma Yin-chu], "Liberty of Conscience," *CSM* 6:267–273. On some campuses, like Yale, the Chinese Student Christian Association was almost synonymous with the Chinese Students' Alliance.

36. See the 1912 conference oration on "National Ideals" by Peng Chun Chang, *CSM* 8:17–21.

37. Hu Shih roomed from 1911 to 1914 in the building that headquartered the Cornell Cosmopolitan Club, and was active in the club affairs during that period. Jerome Grieder, *Hu Shih and the Chinese Renaissance: Liberalism in the Chinese Revolution, 1917–1937* (Cambridge, Mass., 1970), p. 53.

38. *CSM* 11:456–457.

39. Kuo Ping-wen, "A Plea for True Patriotism," *CSM* 5:104.

40. For the debate over Confucianism and state religion among T. I. Dunn, Zuntsoon Zee, and Suh Hu (Hu Shih), see *CSM* 9:331–341, 506–507, and 533–536. For the charge that Hu Shih was guilty of "unpatriotic insanity" for his stance on Japan's Twenty-One Demands in 1915, see the exchange between Hu Shih and H. K. Kwong, *CSM* 10:425–430. Notice Kwong's characterization of Hu: "Fortunately, we are made of different materials from Suh Hu—not of wood and stone but of blood and flesh. We have senses and feelings. We do not pretend to be deaf and dumb, when the situation requires us to express what is in us" (ibid., p. 427).

41. Pusey, p. 235. Pusey's entire section on the struggle against Confucius and the implications of the loss of this central faith (pp. 216–235) merits close reading. The loss mattered terribly to the intelligentsia. "It mattered more than anyone can say, and more than Westerners, perhaps, can ever appreciate, for the revolution against Confucianism really did lead most Chinese to lose the faith of their fathers. Westerners en masse have not been forced from their faith since the Christian conquest of Europe. They have known what it is like to lose the faith of their fathers as individuals, but never as a people" (p. 230).

42. Runtien J. Li, "The Mission of a Chinese Student," *CSM* 5:379.

43. Pingsa Hu, "The Women of China," *CSM* 9:202–203.

44. For one fictional recreation of this moral dilemma, see Woon Yung Chun's short piece entitled "East is East and West is West," *CSM* 9:491–493.

45. Pingsa Hu, p. 203.

46. *CSM* 6:346–347, emphasis mine.

47. Mabel Lee, "Moral Training in Chinese Schools," *CSM* 11:543–547.

48. Yuen R. Chao, p. 580.

49. Feuerwerker, op. cit.

50. Chang Fu-liang, *When East Met West: A Personal Story of Rural Reconstruction in China* (New Haven, 1972), p. 19.

51. Chiang Monlin, *Tides from the West,* p. 43.

52. Chiang Fu-liang, p. 19.

53. Han Suyin, *The Crippled Tree,* p. 158.

54. Ibid., p. 162 (quoting Chou Yentung).

55. Ibid., p. 163.

56. Wang Gungwu, "Early Ming Relations with Southeast Asia: A Background Essay," in Fairbank, ed., *Chinese World Order,* pp. 34–62.

57. Pye, pp. 54–56. Because of this strong identification with the past, Pye feels that the words "pride" and "complex" are inadequate to describe the phenomenon; he chooses to call it an identification with greatness.

58. Ibid., pp. 61–63.

59. Ibid., pp. 4 and 6. See also ch. 4 and ch. 5, esp. pp. 66–67.

60. For a critical review of some of the basic assumptions for Pye's theory, see Cheryl Payer Goodman, in *CCAS Newsletter* 1.3:18–21. For Pye, the Western pluralistic model of development is both the most efficacious and the most moral; other styles of development tend to become irrational, contradictory, self-defeating, if not evil. He stresses unconscious cultural patterns of reaction almost to the exclusion of the conscious responses of men and women to their perceived situation.

61. Wolfgang Franke, *China and the West: The Cultural Encounter, 13th to 20th Centuries,* R. A. Wilson, tr. (New York, 1967), pp. 71–76 and 84–91.

62. Murphey, *The Treaty Ports,* p. 23.

63. Franke, *China and the West,* pp. 138–139.

64. Orville Schell, *"Watch Out for the Foreign Guests!"—China Encounters the West* (New York, 1980). My observations on the relative ease in personal relations are based in part on a year of living, teaching, and traveling in China in 1985–1986; that year, however, may emerge in retrospect as one of the more relaxed and open ones in post-Mao China. The basic pattern is still "cold winds, warm winds," with the anti-spiritual pollution campaign of 1983, the anti-bourgeois liberalism campaign of 1986–1987, and the attack on pro-democracy demonstrators in 1989 setting the tone of defensive wariness about Western cultural influences. See Liang Heng and Judith Shapiro, *Cold Winds, Warm Winds: Intellectual Life in China Today* (Middletown, Conn., 1984).

65. The argument over the psychological effects of imperialism is intertwined with the arguments over the other effects of imperialism. To the extent that the economic or political effects of Western imperialism can be shown to be exaggerated by those who explain modern Chinese history largely in terms of this concept, then the Chinese response increasingly appears less grounded in economic or political reality, and more grounded in internal sociocultural factors. Direct economic effects seem, on the basis of much empirical evidence, to have been quite restricted in scale and extent, while direct and indirect political and intellectual effects are acknowledged to have been considerable. For an insightful review of this recent literature, see Paul Cohen, *Discovering History in China: American Historical Writing on the Recent Chinese Past* (New York, 1984), pp. 97–147. Cohen also argues that the special characteristics of colonialism in China have not been adequately addressed: partial domination by a plurality of foreign nations connected with a full colonization of China by the Manchus during the Ch'ing dynasty. "[T]he failure to scrutinize with care the distinctive colonial environment that prevailed in China has been a major limitation on the productiveness of the entire imperialism controversy—almost as great a limitation as the failure of the proponents of the 'negative effect' position to take

China's internal sociocultural setting with any degree of seriousness" (p. 145). The fixation with the overall problem of economic development, he says, has also limited the debate (pp. 145–147). The exception to most of Cohen's generalizations (except the latter one) is Rhoads Murphey's work: While aware of the negative economic and political effects of imperialism, he has made sociocultural factors, particularly the Chinese self-image, into central explanatory concepts. From the approach of human development and identity formation, the psychological effects of imperialism were not just immediate reactions of anger, hatred, or resentment at acts of national shame and humiliation, but deep-seated feelings of inferiority and "coming up from under." Nevertheless, and here I agree with Murphey, this experience did not seem to lead to deculturation and deep identity confusion; a basic sense of Chineseness persisted within the new framework of Chinese nationalism, no matter how strongly tradition was attacked or how elusive the Way Out seemed. See Rhoads Murphey, *The Outsiders: The Western Experience in India and China* (Ann Arbor, 1977), pp. 131–155 and 221–234. On the methodological question of linking external structures with internal consciousness, see my article "The Human Factor," pp. 105–109.

66. *CSM* 11:43
67. *CSM* 5:9.
68. *CSM* 6:202 and 207.
69. "The Truth about Prohibition Lies," in the Wit and Humor section, *CSM* 16:251.
70. *CSM* 6:208–209.
71. *CSM* 5:7.
72. *CSM* 6:4.
73. C. T. Wang [Wang Cheng-ting], "China and America," *CSM* 6:454–465.
74. Lui-Ngan Chang, "Working for China's Welfare Abroad," *CSM* 5:544–548.
75. Ibid.
76. The problem, although patronizingly conceived, was addressed with vigor by some local clubs, particularly in Boston. There ten students created an "educational mission to the better sort of younger laboring class" by starting a school. Ninety-three Chinatown pupils were enrolled in afternoon and evening sessions, to study English, Chinese, mathematics, and to hear lectures on geography, Chinese history, hygiene, the United States, and Chinese in the United States, especially as they are seen by others. See the Report of the General Welfare Committee of Boston, *CSM* 5:419–431.
77. Y. Tsenshan Wang, "Our Hope and Our Task," *CSM* 5:535–543.
78. *CSM* 6:21. On the dangers in confronting Western learning, by an American professor in the United States and an American born in China, see *CSM* 7:52–60 and 163–168.
79. *CSM* 10:82–84.
80. H. H. Wong, "The Chinese Student and the Study of Law," in *CSM* 10:147.
81. *CSM* 10:594 and 15.3:54.

82. T. H. K. [Telly H. Koo], "Confucius and John Dewey: The Bankruptcy of the East and the West," *CSM* 16:539–541.

83. A *CSM* editorial on the 1916 election said that the American political system was not working very well, for the people were apathetic and materialistic; the American system was not suited to China's needs (*CSM* 12:79–80). See also the critical response to this editorial (ibid., pp. 180–183).

84. *CSM* 13:83.

85. For a powerful statement of China's case at Versailles, see C. K. Chang, "Wilson's Principles of World Reconstruction in their Application to the Far East," *CSM* 14:232–238.

86. Quo Tai-chi, "China's Fight for Democracy," *CSM* 15:37.

87. *CSM* 14:415–416.

88. H. C. Wang, "China and the League of Nations," *CSM* 16:476–478.

89. Editorial, *CSM* 15.3:5–9. On the shift to learning from the actual political situation as opposed to deferential leanings towards parliaments and constitutionalism, see S. K. Wei, "The Immediate Political Problem in China," *CSM* 15.7:28–31, esp. p. 31.

90. Chuan Chao, "China and a Stable Peace," *CSM* 14:114–117.

91. Y. C. Yang [Yang Yung-ch'ing], "Making Patriotism Count Most," *CSM* 13:110. The succeeding article struck a different note of conditional nationalism: "Not until international righteousness dominates the mind of my people will nationalism be saved from selfishness." C. Y. Tang, "The Cycle of Civilization," *CSM* 13:111–115.

92. *CSM* 15.2:18.

93. Y. C. Yang, *CSM* 13:107–111.

8. BREAKING THE HOLD OF THE GROUP

1. Lu Hsun, *Selected Works*, vol. 1, p. 35. See also Tsao Chü-jen, p. 74; William A. Lyell, Jr., pp. 73–75.

2. Lu Hsun, *Selected Works*, vol. 1, pp. 59, 53, 40, and 41.

3. Not only does Ah Q have no name, but the names of the two families in the story—Chao and Chien—are the first two names in the common children's textbook, the *Hundred Family Surnames*. The story's incisiveness is indicated by the reactions of people who read it in serialized form in the literary supplement of the Peking *Morning News* without knowing its author: Many readers thought that they personally were being satirized and that the author must be someone who knew their innermost thoughts and needs. See Tsao Chü-jen, pp. 72–73.

4. Lyell, pp. 233–237 and 244–246.

5. Hsu, *Clan, Caste, and Club*, pp. 162–170.

6. Hsu, "Eros, Affect, and *Pao*," in Francis L. K. Hsu, ed., *Kinship and Culture* (Chicago, 1971), p. 473.

7. Hsu, *Clan, Caste, and Club,* p. 163.

8. "My Secret Self" resulted from group discussions on what "inner life" means to Chinese. These discussions were part of a Research in Contemporary Cultures project conducted at Columbia University from 1947 to 1951. This document has been reprinted and analyzed more fully in my article "Breaking the Hold of Tradition."

9. Boyd R. McCandless, "Childhood Socialization," in David A. Goslin, ed., *Handbook of Socialization Theory and Research,* (Chicago, 1969), pp. 797–800. McCandless lists several areas of power that adults possess in child-rearing: power in the physical sense to overwhelm children, power in the area of knowledge, power in the area of social and economic influence, and power in the area of virility or generativity.

10. "My Secret Self," p. 158.

11. Ibid., p. 159.

12. This distinction is made explicitly in the document; see also Stover and Stover, *China: An Anthropological Perspective,* pp. 202–203; and the related discussion of the "situation orientation" of the Chinese in Hsu, *Clan, Caste, and Club,* p. 164 ff.

13. Leon E. Stover, *Cultural Ecology,* ch. 5. Stover's viewpoint has had a skeptical reception among Western Sinologists. It challenges the more traditional view of the cultural unity of China by postulating two Chinas, elite and folk, connected functionally by a relationship of dominance and subordination rather than by shared cultural beliefs. The traditional view, which itself is derived from earlier Western deference to the Confucian literati as spokesmen for all of Chinese culture, was recently affirmed, at a more sophisticated level, in Richard J. Smith, *China's Cultural Heritage: The Ch'ing Dynasty, 1644–1912* (Boulder, Col., 1983). Smith draws his evidence primarily from the upper-class Confucian elite; but he argues, and to an extent demonstrates, that certain traits (thought patterns reflecting the complementary bipolarity of yin-yang, ethical concerns, and a strong sense of ritual) cut across class and ideology.

   The prospects for breaking new ground on this important question lie with the burgeoning field of Chinese popular culture. Researchers conducting detailed empirical studies are illuminating the in-between area where elite and folk culture met in villages and towns, in order to establish who shared what, and to what degree, with whom. That there were shared elements is taken for granted, as expressed in the preface of a major study edited by David Johnson, Andrew J. Nathan, and Evelyn S. Rawski, *Popular Culture in Late Imperial China* (Berkeley, 1985):

   > Chinese culture in the last centuries of imperial rule was both extremely diverse and highly integrated. The diversity is easy to understand—it was an obvious function of China's great size . . . But—and this is much harder to account for—these diverse elements were integrated into a single complex cultural system. The intellectual and spiritual world of the scholar or official in late imperial times was not utterly alien to the peasant or laborer, nor was the reverse true. There were common elements in the mental worlds of all Chinese. We are far from satisfied with our account of the nature of those elements, but we take it as axiomatic that they existed. If they had not, the

whole idea of Chinese culture dissolves—"China" is reduced to the semantic triviality of "Asia" [pp. xi, xiii].

The evidence in these case studies is drawn from writings (ballads, scriptures, handbooks, almanacs, scripts, novels, folk tales, proverbs, plain explanations of the *Sacred Edict*) intended for non-elite audiences; and the studies focus on local specialists (schoolteachers, letter writers, ceremonial experts, entertainers and the like) who were intermediaries between the illiterate villagers and the educated classes. The portrait of Chinese society that emerges from this research sharply questions the concept of closed peasant communities and the idea of a one-way cultural influence from an elite Great Tradition to a folk Little Tradition. Influences percolated in both directions; and Confucian thought, however differently coded and communicated within villages and towns, was nonetheless present in both traditions. Still, Stover's challenge to our understanding persists, for one major reason: our relative ignorance about the mental world of the peasantry. Even the editors of *Popular Culture in Late Imperial China* acknowledge that "We can seldom hope to form more than the dimmest conception of the attitudes and values of the illiterate majority" (p. ix).

On the *Sacred Edict,* see Victor H. Mair, "Language and Ideology in the Written Popularizations of the *Sacred Edict,"* in Johnson, Nathan, and Rawski, eds., *Popular Culture,* pp. 354–355.

14. Stover, *Cultural Ecology,* ch. 9 and pp. 258–262; see also Stover and Stover, *China: An Anthropological Perspective,* pp. 207–212.

15. Margery Wolf, *The House of Lim: A Study of a Chinese Farm Family* (New York, 1968), pp. 141–142.

16. Ibid., pp. 102–103.

17. Maxine Hong Kingston, *The Woman Warrior: Memories of a Girlhood among Ghosts* (New York, 1977), pp. 3–19, esp. 9 and 14.

18. D. Y. F. Ho [David Yau-fai Ho], "Traditional Patterns of Socialization in Chinese Society," *Acta Psychologica Taiwanica* 23.2:90. Shen Ts'ung-wen relates one tale of how a young woman who had a lover was drowned by community action at the instigation of a jealous, lustful clan elder, who maintained he was only preserving the clan's honor by punishing immoral behavior. See Shen Ts'ung-wen, *Recollections of West Hunan,* Gladys Yang, tr. (Peking, 1982), pp. 144–149.

19. Taiwan Interview No. 14.

20. Hsu, *Under the Ancestors' Shadow,* pp. 247–253.

21. See Ho, "Traditional Patterns," p. 81, n. 2; and Wolf, *The Revolution Postponed,* pp. 8–9.

22. Y. L. Tong, "A Word for the Returned-Students-To-Be," *CSM* 10:560.

23. Hu Ch'iu-yuan, "Fu-ch'in chih hsun," *Min-chu ch'ao* 10.15:15–19.

24. The latter passage is the words of Mencius summarized by Lien-sheng Yang in "The Concept of 'Pao,' " p. 305.

25. Lynd, p. 234.

26. My ignorance here is due to the smaller number of cases that I have uncovered and to my focus on the pattern for boys and young men, who were numerically dominant among those who became educated youth with a bent for reform. The women's story still remains to be told. The outline of women's lives through the life cycle, told from a woman's perspective, has been well sketched by Margery Wolf in *The Revolution Postponed,* pp. 4–13. Mary Backus Rankin has studied the background and life of Ch'iu Chin, whose execution for revolutionary activities in 1907 made her a heroic model for the next generation; see Rankin, *Early Chinese Revolutionaires,* pp. 38–47.

27. Lynd, pp. 230–231 and 234.

28. Lu Hsun, *Selected Works,* vol. 1, pp. 63–65. I have retained the Wade-Giles romanization.

29. Ibid., pp. 77–78.

30. Helen Lynd has expressed this insightfully in *Shame and the Search for Identity* (p. 46):

> Sudden experience of a violation of expectation, of incongruity between expectation and outcome, results in a shattering of trust in oneself, even in one's own body and skill and identity, and in the trusted boundaries or framework of the society and the world one has known. As trust in oneself and in the outer world develop together, so doubt of oneself and of the world are also intermeshed. The rejected gift, the joke or the phrase that does not come off, the misunderstood gesture, the falling short of our own ideals, the expectation of response violated—such experiences mean that we have trusted ourselves to a situation that is not there. We have relied on the assumption of one perspective or *Gestalt* and found a totally different one. What we have thought we could count on in ourselves, and what we have thought to be the boundaries and contours of the world, turn out suddenly not to be the "real" outlines of ourselves or of the world, or those that others accept. We have become strangers in a world where we thought we were at home.

31. Excerpted from Lu Hsun, "Amid Pale Bloodstains," *Selected Works,* vol. 1, p. 362, emphasis mine. In his actions if not in his words and thoughts, Lu Hsun was often cautious. His wariness about the path of violence and open confrontation was evident in his 1925–1926 correspondence with Hsu Kuang-p'ing, one of his students. Yet he judged himself harshly for his protective inaction. In a memorial for another student of his who was killed in the March 18 tragedy, he wrote: "She is no longer the pupil of one dragging on an ignoble existence like myself. She is a Chinese girl who has died for China." Jonathan Spence, *The Gate of Heavenly Peace: The Chinese and Their Revolution, 1895–1980* (New York, 1981), pp. 195–197.

32. Leo Ou-fan Lee, *The Romantic Generation,* pp. 189–190.

33. Ibid., p. 199.

34. Ibid., pp. 295–296. These are questions that Lee asks about the entire generation of romantic writers. He sees the romantic temperament as appearing in cultures undergoing sharp historical transitions (such as China during the Republican era)

and being generated by the very normlessness and chaos that individual persons face in such societies.

35. Kuo Mo-jo, *Wo ti t'ung-nien* (Hong Kong, 1968), pp. 34–35. Following Kuo Mo-jo's death in 1978, his family home in Sha-wan, Szechwan, was restored and opened up as a museum. The Ch'ing-style house, despite its 36 rooms, has the spartan quality of a lower-gentry family about it. The family tutorial school in the back courtyard opened onto a flower garden facing a hill. Today the benches are absent, as is the Confucian memorial tablet.

36. Ho, "Traditional Patterns," pp. 82–83.

37. Kuo Mo-jo, pp. 34–35.

38. This letter, and sixty-five others from the period 1913–1923, have been reprinted with commentary in T'ang Ming-chung, ed., *Ying-hua shu-chien* (Chengtu, 1981). A copy of the letter hangs on a wall of the tutorial room in the Kuo Family Residence Museum in Sha-wan.

39. Roy, pp. 15–20.

40. Kuo Mo-jo, pp. 59 and 84; also Roy, pp. 22–23.

41. Kuo Mo-jo, p. 82; Roy, pp. 24–25. His overall academic performance is recorded in the School Leaving Certificate on display at the Kuo Family Residence Museum in Sha-wan. In Mathematics (100), Physiology (98), Study of the Classics (96), History (87), Geography (92), Botany (78), and Physical Education (85), the young Kuo did very well, whereas in Self-Cultivation *(hsiu-shen),* which was undoubtedly practiced on the basis of traditional moral tenets that he now opposed, and in Painting, which did not interest him, his scores were 35 out of 100.

42. Kuo Mo-jo, pp. 84–85 and 90. Note that in the text itself, the first person voice switches to the third person, reflecting the shift from feeling in control to becoming the target of others.

43. Ibid., p. 85.

44. Ibid., p. 73. For a fuller discussion of the teachers in Kuo's primary school, see Roy, pp. 23–26.

45. Kuo Mo-jo, p. 73.

46. Ibid., pp. 90–95.

47. Ibid., p. 95.

48. Ibid., pp. 100–101.

49. Ibid., p. 102.

50. Ibid., p. 103. As Kuo Mo-jo noted, this strategy of exhibiting the guilty one before others paralleled the parading of criminals publicly through the streets.

51. Ibid., p. 104. Note the role of "literary fame" here in helping build up the expectation of unusual behavior from young Kuo—one of the secondary customs surrounding the "young prodigy."

52. Ibid., pp. 104–107.

53. Kuo also cites a strong element of curiosity involved in these adventures—what he

called his fondness for unfamiliar things *(hao-chi hsin);* ibid., pp. 95–96 and 107–108. Kuo's erotic feelings and leanings during this period may also have intensified his sense of shame. On the basis of several of Kuo's "homosexually tinged" relationships in primary and middle school, as well as association with male prostitutes, David Tod Roy concluded that there might have been "a relatively strong homosexual component in Kuo Mo-jo's make-up"; see Roy, pp. 20–21 and 28–29. While homosexuality may have been the social custom among Kuo's peers at his schools, it was scorned by conventional morality.

EPILOGUE

1. Keniston, pp. 329–345, esp. p. 342. For my speculations on the importance of several "missing pieces" in traditional Chinese socialization, including a separate adolescence, see Saari, "Breaking the Hold of Tradition," pp. 37–40.
2. Taiwan Interview No. 35.
3. Kuo Jen-yuan, "The Anatomy of Chinese Behavior," (unpublished manuscript), pp. 60–63. The following passage conveys the tone and sense of his argument:

> [Between 1911 and 1921] China was a land of poverty, economically, intellectually, and scientifically. Studying the ancient literature was no longer fashionable; students returning from Japan had only superficial knowledge of Western science and technology. Few students returning from America or Europe had graduate training; practically none had had experience in independent research. Instruction in Chinese colleges consisted of teachers giving verbal explanations of textbooks from the West. Outside references were out of the question . . .
>
> China was a virgin land for any intellectual enterprise. But with such a low level of intellectual standards, independent thought and independent research were unthinkable. The Chinese needed authorities to lead them. The young people of that generation were brought up to revere authorities. Since it was no longer fashionable to follow the authority of Confucius and the other ancient greats, the New Authorities naturally were expected to come from the West. *This is how the Antiquity Complex was transformed into the Comprador Complex.* The cultural compradors had no wares of their own to sell to the Chinese, but they had new imported wares from the West. They told the Chinese youth: "Worship no more the ancient greats, but listen to the giants from the West."
>
> When John Dewey came to lecture in China, he was introduced by the President of Peking University as the Western Confucius, and Hu Shih, Dewey's interpreter, immediately achieved national fame as a "high foot (Chinese expression for brilliant pupil)" of the Columbia pragmatist . . . [Other examples from the groups that collected around Bertrand Russell, Hans Driesch, Margaret Sanger, Karl Marx.]
>
> The so-called "New Culture Movement" or May Fourth Movement had revealed China's intellectual immaturity and scientific poverty . . . young students and their leaders had done nothing more than uncritical compradoring.

4. Mao Tse-tung, vol. 3, p. 20. The problem of revering authorities lasted well beyond the 1920s, as Mao was still complaining in 1941 about students in the Com-

munist areas who "give all their hearts to the supposedly eternal and immutable dogmas learned from their teachers" (ibid).

5. See D. W. Y. Kwok, *Scientism in Chinese Thought: 1900–1950* (New Haven, 1965); Lin Yü-sheng, *The Crisis of Chinese Consciousness;* Leo Ou-fan Lee, *The Romantic Generation.*

6. Spence, *The Gate of Heavenly Peace,* p. xiv. Spence has consistently presented through his written works, and in his teaching, an intimate history of China by trying to figure out what was going on in individual minds. In *The Gate of Heavenly Peace,* his final image is that life itself is like a net, entrapping the actors within it (pp. 368–370). See also Norman Oder, "Teachers: Intimate History of China," *Yale Alumni Magazine* 48.1:40–42.

7. This was the judgment of the historian and philosopher Li Tse-hou (Li Zehou) in a 1979 study published in Peking on modern Chinese intellectual history. Among the six generations he distinguished spanning the years from 1898 to the 1970s, the May Fourth generation was the most creative and important one; he called it "the pattern-making, model-building, paradigm-articulating generation" (cited and translated in Vera Schwarcz, *The Chinese Enlightenment,* pp. 25–26 and 313).

8. First used by Peter Berger, Brigitte Berger, and Hansfried Kellner in their study, *The Homeless Mind,* the term in part reflects the widespread erosion of religious definitions of reality that has created a metaphysical homelessness within pluralistic secular societies. High mobility in society and in individual lives imply a more literal loss of a sense of home. The painful experience of homelessness has in turn engendered nostalgias—"nostalgias . . . for a condition of 'being at home' in society, within oneself and, ultimately, in the universe." Socialism is partly understood as the promise of a new home. See Berger, Berger, and Kellner, pp. 82 and 138.

9. Quoted in T. A. Hsia, p. 184.

Bibliography

Alitto, Guy S. *The Last Confucian: Liang Shu-ming and the Chinese Dilemma of Modernity*. 2nd ed. Berkeley, University of California Press, 1986.

Allen, George Cyril and Audrey G. Donnithorne. *Western Enterprise in Far Eastern Economic Development: China and Japan.* New York, Macmillan, 1954.

Amnesty International. *Political Imprisonment in the People's Republic of China.* London, Amnesty International Publications, 1978.

Barnett, H. G. *Innovation: The Basis of Cultural Change*. New York, McGraw-Hill, 1953.

Bastid-Bruguière, Marianne. "Currents of Social Change," in John K. Fairbank and Kwang-Ching Liu, eds., *The Cambridge History of China*, vol. 11, part 2. Cambridge, Cambridge University Press, 1980.

Baum, Carolyn Lee and Richard Baum. "Creating the New Communist Child: Continuity and Change in Chinese Styles of Early Childhood Socialization," in Richard W. Wilson, et al., eds., *Value Change in Chinese Society*. New York, Praeger, 1979.

Becker, Ernest. *Angel in Armor: A Post-Freudian Perspective on the Nature of Man*. New York, G. Braziller, 1969.

———. *The Birth and Death of Meaning: A Perspective in Psychiatry and Anthropology*. 2nd ed. New York, The Free Press, 1971.

———. *The Structure of Evil: An Essay on the Unification of the Science of Man*. New York, G. Braziller, 1968.

Bendix, Reinhard. "Compliant Behavior and Individual Personality," in Neil J. Smelser and William T. Smelser, eds., *Personality and Social Systems*. New York, Wiley, 1963.

Berger, Peter L. and Thomas Luckmann. *The Social Construction of Reality: A Treatise in the Sociology of Knowledge*. Garden City, N.Y., Doubleday, 1966.

————, Brigitte Berger, and Hansfried Kellner. *The Homeless Mind: Modernization and Consciousness*. New York, Random House, 1973. Reference is to the 1974 Vintage Books edition.

Bergere, Marie-Claire. "The Role of the Bourgeoisie," in Mary Clabaugh Wright, ed., *China in Revolution: The First Phase, 1900–1913*. New Haven, Yale University Press, 1968.

Berkhofer, Robert F. *A Behavioral Approach to Historical Analysis*. New York, The Free Press, 1969.

Bodde, Derk, and Clarence Morris. *Law in Imperial China, Exemplified by 190 Ch'ing Dynasty Cases*. Cambridge, Harvard University Press, 1967.

Boorman, Howard L., and Richard G. Howard, eds., *Biographical Dictionary of Republican China*. 4 vols. New York, Columbia University Press, 1967–1971.

"Brighter Horizons for Children," *China Reconstructs* 37.6:5 (June 1988).

Brown, L. B. *Psychology in Contemporary China*. Oxford, Pergamon Press, 1981.

Brunnert, H. S., and V. V. Hagelstrom. *Present Day Political Organization of China*. A. Beltchenko and E. E. Moran, tr. Shanghai, Kelly and Walsh, 1912.

Bryson, Mrs. [Mary Isabella]. *Child Life in Chinese Homes*. London, The Religious Tract Society, 1885.

Butterfield, Fox. *China: Alive in the Bitter Sea*. New York, Times Books, 1982.

Butterfield, Herbert. *History and Human Relations*. London, Collins, 1951.

Chai, Ch'u and Winberg Chai, eds., *The Sacred Books of Confucius and Other Confucian Classics*. New Hyde Park, N.Y., 1965. Reference in the text to Taiwan reprint entitled *The Humanist Way in Ancient China: Essential Works of Confucianism*.

Chan, Anthony B. "The Failure of Theory: Psychohistory and the Study of China." University of Toronto-York University Joint Centre on

Modern East Asia Discussion Paper, No. 3. Downsview (Ontario), 1979.

Chan, Wing-tsit, comp. and tr. *A Sourcebook in Chinese Philosophy*. 2 vols. Princeton, Princeton University Press, 1963.

Chang, C. K. "Wilson's Principles of World Reconstruction in their Application to the Far East," *CSM* 14:232–238 (1918–1919).

Chang, Carson. *The Development of Neo-Confucian Thought*. 2 vols. New York, Bookman Associates, 1957.

Chang, Chung-li. *The Chinese Gentry: Studies on Their Role in Nineteenth-Century Chinese Society*. Seattle, University of Washington Press, 1955.

Chang, Ch'i-yun 张其昀 . *Chung-hua wu-ch'ien nien shih* 中华五千年 史 (Fifty centuries of Chinese history). Taipei, 1960.

Chang Fu-liang. *When East Met West: A Personal Story of Rural Reconstruction in China*. New Haven, Yale-China Association, 1972.

Chang, Hao. *Liang Ch'i-ch'ao and Intellectual Transition in China, 1890–1907*. Cambridge, Harvard University Press, 1971.

———. "New Confucianism and the Intellectual Crisis of Contemporary China," in Charlotte Furth, ed., *The Limits of Change: Essays on Conservative Alternatives in Republican China*. Cambridge, Harvard University Press, 1976.

———. "Intellectual Change and the Reform Movement, 1890–8" in John K. Fairbank and Kwang-Ching Liu, eds., *The Cambridge History of China*. vol. 11, part 2. Cambridge, Cambridge University Press, 1980.

Chang, Lui-Ngan. "Working for China's Welfare Abroad," *CSM* 5:544–548 (1909–1910).

Chang, Loy. "The Need of Experts," *CSM* 11:467–471 (1915–1916)

Chang Po-hsing 张伯行 , comp. *Hsiao hsueh chi-chieh* 小学集解 (Commentary on *Learning for the young*). Taipei reproduction of 1713 edition, 1962. *See also* Chu Hsi.

Chang, Peng Chun. "National Ideals," *CSM* 8:17–21 (1912–1913).

Chao, Chuan. "China and a Stable Peace," *CSM* 14:114–117 (1918–1919).

Chao Yang Buwei. *Autobiography of a Chinese Woman*. Yuenren Chao, tr. New York, The John Day Company, 1947.

Chao, Yuen R. [Y. R. Chao, Chao Yuanren]. "Proposed Reforms," *CSM* 11:572–593 (1915–1916).

Chao Yuanren 赵元任. "Tsao-nien hui-i" 早年回忆 (Childhood reminiscences), *Chuan-chi wen-hsueh* 15.3; 15.4; and 15.5.

Chen, Ivan. *The Book of Filial Duty*. London, John Murray, 1908.

Ch'en, Ta. *Population in Modern China*. Chicago, University of Chicago Press, 1946.

Ch'en Ch'i-t'ien 陈啟天. *Chi-yuan hui-i lu* 记圆回忆录 (Recollections at Chi-yuan). Taipei, 1965.

Ch'en, Jerome. *Mao and the Chinese Revolution*, with thirty-seven poems by Mao Tse-tung, translated from the Chinese by Michael Bullock and Jerome Ch'en. London, Oxford University Press, 1965.

Ch'en Tu-hsiu 陈独秀. *Shih-an tzu-chuan* 实庵自传 (Autobiography of Shih-an). Chuan-chi wen-hsueh ts'ung-shu 20. Taipei, 1967.

Cheng, F. T. [Cheng T'ien-hsi]. *East and West: Episodes in a Sixty Years' Journey*. London, Hutchinson, 1951.

———. *Reflections at Eighty*. London, Luzac, 1966.

Chiang Monlin. *Tides from the West: A Chinese Autobiography*. New Haven, Yale University Press, 1947.

———. *A Study in Chinese Principles of Education*. Shanghai, 1918. Reprinted under title *Chinese Culture and Education: A Historical and Comparative Survey*, with new introduction. Taipei, 1963.

Chiang Yee. *A Chinese Childhood*. London, Methuen, 1940.

Chin, C. Y. "The Proper Meaning of the Chinese Students' Alliance," *CSM* 8:527–531 (1912–1913).

Chinese Students' Monthly. New York, 1909–1921. Abbreviated in the Notes and Bibliography as *CSM*.

Chou Yentung [Chou Yen-t'ung]. Autobiographical excerpts in Han Suyin, *The Crippled Tree: China—Biography, History, Autobiography*, pp. 57–60, 62–77, 88–108, 160–163, 187–191, 211, 277–291, 309–312. New York, Putnam, 1965.

Chow Tse-tsung. *The May Fourth Movement: Intellectual Revolution in Modern China*. Cambridge, Harvard University Press, 1960.

Chow Yung-teh. "Life Histories," in Fei Hsiao-t'ung, *China's Gentry: Essays in Rural-Urban Relations*. Rev. and ed. by M. P. Redfield.

Chicago, University of Chicago Press, 1953. Reference in the text to Phoenix reprint, 1968.

————. *Social Mobility in China: Status Careers Among the Gentry in a Chinese Community.* New York, Atherton, 1966.

Chu Hsi 朱熹. *Hsiao hsueh* 小学 (Learning for the young), in Chang Po-hsing, comp., *Hsiao hsueh chi-chieh,* 6 chüan with prefaces. Reprinted in series Chung-kuo hsueh-shu ming-chu 中国学术名著 (Famous works of Chinese scholarship), ed. Yang Chia-lo 杨家骆. Taipei, 1962.

Chuan-chi wen-hsueh 传记文学 (Biographical literature). Taipei, 1962–.

Ch'ü Ch'iu-pai 瞿秋白. *O-hsiang chi-ch'eng* 饿乡记程 (Journey to the land of hunger), vol. 1 in *Ch'ü Ch'iu-pai wen-chi* 瞿秋白文集 (Collected works of Ch'ü Ch'iu-pai). 4 vols. Peking, 1953.

Ch'ü, T'ung-tsu. "Chinese Class Structure and its Ideology," in John K. Fairbank, ed., *Chinese Thought and Institutions.* Chicago, University of Chicago Press, 1957.

Chun, Woon Yung. "East is East and West is West," *CSM* 9:491–493 (1913–1914).

Cohen, Paul A. "Ch'ing China: Confrontation with the West, 1850–1900," in James B. Crowley, ed., *Modern East Asia: Essays in Interpretation.* New York, Harcourt, Brace & World, 1970.

————. *Between Tradition and Modernity: Wang T'ao and Reform in Late Ch'ing China.* Cambridge, Harvard University Press, 1974.

————. *Discovering History in China: American Historical Writing on the Recent Chinese Past.* New York, Columbia University Press, 1984.

Coles, Robert. *Erik H. Erikson: The Growth of His Work.* Boston, Little Brown, 1970.

Confucius. *Analects.* Arthur Waley, tr. New York, Random House, 1960.

Crowley, James B., ed. *Modern East Asia: Essays in Interpretation.* New York, Harcourt, Brace and World, 1970.

de Bary, Wm. Theodore. *The Liberal Tradition in China.* Hong Kong, The Chinese University Press, 1983.

deMause, Lloyd. "The Evolution of Childhood," in Lloyd deMause, ed., *The History of Childhood.* New York, Psychohistory Press, 1974.

deMause, Lloyd. *Foundations of Psychohistory*. New York, Creative Roots, 1982.

Doleželová-Velingerová, Milena. "Kuo Mo-jo's Autobiographical Works," in Jaroslav Průšok, ed., *Studies in Modern Chinese Literature*. Berlin, Akademie-Verlag, 1964.

Doolittle, Rev. Justus. *Social Life of the Chinese*. New York, Harper & Brothers, 1885.

Doré, Henry. *Researches into Chinese Superstitions*. M. Kennelly, S. J., tr. Shanghai, T'usewei Printing Press, 1914.

Douglass, Bruce, and Ross Terrill, eds. *China and Ourselves: Explorations and Revisions by a New Generation*. Boston, Beacon Press, 1969, 1970.

Drake, Fred W. *China Charts the World: Hsu chi-yü and his Geography of 1848*. Cambridge, East Asian Research Center, Harvard University, 1975.

Dunn, Patrick. " 'That Enemy is the Baby': Childhood in Imperial Russia," in Lloyd deMause, ed., *History of Childhood*. New York, Psychohistory Press, 1974.

Eberhard, Wolfram. *Guilt and Sin in Traditional China*. Berkeley, University of California Press, 1967.

Erh-shih-ssu hsiao 二十四孝 (Twenty-four examples of filial piety). Taipei, Hsin min chiao-yü she, 1964.

Erikson, Erik H. *Childhood and Society*. 2nd ed. New York, Norton 1963.

———. *The Challenge of Youth*. New York, Doubleday, 1965.

———. *Identity: Youth and Crisis*. New York, Norton, 1968.

———. "On the Nature of Psycho-Historical Evidence: In Search of Gandhi," *Daedalus* 97.3:695–730 (Summer 1968).

Fairbank, John King. *The United States and China*. 4th ed., enlarged. Cambridge, Harvard University Press, 1983.

———. *Trade and Diplomacy on the China Coast: The Opening of the Treaty Ports, 1842–1854*. 1953; rpt. Stanford, Stanford University Press, 1969 .

———, Alexander Eckstein, and L. S. Yang. "Economic Change in Early Modern China: An Analytic Framework," *Economic Development and Cultural Change* 9.1:1–26 (October 1960).

———, Edwin O. Reischauer, and Albert M. Craig. *East Asia: The Modern Transformation*. Boston, Houghton-Mifflin, 1965.

————, ed. *The Chinese World Order: Traditional China's Foreign Relations*. Cambridge, Harvard University Press, 1968.

————, and Kwang-Ching Liu, eds. *The Cambridge History of China*, vol. 11: *Late Ch'ing, 1800–1911*, Part 2. Cambridge, Cambridge University Press, 1980.

Fei Hsiao-t'ung. *Peasant Life in China: A Field Study of Country Life in the Yangtze Valley*. London, Dutton, 1939.

————. "Peasantry and Gentry: An Interpretation of Chinese Social Structure and its Changes," *The American Journal of Sociology* 52.1:1–17 (July 1946).

————. *China's Gentry: Essays in Rural-Urban Relations*. Rev. and ed. by M. P. Redfield, with six life-histories of Chinese gentry families collected by Yung-teh Chow. Chicago, University of Chicago Press, 1953. Reference in the text to Phoenix reprint, 1968.

————, and Chih-i Chang. *Earthbound China: A Study of Rural Economy in Yunnan*. Rev. English ed. prepared in collaboration with Paul Cooper and M. P. Redfield. Chicago, University of Chicago Press, 1945.

Feng Yu-lan. *A Short History of Chinese Philosophy*. Derk Bodde, tr. New York, Macmillan, 1948.

Feuerwerker, Albert. *The Foreign Establishment in China in the Early Twentieth Century*. Ann Arbor, Center for Chinese Studies, University of Michigan, 1976.

Foster, George. "Peasant Society and the Image of Limited Good," *American Anthropologist* 67:293–315 (April 1965).

Franke, Wolfgang. *China and the West: The Cultural Encounter, 13th to 20th Centuries*. R. A. Wilson, tr. New York, Harper and Row, 1967.

————. ed. *China Handbuch: Gesellschaft, Politik, Staat, Wirtschaft*. Düsseldorf, Bertelsman, 1973. References in the text to Rowohlt edition, 1977.

Frankel, Victor. *The Search for Meaning*. New York, Pocket Books, 1963.

Furth, Charlotte. *Ting Wen-chiang: Science and China's New Culture*. Cambridge, Harvard University Press, 1970.

————. "Concepts of Pregnancy, Childbirth, and Infancy in Ch'ing Dynasty China," *Journal of Asian Studies* 46.1:7–35 (February 1987).

————, ed. *The Limits of Change: Essays on Conservative Alternatives in Republican China*. Cambridge, Harvard University Press, 1976.

Gallin, Bernard. *Hsin Hsing, Taiwan: A Chinese Village in Change.* Berkeley, University of California Press, 1966.

Gamble, Sidney. *Ting Hsien: A North China Rural Community.* Stanford, Stanford University Press, 1954.

Gates, Hill. *Chinese Workingclass Lives: Getting by in Taiwan.* Ithaca, Cornell University Press, 1987.

Geertz, Clifford. "The Impact of the Concept of Culture on the Concept of Man," in John R. Platt, ed., *New Views on the Nature of Man.* Chicago, University of Chicago Press, 1965.

Geertz, Hildred. "The Vocabulary of Emotion: The Study of Javanese Socialization Processes," *Psychiatry* 22.3:225–237 (August 1959).

Grieder, Jerome B. *Hu Shih and the Chinese Renaissance: Liberalism in the Chinese Revolution, 1917–1937.* Cambridge, Harvard University Press, 1970.

————. *Intellectuals and the State in Modern China: A Narrative History.* New York, Free Press, 1981.

Hagen, Everett E. *On the Theory of Social Change: How Economic Growth Begins.* Homewood, Ill., Dorsey Press, 1962.

Hallowell, Irving A. *Culture and Experience.* New York, Schocken Books, 1967.

Han Suyin, pseud. *The Crippled Tree: China—Biography, History, Autobiography.* London, Putnam, 1965.

————. *A Mortal Flower: China—Autobiography, History.* London, Putnam, 1965.

————. *A Birdless Summer: China—Autobiography, History.* London, Putnam, 1968.

Hankiss, Agnes. "Ontologies of the Self: On the Mythological Rearranging of One's Life History," in Daniel Bertaux, ed., *Biography and Society: The Life History Approach in the Social Sciences.* Beverly Hills, California, Sage Publications, 1981.

Hao, Yen-p'ing. *The Comprador in Nineteenth Century China: Bridge between East and West.* Cambridge, Harvard University Press, 1970.

———— and Erh-min Wang, "Changing Chinese Views of Western Relations, 1840–95," in John K. Fairbank and Kwang-Ching Liu, eds., *The Cambridge History of China,* vol. 11, part 2. Cambridge, Cambridge University Press, 1980.

Hardy, E. J. *John Chinaman at Home: Sketches of Men, Manners, and Things in China*. London, T. Fisher Unwin, 1906.

Harvey, Edwin D. *The Mind of China*. New Haven, Yale University Press, 1933.

Hayes, James. "Specialists and Written Materials in the Village World," in David Johnson, Andrew J. Nathan, and Evelyn Rawski, eds., *Popular Culture in Late Imperial China*. Berkeley, University of California, 1985.

Headland, Isaac Taylor. *The Chinese Boy and Girl*. New York, Fleming H. Revell, 1901.

Ho, David Yau-fai [David Y. F. Ho, D. Y. F. Ho]. "On the Concept of Face," *American Journal of Sociology* 81.4:867–884 (January 1976).

———. "Childhood Psychopathology: A Dialogue with Special Reference to Chinese and American Cultures," in Arthur Kleinman and Tsung-yi Lin, eds., *Normal and Abnormal Behavior in Chinese Culture*. Dordrecht, The Netherlands, D. Reidel, 1981.

———. "Traditional Patterns of Socialization in Chinese Society," *Acta Psychologica Taiwanica* 23.2:81–95 (1981).

Hommel, Rudolf P. *China at Work: An Illustrated Record of the Primitive Industries of China's Masses, Whose Life is Toil, and Thus an Account of Chinese Civilization*. New York, The John Day Company, 1937.

Howard, Richard Campbell. "The Early Life and Thought of K'ang Yu-wei, 1858–1895. Columbia Ph.D. diss., 1972.

Hsia, T. A. [Hsia Tsi-an]. "Ch'ü Ch'iu-pai's Autobiographical Writings: The Making and Destruction of a 'Tender-hearted' Communist," *The China Quarterly* 25:178–212 (January–March 1966).

———. *The Gate of Darkness: Studies on the Leftist Literary Movement in China*. Seattle, University of Washington Press, 1968.

Hsiao, Harry Hsin-i. "A Study of the *Hsiao-Ching:* with an emphasis on its intellectual background and its problems." Harvard Ph.D. diss., 1973.

Hsiao, Kung-ch'uan. *A Modern China and a New World: K'ang Yu-wei, Reformer and Utopian, 1858–1927*. Seattle, University of Washington Press, 1975.

Hsieh Ping-ying. *Autobiography of a Chinese Girl: A Genuine Autobiogra-*

phy. Tsui Chi, tr. London, G. Allen & Unwin, 1943. American Edition entitled *Girl Rebel, The Autobiography of Hsieh Ping-ying, with Excerpts from her New War Diaries,* Adet and Anor Lin, tr. New York, The John Day Company, 1940.

Hsu, Francis L. K. *Under the Ancestors' Shadow: Kinship, Personality, and Social Mobility in Village China.* Rev. ed. Garden City, N. Y., Doubleday, 1967. Originally published as *Under the Ancestors' Shadow: Chinese Culture and Personality,* New York, Columbia University Press, 1948.

————. *Religion, Science and Human Crisis.* London, Routledge & K. Paul, 1952.

————. *Clan, Caste, and Club.* Princeton, Van Nostrand, 1963.

————. *Americans and Chinese: Passage to Differences.* 3rd ed. Honolulu, University of Hawaii Press, 1981.

————. *Rugged Individualism Reconsidered: Essays in Psychological Anthropology.* Knoxville, University of Tennessee Press, 1983.

————, ed. *Kinship and Culture.* Chicago, Aldine, 1971.

Hsueh Chun-tu, ed. *Revolutionary Leaders of Modern China.* New York, Oxford University Press, 1971.

Hu Ch'iu-yuan 胡秋原. *Shao tso shou-ts'an chi* 少作收残集 (Collected fragments of early works), 3 chüan. Taipei, 1959.

————. "Fu-ch'in chih hsun" (Father's teachings), *Min-chu ch'ao* 10.15:15-19 (1960).

————. "*Shao tso shou-ts'an chi* tzu-hsu: Ch'ing-nien shih-tai ssu-hsiang chih hui-i" 少作收残集自序：青年时代思想之回忆 (Introduction to "Collected Fragments of early works": Recollecting thoughts from the period of youth), *Min-chu ch'ao* 民主潮, vol. 9, nos. 13-17, 21, 22 (1959); vol. 10, nos. 3-7, 9, 10, 12-18, 21, 23, 24 (1960); vol. 11, nos. 4, 7, 9, 12, 17 (1961).

Hu Hsien Chin. "The Chinese Concepts of Face," *American Anthropologist* 46.1:45-64 (January–March 1944).

Hu Kuang-piao 胡光麃. *Po-chu liu-shih nien* 波逐六十年 (Riding the waves for sixty years). Hong Kong, 1964.

Hu, Pingsa. "The Women of China," *CSM* 9:202-203 (1913–1914).

Hu Shih. "My Credo and its Evolution," in Clifton Fadiman, ed., *Living*

Philosophies: A Series of Intimate Credos. New York, Simon and Schuster, 1931.

Hu Shih 胡適 . *Ssu-shih tzu-shu* 四十自述 (Autobiography at forty). Shanghai, 1933. References in text to Hong Kong, 1954, overseas Chinese edition.

———. *Hu Shih wen-ts'un* 胡適文存 (Collected essays of Hu Shih). 4 vols. Taipei, 1953.

———. "Dr. Hu Shih's Personal Reminiscences." Interviews comp. and ed. by Te-kong Tong, with Dr. Hu's corrections in his own handwriting, 1958. Typescript in the archive of the Oral History Project, Columbia University.

Huang Hsun-chu 黃旭初 . *Wo ti mu-ch'in* 我的母亲 (My mother). Ch'un-ch'iu ts'ung-shu 1. Hong Kong, 1968.

Huang, Philip C. *Liang Ch'i-ch'ao and Modern Chinese Liberalism.* Seattle, University of Washington Press, 1972.

Hummel, Arthur W., ed. *Eminent Chinese of the Ch'ing Period.* 2 vols. Washington, D.C., United States Government Printing Office, 1943.

Hyatt, Irwin T., Jr. "Protestant Missions in China, 1877–1890: The Institutionalization of Good Works." *Papers on China* 17:67–100. Cambridge, East Asian Research Center, Harvard University, 1963.

Ichiko, Chūzō. "Political and Institutional Reform, 1901–11" in John K. Fairbank and Kwang-Ching Liu, eds., *The Cambridge History of China,* vol. 11, part 2. Cambridge, Cambridge University Press, 1980.

Israel, John. *Student Nationalism in China: 1927–1937.* Stanford, Stanford University Press, 1966.

——— and Donald W. Klein. *Rebels and Bureaucrats: China's December 9ers.* Berkeley, University of California Press, 1976.

Jahoda, Gustav. "Theoretical and Systematic Approaches in Cross-Cultural Psychology," in Harry C. Triandis and Alastair Heron, eds., *Handbook of Cross-Cultural Psychology,* vol. 1: *Perspectives.* Boston, Allyn and Bacon, 1980.

Johnson, David. "Communication, Class, and Consciousness in Late Imperial China," in David Johnson, Andrew J. Nathan, and Evelyn S. Rawski, eds., *Popular Culture in Late Imperial China.* Berkeley, University of California Press, 1985.

Johnson, David, Andrew J. Nathan, and Evelyn S. Rawski, eds. *Popular Culture in late Imperial China*. Berkeley, University of California Press, 1985.

Johnson, Elizabeth. "Women and Childbearing in Kwan Mun Han Village: A Study of Social Change," in Margery Wolf and Roxanne Witke, eds., *Woman in Chinese Society*. Stanford, Stanford University Press, 1975.

K., T. H. [Telly H. Koo]. "Confucius and John Dewey: The Bankruptcy of the East and the West," *CSM* 16:539–541 (1920–1921).

Keniston, Kenneth. "Psychological Development and Historical Change," *The Journal of Interdisciplinary History* 2:329–345 (Autumn 1971), as reprinted in Robert Jay Lifton with Eric Olson, eds., *Explorations in Psychohistory: The Wellfleet Papers*. New York, Simon and Schuster, 1974.

Kennedy, John G. "Peasant Society and the Image of Limited Good: A Critique," *American Anthropologist* 68:1212–1225 (October 1966).

Kiang, Wen-han. *The Chinese Student Movement*. Morningside Heights, N.Y., King's Crown Press, 1948.

Kingston, Maxine Hong. *The Woman Warrior: Memories of a Girlhood among Ghosts*. New York, Alfred Knopf, 1977.

Kleinman, Arthur. *Social Origins of Distress and Disease: Depression, Neurasthenia, and Pain in Modern China*. New Haven, Yale University Press, 1986.

—— and Tsung-yi Lin, eds. *Normal and Abnormal Behavior in Chinese Culture*. Dordrecht, The Netherlands, D. Reidel, 1981.

Koo, V. K. Wellington. "An Account of the History of the Chinese Students' Alliance in the United States," *CSM* 7:420–431 (1911–1912).

——. "Address made at the Platform Meeting of the Chinese Students' Conference at Brown University, September 6, 1917," *CSM* 13:20–28 (1917–1918).

Ku Chieh-kang. *The Autobiography of a Chinese Historian, Being the Preface to a Symposium on Ancient Chinese History (Ku Shih Pien)*. Arthur W. Hummel, tr. Leiden, E. J. Brill, 1931.

Kuei Wen-ts'an 桂文燦 ed. *Hsiao ching chi-chieh* 孝经集解 (Commentary on the *Classic of filial piety*). Taiwan reproduction of nineteenth-century text, Cheng yan, 1968.

Kuo Jen-yuan [Zing Yang Kuo]. "The Anatomy of Chinese Behavior." Unpublished manuscript in author's possession.

———. "The Confessions of a Chinese Scientist." Unpublished manuscript in author's possession.

———, and Lam Yut-hand. "Chinese Religious Behavior and the Deification of Mao Tse-tung," *Psychological Record* 18:455–468 (1969).

Kuo Mo-jo 郭沫若. *Wo ti t'ung-nien* 我的童年 (My boyhood years). Part 1 of *Shao-nien shih-tai* 少年时代 (The period of youth). Shanghai, 1956; references to Hong Kong reprint, 1968. Original edition entitled *Wo ti yu-nien* 我的幼年 (The years of my youth). Shanghai, 1929.

Kuo Ping-wen [Kuo P'ing-wen]. "A Plea for True Patriotism," *CSM* 5:104 (1909–1910).

Kwok, D. W. Y. *Scientism in Chinese Thought: 1900–1950*. New Haven, Yale University Press, 1965.

Lang, Olga. *Pa Chin and His Writings: Chinese Youth Between the Two Revolutions*. Cambridge, Harvard University Press, 1967.

Latourette, Kenneth Scott. *A History of Christian Missions in China*. New York, Russell & Russell, 1929.

Laue, Theodore H. Von. *The Global City: Freedom, Power, and Necessity in the Age of World Revolutions*. Philadelphia, Lippincott, 1969.

Lee, Leo Ou-fan. *The Romantic Generation of Modern Chinese Writers*. Cambridge, Harvard University Press, 1973.

———. "Genesis of a Writer: Notes on Lu Xun's Educational Experience, 1881–1909," in Merle Goldman, ed., *Modern Chinese Literature in the May Fourth Era*. Cambridge, Harvard University Press, 1977.

Lee, Mabel. "Moral Training in Chinese Schools," *CSM* 11:543–547 (1915–1916).

Lee, Yan Phou. *When I was a Boy in China*. Boston, D. Lothrop, 1887.

Legge, James. *The Chinese Classics*. 5 vols. 1893–1895; rpt. Taipei, 1966.

Levenson, Joseph R. *Liang Ch'i-ch'ao and the Mind of Modern China*. Cambridge, Harvard University Press, 1953.

———. *Confucian China and its Modern Fate*. 3 vols. Berkeley, University of California Press, 1958–1965.

———, ed. *Modern China: An Interpretive Anthology*. London, Macmillan, 1971.

LeVine, Robert A. *Culture, Behavior, and Personality*. Chicago, Aldine, 1973.

Levy, Howard. *Footbinding: The History of an Erotic Custom*. New York, Bell Publishing, 1967.

Levy, Marion J., Jr., *The Family Revolution in Modern China*. Cambridge, Harvard University Press, 1949. References in the text to Atheneum edition, 1968.

Lewis, Charlton M. *Prologue to the Chinese Revolution: The Transformation of Ideas and Institutions in Hunan Province, 1891–1907*. Cambridge, East Asian Research Center, Harvard University, 1976.

Li Chi 李济 . *Kan chiu lu* 感旧录 (Record of feelings for the past). Chuan-chi wen-hsueh ts'ung-shu 16. Taipei, 1967.

Li Pu-sheng 李朴生 . *Wo pu-jen-tzu ti mu-ch'in* 我不认字的母亲 (My illiterate mother). Chuan-chi wen-hsueh ts'ung-kan 4. Taipei, 1966.

Li, Runtien J. "The Mission of a Chinese Student," *CSM* 5:379 (1909–1910).

Li, T. L. "What Chinese Students Should Do When They Return," *CSM* 13:163–167 (1917–1918).

Li Tsung-t'ung 李宗侗 . "Yu Kuangchou ch'ung hui Peiching" 由 广州重回北京 (Return from Canton to Peking), *Chuan-chi wen-hsueh* 4.1:26 (January 1964).

Li Tung-fang 黎東方 . *P'ing-fan ti wo* 平凡的我 (My commonplace self). 2 vols. Chuan-chi wen hsueh: wen shih hsin-kan 62. Taipei, 1969.

Liang Heng and Judith Shapiro. *Cold Winds, Warm Winds: Intellectual Life in China Today*. Middleton, Conn., Wesleyan University Press, 1984.

Lien Shih-sheng 连士升 . *Hui-shou ssu-shih nien* 回首四十年 (Looking back over forty years). Singapore, 1952. This is vol. 3 in *Lien Shih-sheng wen-chi* 连士升文集 (Collected essays of Lien Shih-sheng). 10 vols. Singapore, 1963.

Lifton, J. Robert. *Thought Reform and the Psychology of Totalism: A Study of "Brainwashing" in China*. New York, Norton, 1963.

———. *Revolutionary Immortality: Mao Tse-tung and the Chinese Cultural Revolution*. New York, Vintage Books, 1968.

————. "Psychohistory," *Partisan Review* 37.1:11–32 (1970).

————. *History and Human Survival.* New York, Vintage Books, 1971.

————. *The Broken Connection: On Death and the Continuity of Life.* New York, Simon and Schuster, 1979.

Lin Yü-sheng, "The Suicide of Liang Chi: An Ambiguous Case of Moral Conservatism," in Charlotte Furth, ed., *The Limits of Change: Essays on Conservative Alternatives in Republican China.* Cambridge, Harvard University Press, 1976.

————. *The Crisis of Chinese Consciousness: Radical Antitraditionalism in the May Fourth Era.* Madison, University of Wisconsin Press, 1979.

Lin Yutang. *From Pagan to Christian.* Cleveland, The World Publishing Company, 1959.

Liu, Hui-chen Wang. *The Traditional Chinese Clan Rules.* Locust Valley, N.Y., J. J. Augustin, 1959.

Liu Kwang-ching. "Nineteenth Century China: The Disintegration of the Old Order and the Impact of the West," in Ping-ti Ho and Tang Tsou, eds., *China in Crisis.* vol. 1, book 1 (vol. 1 in 2 books in pb. edition). Chicago, University of Chicago Press, 1968.

Liu Ta-chieh 刘大杰. *San-erh k'u-hsueh chi* 三儿苦学记 (Record of the bitter study of Third Son). Shanghai, 1935.

Lo, Jung-pang, ed. *K'ang Yu-wei: A Biography and Symposium.* Tucson, University of Arizona Press, 1967.

Lo Tun-wei 罗敦伟. *Wu-shih nien hui-i lu* 五十年回忆录 (Recollections at fifty). Taipei, 1952.

Loh, Pinchon P. Y. *The Early Chiang Kai-shek: A Study of His Personality and Politics, 1887–1924.* New York, Columbia University Press, 1971.

Lu Hsun [Lu Xun]. *Selected Works.* 4 vols. Yang Xianyi and Gladys Yang, tr. Peking, Foreign Languages Press, 1980.

————. *Na-han* 呐喊 (Outcry). Peking, Ren-min wen-hsueh ch'u-pan-she, 1973.

Lyell, William A., Jr. *Lu Hsun's Vision of Reality.* Berkeley, University of California Press, 1976.

Lynd, Helen Merrill. *Shame and the Search for Identity.* New York, Harcourt Brace & World, 1958.

Ma, Y. C. [Ma Yin-chu]. "Liberty of Conscience," *CSM* 6:267–273 (1910–1911).

Macgowan, J. [Rev.] *Men and Manners of Modern China.* London, T. F. Unwin, 1912. Originally published in China under the title *Lights and Shadows of Chinese Life.*

Mair, Victor H. "Language and Ideology in the Written Popularizations of the *Sacred Edict,*" in David Johnson, Andrew J. Nathan, and Evelyn Rawski, eds., *Popular Culture in Late Imperial China.* Berkeley, University of California Press, 1985.

Mao Tse-tung. *Selected Works of Mao Tse-tung.* 4 vols. Peking, Foreign Languages Press, 1975.

May, K. T. [Mei Kuang-ti]. "The Task of Our Generation," *CSM* 12:152–154 (1916–1917).

———. "The New Chinese Scholar," *CSM* 12:342–351 (1916–1917).

McCandless, Boyd R. "Childhood Socialization," in David A. Goslin, ed., *Handbook of Socialization Theory and Research.* Chicago, Rand McNally, 1969.

Meskill, John. *Academies in Ming China: A Historical Essay.* Tucson, University of Arizona Press, 1982.

Metzger, Thomas A. "On Chinese Political Culture," *Journal of Asian Studies* 32.1:101–105 (November 1972).

———. *Escape from Predicament: Neo-Confucianism and China's Evolving Political Culture.* New York, Columbia University Press, 1977.

———. "Selfhood and Authority in Neo-Confucian Political Culture," in Arthur Kleinman and Tsung-Yi Lin, eds., *Normal and Abnormal Behavior in Chinese Culture.* Dordrecht, The Netherlands, D. Reidel, 1981.

Meyer, Jeffrey E. "Teaching Morality in Taiwan Schools: The Message of the Textbooks," *The China Quarterly* 114:267–284 (June 1988).

Miller, Perry. *The New England Mind: From Colony to Province.* Cambridge, Harvard University Press, 1953.

Miyazaki, Ichisada. *China's Examination Hell: The Civil Service Examination of Imperial China.* New Haven, Yale University Press, 1981.

Mok, K. F. "Culture," *CSM* 11:276–279 (1915–1916).

Monkey. Arthur Waley, tr. London, Allen & Unwin, 1965.

Monroe, Harriet. "The Training of Chinese Children," *The Century Magazine* 83:64 (March 1912).

Morse, Hosea Ballou. *The Trade and Administration of China*. London, Longmans Green, 1908.

Mote, Frederick W. "China's Past in the Study of China Today—Some Comments on the Recent Work of Richard Solomon," *Journal of Asian Studies* 32.1:107–120 (November 1972).

Munro, Donald J. *The Concept of Man in Early China*. Stanford, Stanford University Press, 1969.

Murphey, Rhoads. *The Treaty Ports and China's Modernization: What Went Wrong?* Ann Arbor, University of Michigan Press, 1970.

———. *The Outsiders: The Western Experience in India and China*. Ann Arbor, University of Michigan Press, 1977.

"My Secret Self," Document RCC-C11689, Informant 45F, in Margaret Mead and Rhoda Metraux, eds., *The Study of Culture at a Distance*. Chicago, University of Chicago Press, 1953.

Myrdal, Jan. *Report from a Chinese Village*. Maurice Michael, tr. New York, Pantheon, 1965.

Needham, Joseph, with the research assistance of Wang Ling. *History of Scientific Thought,* vol. 2 of Joseph Needham, ed., *Science and Civilization in China*. Cambridge, Cambridge University Press, 1956.

Nietzsche, Friedrich. *The Use and Abuse of History*. Adrian Collins, tr. 1874; rpt. Indianapolis, Bobbs-Merrill, 1957.

Oder, Norman. "Teachers: Intimate History of China," *Yale Alumni Magazine,* 48.1:40–42 (October 1984).

Osgood, Cornelius. *Village Life in Old China: A Community Study of Kao Yao, Yunnan*. New York, Ronald Press, 1963.

Parsons, Talcott. "Social Structure and the Development of Personality: Freud's Contribution to the Integration of Psychology and Sociology," *Psychiatry* 21.4:321–340 (November 1958).

———. *Societies: Evolutionary and Comparative Perspectives*. Englewood Cliffs, N.J., Prentice-Hall, 1966.

Payne, Robert. *Chiang Kai-shek*. New York, Weybright and Tallery, 1969.

Perry, Elizabeth. "Rural Violence in Socialist China," *The China Quarterly* 103:414–440 (September 1985).

Pruitt, Ida, from the story told her by Ning Lao T'ai-t'ai. *A Daughter of*

Han: The Autobiography of a Chinese Working Woman. New Haven, Yale University Press, 1945.

————. *A China Childhood.* San Francisco, China Materials Center, 1978.

Pu Yi [P'u Yi], Aisin-Gioro. *From Emperor to Citizen: The Autobiography of Aisin-Gioro Pu Yi.* W. J. F. Jenner, tr. 2 vols. Peking, Foreign Languages Press, 1964–1965.

Pusey, James Reeve. *China and Charles Darwin.* Cambridge, Council on East Asian Studies, Harvard University, 1983.

Pye, Lucian W. *The Spirit of Chinese Politics: A Psychocultural Study of the Authority Crisis in Political Development.* Cambridge, Massachusetts Institute of Technology Press, 1968.

Quo Tai-chi. "China's Fight for Democracy," *CSM* 15.3:37 (1919–1920).

Raddock, David M. *Political Behavior of Adolescents in China: The Cultural Revolution in Kwangchow.* Tucson, University of Arizona Press, 1977.

Rankin, Mary Backus. "The Revolutionary Movement in Chekiang: A Study in the Tenacity of Tradition," in Mary Clabaugh Wright, ed., *China in Revolution: The First Phase, 1900–1913.* New Haven, Yale University Press, 1968.

————. *Early Chinese Revolutionaries: Radical Intellectuals in Shanghai and Chekiang, 1902–1911.* Cambridge, Harvard University Press, 1971.

Ridley, Charles P. "Educational Theory and Practice in Late Imperial China: The Teaching of Writing as a Specific Case." Stanford Ph.D. diss., 1973.

Riesman, Paul. "On the irrelevance of child rearing practices for the formation of personality," *Culture, Medicine and Psychiatry* 7.2:103–129 (June 1983).

Roazen, Paul. *Erik Erikson: The Power and Limits of a Vision.* New York, The Free Press, 1976.

Roy, David Tod. *Kuo Mo-jo: The Early Years.* Cambridge, Harvard University Press, 1971.

Saari, Jon L. "Breaking the Hold of Tradition: The Self-Group Interface in Transitional China," in Sidney L. Greenblatt, Richard W. Wilson, and Amy Auerbacher Wilson, eds., *Social Interaction in Chinese Society.* New York, Praeger, 1982.

————. "The Human Factor: Some Inherent Ambiguities and Limitations in Scholarly Choices," in Amy Auerbacher Wilson, Sidney Leonard

Greenblatt, and Richard W. Wilson, eds., *Methodological Issues in Chinese Studies*. New York, Praeger, 1983.

Sacred Edict, Containing Sixteen Maxims of the Emperor Kang-he, Amplified by his Son, the Emperor Yeong-Ching, Together with a Paraphrase on the Whole by a Mandarin. Rev. William Milne, tr. London, 1817.

Sah Meng-wu 薩孟武．*Hsueh-sheng shih-tai* 學生時代 (Student years). San-min wen-k'u 16. Taipei, 1967.

——. *Chung-nien shih-tai* 中年時代 (Middle years). San-min wen-k'u 26. Taipei, 1967.

San Tzu Ching: Elementary Chinese. Annotated by Herbert A. Giles, tr. 2nd ed., rev. 1910; rpt. New York, Frederick Ungar, 1963.

Schachtel, Ernest. "The Development of Focal Attention and the Emergence of Reality," *Psychiatry* 7.4:309–324 (November 1954).

Schell, Orville, *"Watch Out for the Foreign Guests!"—China Encounters the West*. New York, Pantheon, 1980.

Schneider, Laurence A. *Ku Chieh-kang and China's New History: Nationalism and the Quest for Alternative Traditions*. Berkeley, University of California Press, 1981.

——. "National Essence and the New Intelligentsia," in Charlotte Furth, ed., *The Limits of Change: Essays on Conservative Alternatives in Republican China*. Cambridge, Harvard University Press, 1976.

Schram, Stuart. *Mao Tse-tung*. Baltimore, Penguin, 1966.

Schwarcz, Vera. *The Chinese Enlightenment: Intellectuals and the Legacy of the May Fourth Movement of 1919*. Berkeley, University of California Press, 1986.

Schwartz, Benjamin. "The Intellectual History of China: Preliminary Reflections," in John K. Fairbank, ed., *Chinese Thought and Institutions*. Chicago, University of Chicago Press, 1957.

——. *In Search of Wealth and Power: Yen Fu and the West*. Cambridge, Harvard University Press, 1964.

——. "A Brief Defense of Political and Intellectual History with Particular Reference to Non-Western Cultures," in Felix Gilbert and Stephen R. Graubard, eds., *Historical Studies Today*. New York, Norton, 1971. Originally in *Daedalus* 100.1:98–112 (Winter, 1971).

——. *Reflections on the May Fourth Movement: A Symposium*. Cambridge, East Asian Research Center, 1973.

Shen Congwen [Shen Ts'ung-wen]. *Recollections of West Hunan*. Gladys Yang, tr. Peking, Panda Books, 1982.

Shen Kang-poh 沈刚伯 . "Wo yu-shih suo shou ti chiao-yü" 我幼年所受的教育 (The education I received in my youth), *Chuan-chi wen-hsueh* 1.1:12–15 (June 1962).

Shen Tsung-han 沈宗瀚 . *K'o-nan k'u-hsueh chi* 克唯苦学记 (Record of overcoming difficulties and bitter study). Taipei, 1954.

———. *Chung-nien tzu-shu* 中年自述 (Autobiography of the middle years). Taipei, 1957.

Shen Ts'ung-wen 沈從文 . *Ts'ung-wen tzu-chuan* 從文自传 (Autobiography of Ts'ung-wen). Shanghai, 1948. References in text to Hong Kong, 1960 edition.

Sheng Cheng. *A Son of China*. M. M. Lowes, tr. New York, W. W. Norton, 1930. Original French edition *Ma Mere et moi à travers la Revolution Chinoise*. Paris, 1929.

Shu Hsin-ch'eng 舒新城 . *Wo ho chiao-yü* 我和教育 (My life in education). Shanghai, 1945.

Sie, Cheou-kang. *President Chiang Kai-shek: His Childhood and Youth*. Taipei, China Cultural Service, 1954.

Smith, Arthur H. *Village Life in China: A Study in Sociology*. London, Oliphant, Anderson, and Ferrier, 1899.

Smith, Richard, J. *China's Cultural Heritage: The Ch'ing Dynasty, 1644–1912*. Boulder, Col., Westview, 1983.

Snow, Edgar. *Red Star Over China*. 1938; rpt. New York, Grove Press, 1968.

Solomon, Richard H. *Mao's Revolution and the Chinese Political Culture*. Berkeley, University of California Press, 1971.

Spence, Jonathan D. *The Death of Woman Wang*. New York, Viking Press, 1978.

———. *The Gate of Heavenly Peace: The Chinese and Their Revolution, 1895–1980*. New York, Viking Press, 1981.

Sprenkel, Sybille van der. *Legal Institutions in Manchu China: A Sociological Analysis*. London, Athlone, 1962.

Stauffer, Milton Theobald, ed. *The Christian Occupation of China; A General Survey of the Numerical Strength and Geographical Distribution of the*

Christian Forces in China Made by The Special Committee on Survey and Occupation; China Continuation Committee, 1918–1921. Shanghai, 1922.

Stover, Leon E. *The Cultural Ecology of Chinese Civilization: Peasants and Elites in the Last of the Agrarian States.* New York, New American Library, 1974.

———— and Takeko Kawai Stover. *China: An Anthropological Perspective.* Pacific Palisades, Cal., Goodyear, 1976.

Super, Charles M. "Cross-Cultural Research on Infancy," in Harry C. Triandis and Alastair Heron, eds., *Handbook of Cross-Cultural Psychology,* Vol. 4: *Developmental Psychology.* Boston, Allyn and Bacon, 1981.

Sze, Sao-ke Alfred. *Sao-ke Alfred Sze: Reminiscences of his Early Years as Told to Anming Fu.* Amy C. Wu, tr. Washington D.C., 1962.

Tan Shih-hua. *A Chinese Testament: The Autobiography of Tan Shih-hua, as Told to S. Tretiakov.* New York, Simon and Schuster, 1934.

Tang, C. Y. "The Cycle of Civilization," *CSM* 13:111–115 (1917–1918).

T'ang Ming-chung 唐明中 ed. *Ying-hua shu-chien* 樱花书简 (Letters from Japan). Chengtu, Szechwan jen-min ch'u-pan-she, 1981.

T'ang Chün-i . "The Reconstruction of Confucianism and the Modernization of Asian Countries," in *Report: International Conference on the Problems of Modernization in Asia.* Seoul, 1965.

T'ang Chün-i 唐君毅 . *Ch'ing-nien yü hsueh-wen* 青年与学文 (Youth and learning). Taipei, San min ch'u-pan-she, 1973.

T'ao Hsi-sheng 陶希聖 . *Ch'ao-liu yü tien-ti* 潮流与点滴 (One drop in the floodtide). Chuan-chi wen-hsueh ts'ung-kan 2. Taipei, 1964.

Tawney, R. H. *Land and Labor in China.* London, George Allan & Unwin, 1932.

Tcheng Ki-Tong [Ch'en Chi-t'ung]. *The Chinese Painted by Themselves.* James Millington, tr. London, 1885.

Teng Ssu-yü [Teng, S. Y.]. *Family Instructions for the Yen Clan, An Annotated Translation with Introduction.* Leiden, Brill, 1968.

————. "Wang Fu-chih's views on History and Historical Writing," *Journal of Asian Studies* 28.1:111–123 (November 1968).

———— and John K. Fairbank, eds. *China's Response to the West: A Documentary Survey, 1839–1923.* Cambridge, Harvard University Press, 1961.

Tomkins, Silvan S. "Affect and the Psychology of Knowledge," in Silvan S. Tomkins, ed., *Affect, Cognition and Personality: Empirical Studies*. New York, Springer, 1965.

Tong, Y. L. "A Word for the Returned-Students-To-Be," *CSM* 10:560 (1914–1915)

Ts'ai T'ing-k'ai 蔡廷鍇 . *Ts'ai T'ing-k'ai tzu-chuan* 蔡廷鍇自传 (Autobiography of Ts'ai T'ing-k'ai). 2 vols. Hong Kong, 1946.

Ts'ao Chü-jen 曹聚仁. *Lu Hsun p'ing-chuan* 鲁迅评传 (Critical biography of Lu Hsun). Hong Kong, Hsin wen-hua, 1957.

Tseng Ch'i-fen 曾纪芬 . "Tzu-ting nien-p'u" 自订年谱 (Self-chronology), in *Ch'ung-te Lao-jen chi-nien ts'e* 崇德老人纪念册 (Memorial volume to Elder Ch'ung-te). Private publication, 1931.

Tu Wei-ming. *Confucian Thought: Selfhood as Creative Transformation*. Albany, State University of New York Press, 1985.

Tuan, Yi-fu. *Segmented Worlds and Self: Group Life and Individual Consciousness*. Minneapolis, University of Minnesota Press, 1982.

van Norden, Warner M., ed. *Who's Who of the Chinese in New York*. New York, 1918.

von Brandt, M. *Der Chinese in der Offentlichkeit und der Familie wie er sich selbst sieht und schildert*. Berlin, n.d.

Wakeman, Frederic, Jr. "The Opening of China," in Joseph R. Levenson, ed., *Modern China: An Interpretive Anthology*. London, Macmillan, 1971.

———. "The Price of Autonomy: Intellectuals in Ming and Ch'ing Politics," *Daedalus* 101.2:35–70 (Spring 1972).

Wales, Nym [Helen Foster]. *Red Dust: Autobiographies of Chinese Communists as Told to Nym Wales*. Stanford, Stanford University Press, 1952.

Wang, C. T. [Wang Cheng-t'ing]. "China and America," *CSM* 6:454–465 (1910–1911).

Wang Gungwu. "Early Ming Relations with Southeast Asia: A Background Essay," in John K. Fairbank, ed. *The Chinese World Order*. Cambridge, Harvard University Press, 1968.

Wang, H. C. "China and the League of Nations," *CSM* 16:476–478 (1920–1921).

Wang Ming-tao 王明道 . *Wu-shih nien lai* 五十年来 (The last fifty years). Preface dated Peking, 1950. Hong Kong, 1967.

Wang, Y. C. *Chinese Intellectuals and the West: 1872–1949.* Chapel Hill, University of North Carolina Press, 1966.

Wang, Y. Tsenshan. "Our Hope and Our Task," *CSM* 5:535–543 (1909–1910).

Wang Yun-wu 王云五 . *Wo ti sheng-huo p'ien-tuan* 我的生活片段 (Snippets of my life). Hong Kong, 1952.

Weber, Max. *The Religion of China: Confucianism and Taoism.* Hans H. Gerth, tr. and ed. New York, Macmillan, 1964.

Wei, S. K. "The Immediate Political Problem in China," *CSM* 15.7:28–31 (1919–1920).

Whiting, John W. M., and Irwin L. Child. *Child Training and Personality: A Cross-cultural Study.* New Haven, Yale University Press, 1953.

Wilson, Richard W. *Learning to be Chinese: The Political Socialization of Children in Taiwan.* Cambridge, Massachusetts Institute of Technology Press, 1970.

Wolf, Margery. *The House of Lim: A Study of a Chinese Farm Family.* New York, Appleton-Century-Crofts, 1968.

———. "Child Training and the Chinese Family," in Arthur P. Wolf, ed., *Studies in Chinese Society.* Stanford, Stanford University Press, 1978.

———. *Revolution Postponed: Women in Contemporary China.* Stanford, Stanford University Press, 1985.

Wong, H. H. "The Chinese Student and the Study of Law," *CSM* 10:147 (1914–1915)

Woo, C. C. "The Value of Industrial Scientific Research to the Advancement of Manufacturing Methods," *CSM* 16:80–81 (1920–1921).

———. "Some Suggestions on the Preparation of the Chinese Technical Students in the United States," *CSM* 16:168–172 (1920–1921).

Wright, Mary Clabaugh, ed. *China in Revolution: The First Phase, 1900–1913.* New Haven, Yale University Press, 1968.

———. "Introduction: The Rising Tide of Change,"in Mary C. Wright, ed., *China in Revolution: The First Phase, 1900–1913.* New Haven, Yale University Press, 1968.

Wu, John C. H. *Beyond East and West*. New York, Sheed and Ward, 1951.

Wu Yü 吴虞 . Wu Yü wen-lu 吴虞文录 (Collected essays of Wu Yü). 5 vols. Shanghai, 1927.

Yang, C. K. *Religion in Chinese Society: A Study of Contemporary Social Functions of Religion and Some of Their Historical Factors*. Berkeley, University of California Press, 1961.

Yang Lien-sheng. "The Concept of 'Pao' as a Basis for Social Relations in China," in John K. Fairbank, ed., *Chinese Thought and Institutions*. Chicago, University of Chicago Press, 1957.

Yang, Martin C. *A Chinese Village: Taitou, Shantung Province*. New York, Columbia University Press, 1945.

Yang, Y. C. [Yang Yung-ch'ing]. "Making Patriotism Count Most," *CSM* 13:107–111 (1917–1918).

Young, Ernest P. "Nationalism, Reform, and Republican Revolution: China in the Early Twentieth Century," in James B. Crowley, ed., *Modern East Asia: Essays in Interpretation*. New York, Harcourt, Brace & World, 1970.

Yu, P. K., ed. *Research Materials on Twentieth-Century China: An Annotated List of CCRM Publications*. Washington, D.C., Center for Chinese Research Materials, Association of Research Libraries, 1975.

Yu Tzu-i, *"Erh-shih nien ch'ien hsiang-ts'un hsueh-hsiao sheng-huo-li ti wo"* 二十年前乡村学校生活里的我 (My life inside a village school twenty years ago), *Chiao-yü tsa-chih* 19:30533–30545 (December 20, 1927), partially translated by Jane Chen in Patricia Buckley Ebrey, ed., *Chinese Civilization and Society: A Sourcebook*. New York, The Free Press, 1981.

Yung Wing. *My Life in China and America*. New York, 1909.

Zee, Zuntsoon. "Scientific Training for Efficiency," *CSM* 9:186–187 (1913–1914).

———. "Learning and Unlearning," *CSM* 9:525 (1913–1914).

Zigler, Edward, and Irwin L. Childs. "Socialization," in Gardner Lindzey and Elliot Aronson, eds., *Handbook of Social Psychology*, 2nd ed., vol. 3. Reading, Mass., Addison-Wesley, 1969.

Glossary

Ch'en Tu-hsiu 陈独秀

cheng-hsin 正心

cheng-t'u 正途

Ch'eng I 程頤

ch'eng jen 成人

Ch'eng Tuan-meng 程端蒙

ch'i 气

chia 家

chiao 教

chiao-tzu 餃子

Ch'ien Mu 錢穆

chih-shih fen-tzu
  知识分子

chih-shih wei k'ai
  知识未开

ch'ih k'u 吃苦

ch'ih k'uei 吃亏

chin-shih 进士

Chin ssu lu 近思录

ch'in 亲

ching 矜

ching hsueh 敬学

ch'ing huang pu chieh
  青黄不接

ch'ing-i 清議

ch'ing-nien 青年

ch'ing-nien jen 青年人

Chou Tso-jen 周作人

ch'u-lu 出路

chü-jen 举人

Chü Yuan 屈原

Chuan-chi wen-hsueh 传记文学

chüan 卷

chuang-yuan 狀元

chün-tzu 君子

ch'ün 群

fa 法

fa-cheng hsueh-t'ang 法政学堂

Fan Chen 范縝

feng-liu 风流

feng-shui 风水

hao-ch'i hsin 好奇心

hsi-hsueh 西学

hsiang-yuan 乡愿

hsiang-yueh 乡约

hsiao　孝
hsiao hsueh　小学
hsiao jen　小人
hsiao ta-jen　小大人
hsiao-wo　小我
hsien ju wei chu　先入为主
hsien-sheng　先生
hsin-hsueh　新学
hsing-ling　性灵
hsiu-shen　修身
hsiu-ts'ai　秀才
hsiu-yang　修养
Hsiung Shih-li　熊十力
Hsu Chi-yü　徐继畲
Hsu Fu-kuan　徐復观
hsueh-hui　学会
Hsun-tzu　荀子
Huang-p'i　黄陂
Huang Tsung-hsi　黄宗羲
hun-po　魂魄

jen　仁
jen-lun　人伦

k'ao t'ien ch'ih-fan　靠天吃饭
k'ou-t'ou　叩头
kuai hai-tzu　乖孩子
kuan-shu　管束
kuei　鬼
kuei-shen　鬼神
Kuo Sung-tao　郭嵩燾

li　礼
li*　理
li-hsueh　理学
Liang Chi　梁濟

Liang Ch'i-ch'ao　梁啟超
Liang Shu-ming　梁漱溟
lien　脸
Liu Tsung-chou　劉宗周
luan　乱

mei yu lien　没有脸
mi　糜
mi-hsin, mi-hsin, pu te pu hsin
　　迷信迷信, 不得不信
mien-tzu　面子
ming　命
mo-teng　摩登
mou　亩
Mou Tsung-san　牟宗三
Mu-lien chiu-mu　目连救母

nai-ma　奶妈
nien-p'u　年谱
nan fu hsueh-t'ang, nü fu chia
　　男服学堂, 女服家
Pa Chin　巴金
Pai-lu-tung shu-yuan
　　白鹿洞书院
pai-erh kuan　白儿关
pao　抱
pu-hsiao　不孝
pu yao lien　不要脸
pu yen chih chiao　不言之教
P'u Chieh　溥杰
p'u-shih　朴实
P'u Yi　溥仪

Sha-wan　沙湾
shan jen　善人
shan-shu　善书

shang-shen 商绅

shao-yeh 少爷

shao-yeh ti pai-tou
    少爷的派头

shen 神

Shen Huan-chang 沈焕章

shen-kuei 神鬼

shen-t'ung 神童

Sheng-yü 聖谕

sheng-yuan 生员

shih 时

shih-chung 示众

shih-fei 是非

shih-lin 士林

shu-hsiang shih chia
    书香世家

shu-yuan 书院

Ssu-ma Kuang 司马光

ssu-shu 私塾

Su Man-shu 蘇曼珠

suan-ming 算命

sui 岁

sui-yuan chin-li 随缘尽力

ta chung-hua lao ta kuo-chia
    大中华老大国家

Ta ch'eng tien 大成殿

ta hsueh 大学

ta-t'ung 大同

Ta-t'ung shu 大同书

ta-wo 大我

Tai Chen 戴震

tao 道

t'ao-ch'i 淘气

T'ao Yuan-ming 陶源明

t'i 悌

t'iao-p'i 调皮

t'ien 天

t'ien chih chiao-tzu
    天之骄子

t'ien hsing 天性

tiu lien 丢脸

t'ou-sheng kuei 偷生鬼

ts'ai-tzu 才子

ts'e lun ching-i 测论经义

Tseng Kuo-fan 曾国藩

tso ch'ih shan k'ung 坐吃山空

tso jen 作人

tso jen yang-tzu 做人樣子

tsu-kuei 族规

ts'u-yeh 粗野

tsui 罪

Tu Shao-shang 杜少裳

Tung Shu 董銖

tung shih 懂事

Tung Ya ping-fu 东亚病夫

T'ung-tzu li 童子礼

T'ung-meng hui 同盟会

T'ung-wen kuan 同文馆

tzu-hsiu 自修

tzu-jan 自然

wan-p'i 顽皮

Wang Ch'ung 王充

Wang Fu-chih 王夫之

Wang Kuo-wei 王国维

Wang T'ao 王韜

Wang Yang-ming 王陽明

Wang Yun 王筠

wen 文

wen chou-chou-ti 文绉绉的

wen-hua 文化

wen-jen 文人

Wu T'ing-fang 伍廷芳

wu-chün 无君

wu-fu 无父

wu-kuei wu-shen ti jen
　　　无鬼无神的人

wu-lun 五伦

yang hsueh-t'ang 洋学堂

yen 严

Yen Fu 严復

Yen Yuan 颜元

yi 义

Yi Shu-hui 易曙辉

ying-erh 婴儿

ying-erh shih-ch'i 婴儿时期

yü-hsiao 愚孝

yu-nien 幼年

yu-nien shih-ch'i 幼年时期

Yü-li chao-chuan 玉歷钞传

Yuan Shih-k'ai 袁世凱

yun 运

yun-ch'i 运气

Yung Wing 容閎

Index

Harvard East Asian Monographs

49. Endymion Wilkinson, *The History of Imperial China: A Research Guide*

50. Britten Dean, *China and Great Britain: The Diplomacy of Commercial Relations, 1860–1864*

51. Ellsworth C. Carlson, *The Foochow Missionaries, 1847–1880*

52. Yeh-chien Wang, *An Estimate of the Land-Tax Collection in China, 1753 and 1908*

53. Richard M. Pfeffer, *Understanding Business Contracts in China, 1949–1963*

54. Han-sheng Chuan and Richard Kraus, *Mid-Ch'ing Rice Markets and Trade, An Essay in Price History*

55. Ranbir Vohra, *Lao She and the Chinese Revolution*

56. Liang-lin Hsiao, *China's Foreign Trade Statistics, 1864–1949*

57. Lee-hsia Hsu Ting, *Government Control of the Press in Modern China, 1900–1949*

58. Edward W. Wagner, *The Literati Purges: Political Conflict in Early Yi Korea*

59. Joungwon A. Kim, *Divided Korea: The Politics of Development, 1945–1972*

60. Noriko Kamachi, John K. Fairbank, and Chūzō Ichiko, *Japanese Studies of Modern China Since 1953: A Bibliographical Guide to Historical and Social-Science Research on the Nineteenth and Twentieth Centuries, Supplementary Volume for 1953–1969*

61. Donald A. Gibbs and Yun-chen Li, *A Bibliography of Studies and Translations of Modern Chinese Literature, 1918–1942*

62. Robert H. Silin, *Leadership and Values: The Organization of Large-Scale Taiwanese Enterprises*

63. David Pong, *A Critical Guide to the Kwangtung Provincial Archives Deposited at the Public Record Office of London*

64. Fred W. Drake, *China Charts the World: Hsu Chi-yü and His Geography of 1848*

65. William A. Brown and Urgunge Onon, translators and annotators, *History of the Mongolian People's Republic*

66. Edward L. Farmer, *Early Ming Government: The Evolution of Dual Capitals*

67. Ralph C. Croizier, *Koxinga and Chinese Nationalism: History, Myth, and the Hero*

68. William J. Tyler, tr., *The Psychological World of Natsumi Sōseki*, by Doi Takeo

69. Eric Widmer, *The Russian Ecclesiastical Mission in Peking during the Eighteenth Century*

70. Charlton M. Lewis, *Prologue to the Chinese Revolution: The Transformation of Ideas and Institutions in Hunan Province, 1891–1907*

71. Preston Torbert, *The Ch'ing Imperial Household Department: A Study of its Organization and Principal Functions, 1662–1796*

72. Paul A. Cohen and John E. Schrecker, eds., *Reform in Nineteenth-Century China*

73. Jon Sigurdson, *Rural Industrialism in China*

74. Kang Chao, *The Development of Cotton Textile Production in China*

75. Valentin Rabe, *The Home Base of American China Missions, 1880–1920*

76. Sarasin Viraphol, *Tribute and Profit: Sino-Siamese Trade, 1652–1853*